INSIDE THE ANTISEMITIC MIND

The Tauber Institute Series for the Study of European Jewry

The Tauber Institute Series is dedicated to publishing compelling and innovative approaches to the study of modern European Jewish history, thought, culture, and society. The series features scholarly works related to the Enlightenment, modern Judaism and the struggle for emancipation, the rise of nationalism and the spread of antisemitism, the Holocaust and its aftermath, as well as the contemporary Jewish experience. The series is published under the auspices of the Tauber Institute for the Study of European Jewry—established by a gift to Brandeis University from Dr. Laszlo N. Tauber—and is supported, in part, by the Tauber Foundation and the Valya and Robert Shapiro Endowment.

For the complete list of books that are available in this series, please see www.upne.com

*Monika Schwarz-Friesel
and Jehuda Reinharz
Inside the Antisemitic Mind: The Language of Jew-Hatred in Contemporary Germany

Elana Shapira
Style and Seduction: Jewish Patrons, Architecture, and Design in Fin de Siècle Vienna

ChaeRan Y. Freeze, Sylvia Fuks Fried, and Eugene R. Sheppard, editors
The Individual in History: Essays in Honor of Jehuda Reinharz

Immanuel Etkes
Rabbi Shneur Zalman of Liady: The Origins of Chabad Hasidism

*Robert Nemes and Daniel Unowsky, editors
Sites of European Antisemitism in the Age of Mass Politics: 1880–1918

Sven-Erik Rose
Jewish Philosophical Politics in Germany, 1789–1848

ChaeRan Y. Freeze and Jay M. Harris, editors
Everyday Jewish Life in Imperial Russia: Select Documents, 1772–1914

David N. Myers and Alexander Kaye, editors
The Faith of Fallen Jews: Yosef Hayim Yerushalmi and the Writing of Jewish History

Federica K. Clementi
Holocaust Mothers and Daughters: Family, History, and Trauma

*Ulrich Sieg
Germany's Prophet: Paul de Lagarde and the Origins of Modern Antisemitism

David G. Roskies and Naomi Diamant
Holocaust Literature: A History and Guide

*Mordechai Altshuler
Religion and Jewish Identity in the Soviet Union, 1941–1964

Robert Liberles
Jews Welcome Coffee: Tradition and Innovation in Early Modern Germany

Sharon Faye Koren
Forsaken: The Menstruant in Medieval Jewish Mysticism

Nils Roemer
German City, Jewish Memory: The Story of Worms

David Assaf
Untold Tales of the Hasidim: Crisis and Discontent in the History of Hasidism

Jehuda Reinharz and Yaacov Shavit
Glorious, Accursed Europe: An Essay on Jewish Ambivalence

Eugene M. Avrutin, Valerii Dymshits, Alexander Ivanov, Alexander Lvov, Harriet Murav, and Alla Sokolova, editors
Photographing the Jewish Nation: Pictures from S. An-sky's Ethnographic Expeditions

* A Sarnat Library Book

INSIDE THE ANTISEMITIC MIND

THE LANGUAGE OF JEW-HATRED IN CONTEMPORARY GERMANY

MONIKA SCHWARZ-FRIESEL AND JEHUDA REINHARZ

A Sarnat Library Book | *Brandeis University Press Waltham, Massachusetts*

Brandeis University Press
An imprint of University Press of New England
www.upne.com

Manufactured in the United States of America
Designed by Mindy Basinger Hill
Typeset in Garamond Premier Pro

Library of Congress Cataloging-in-Publication Data appear at the end of the book.

This publication was made possible by the generous support of Brandeis University's Bernard G. and Rhoda G. Sarnat Center for the Study of Anti-Jewishness, which aims to promote a deeper understanding of anti-Jewish prejudice, as well as Jewish and non-Jewish responses to this phenomenon, from both a historical and contemporary perspective.

CONTENTS

For an additional appendix of selected complete texts included in the corpus, visit http://bir.brandeis.edu/handle/10192/26034

PREFACE TO THE ENGLISH EDITION (2016)

The broad public and academic reaction to the German edition of this book, published early in 2013, was bewilderment, almost shock. In spite of people's knowledge of the Holocaust and what consequences a rhetoric of hate and hostility might have, Jews are frequently attacked verbally in contemporary discourse. The experience of the lethal worldview that led to Auschwitz did not bring the strategies of verbally dehumanizing and demonizing the Jews to an end. Such strategies prevail and are frequently used in modern discourse, even by highly educated people from mainstream society. Further, in the twenty-first century, the official ban on antisemitic utterances has lost its influence, and the articulation of traditional antisemitic stereotypes by projecting them on Israel has increased significantly.

How is it possible that in the seventy years since the end of the Holocaust, years of coping with the past, years of remembrance and education, of making antisemitic utterances socially taboo and legally banned from public discourse, Judeophobic thought and feeling have not been driven from the heart of society? Why has the hatred of Jews not been erased from the collective and communicative memory?

The rich body of empirical data this book is based on shows that the old resentment is still very much alive, not only on the edges of society, but also in the mainstream of German and European society. In fact, antisemitism turns out to be a worldwide phenomenon on the rise, as recent years have shown: In Hungary, the Jobbik party is part of the government and openly antisemitic. In Sweden, the Jewish community is under pressure because of the growing hatred of Jews stemming mainly from the Muslim community. Jews have been attacked and killed in Belgium and in France, spit upon in Rome and in London, and more. In Berlin, a rabbi was knocked down on the street in front of his little daughter. Jewish cemeteries and synagogues have been desecrated. Jewish institutions in Germany have to be kept under constant police supervision.

International polls show that the attitude toward the Jewish state of Israel has become extremely hostile and aggressive everywhere; this hostility is based on Judeophobic stereotypes and an age-old bias in new garb.

All over the world, frantic and obsessive anti-Israel boycott movements have spread, gaining influence especially in left-wing circles, but also in parts of the Christian Church. There is a virulent campus antisemitism in both U.S. and British colleges and universities that claims to be critical of Israel but in fact is based on hostility toward Jews and uses the same demonizing verbal strategies as do right-wing extremists and neo-Nazis.

Hatred of the Jewish state of Israel is at the center of the activities of antisemites no matter whether from the right, left, or mainstream. Demonizing Israel "as the most dangerous peril" on earth, delegitimizing and derealizing the Jewish state as an "apartheid regime practicing state terror," calling it a "child-murderer" and a "disgrace to humankind," asking people to boycott its products because of its "state racism" is not criticism; it is antisemitism in its current, most dominant manifestation. In fact, there is an "Israelization" of modern Judeophobic discourse.

Here, once again, antisemitism proves to be a chameleon: it changes its colors according to the social and political situations, but stays the same at its cognitive and emotional core. Hatred of and hostility toward Jews are deeply engraved in the collective memory. Over the centuries, the surface has changed, but the core of hateful feelings and mental stereotypes has remained unaltered. And Judeophobia proves to be resistant to education, to argument, to reasoning, to facts. In spite of all the efforts to erase the distorted and false picture of Jews and Judaism after the Holocaust, our data reveal the shocking truth about the continuity and persistence of the age-old hostility toward Jews, the stereotypes on which it rests, and its most current linguistic manifestations. Deeply rooted in the Western tradition of thinking and feeling for almost two thousand years, it proves to be a central part of Western culture and therefore should not be seen as one prejudice among others, not some kind of xenophobia, but as a way of explaining the world according to Western culture. To cope with contemporary hatred of Jews, to find a solution so as to seriously and effectively fight it, one must take this into account.

Further, one has to acknowledge the persuasive and mind-manipulating power of verbal antisemitism. Judeophobic phrases and structures are kept alive in communicative memory and still influence the collective human mind, sometimes quite subconsciously and unintentionally. This influence is often underestimated. But language is powerful; in fact, it is the most powerful tool with which to influence and manipulate the human mind. It can be used to offend, to hurt, and to threaten people, to keep alive grudges and hatred. Some words are like weapons: they wound like bullets; some are like poison: they slowly get into the mind and activate a lethal semantics. Using language as a tool in order to discriminate against and demonize Jews can lead to radical political and social consequences in a society. This was shown in the Nazi era, when Jewish citizens were first stigmatized and threatened verbally, then mistreated physically, and finally brutally murdered.

However, as we demonstrate here, the experience of the Holocaust and dealing with the past has not brought the strategies of verbally dehumanizing and demonizing Jews to an end. We still find them very much alive in modern discourse. And as observed, verbal antisemitism is on the rise. This book describes and explains the verbal manifestations of contemporary antisemitism in Germany and Europe on the basis of a longitudinal corpus-based study. Further, the approach we have developed here can be used as an analytical tool to distinguish between verbal antisemitism and mere political critique. Although the examples are predominantly from German discourse, the results are arguably representative of antisemitic discourse worldwide. Thus the classification presented in this book can help to identify Judeophobic utterances and might also serve as a means of evaluating contested language in an arbitrational or legal context.[1]

Verbal antisemitism can take many forms—from allusion and citation, jokes, mocking, or contemptuous ill-will to generically discriminating sentences, from condemnation and dehumanizing metaphors to death threats and the articulation of solution plans. The analysis of direct and indirect verbal threats reveals the power of language as a weapon with far-reaching emotional and cognitive consequences. As a contrastive analysis (work in progress) of data from the World Wide Web reveals—the same linguistic features and patterns of argument are found to be widely evident here, too.

In spite of overwhelming praise for the book from both the press and the academic world, the following question hung, stated or hinted, in the air: Is the anti-Jewish attitude in Germany and Europe really as serious a problem as the data would suggest? Could it not be that the texts we analyzed were exceptional and not representative?

Little more than a year after publication of the book, that query met with an unsettling response: the Gaza conflict in the summer of 2014 brought about an eruption of anti-Jewish and anti-Israeli utterances and manifestations in Germany and in other European countries, as well as on many U.S. campuses (mostly in the framework of the boycotts, divestment, and sanctions campaign [BDS]). On the streets of German cities one could read and hear utterances like "Stop the Jewish terror!"; "Supposedly former victims. Now themselves perpetrators"; "Hamas, Hamas, Jews to the gas chambers"; "Child-murderer Israel." The same slogans could be heard in London, Paris, Washington, Istanbul—throughout the world.

At the same time, a flood of antisemitic hate speech appeared on the World Wide Web that continues today. In the meantime, the Internet has become the main and most influential propagator of anti-Jewish utterances, especially in social media: "You ugly little Jews, mankind's rats, one should gas all genetically declared Jewish criminals." Or "The Jews are to be blamed for everything. Therefore we should eliminate the Jews, in whatever way we can." These are two examples among thousands in online comments, in chat forums, on Twitter accounts, on Facebook, and so on.

"Across Europe and the whole world, the conflict in Gaza is breathing new life into some very old, and very ugly, demons," wrote the *Guardian* on 7 August 2014. It went on: "This is not unusual; police and Jewish civil rights organizations have long observed a noticeable spike in anti-Semitic incidents each time the Israeli–Palestinian conflict flares. . . . But according to academics and Jewish leaders, this time it is different. More than simply a reaction to the conflict, they say, the threats, hate speech and violent attacks feel like the expression of a much deeper and more widespread anti-Semitism, fuelled by a wide range of factors, that has been growing now for more than a decade."

Several European governments recognized and rebuked the anti-Jewish/anti-Israeli outbreaks. This was especially so in Germany. The highest political personages in the country, President Gauck and Chancellor Merkel, and many other important figures participated in a demonstration under the banner "Stand Up: Hatred of Jews—Never Again!" that took place at the Brandenburg Gate in Berlin on 14 September 2014, organized by the Central Council of the Jews in Germany.

At the same time, however, people wrote against this official attitude and articulated their hostile feelings toward Jews. It seems that there is a disparity between the official position, which is highly supportive of Jews and Israel, and the views among the broader public. The deluge of critical and venomous e-mails against Jews and Israel sent to German-Jewish and Israeli institutions during the summer of 2014 indicates that mainstream social opinion is moving in a different direction.

Its vehemence aside, the outstanding characteristic of the current phenomenon, the combination of Judeophobia and anti-Israelism—the two have become practically indistinguishable—is not new. For people with a Judeophobic propensity, there is no difference between the 'Jewish question' and the 'Israeli question,' even if they deny it heatedly. Denial of antisemitism is in the meantime one of the most dominant strategies in modern antisemitic discourse: 'I am not an antisemite' is an almost classical beginning to many an e-mail sent to Jewish institutions by obviously educated people. 'It is only Israel that I abhor' is the usual continuation of such messages, with this or that anti-Israeli justification added. The by-now-well-known poem by Günther Grass, from April 2012, "Was gesagt werden muss" ("What must be said"), has many of the characteristics of such an attitude.

A certain attitude hovers over the academic debate in the form of denial among educated Europeans and Americans regarding actual anti-Judaism. Frequently, both informed citizens and respected scholars reject out of hand that a Judeophobic problem exists. 'They are just extremists of some kind,' or 'merely some immigrants,' or 'People don't really mean it' are expressions one hears repeatedly. In a sense, such a mindset is understandable. For a thinking Western person, and especially a German one, the very possibility that, since the unique crime committed against European Jewry in the mid-twentieth century, no deeper change has occurred in the relationship between non-Jews and Jews is a notion hard to accept. This attitude of denial was severely shaken by the events of the summer of 2014, and yet it still surfaces. Researchers and commentators seem unwilling to recognize the immense resilience of historical Judeophobia. Therefore, the stance of denial should be recognized for what it ultimately is: a most serious factor in the present-day negative attitudes toward Jews.

Altogether, the upheavals of the summer of 2014 and the debates they caused strengthen and underline the conclusions of our book. What occurred was a reemergence of the historically known negative stereotype of Jews, deeply rooted in Western culture, now emerging in the attire of concepts and events of our days. Its more dangerous spokespersons are not right-wing radicals, who enjoy no public support or legitimacy; rather, as in the past, the resentment is anchored in and carried by the educated mainstream, among them nowadays many liberals and leftists. Therefore, what is needed is a greater public awareness of the scope of everyday antisemitism. We have to overcome the illusion that Judeophobia is primarily a phenomenon among neo-Nazis. We find verbal antisemitism explicitly and implicitly, intentionally and unintentionally among "normal" people, our neighbors, our colleagues, our doctors, bankers, teachers, editors, journalists. Anti-Judaism proves to be both a persistent and a central way of thinking and feeling in the Western tradition—neither shaken nor destroyed by the experience of Auschwitz.

As it happens, only recently has the spread of this everyday antisemitism in the United States been saliently summed up by J. J. Goldberg: "You don't have to be paranoid to sense a new strain of anti-Semitism surfacing in American politics of late" (*The Forward*, 24 September 2015).

■

In the past two years, the authors of the present work have been frequently confronted by the question of how to react to the present wave of hatred of Jews. In fact, it is difficult to suggest what steps to take when there is so much disagreement about the very character of this hatred. Perhaps the recognition that the public has an entrenched and continuing problem regarding Jews would be a first and indispensable step toward a change in Western attitudes. What seems especially worrisome is that there are reasons to ask whether the current trends in Western public opinion do not point in the opposite direction, toward a Judeophobic radicalization.

Today, it's impossible to distinguish between antisemitism and anti-Israelism. Bashing Israel by evoking traditional Judeophobic stereotypes has in the meantime become the most common strategy of contemporary antisemitism. Modern antisemites have turned 'the Jewish problem' into 'the Israeli problem.' They have redirected the 'Final Solution' from the Jews to the state of Israel, which they see as the embodiment of evil.

Lately, commentators have begun to look for the "roots" of the so-called Israel problem, and it hasn't taken them long to "discover" that it started with the creation of a Jewish state, the usual corollary being that Israel should never have been established. This has set off an intellectual logic that is akin to riding a downhill slope into the unthinkable. First comes a criticism of the characteristics of the Jewish state and all it stands for. "Israel is a European colony on Arab land," stated the German publicist and former parliamentarian Jürgen Todenhöfer in a television debate in July 2014. Or, as the British professor Brian Klug (he himself a Jew) put it, Israel is "a splintered state." The next typical step is: "In a free country it must be possible to question with impunity the right of Israel to exist" ("Es muss in einem freien Land möglich sein, straflos das Existenzrecht Israels infrage zu stellen"), this by Stefan Reinecke, a journalist at the well-known leftist *Tageszeitung* of Berlin (*TAZ*) in July 2014, in the name of freedom of expression (*Meinungsfreiheit*). Israel, the only really modern and functioning state in the Middle East, is the only nation among all the recognized countries of the world whose existence is constantly being called into question (or at least its "transformation" has been called for, as, for example, by the American-Jewish professor Judith Butler). In the meantime, this has become a discourse ritual that is no longer reflected on in its uniqueness, brutality, and potential radical consequences; indeed, it has become a habitus among intellectuals, something "normal." The next step has a sense of ominous inevitability about it. A German academic (name provided), who declared himself to be politically left-leaning and not antisemitic, wrote in an e-mail sent to the Israeli Embassy in Berlin in February 2013:

> From a realpolitik German perspective à la Merkel, I must say that seven million dead [Israeli] Jews, as horrible as this might be, yet soberly considered, is still better than seven billion dead people caused by the Jews' brutal world domination. (Aus Sicht eines realpolitischen Deutschlands à la Merkel muss man sagen, dass sieben Millionen tote Juden, so schlimm das auch wäre, aber nüchtern betrachtet besser wären als sieben Milliarden tote Menschen wegen der jüdischen brutalen Weltherrschaft.)

This, seventy years after the Holocaust . . .

■

This English edition was made possible by the support of the Bernard G. and Rhoda G. Sarnat Center for the Study of Anti-Jewishness at Brandeis University. Sylvia Fuks Fried, associate editor of the Tauber Institute Series for the Study of European Jewry, in which the volume appears, oversaw the preparation of the English version, and Phyllis Deutsch, editor in chief of Brandeis University Press / University Press of New England, offered valuable suggestions on the organization of the book for an American readership. The volume benefited greatly from Catherine Schwerin's review of the translation, Mary Becker's thoughtful editing under the guidance of managing editor Amanda Dupuis, as well as Golan Moskowitz's careful read and Talia Graff's meticulous proofreading. Here, as in the case of the German edition, we owe a debt of gratitude to Evyatar (Sigi) Friesel.

Monika Schwarz-Friesel and Jehuda Reinharz

PREFACE TO THE GERMAN EDITION (2013)

This scholarly investigation looks at present-day hostility toward Jews in Germany as expressed through the medium of language. Anyone presenting such a study must anticipate the question "What, yet another book on antisemitism?" Recent years have certainly seen a spate of studies on this topic. But this book is different. For one thing, the data that constitute its empirical basis differ markedly, both in quantity and in authenticity, from the data used in any other analysis of antisemitic discourse known to us. For another, the focus on the crucial significance of linguistic manifestations of hostility toward Jews and on the reciprocal effects of cognitive stereotypes and emotional attitudes that can be discerned in verbal antisemitic formulations sets this study apart. The specific characteristics of linguistically coded antisemitic attitudes generally do not receive the attention they deserve. Lastly, this investigation has an unusual interdisciplinary dimension in that it combines historical reflection with linguistic and cognitive textual analysis.

When we set out in 2002 to collect, classify, and analyze the thousands of e-mails, letters, postcards, and faxes sent from all regions of Germany by all sorts of individuals to the Central Council of Jews in Germany and the Israeli Embassy in Berlin, we did not know what to expect. In the intervening years, these linguistic manifestations have given us remarkable insights into the cognitive and emotional conceptualizations manifested by antisemitically oriented contemporary Germans. We encountered thousands of messages that verbalized irrational hatred and obsessive rage directed at Jews, in combination with ancient stereotypes that one might have expected to have been thoroughly exposed and discredited after the experience of the Holocaust. What came to light were forms of rejection, hostility, and defensiveness that all the decades devoted to memory work and education seem to have done remarkably little to dispel. As depressing as the crude and violent antisemitic ravings of right-wing extremists were to all of us who worked on the project, we were far more appalled to encounter the hostile utterances by members of mainstream society. Scholars, lawyers, doctors, bank employees, clergymen, and students used language that revealed age-old Judeophobic resentments apparently impervious to education or reflection on the experience of Auschwitz; the language in which these resentments found expression revealed naked intolerance and delusion. To make things worse, when we spoke of our undertaking to colleagues, our findings elicited astonishment and disbelief, sometimes paired with rather ineffectual attempts to minimize our results or to pooh-pooh them with the assertion that the authors of such utterances must be "fossils," "nut cases," or members of the "lunatic fringe." The conclusion forced itself on us that most Germans find it extremely difficult to acknowledge that for many of their countrymen the Holocaust and study of its origins and impact did not bring about a clean break in mindset when it came to hostile attitudes toward Jews.

Our data, together with analyses of thousands of views expressed in public venues, as well as on social media and in Internet chat rooms, show that the verbal expressions of antisemitism we describe cannot be passed off as marginal phenomena; indeed, they form part of largely habitual and widely accepted patterns. Hostility toward Jews was not, and is not, encountered only on the margins of society; it could not, and cannot, be classified exclusively as a form of psychopathology. It occupies a solid position in the very middle of society and can be observed among intelligent, highly educated, sensitive persons. Verbal expressions of this hostility have manifested themselves in Germans' communicative and cultural memory for centuries. The linguistic patterns we analyzed are used widely—sometimes consciously, sometimes unconsciously—in everyday discourse. Their unreflexive (re)production transmits Judeophobic thinking to the entire realm of social communication. Linguistic utterances that convey anti-Jewish stereotypes have the potential to influence—decisively yet subliminally—content of consciousness, attitudes, and feelings. Language must thus be recognized as a dangerous tool of manipulation. Habitualized patterns of language usage can have a powerful effect on individual and collective thought and valuation processes.

On the one hand this book presents many variants of verbal hostility toward Jews that are remarkably homogeneous as far as their semantic content is concerned, while on the other it appeals for critical awareness of, and reflection on, the potential of language to exert power and promote violence. If verbal expressions of hostility toward Jews have transmitted resentment and dislike from one generation to the next for centuries, showing how this mechanism works represents the only hope for defeating these patterns.

We would like to thank all our collaborators, who, despite the immense emotional burden imposed by working with this material, accepted the challenge and with unwavering dedication labored side by side with us for years to classify and analyze the texts. Although the devastating content of those texts often pushed us to the limits of our professional perspective as scholars, what sustained us was the conviction that it was crucially important to make our results available to the public.

We owe thanks to Robert Beyer, who for more than three years participated as a scholarly expert in the project "Conceptualization and Verbalization of Contemporary Antisemitism in Germany," cataloging and classifying thousands of texts. We would also like to thank the members of the project team—Dirk Hertrampf, Judith Malicke, Eva Leuschner, John Reichel, Franziska Schmidtke, and Patrick Schneider. In the final phase, Matthias Becker, Konstanze Marx, Gerrit Kotzur, Jan-Henning Kromminga, Jonas Nölle, Stephan Peters, and Sabine Reichelt helped with meticulous proofreading. Marie-Luise and Wolfgang Höbelt served as patient test-readers, offering useful suggestions for making the text more readable. In stimulating conversations in Jerusalem, Joseph Shatzmiller and Moshe David Herr provided valuable sources on historical manifestations of hostility toward Jews. We thank Laura Sturm and Matthias Becker for translating e-mails written in Spanish, and Annick Trellu for translating the French texts. Helge Skirl read and commented on all the chapters with great thoroughness, also performing yeoman service as an editor.

We are grateful to the Central Council of Jews in Germany as well as the Israeli Embassy in Berlin, at the latter especially Janine Khoschlessan, for making the correspondence available to us. We are likewise indebted to the Israeli Embassy staffs in Vienna, Berne, The Hague, Madrid, Brussels, London, Dublin, and Stockholm, and to the Forum against Antisemitism in Vienna. We are grateful to the Tauber Institute at Brandeis University for its support and cooperation through the years.

Our thanks go also to staff members at the de Gruyter publishing house, especially Julia Brauch and Alice Keller, for the productive and pleasant collaboration we have enjoyed with them.

Above all, we owe our deepest gratitude to Evyatar (Sigi) Friesel not only for his helpful and always constructively critical comments on every chapter of the book but especially for his love and friendship, as well as his unshakable belief in our work and his conviction that our analyses were significant and relevant. We dedicate this book to him.

Monika Schwarz-Friesel and Jehuda Reinharz

NOTATIONAL CONVENTIONS

In this book, all orthographic, grammatical, and spelling mistakes in the examples quoted appear in the original texts.

Following the conventions of cognitive science and linguistics, examples drawn from the corpus to make specific points are set off from the main text and numbered. Specific linguistic formulations discussed in the running text appear in italics. Conceptual (i.e., mental) entities and structures appear in small capitals. Paraphrases of meaning, arguments, and conclusions appear in single quotation marks.

Throughout, the communications under discussion were anonymized and are cited using basic information (e.g., ZJD_29.05.2007_Sch_002) to allow for uniform citation and searchability within the corpus as a whole. The label provides basic information. ZJD stands for Zentralrat der Juden in Deutschland—the Central Council of Jews in Germany—while IBD stands for Israeli Botschaft Deutschland—the Israeli Embassy in Germany. The date, in day/month/year order, indicates when the communication was received. The abbreviation that follows represents the first three letters of the author's name, and the number indicates whether the letter was the first or a subsequent message from that writer. This system makes it possible to identify repeat correspondents.

INSIDE THE ANTISEMITIC MIND

1 INTRODUCTION
The Need for This Book

Hostility toward Jews has manifested itself over many centuries not only through physical violence and social discrimination but also through language that stigmatizes and defames its objects. Verbal antisemitism is a form of mental violence that uses language as a weapon to express discriminatory and insulting attitudes and distort reality. Such language creates and maintains images of the Jew as the enemy, passing such negative images and ancient stereotypes from generation to generation. Language plays a unique role in preserving and transmitting antisemitic resentments: linguistic utterances activate or construct specific concepts of Jews as alien, odd, and evil beings, thereby evoking negative feelings. Language functions to preserve knowledge over the course of history, maintaining collectively established concepts, and in this way many Judeophobic ideas have been kept alive over the centuries. Among the demonizing characterizations applied to Jews are *monsters*, *devils*, and *fiends*. According to this usage, Jews are *greedy usurers*, *devious conspirators*, and *vengeful exploiters*, epithets that discredit Jews' morality. Describing them as *alien*, *arrogant*, *obstinate*, and *different* discriminates against them as a minority. Judaism is associated with attributes such as *atavistic*, *brutal*, *strange*, and *heretical* with respect to Christianity—the *one true faith*—and thereby delegitimized as a religion. Repeated exposure to such clichés and stock phrases results in the construction of partially conscious, partially unconscious mental representations that can solidify into permanent attitudes, belief systems, and even worldviews. Often, however, those who appropriate these long-standing usages have no awareness of their lineage or their potential to exclude and degrade those to whom they are applied. Yet in both the past and the present, negative attitudes toward Jews and images of them as the enemy are by no means found only on the margins of society; they occur frequently among mainstream individuals who are educated, comfortably situated economically, and not politically radical.[1] In this connection, many fail to notice or recognize how dangerous it is to use such formulations, especially those that unthinkingly express and reproduce age-old patterns of hostility toward Jews.

It is therefore an important concern of this book to raise awareness of the power and the violence that can emanate from language, especially when used in a particular way. Drawing on a wealth of empirical examples, we will show that current linguistic usage still incorporates the entire range of traditional anti-Jewish stereotypes and emotional resentments—despite all the education Germans have received since the Holocaust—and that antisemitic notions are not exclusively the province of extremists on the far right and left. Educated people in Germany also produce utterances with content hostile toward Jews—sometimes intentionally, sometimes unconsciously. One can identify different types of verbal antisemitism: in a communicative sense Judeophobia can be explicit—in other words, overt—or implicit, meaning indirect and recognizable from the conclusions that can be drawn and from knowledge of the context. Up to now the specific features of current Judeophobic usage have been inadequately analyzed and described.[2] Especially prominent among the inadequately known and investigated phenomena are the implicit forms of verbal antisemitism that can be heard or read increasingly in public discourse. Such forms can be detected contextually by means of implicatures: the word *Jew(s)* need not occur in an utterance for it to count as antisemitic. Hostility toward Jews can find expression in many different ways—through allusions, paraphrases, or a combination of specific arguments.

This book treats the various verbal manifestations of contemporary hostility toward Jews, and the underlying conceptions of Jews and Judaism, using the tools of historical discourse analysis and of linguistics and cognitive science.

An analysis of the specific lexical, semantic, syntactic, and argumentative-conceptual traits of antisemitic language thus provides the basis not only for a better understanding of the stereotypes and the emotionally colored prejudices such language expresses, but also for a comprehensive picture of the cultural, social, cognitive, and affective phenomenon of hostility toward Jews.[3] Because debates—some of them fierce and highly emotional—continue to flare up in German society over whether a given oral or written expression deserves to be categorized as antisemitic, it is also critically important to achieve clarity and to establish unambiguous criteria for classification that will make it possible to resolve the question when it arises. In addition to describing the specific ways in which current hostility toward Jews finds verbal expression, this book therefore also aims to establish indicators drawn from the methodology of textual analysis that will address the question "When is a linguistic utterance antisemitic?"[4]

The empirical basis for our study is the analysis of an extensive corpus; while primarily qualitative, this analysis also allows us to include certain quantitative elements when they help us present a more comprehensive picture of modern manifestations of antisemitism in verbal utterances.[5] The study rests on the analysis of more than fourteen thousand communications received by the Central Council of Jews in Germany (sent between 2002 and 2009) and the Israeli Embassy in Berlin (sent between 2004 and 2012). These communications offer insight into the authors' attitudes, thoughts, and feelings, and thereby into the forms in which hostility toward Jews manifests itself in the twenty-first century.[6] We augmented the analysis of this corpus of e-mails, faxes, and letters by examining representative examples of the language found in the mass media, for example in letters to the editor and newspaper articles, on posters, and in blog posts. These data, sampled at random, demonstrate that the stereotypes and arguments we have identified, far from being confined to the specific genres of the e-mail and the letter, turn out to be typical of a broad spectrum of public communication. Thus we are in a position to use a representative study to show how hostility toward Jews manifests itself in current language usage,[7] and to discuss the extent to which the interaction of cognitive categorization and emotional reactions can be discerned on various structural levels of these patterns. We can thereby capture not only the verbal characteristics of antisemitic usage but also the conceptual frameworks within which that usage operates. It is particularly important to render these frameworks visible, because only by bringing them to light can we identify hostility toward Jews as a distinctive mental and affective phenomenon. In the future, modern research on antisemitism must respond more attentively to this requirement and produce more qualitative discourse analyses.

The questions that come to the fore in textual analysis of the corpus bear on the verbal characteristics of antisemitic usage as well as the underlying intellectual structures within which categorization and evaluation take place. We address the following questions: Which (traditional) anti-Jewish stereotypes are reflected explicitly or implicitly in the texts themselves, and in what (new) conceptual combinations do they occur? What emotional attitudes underlie the verbalization of attitudes hostile toward Jews? What strategies of argumentation are employed to articulate and justify antisemitic contents? What modalities and structures in the texts serve to portray and express attitudes hostile toward Jews? Which of these forms of expression automatically convey antisemitism through their semantic features alone, independent of context, and which, on the other hand, lend themselves to an anti-Jewish reading only in context and when analyzed from a cultural standpoint?

All of our analyses proceed on the assumption that linguistic utterances provide insight into the cognitive and affective activity of those who produce them. Accordingly, the texts offer a picture of their authors' mental structures, attitudes, and feelings. This book employs an interdisciplinary approach to analysis: we combine historiological reflection and linguistic textual analysis in order to capture the phenomenon of hostility toward Jews as comprehensively and as precisely as possible, in all its varied forms. Up to now such an approach has not been employed in research on antisemitism, despite its having been put forward as a desideratum a number of times. Historical, sociological, or philologically oriented treatments of hostility toward Jews usually lack detailed analysis of texts. Furthermore, many important aspects do not undergo sufficiently precise explication. Instead one often finds only very general and vague statements about antisemitic utterances, and many phenomena do not receive adequate explanation, with terms such as *code*, *cliché*, and *stereotype* (often used almost interchangeably) applied without clear definitions or distinctions. Concepts such as "latent," "manifest," "implicit," "explicit," "direct," "indirect," and the like are usually used imprecisely outside of linguistics, which contributes to confusion and lack of clarity. On the other hand, purely linguistic investigations of verbal antisemitism often limit themselves to descriptive catalogs of stylistic or rhetorical, lexical, and syntactic features, without taking into consideration their dependence on contextual factors, their long-term and deep-seated cultural embeddedness and cognitive connections, or their relevance to communicative and manipulative mechanisms. A further complicating factor is the use of highly specific technical jargon, which makes it difficult for nonlinguists to understand detailed linguistic analyses and renders them inaccessible or off-putting. In this book we aspire to maintain the precision necessary for scholarly analysis of the textual material, offering clear explanations and accurate use of technical terminology, while formulating these explanations as accessibly and clearly as possible. All the relevant theoretical and scholarly aspects are explored with reference to concrete examples from the corpus. We are convinced that the wealth of authentic examples makes it possible to give the reader a particularly vivid impression of the modalities and import of language expressing hostility toward Jews. The meta-observations incorporating historical and cognitive perspectives are intended to bring into clear focus the phenomenon of modern hostility toward Jews in its sociocultural, cognitive, and emotional contexts.

After a brief discussion of the relevance and function of language when it comes to establishing and transmitting beliefs and attitudes hostile toward Jews, we will draw on historical texts to establish the extent to which certain mental stereotypes have persisted in cultural memory and have been repeated in communicative practice and language with remarkable consistency. In this connection we will examine the genesis of the hatred to which Jews have been subjected over many centuries. After characterizing the forms in which this hostility found expression in the nineteenth and twentieth centuries, knowledge of which is essential to any recognition of antisemitism as a phenomenon that rears its head repeatedly, we will concentrate on current verbal instances of antisemitic thinking from the first decade of the twenty-first century in Germany. It should be noted that, contrary to common assumptions, the Holocaust by no means constitutes a break with inherent prejudices and hatred directed toward Jews; after 1945 no truly probing self-critical reflection or processing of the recent past with respect to all societal structures took place of the sort that the recent caesura in civilization would have called for.

Accordingly, most of the conceptual patterns that characterize two millennia of hostility toward Jews reappear, sometimes in traditional, sometimes in new forms of expression. In this connection we will also show that to this day many components (words, phrases, metaphors) of the Nazis' ideologically colored terminology continue to crop up. Modern stereotypes, arguments, and strategies, as well as the linguistic forms they take, will be described and explained in context. We will also show the extent to which anti-Israel sentiment has become the dominant form of contemporary verbal antisemitism, such that references to the Jewish state function as proxies for a general hatred of Jews. A brief comparative study of verbally antisemitic texts in other European countries follows, calling attention to the significant conceptual commonalities to be found in hostile attitudes toward Jews elsewhere in Europe. In German discourse this hostility appears to be invested with a greater intensity, occasioned by the Nazi past, of guilt, shame, denial of memory and responsibility, and compassion fatigue. For that reason, we will also explore the emotional dimension of modern antipathy to Jews and show what sentiments (interacting with stereotyped thinking) shape the affective and irrational basis of hostility toward Jews. This hostility rests primarily on a deep-seated resentment, endemic to Western culture, that turns out to be highly resistant to facts, education, and argumentation. That makes it all the more important not merely to describe the diverse forms of repression, denial, and reinterpretation in modern antisemitic discourse but also to create widespread critical awareness of its existence and prevalence and thereby to develop possibilities for combating it.

2 HOSTILITY TOWARD JEWS AND LANGUAGE

Verbal Imposition of Power and Violence

Language as a Cognitive System and Communicative Instrument for Action

The ability to communicate through language represents one of human beings' most important intellectual and social functions. All significant social interactions, structures, and institutions are based on linguistic processes. Language fulfills a wide range of functions: it transmits general and individual knowledge, preserves collective knowledge, expresses political and ideological positions, and makes possible complex thought processes. It passes on bodies of information, activates emotions, influences awareness, expands representations of knowledge, and triggers associations and learning. Through language systems shaped by cognition and culture, human beings share their perceptions, impressions, and judgments, as well as their ideas, mental images, and convictions, their wishes, expectations, and intentions. Language constitutes a system for conveying knowledge and understandings that all members of a community share and use; it transcends a multitude of individual differences and subjective orientations.[1] It is a system that makes it possible not only to store information about the world over long periods of time by means of symbolic structures that follow recognizable rules but also to pass this information on to fellow human beings. This system facilitates the exchange of information by means of signs, thereby ensuring that subjects can establish contact with other subjects and communicate in complex ways. The products of mental and affective processes—that is, nonembodied thoughts—can be expressed in a concrete medium, which allows them to be objectified. That which is thought can be conveyed through that which is said, thereby becoming a part of social processes and social interactions.

Through language we relate to the extralinguistic world. We relate to persons, things, and situations. We represent structures of reality, create causal, temporal, and spatial verbal connections. We convey judgments as to the truth or falsity of statements. Yet language never merely portrays reality, since the choice of means and the way in which information is presented always reflect a specific perspective and judgment on what is conveyed. Thus every verbal portrayal of reality can be varied through the forms of expression chosen and the speaker's intentions. A specific language's lexicon and grammar provide a storehouse of words and syntactic structures that afford the speaker great flexibility.

Looking at our corpus, we can see that depending on a correspondent's perspective, references to Jews can be neutral, meliorative, pejorative, vague, or simply wrong, as in such expressions as *Jewish fellow citizens*, *Jews*, *filthy Jews*, *Jewish sows*, *Jewish swine*, *Jewish parasites*, *certain circles*, *that religious community*, *East Coast lobby*, *Zionists*, *Israelis*, and *Semites*. Use of the words *Jew(s)* and *Israeli(s)* synonymously, terms that have two different meanings and refer to different reference groups, expresses an identification that is factually incorrect.[2]

Thus any linguistic construction always creates a subjectively inflected representation of reality. Verbal utterances in part generate their own realities, and through semantics, or in other words the meaning of the structures involved, entire mental models are produced that have nothing in common with extralinguistic reality.[3] An example is the sentence formulated in 1879 by Heinrich von Treitschke, an assertion that can be described as a classic example of Judeophobic fiction, picked up by the Nazis fifty years later and used as a headline in their party organ, *Der Stürmer*:

> (1) The Jews are our misfortune! [Treitschke 1879, 575]

This statement makes all Jews collectively responsible for the problems and the future of the German people, a judgment that in light of the reality at that time is as wrong as it is grotesque (see chapter 3, under Survival and Resistance of Judeophobic Stereotypes in Modern Times).[4] Furthermore, the additive contrast verbalizes grammatically the demarcation of Jews from Germans. A comment from the year 2007 likewise reflects a distortion of reality:

> (2) Jews are the scourge of humanity and threaten world peace. [ZJD_29.05.2007_Sch_002]

At the same time, this formulation creates its own reality through the use of hyperbolic and generic language. It establishes an enemy- and threat-scenario that exists only in the author's mind but is communicated through verbalization as an accurate depiction of the world.

Linguistic expressions thus generate textual worlds expressive of the observer's perspective. These worlds occupy intermediate cognitive levels that often have no equivalent in the real world.[5] The ability of language to constitute reality and objects becomes particularly clear when we look at fictional texts. The author of a literary work uses linguistic structures to create an independent, complex, internally coherent but fictive reality. The constructs of Judeophobia are not that different: most of the Judeophobic stereotypes, some of which have existed for centuries, have no basis in reality but are cognitively produced and linguistically transmitted fictions (see chapter 3), stored as conceptualization patterns in the heads of their users (or conserved culturally as communicative codes in verbal forms). The notion of a worldwide conspiracy articulated in *The Protocols of the Elders of Zion* or the coded conception of Jews in circulation since the Middle Ages as adherents of a blood cult who murder little children: these constructs can be shown to be pure figments of the imagination, yet millions of people around the world believe them to be true, preserve them in a variety of texts, and pass them along.[6] When Judeophobic concepts coalesce into a complex belief system, a worldview immune to facts results in which everything fits together in a coherent, pseudo-rational fashion. Within this system every piece of information is integrated plausibly or reinterpreted to suit the occasion. If, for example, Jews become the victims of verbal or nonverbal violence, from the point of view of the antisemitic observer who subscribes to the system the Jews have brought the problem on themselves.

Aggressive language and Judeophobia coexist in a long-standing symbiosis. The history of linguistic usage shows that for centuries Jews have been discredited and excluded largely in semantically homogeneous ways, despite changing social constellations. Language maintains a cultural heritage and serves as a reservoir of collective knowledge, preserving myths and stereotypes that are passed along without critical reflection and become part of a society's collective knowledge even though their claim to validity has no empirical basis. Language carries, directs, and shapes our thinking to a great extent. Language makes it possible to express one's identity (*I, as a young German of the postwar generation*), to experience national self-awareness (*I am proud of Germany, my country*), to feel part of a community and a larger identity, and at the same time to differentiate oneself from members of other groups. One's individual and collective ego and alter ego are defined through language in terms of specific markers ('we Germans versus you Jews'). Language conveys assessments and value judgments (*Israel is a state that perpetrates injustice and apartheid*), guides processes of opinion formation (*We are not allowed to express criticism*), transmits or reactivates stereotypes (*All Jews are avaricious*), describes, awakens, or influences emotions (*Out of great concern for the threat to world peace I feel compelled to write*), constructs extremely negative images (*the Jewish plague of boils*), threats (*international Judaism wants to destroy us*), and fictitious analogies (*The Israeli military employs SS methods*). Language can produce images of an enemy that turn an individual or a group into a baleful, evil figure or agent (as in "*The Jews are destroying Germany*," in a 2009 e-mail to the Central Council).[7] Texts often create not only their own reality structures ("*All Israelis are murderers*," in a 2008 e-mail to the Embassy, or "*Jews control the media*," addressed to the Central Council in 2002), but at the same time present very specific valuation metrics or systems that clearly define such categories as good and evil ("*Jews are the scourge of humanity*").

If, however, one wants to capture the entire potential of linguistic utterances to convey information and affect perceptions, it does not suffice to analyze the referential descriptive function of language and the conceptualizations on which that function relies. Beyond the explicit referential effects conveyed verbally, texts often implicitly communicate information whose effortless reconstruction can be assumed. A sentence like (3), which appears in a number of forms in right-wing publications such as the *National-Zeitung*, does not contain a single expression that mentions Jews explicitly:

(3) East Coast bankers influence U.S. policy.

The expression "East Coast bankers" obviously alludes to American Jews and has come into use as a recognizable formula. Other referential formulas include expressions such as *the lobby that calls the shots in our country* or *the religious community that has us over a barrel.* Readers of these texts immediately recognize, on the basis of their general knowledge and the context, who is meant by such phrases.

A question often posed to the Central Council during the last few years, like

(4) Why don't you move to Israel?

implies that the person asking the question does not view German Jews as Germans but rather as Israelis. Such indirect speech acts are often employed to circumvent taboos and avoid sanctions.[8] Since 1945, overt antisemitism and denial of the Holocaust have been not only frowned upon in Germany but also legally prohibited; as a result, indirect forms of conveying information have been adopted, for instance rhetorical questions (*Must we Germans do penance forever? Who seriously needs a memorial?*) as well as allusions and puns (*USrael, IsraHell, Schwindler's List*). Referential shifting occurs often: when Israel is referred to, all Jews are meant. Thus the word *Jew* or *Jewish* need not occur even once in a statement for hostility toward Jews to be expressed. Those making the statements count on those hearing them to recognize what is implied. Since purely mental conclusions are involved, they can readily be denied or withdrawn by the speaker if a prickly situation arises. In such cases the speaker points to the literal statement, pretending that nothing else was implied. Thus after an assertion such as *The Israelis are a criminal, bloodthirsty gang of murderers operating under the Star of David!* the implied conclusion—'Israel has no right to exist' or 'Israelis are Jews, and Jews are murderers'—can be negated if necessary. Resorting to indirect speech acts thus represents a precautionary measure on the part of the speaker.

Language not only serves to describe reality; it also intervenes directly in reality. Language is an instrument of action and can be used as a weapon to harm people, to upset them, to offend them, to libel them, to exclude them, and to threaten them (see chapter 9, under Abuse, Insults, Threats, Curses).[9] One can employ language not merely to invoke violence but actually to perpetrate violence. Different types of verbal acts can be identified (cf. Searle 1969; Meibauer 2001; Bublitz 2009; Schwarz-Friesel 2007).

Directives convey an immediate appeal to the addressee; saying "*Get out of Germany!*" (to the Central Council) demands action; the extralinguistic world is supposed to obey language, be oriented toward it. With commissives such as threats ("*I will do everything in my power to stir up my fellow human beings against Jews,*" in a 2007 e-mail to the Central Council, or "*We will kill you all!*" from a 2005 e-mail to the Central Council), an attempt is likewise made to force reality to conform to language by predicting something about the future and thereby frightening the addressees or putting them under pressure. Assertives have the function of portraying reality; language both takes its cue from the world and describes it. The speaker commits to the truth or falsehood of what is expressed. But when speech acts are used to distort or falsify reality, they function as insults, defamation, and discrimination, as in *All Jews are avaricious* or *Israel is a Nazi state*. An assertion such as *The Holocaust never happened* twists reality but also inflicts affective wounds on the victims (or their descendants). Holocaust denial not only falsifies history; it always implies that those who think otherwise are liars, and it mocks the victims' suffering. Thus one assertion can perform several actions simultaneously. Language's potential for action also manifests itself in expressives—that is, speech acts that convey emotions in which the speaker articulates his or her attitude toward a certain state of affairs, as in "*I feel sick to my stomach when I think of Jews*" (postcard to the Embassy, 2006) or "*Sickening, that Jewish riffraff!*" (to the Central Council, 2003). Such speech acts also perpetrate violence, insulting and wounding those at whom they are aimed, attacking their dignity.

The Power of Language as Violence through Language

Although power and violence are not identical, they are nonetheless inseparable from one another.[10] Violence is a certain subtype of possible exercises of power involving a perpetrator and a victim.[11] In such situations language becomes a weapon. Verbal violence is a destructive form through which to exercise power. It is deployed consciously and intentionally with the goal of upsetting, insulting, excluding the other. This is characteristic of both verbal and nonverbal violence.[12] As a means of action, language has the potential to injure human beings cognitively as well as emotionally and to inflict harm on them not just individually but also socially. Language of this sort aims not only to exploit the vulnerability of its victims, but also to influence or win over those of a similar persuasion. Verbal utterances activate, reactivate, and construct ideas that can massively affect and lastingly influence public opinion and the collective consciousness.

Verbal utterances attack, insult, mock, threaten, and defame human beings as individuals and/or as members of groups. In everyday communicative situations, various forms of aggressive exercise of power through language occur repeatedly. Aggression (whose basis is a negative, emotional attitude that can be directed inward or outward) manifests itself verbally in hostile actions intended to harm someone cognitively, emotionally, or socially. Verbal discrimination is a form of violence that exploits the potential of language to devalue social groups on the basis of their ethnicity, gender, sexual preference, religion, age, or origin and exclude them from what the aggressor has defined as the social majority. Exclusion based on group identity grows out of the fundamental psychosocial distinction between one's own group and another group that manifests itself at all levels of human socialization. Discrimination as a verbal action differs from aggressive but not necessarily discriminatory speech acts in that it 'pertains to groups.' This semantic characteristic is crucial for determining whether a speech act should be categorized as criticism, insult, or discrimination (emphasizing the social or ethnic identity of a group).

Actions that are carried out consciously by means of verbal utterances constitute only one dimension of language's potential for exerting power and perpetrating violence. Language also has power because it is an instrument that can influence and guide our thoughts and feelings, that can manipulate us without our being aware of it. The meaning of words often sneaks into our minds and leaves traces, triggers associations, and shapes lasting attitudes and feelings. By way of semantics, words and sentences such as "*The vengeful Jews are shamelessly exploiting us Germans!*" (from a 2009 e-mail to the Embassy) activate specific representations and value judgments that can shape opinions. In this sense language exerts cognitive power that can have social consequences.[13] The power of the word of which Freud spoke (1926, 13) has today been established empirically: within fractions of a second, words activate mental representations in our long-term memory, unleash feelings, and create specific mental images (see, e.g., Miller 1995; Schwarz-Friesel 2007, 2008; Aitchison 2012).[14] People are more vulnerable to influence than they think, since many processes take place unconsciously and are not subject to control.[15] Assigning meaning is a mental process that cannot be suppressed: human reactions to language take place automatically, like a reflex. We cannot do anything to stop them except cover our ears and close our eyes. Our brain reacts in milliseconds to linguistic impulses and instantly assigns contents to the forms of expression. Linguistic utterances promptly activate mental representations in our memory. Controlling our receipt of influences is not possible (see Fodor 1983; Schwarz 2008, 167ff.). Only after automatically assigning significance are we cognitively in a position to subject the notions we have received to critical and controlled consideration. But these notions have already been stored in our working memory and can exercise an unconscious influence over us. Linguistic processing takes place on many levels, some of which are not directly accessible to consciousness. Thus it is possible for words or phrases that activate emotions to leave traces in our long-term memory or establish associations of which the listener or reader remains completely unaware.

A single word can activate a complex scenario in the human mind. *Apartheid* means 'institutionalized government separation of races or ethnic groups.' If we hear or read this word, we promptly activate a mental and prototypical image of South Africa as it used to be, with separate schools, restaurants, and park benches, with discriminatory laws and government repression. Empirical cognitive science tells us that the mental process of drawing comparisons is an essential activity in human cognition. By means of conscious or unconscious comparisons, the human mind tries to make sense of new or difficult experiences or objects, using analogies, for instance, to render the unfamiliar comprehensible. If Israel is described as an *apartheid regime*, therefore, a false analogy is quickly established that crudely stigmatizes that country. Words can often act like arrows; they bore their way into our consciousness. To describe Jews as *parasites*, *a nest of rats*, or *subhumans* means categorizing them as less than human and devaluing them as human beings. But words can also act as poison, dripping judgments into people's brains that do lasting harm. Expressions such as *beating people over the head with Auschwitz* and *Holocaust industry* have this potential, consigning any reminder of the Holocaust to the semantic context of instrumentalization. The focus shifts from the caesura in civilization and the suffering of the victims to the supposed advantages derived from victimhood. As a result, the crime is stripped of its decisive dimension of relevance, or its relevance is ignored. Frequent repetition of certain formulas can have the effect of normalizing the concepts they represent. When drastic expressions (*criminal state*, *murderous regime*, *orgies of violence*), hyperbolic phrases (*ferocious war criminals*, *appalling atrocities*), and comparisons to the Nazis are used repeatedly for so-called criticism of Israel without being challenged, after a while their inappropriateness goes unnoticed and habituation sets in. Comparisons to the Nazis also occur in conjunction with relativizing the Holocaust and mocking its victims (see Schwarz-Friesel 2007, 195ff.). Inflated use of the term *Holocaust* does not merely call into question the singularity of this criminal undertaking; it can also result in shifts in meaning from 'murder of European Jews' to 'murder, violence, ethnic cleansing' in general. One effect of this shift would be that the memory and awareness of the unique dimensions of this caesura in civilization would gradually be lost. When the lexeme *Jew* occurs in various discourses (Internet forums, school slang, etc.) as an insult rather than as a designation for 'a member of the Jewish faith community,' the shift in meaning that occurs can turn the concept into a stigma, and in everyday usage negative connotations can attach to it.[16] Frequent combinations of the adjective *Jewish* with nouns referring to violence, military actions, and war can cause such combinations to become customary and thereby create visual images and a semantic network of anti-Jewish notions or reactivate old structures of prejudice. The "rumor about the Jews," as Adorno described the phenomenon of antisemitism (1951/1980, 123), is kept alive by means of such discursive markers and reinforced by way of speculation, conjecture, deliberate slander, but also unconscious linguistic patterns. Such patterns leave conceptual traces in memory, at the very least in the form of suspicion.

The mass media play a particularly influential role in this area. It is well known that persuasive rhetoric was and is part of all propaganda in a dictatorial system, its goal being to shape public opinion. Examination of the Nazis' use of language clearly shows how institutionalized management of language can create an image of enemy and convey a specific view of the world (see also chapter 3, under Antisemitism as State Doctrine). Ready-made linguistic classifications (such as *Aryan*, *degenerate art*, *Jewification*, *international Jewish control of finance*) determine understandings of reality and encode absolutist value judgments. In this sense language becomes not only an important vehicle of cultural and cognitive categorization but also a source of such categorization. On the other hand, the use of euphemisms (such as *Final Solution*, *special treatment*, *euthanasia*, *Jew-free*) that do not designate semantically what they actually refer to, but activate nebulous concepts, have the effect of rendering extralinguistic phenomena anodyne and unreal, at least where acts of cruelty and violence are concerned.

But the mass media that disseminate information in our democracy also have the potential to shape negatively the thoughts and feelings of many, especially because the majority trust the media to meet the criteria of truthfulness and objectivity. When reporting in the mass media treats the Middle East conflict for years in a one-sided emotional manner and creates images of perpetrators and victims by means of pejorative lexemes and analogies, stereotypes can arise and old resentments can be (re)activated (cf. chapter 6, under "*As I just read in my paper . . .*"). Regardless of whether language occurs in everyday discourse or in public communication, it always has the power to influence the recipients' consciousness and attitudes. This capacity for influence constitutes the potential power of language.

The Reconstruction of Antisemitic Conceptualizations: Linguistic Utterances as Traces of Cultural, Cognitive, and Emotional Processes

For centuries hostile attitudes toward Jews have been represented and passed down in specific forms through language.[17] Words express and name, awaken, intensify, or create stereotypes and emotional attitudes. Representations through language transmit resentments and pass these along to others as externally perceptible value judgments. If we want to understand modern hostility toward Jews, it is relevant to examine the images and value judgments that find expression in verbal formulations. In all analyses of language we proceed from the basic assumption of cognitive linguistics that utterances carry traces of the mental activity of those who have produced them.[18] These traces are like footprints in the sand: we draw conclusions from the character of the footprint about the person who left it. Correspondingly, concrete manifestations in language are traces of mental activity. Since circumstances in reality are always represented in a specific way through language, these referents can reveal the conceptualizations (in the sense of mental images) of the producer of the language.[19] On the basis of linguistic manifestations, we reconstruct the underlying intellectual and emotional representations of those who created or motivated them. Thus texts provide insight into the mental structures, attitudes, and feelings of their authors. In this way we can form an impression of attitudinal antisemitism. Up to now, however, linguistic analyses with few exceptions (cf. Bering 2004) have played no important, let alone prominent, role in research on antisemitism. In this book we will show the great relevance of detailed linguistic and cognitive analysis, which has the capacity to uncover in a precise and reproducible fashion formal and mental components of hostility toward Jews and to establish criteria for the classification of modern antisemitism conveyed by verbal means. Since nowadays Judeophobic thinking and feelings find expression primarily through language, it is important to analyze and explicate the characteristics of antisemitic usage and to make this information available to international interdisciplinary research on antisemitism, providing a precise apparatus for analysis and classification that meets scholarly criteria for determining when a given utterance deserves to be considered antisemitic. In view of the debates that keep cropping up, the numerous libel suits, and even trials, it can prove significant when scholarship is in a position to provide clear information as to whether a given utterance is antisemitic. At present an attempt is made in the case of almost every "verbal misdemeanor" to find an excuse or an alternative interpretation, and the producers of the offensive language often style themselves victims of the alleged *antisemitism bludgeon* (see chapter 4, under Current Stereotypes and Their Verbal Manifestations). A widely disseminated and reputable scientific classification of verbal antisemitism can clarify this state of affairs.

An antisemitic attitude usually rests on a conceptualization of JEWS characterized by negative emotions and stereotypes.[20] A sentence such as *The Jews are subhuman* makes the racist ideology obvious. A sentence such as *The Jews want to rule the world* reveals that the speaker has obviously stored the traditional stereotype of the JEWISH WORLD CONSPIRACY in his or her mental belief system and is convinced of the truth of this belief. One of the fundamental principles of our communicative practice is that we always attribute cooperativeness and therefore rationality to the other person; that is, we proceed on the assumption that our interlocutor will observe certain criteria of quality (truthfulness) and relevance. We thus also assume that what a person says conveys his or her intentions precisely. In communicative practice, rational and moral claims (with respect to truth, correctness, and honesty) are always asserted (cf. Grice 1975; Habermas 1981, 525ff.). When we read sentences such as "*Jews dominate the financial sector*" (to the Central Council, 2002) or "*Jews control the media*" (to the Embassy, 2007), without being able to influence or block them, we activate the corresponding meanings and images and also automatically assume that the statement represents the actual opinion of the person making it. Thus language provides a window into the mind of the speaker, or "the key to the world of the speaker" (Edelman 1976, 168) and at the same time the path into the mind of the listener, who can be significantly influenced by such statements, whether willingly or not. Accordingly, every linguistic utterance mirrors a particular conceptual world corresponding to the worldview of its producer. In linguistic production a conceptual structure comes into focus that determines the choice of stored words. What words are considered appropriate depends on the producer's intentions as well as general attitude. For instance, in an antisemitic text, *rats' nest* is considered a suitable descriptor to apply to Jewish fellow citizens, since the speaker's emotional attitude toward and conceptualization of this community are marked by hatred, defensiveness, and an intent to discriminate.

Textual analyses employing the methodology of cognitive linguistics can, on the one hand, help us make transparent the conceptualization patterns of those producing a text and, on the other hand, contribute to critical awareness of the potential of such utterances to shape opinion and intensify prejudice. In the case of modern antisemitism, cognitive, emotional, and social aspects come together. The timeless components of pejorative antisemitic semantics are usually overlaid with informational components referring to current events such as the Middle East conflict, reassessments of Nazism, libel charges, and debates taking place. As a result, antisemitic texts often go unrecognized.[21] Reconstructing and explicating linguistic evaluation as a blend of old and new information ultimately offers a way to understand better the interaction of cultural knowledge and emotive judgments when Judeophobia is perpetuated through communication.

Conceptual and Verbal Antisemitism

Antisemitism as a mental system of belief and of interpretation of the world has been passed down through the centuries, always adapted to current conditions and correspondingly modified, yet without changes in the underlying conceptual constants, according to which Jews categorically function as THE OTHER. This conceptual antisemitism is based on stereotypes that represent mental constructs—that is, have no empirical basis but consist purely of projections by non-Jews onto Jews (see chapter 3). The essential aspect is that it is not individual characteristics or features of Jews that are rejected. Rather it is Jewish existence itself that is viewed as a provocation, an annoyance, an evil in the world (see chapter 8):

(5) Get out of our world, you Jewish scum! [ZJD_11.02.2005_Her_003]

(6) Jews—you are the cancerous growth on our world! [IBD_01.08.2006_001_Postcard]

In antisemites' mentally fixed binary construction of the world, Judaism figures as the ultimate opposite of their own form of existence. Accordingly Jews, with the imagined characteristics imputed to them, embody that which is categorically non-normal and bad. Antisemitism thus signifies exclusion of Jews and Judaism by labeling them as the absolute and total negation of the world order defined as normal. The fundamental principle by which humans establish meaning, "Omnis determinatio est negatio" (Spinoza), is thus taken as an absolute: the contents of the concept of the JEW are fixed and defined as a totality *ex negativo* (see Schwarz and Chur 2007, 38ff.). Beyond the normal contrasting distinctions inherent in any cognitive classification, Jews are assigned the status in antisemitic systems of conceptualization of NOT ONE OF US. In a categorical sense, therefore, JEW is an existential form that must not be accepted. The devaluation that accompanies this unique categorization has been reflected for centuries in numerous verbal manifestations in which Jews are dehumanized (*Jewish swine, parasites*), demonized (*monsters, ogres, devil's brood*), delegitimized (*worthless, noxious vermin, Final Solution of the Jewish question*), and therefore cognitively (in the literal sense of the word) localized as "nonhuman beings" outside the world order. Conceptual antisemitism is thus inextricably coupled with a derealizing worldview (see chapter 6, under Derealization). The image of the JEW as enemy is a concept beyond the reach of all experience, a negative construction that arises from a mental belief system, as well as from profound emotional resentment of Jews (see chapter 8).

All linguistic utterances that devalue, stigmatize, discriminate against, and defame Jews *qua* Jews can be considered forms of verbal antisemitism. These are utterances, in other words, that can be coded as stereotypes hostile toward Jews and that are used to transmit resentments. Verbal antisemitism can thus be defined as consisting of all formulations that explicitly and/or implicitly express stereotypes about Jews, share anti-Jewish conceptualizations and feelings, and pass along traditional Judeophobic images of the world. Conceptual representations formed from stereotypical constructs of categories thus always serve as the basis for verbal expressions of antisemitism.

In the case of intentional verbal antisemitism, the articulation of such notions at the level of conceptualization rests on a conscious anti-Jewish representation, and the verbalization process is determined largely by this conceptual representation. Additionally, the utterance has the specific purpose of intentionally discriminating against and defaming Jews.

Whether the person producing verbal antisemitic utterances styles himself or herself as an antisemite[22] and/or whether an utterance is articulated consciously and intentionally as hostile toward Jews (which can be reconstructed empirically only to a limited degree) does not affect its classification (see also Rensmann and Schoeps 2008, 15). Unintentionally produced verbal antisemitic expressions also draw on traditional conceptualizations hostile toward Jews and contribute to the preservation of stereotypes in the cultural and communicative memory (on intentional and unintentional verbal antisemitism, see Schwarz-Friesel 2007, 347, 2010a, 30).[23] Certain stock phrases, like the expressions *Jewish usury* and *Jewish rashness*, encode stereotypic images of Jews that have persisted over centuries and thereby form, for the most part unconsciously and in uncontrolled fashion, collective processes of societal consciousness formation; they have become habitual, often produced unthinkingly, without necessarily emanating from conceptual hatred of Jews. Using the terms *Jew(s)* and *Israeli(s)* synonymously, or a phrase like *Jews and Germans* that semantically creates two separate reference groups,[24] need not derive from an explicit intention to discriminate or express aggression. Nonetheless, such stereotype-reinforcing usage contributes to the maintenance of Judeophobic patterns of expression, along with the associated thought contents, in the society. Verbal antisemitisms can be described and explained by means of objective, reproducible criteria—unlike the underlying mental attitudes or intentions, which can be reconstructed only hypothetically. As presumably authentic traces of the cognitive and emotional activity taking place in the persons who use them, these phrases also provide insight into mental processes and states or allow plausible theories about them to be formulated.

Analysis of expressions with respect to their verbally antisemitic status and communicative place value requires prior response to three questions that involve three different aspects or levels of analysis:[25]

(1) Whether a given expression conveys antisemitic conceptualization, and thus constitutes actual verbal antisemitism, not merely a communicative act of criticism or individual insult.

(2) Where the verbal antisemitism occurs, whether in a private or public space (public/ semipublic/private). When antisemitic contents are expressed, it is relevant to establish the discursive situation and the degree to

which it is public; at stake is the question of accessibility and dissemination as well as the potential societal impact of antisemitic utterances.

(3) How a given verbal antisemitism is expressed (explicitly vs. implicitly). This contrasting pair designates the differentiation between direct and indirect speech acts and thus the way in which antisemitic thinking finds expression through language. Explicit expression makes use of semantics—that is, literal formulations of antisemitic thinking; implicit expression conveys such thinking through contextually determined meanings that can be decoded pragmatically and detected through the conclusions that the recipient draws (see the previous discussion of indirect speech acts and implicatures in this chapter, under Language as a Cognitive System and Communicative Instrument for Action, and endnote 9 in this chapter). The conclusions derive from the meaning but are not articulated *expressis verbis*. They are informational components of linguistic utterances that are not verbalized but can be understood without difficulty.

When, for example, an e-mail to the Central Council asks (rhetorically) "*whether the excessive violence in Israel that is perpetrated especially often on children corresponds to a long-standing tradition of your people*" (ZJD_06.09.2002_Sch_001), information is conveyed through implicatures that German Jews share responsibility for violence in the Middle East and that Jewish tradition in general involves violence. The notion implied in the reference to children is the Judeophobic stereotype of JEWS AS CHILD-MURDERERS.

Since verbal utterances must always be examined and assessed in context and in consideration of both the collective knowledge inherent in the given discourse and the action- and effect-oriented communicative sense, an analysis that attended only to external forms and literal meanings would be not only incomplete but also unscientific.

The pairs designed for differentiation are not mutually exclusive; rather, an expression in any communicative situation (public as well as private) can convey both explicit and implicit antisemitism.

In nonlinguistic, noncognitive research on antisemitism, these three levels of analysis are often employed in an undifferentiated fashion, in combination with highly heterogeneous and inconsistent terminology and a lack of clear definitions and distinctions. For the most part, no distinction is made between conceptual and verbal antisemitism. Furthermore, in the literature the rather confusing concepts "manifest" and "latent" are used with shifting meanings to make a distinction between, on the one hand, (verbal) antisemitism that is expressed in public and in private communication[26] and, on the other hand, the form in which it finds articulation (cf., e.g., Benz 2004, 20).[27] The circumstances of the communicative situation and the linguistic form in which the utterance is expressed must, however, be designated unambiguously as separate phenomena and distinguished from one another.

Whether an utterance should be characterized as antisemitic can be established unambiguously by means of criteria employed for textual and discourse analysis, as well as those used in cognitive linguistics (as we will demonstrate thoroughly in this book). Everyday verbal aggression such as any individual can encounter in the form of scolding, mocking, threatening, and so on differs markedly from verbal antisemitic speech in that, in the latter, membership in a specific group becomes a decisive component of the verbal violence: people are rejected, attacked, and judged negatively because of their identity as Jews, as in the following passage:

> (7) Obviously Möllemann is right! Sharon is historically a mass murderer! Friedmann is a provocative, intolerant, and arrogant Jew, or in plain German, insolent and shameless. Reich-Ranicki is no literary pope the way the media portrays him but an insolent, slimy Polish Jew! [ZDJ_10.06.2002_ano_001]

The basis for denigrating comments is not these individuals' characteristics or behavior but their Jewishness. The conceptual characteristic JEWISH is the determining factor and provides the mental basis for classification and evaluation expressed through language. Thus verbal antisemitisms are specific forms of linguistic discrimination (see chapter 3, under Survival and Resistance of Judeophobic Stereotypes in Modern Times). The mental image inscribed by means of the concept JEW can refer to a specific person as in (7) but can also be depersonalized. In that case, behavioral patterns classified as typically Jewish can be cited, as in (8), where a connection is made between Israeli military actions and the Jewish mentality, explicitly through the word "*Jewish*" and implicitly through the reference to "*two thousand years*":

(8) Recently the Ambassador denied that the Jewish state's air force fired on a German intelligence-gathering vessel. [. . .] The Ambassador was merely engaging in behavior that Jewish tradition has always sanctioned. [IBD_31.10.2006_Koe_001]

(9) For two thousand years you have been engaged in stealing land and committing murder! [IBD_11.09.2007_Mar_001]

Precisely those modern forms of verbal antisemitism that achieve a referential shift (from the reference object 'Jew' to the reference object 'Israel') work primarily by means of these depersonalized assignments of stereotypes (see chapter 6 for a more thorough discussion).

Verbal antisemitisms take numerous forms, among them invective, Holocaust denial, threats of violence, comparisons to the Nazis, innuendo, and allusions, expressed by means of rhetorical questions, quotations, and the like. It becomes apparent how large a repertory of anti-Jewish stereotypes and feelings exists; Judeophobic contents can be conveyed in the most varied verbal forms. Invective generally considered typical of verbal antisemitism such as *Jewish usurers*, explicit Holocaust denials such as *the Auschwitz lie*, and generic statements such as *All Jews are avaricious* represent only a very small portion of the many types of verbal antisemitism. Despite the multiple lexical, grammatical, and stylistic differences, despite all the nuances and variations in which these notions find expression, several fundamental categorical characteristics of verbal antisemitism can be recognized (in addition to the previously mentioned semantics and pragmatics of dehumanization and delegitimation): collective demarcation, fixation, and devaluation.[28] The demarcation of Jews can be indicated in many different ways (see chapter 4 for a more thorough discussion):

(10) Isn't it time the Jews left us Germans in peace? [ZJD_29.07.2006_Bur_001]

The premise of such a comment is that Jews are fundamentally different and in no sense belong to the speaker's in-group. The imputed difference or foreignness is established through the assignment of negative stereotypes and thereby legitimated or pseudo-rationalized:

(11) You Jews always were and still are thieves, murderers, traitors, and land-grabbers! [ZJD_05.08.2008_Dro_001]

A variant of this verbal antisemitism occurs when stereotypes are assigned, in the process of which conclusions about individuals are applied to all Jews, for instance in utterances like (12) and (13):

(12) That is especially true of your extremely arrogant and presumptuous VP, Friedmann. The way he comports himself and the things he says makes me feel, to put it mildly, extremely uneasy about Judaism, a sensation I never had before in any way. [ZJD_18.06.2002_Neu_001]

(13) You Israelis are completely callous. In the last days of the war you drop cluster bombs over inhabited areas and accuse people who criticize that action of antisemitism. That's typical of you Jews! [ZJD_01.09.2006_Wei_001]

On the basis of their membership in a group, Jews are associated with certain characteristics, qualities, and forms of behavior; they are assigned by way of stereotypes to a conceptually circumscribed category. This category receives a negative value. Every collective attribution thus conveys devaluation. This devaluation occurs with significant frequency in tandem with the semantics of dehumanization:

(14) No thoughtful, humane person can be on your side. [...] You will be [...] combatted wherever and in whatever manner possible. [IBD_20.02.2009_Gut_001]

(15) Can you be considered human beings? You don't even have the socialized behavior of animals, rats, or microbes! [ZJD_Gaza2009_300/816_Mon_001]

Verbal antisemitism is at work when a nationalist and racist definition constitutes the basis for classifying someone or something as Jewish, in the sense that a Jew always remains a Jew and that being Jewish is considered inseparable from certain unchanging markers or characteristics.

(16) You Jews never change. Miserable wretches!!! [IBD_07.11.2006_ano_001]

(17) That's just how Jews have been for more than 2 thousand years. [ZJD_12.03.2007_Kli_001]

Verbal antisemitism also comes into play when the Germans' responsibility for the Holocaust is denied or relativized, when historical facts having to do with the extermination of the Jews are distorted or portrayed falsely, when a reversal of perpetrators and victims takes place or is implied, when arguments are adduced for terminating the culture of memory work and responsibility, and when comparisons are made with the Nazis:

> (18) But the Israelis murder little children—it's horrendous. Worse than the Holocaust, if in fact that even happened. The world's worst criminals are the Jews. The bad part is that the Jews still take pleasure in such things. Simply horrendous what the Jews think they can get away with in the world. First blubber about Hitler and now do the very same thing—how ridiculous can you get? So: PRO HAMAS and down with the criminal GANG OF JEWS. [ZJD_Gaza2009_153/816_Rie_001]
>
> (19) Hey, there, you Jews [. . .] Among the many lies like the one about the 6 million 'Holocaust' victims. Your own Yad Vashem hasn't been able to trace more than 3 million names in all this time. Just another of those lies, cashing in for 6 million—typical Jewish. Fits right in with the cliché about all of you. [IBD_28.10.2006_ano_001]
>
> (20) No one elected the Jewish Central Council! Why do we keep on paying reparations for something that happened over 50 years ago??? That debt's been paid!!!!! [ZJD_26.08.2007_Kar_001]

Verbal antisemitism also occurs when the concepts ISRAELI(S), ZIONISM/ZIONISTS, and JEW(S)/JEWRY are used interchangeably or are intermingled to express a critical or hostile attitude toward all Jews:

> (21) My hat off to the Jewish people. They've learned well from Hitler and his Nazi regime. What the Zionists are doing to the Palestinians today is no better than what they endlessly accuse the Germans of, in order to divert attention from their own atrocities. [ZJD_09.03.2008_Stra_001]
>
> (22) When innocent little children, mothers, and fathers lose their lives in attacks by the Israelis, that's much worse than if now and then anti-Jewish statements are made! [. . .] I'm ashamed for all Jews. [ZJD_05.01.2009_Kil_001]

It is also antisemitic to blame all Jews for Israel's policies and to saddle them with collective guilt:

(23) You, Herr Spiegel, personally support, advocate for, and tolerate a massacre in Israel. You're to blame, Herr Spiegel. [ZJD_08.04.2005_Hah_001]

Here we see an unjustifiable generalization along the lines of 'Jews are responsible for the actions of the Jewish state.' One would never blame all Catholics for the policies of the Vatican, for instance. These assignments of collective guilt also rely on the old antisemitic stereotype of JEWS ARE NO GERMANS (in the current variant JEWS ARE ISRAELIS).

We have a further instance of verbal antisemitism when negative Judeophobic stereotypes are applied to Israel and arguments are deployed that attribute general negative qualities to both Jews and Israelis:

(24) Christ-murderers, thieves, traitors, Jewish rabble: "chosen people"! [IBD_31.07.2006_Luh_001]

(25) Free the Near East from the Jewish plague! [IBD_12.07.2006_ano_003]

(26) let iran get the atom bomb and bomb israel off the map. that'll serve that fucking gang of child-murderers right. go to hell, all of you Jewish assholes. [ZJD_31.01.2006_ano_001]

In the chapters that follow we will investigate thoroughly the different verbal manifestations of hostility toward Jews, citing numerous examples in order to identify their specific characteristics and explaining the historical discursive context, as well as making transparent the conceptual and emotional representations that underlie these linguistic patterns.

Conclusion

Linguistic utterances do not merely depict extralinguistic reality; they also create their own realities through a specific semantics. In the collective communicative memory, Judeophobic patterns of verbal usage constitute and transmit mental models that conceptually represent Jews as THE OTHER. Verbal hostility toward Jews displays a destructive semantics based on the processes of demarcation, hardening of stereotypes, and devaluation. A crucial aspect of the phenomenon is that it does not simply mean the rejection of certain markers or characteristics of Jews; indeed, the very existence of Jews is viewed as a provocation, an annoyance, the force of evil in the world. Antisemitic resentment is directed not toward a specific concrete referent in the real world but toward the concept of the JEW stored in the head of the person producing the speech, a concept that has no empirical foundation.

3 HOSTILE STEREOTYPES OF JEWS AND THEIR HISTORICAL ROOTS

> Such a desperate / through and through evil / poisonous / devilish thing are these Jews / being our plague / pestilence / and all misfortune for 1400 years / and continuing to this day. Summa we have veritable devils in them / no other means to say it / They have no human heart toward us heathen / Such things they learn from their rabbis in the devilish nests of their schools. [Luther 1543/1577, 371f.]

> I call this foreign element a plague and a bane unto itself. It can be called much more, for the Jews are a corrupted and degenerate people. [Arndt 1814, 193]

On the Genesis of Resentment toward Jews: Why the Jews?

To understand how deep the roots of the cognitive stereotypes and emotional resentments of Jews go, one must delve into history. The historical and contemporary patterns of hostility toward Jews resemble each other strikingly, both in semantics and in form. Yet many people do not know, or are not aware, that some of the current negative formulations applied to Jews and/or Israelis belong to the standard repertory used for centuries by antisemites. Accordingly, many lack a critical awareness of how inflammatory some expressions can be. The current forms in which verbal antisemitism appears can be accurately described and fully explained only if one becomes aware of the underlying traditional conceptualizations and linguistic patterns. To demonstrate the unbroken continuity in Judeophobic thinking, we will therefore offer a brief sketch and historical background of the relevant stereotypes, some of which have existed for centuries and remain encoded in language and visual images to this day.[1]

Hostility toward and hatred of Jews have manifested themselves for two millennia both verbally and nonverbally, taking forms that include discrimination, intimidation, persecution, humiliation, and murder. This complex phenomenon involves religious, historical, economic, political, psychological, communicative, and philosophic aspects (cf. Bauer 1985, 1992; Reinharz 1987; Wistrich 1991, 2010; Bergmann 2006; Laqueur 2006; Nonn 2008). All types and variants of hostility toward Jews grow out of specific, timeless conceptual patterns representative of non-Jews' mental constructs about Jews. If in the course of history the particular manifestations and expressions of Judeophobia kept changing, what persisted was a conceptually and emotionally deep-seated resentment, independent of all current political, economic, social, and/or ideological motives, epiphenomena, and influences (cf. Grammel 2002, 9).

But why Jews? Why of all the communities and groups in the world have the Jews incurred so much hatred and violence over the centuries? Why was every misfortune, every plague, every atrocity ascribed to them (see Prager and Telushkin 2003)? Why did this hostility ultimately result in the Nazis' radical policy of extermination? And why does modern antisemitism survive to this day, also in educated circles, despite the experience of Auschwitz and all the efforts to get at the roots of the phenomenon?[2] These questions, often and intensely discussed—and always answered by enemies of the Jews in terms of the character and actions of Jews themselves—can be resolved only if one recognizes that hostility toward Jews is not simply one prejudice among many but something unique. It is unique because it has its origins in a moral and conceptual interpretation of the world that exists in no other form of hostility toward a group. Hatred of Jews does not mean hatred of a specified Other, of something clearly foreign, but of an alleged evil in the world. The genesis of an interpretation of the world that specifically targets the existence of the Jews lies in the split between Judaism and Christianity.

The oldest stereotype about Jews arose in antiquity.[3] In pre-Christian times, Greek and Roman anti-Judaism rested primarily on the idea of Jews as "aliens" (Horkheimer 1946/2002, 30; Grunberger 1962, 265; Grunberger and Dessuant 2000, 264; Wistrich 2010, 81). This conceptualization, expressive not only of general xenophobic tendencies but also of specific ideas about Jews, turns up in Greek writings (see Heinemann 1931; Herr 1988) and functions through the centuries as a basic stereotype that promoted differentiation and segregation of Jews and remained a constant.[4] The concept of the OTHER and the ALIEN did not, however, develop into a genuinely Judeophobic conceptualization (JEWS AS REJECTORS OF THE TRUE FAITH,[5] JEWS AS THE MURDERERS OF CHRIST,[6] JEWS AS THE EPITOME OF EVIL) until after the split between Judaism and Christianity had occurred, when it went hand in hand with religiously motivated hatred. Here we have the origin of the hatred of Jews that has persisted for two thousand years. The early Christians, a Jewish group who initially differed from the rest of Jews only in their belief in Jesus as the Messiah, increasingly set themselves apart from Judaism, emphasizing their differences. It was Paul, not Jesus and his disciples, who created the split, asserting that only someone who believed in Jesus as the Savior represented the true faith. Only this belief, he claimed, not observance of the traditions, determined what was true Judaism. Anyone who did not accept this faith would suffer damnation. Paul's theological writings became the basis for the strict separation between Jews, seen as apostates, and Christians, the only true believers. This dichotomy found its most drastic expression in the Gospel According to John, where the Jews are demonized and damned as unbelievers. Furthermore, the version that contends that Jesus was killed by Jews and in conformity with Jewish law, which was historically implausible in view of the existing political situation in Israel under Roman occupation and absolute rule (see Cohen 1977), led to the establishment of the stereotype of Jews as the murderers of God (see also, e.g., Parkes 1981; Simon 1996; Laqueur 2006; Wistrich 2010). Thus the foundation was laid for the distinction between the true and the false (demonic) Israel.

The radical split from the original religion and the rejection of Judaism were based among other things on disappointment at the lack of insight on the part of those Jews who did not recognize that Jesus, the Jew who came from their midst, was the Messiah, the Savior. This disappointment gave rise to the grudge that laid the foundation for the early resentment of Jews.[7] By making their belief absolute, the Christians excluded any possibility that they might be fallible: accepting the Jews and their religion would have meant granting the cognitive possibility, at least hypothetically, that doubt might attach to their own faith, for the chief justification of the existence of Jewish life included the consideration that under some circumstances Jesus might not be viewed as the son of God. Such a doubt had to be prevented at all costs. Accordingly the Jews came to be identified as the complete opposite of the Christians' existence, the absolute Other, as evil, and thus beyond the pale of all positive values.

The genesis and spread of Christianity as a comprehensive world religion goes hand in hand with the development of hostility toward Jews, their stigmatization and exclusion. Thus arose and became established the image of the Jewish person who remains obstinate, opposing the majority community of faith, closing him- or herself off, insisting on his or her own form of existence and belief. All further forms of anti-Judaism (including those having nothing to do with religion) ultimately hark back to this conceptualization, which divides the world into 'right' and 'wrong.' The long history of hostility toward Jews cannot, of course, be explained monocausally, since this hostility has changed repeatedly over the course of two thousand years, adjusting to current dispositions and situations (see, e.g., Parkes 1963; Poliakov 1985; Almog 1988; Laqueur 2006). But the genesis of Judeophobia goes back to the separation of Judaism from Christianity. Genuine hatred of Jews begins with the assertion by Christians, especially theologians, that they represent the one true faith, and it accompanies the institutional expansion of Christianity as a world religion (cf. Parkes 1981).

The specific features of Christian hatred of Jews grew out of the competition between Judaism and Christianity, as the latter struggled over centuries to establish itself as the leading world religion.[8] According to Christian doctrine, Judaism had to cease to exist once the Messiah appeared (cf. Bauer 1992, 83).

To establish itself as the one true and indubitable religion, Christianity had to completely negate the religion from which it sprang. This negation produced a radical counterversion and resulted in damnation of Judaism as a religion, as well as of the people who remained loyal to it. This negation also laid the groundwork for all further nonreligious variants of hostility toward Jews. Research on hatred (see Haubl 2007) shows accordingly that particularly profound feelings of defensiveness arise and persist when an affinity exists between the object of hatred and the hatred-filled subject; precisely this affinity characterizes the relationship between the Jewish and Christian religions.

Why the Jews? Because Jesus, who promulgated the first Christian doctrines, was a Jew, bound up inseparably with Judaism, with its belief in God and with its laws, and laid out a new path to human existence and to God on the basis of the Jewish religion, and because those who came after him and developed Christianity into a world religion either could not or would not practice the tolerance he preached or embrace his message of love and mercy, but instead fell into rage and hatred toward their own roots, which they wanted to extirpate with blazing intolerance or refused to accept.[9] Jesus the Jew becomes Christ the Savior, who is murdered by the Jews, released from his Jewish roots, transformed into a being separate from Judaism; the former brothers in the faith become anti-Christs who reject the true faith; Judaism becomes a source of damnation. The coexistence of two religions with a common foundation cannot be tolerated: the existence of Jews becomes apostasy. From this apostasy springs the total devaluation of everything Jewish. Jews become the archetype of all that is evil and reprehensible in the world. In the course of the centuries, a theological interpretation becomes an all-encompassing ethos; a religious interpretation and doctrine becomes a system for determining the meaning of the world, a system in which Jews and Judaism on principle come to figure as the negative dimension.

If one considers that the institution of the Christian Church, with its doctrines and New Testament, exercised primary influence on all spheres of life, all social, cultural, and political structures and processes for more than eighteen hundred years as the most powerful societal and ideological force, that it dominated all literary and artistic forms, that it accompanied or shaped all hegemonic structures (and to this day remains a factor in broad sectors of society), it is not surprising that the image it created of the JEW AS ENEMY should have survived through the centuries despite all historical changes. Hostility toward Jews belongs to a mentality with deep roots in Western culture, passed down from generation to generation as a fixed component of Christian tradition and identity.

> (1) The Jew pondereth night and day / how to harm the cristian in any way [Title of an anonymous pamphlet from the fifteenth century, quoted by Hortzitz 1999, 37]

Jews are accordingly not *an* enemy, they are *the* enemy. In addition to being a metaphysical evil, on earth they represent the epitome of evil, the human embodiment of all that is bad, the anti-Christ, and are therefore often described as *devil('s brood) and Satan('s spawn)* (see Trachtenberg 1943).[10]

The schism in the Christian Church caused by Martin Luther does not bring about any reversal. On the contrary: in his writings, Luther, enraged at the Jews' loyalty to their religion, hurls furious accusations at Jewish people, thus exacerbating their demonization,[11] and thereby plays a major part in poisoning the relationship of Protestantism to Judaism for centuries to come:[12]

> (2) That is / what I said heretofore / that a Christian, excepting the devil / has no more poisonous / bitter enemy / than a Jew. [Luther 1543/1577, 378]
>
> (3) But all matches the judgment of Christ / that they are poisonous / bitter / vengeful / secretive vipers / murderers & devil's spawn / who stab in secret and do harm / because they cannot do it openly. Therefore I would wish / they were there /where no Christians are. [Luther 1543/1577, 377]

The conceptualization of Jews as JESUS-MURDERERS, MURDERERS OF THE SAVIOR, as having blood on their hands and still opposing the true faith provided the basis for numerous further negative concepts, some of which derived from the economic and social conditions imposed upon the Jews, some of which were inventions reflective of a perspective oriented toward an image of the enemy (e.g., RITUAL MURDERS AND USE OF BLOOD BY JEWS; cf. Erb 1999; von Braun 1999).[13]

> (4) Herefrom thou mayest wel see / . . . that they are bloodthirsty dogs and murtherers / to all of Christianity . . . How they have then been found guilty / of having poisoned water and fountaine / stolen children / and stabbed them through / and now dismembered them with flax combs / that they might secretly cool themselves with Christians' blood. [Luther 1543/1577, 345]
>
> (5) The godless, blaspheming, thieving, robbing, and murthering [Jews] [Nigrinus 1570, 177]
>
> (6) In what unspeakable way the Jews have stolen Christian children, then martyred, flayed, and crucified them, and sucked out their blood with quills, thereof the most trustworthy exempla may be read . . . in the most believable writers. [Grattenauer 1803, 12f.]

This systematic devaluation of Jewish existence per se provided the basis for all subsequent collective attributes that developed during the following centuries (JEWS AS STUBBORN, VENGEFUL, DIABOLICAL, etc.) and extended far beyond religious differences and created the foundation for a strictly binary image of the world, which persists to this day in the minds of many people, as a current example, a 2009 e-mail to the Central Council, clearly shows (for a more thorough discussion, see chapter 4, under Current Stereotypes and Their Verbal Manifestations):

(7) you are proud of gaza?? what human being can be proud of murder? an antichrist. jesus already said 'you have the devil for a father.' thats in the bible! you can recognize arihmans children by their deeds. thanks israel youve opened my eyes. you reap what you sow! you have three guesses what israel will reap in the future. im looking forward to that day. that day will go down in cosmic history as the day when EVIL was beaten. [ZJD_Gaza2009_84/816_Dar_001]

According to this view of the world, Jews do not merely differ from non-Jews in one way or another; they are fundamentally different and fundamentally bad. This mental construct results in the creation of a categorical, collective image of the enemy. The Judeophobic stereotype projections of JEWS AS CHILD-MURDERERS, BLOOD CULTISTS, and so on have nothing to do with actual circumstances but are constructs in the minds of non-Jews.[14] As a result, everything Jews do or do not do as Jews is by definition wrong, and all judgments about Jews are a priori precondemnations, all resting on the characterization of Jews as BAD. According to this interpretation of the world, all evils were and are attributed to the hated Jews: children's disappearance or murder, crooked deals, poisoned wells, illnesses, the plague, crop destruction, personal misfortunes, lost wars, financial crises. Thus Jews serve as the universal scapegoats in predominantly Christian social structures.

In the case of some traditional stereotypes, real historical circumstances are invoked, for instance when it comes to the Jew as HOMELESS WANDERER. After the destruction of Jerusalem by the Romans in 70 CE, many Jews went into exile and formed communities in the diaspora. The rejection by the inhabitants of the host countries, who did not want the Jews to become integrated, was transformed by way of projection into a negative characteristic of the Jews. Since then the stereotype of the Jews as RESTLESS WANDERERS has become commonplace; they are said to be unwilling to make themselves at home, preferring to remain foreign among their hosts and therefore never developing solidarity with them:

(8) The Jew may be counted among other dead nations; but to the Germans . . . the Jew does not belong. [Sauerwein 1831, 10]

(9) I do not want [the Jews' procreation] also for this reason, that they are a thoroughly alien people and I wish to keep the Germanic tribe as free as possible of alien admixtures. [Arndt 1814, 188]

Because non-Jews prohibited Jews from pursuing normal economic enterprises such as the skilled crafts, Jews were excluded from all social enterprises other than dealing in money (see Raphael 1999, 115). The reproach of being usurers and money-grubbers that non-Jews leveled against Jews thus derived from a situation that non-Jews had created themselves.[15] In the course of history, pursuit of these activities came to be conceptualized as typically Jewish and was cited as a justification for defamatory and discriminatory treatment.

> (10) But what be the Jews? in truth no confessors / but blasphemers and defilers of God and Christ . . . They be also lazy layabouts / for they be idle usurers / that have neither fields nor pastures / can do no trades / nor any handiwork / but go idle / letting us toil and in the sour sweat of our brows earn our victuals / they meanwhile nourish themselves all from the poor Christians' sweat and blood /and live well from / pressing us through usury and cozenage. [Salzmann 1661, cited in Hortzitz 2005, 66f.]

The cliché of the Jewish haggler and usurer became a permanent fixture in the collective frame of reference and established itself by way of language in corresponding stock phrases (see chapter 4, under Current Stereotypes and Their Verbal Manifestations). In world literature the stereotype of the MERCILESS MONEY-GRUBBER has become known through the figure of Shylock in Shakespeare's *Merchant of Venice*.[16] The negative opinion of Jews turns up across the centuries in numerous texts and occurs in all sectors of society, by no means only among the rabble, the uneducated, but also among writers, thinkers, priests, scholars, and philosophers. In Goethe's *The Annual Fair in Plundertown* the clichés are presented satirically by means of stock phrases representing the perspective of one who hates Jews.[17] Nonetheless, they mirror the culturally established knowledge of the time:

> (11) You know the people they call the Jews . . . they have a belief / that gives them the right to rob strangers . . . The Jew loves money and fears danger. He knows how, with little effort and without risking much / to wring money from the land through commerce and interest . . . Yet through money they find the key to all hearts, / And no secret is well kept from them . . . They know how to capture everyone through loans and exchanges; / He who lets himself be drawn in never gets free. [Goethe 1773/1973, 133f.]

Not even the Enlightenment, with its rational critique of religion, which cited rational principles in calling for equal rights for all and the elimination of distinctions according to rank and class, broke through the culturally established anti-Jewish thinking; Voltaire viewed Jews as the natural enemies not only of certain nations but of all humanity and thus succumbed to the traditional, religiously based, conceptualization:[18]

> (12) by virtue of their own laws, natural enemies of these nations and ultimately of humanity. [Voltaire 1761, quoted in Hentges 1999, 45]

In several articles in his *Dictionnaire philosophique*, Voltaire also mentions the Jews very disparagingly, calling them, among other things, "*the most despicable people of the earth*" (see Poliakov 1983, 101; see also Laqueur 2006, 88: "*I would not be the least bit surprised if this people one day were to become deadly to the human race.*")

The assumption that enmity toward Jews can be attributed primarily to lack of enlightenment and education must thus be rejected: even highly intelligent and cultivated persons were and are not immune to Judeophobic resentments (see chapter 8). A glance at the writings of the great German philosophers of Idealism, who were dedicated to seeking the truth through reason, makes this particularly clear:

> (13) Since their exile, the Palestinians living in our midst have gained the not undeserved reputation for fraud, also amongst the great majority, thanks to their spirit of usury. [Kant 1798/1839, 218]
>
> (14) Do you then not recall the state within the state, my friends? Does not the understandable thought come to you that the Jews, who without you are citizens of a state that is more solid and mighty than all of yours, if you vouchsafe them also the right to citizenship in your states, will completely trample upon the rest of you citizens? . . . But to give them citizenship I truly see no other way than to cut off all their heads one night and put in their place others in which not one single Jewish idea can be found. To protect ourselves against them, I also see no other means than to conquer their promised land for them and to dispatch them all thither. [Fichte 1793/1845, 150]

Similar statements can be found in Herder and Hegel. Hegel, the most important philosopher of Idealism, manifests in his early writings a particularly virulent form of hatred toward Jews, expressed by means of almost all the traditional stereotypes yet integrated into his philosophical reflections on the World Spirit (see the thorough discussion in Hentges 1999):

> (15) Not to be denied are the Jews' twisted and immoral conceptions of the anger, partisanship, and hatred toward other peoples, yea, the intolerance of their Jehovah, conceptions that unfortunately made their way into the practice and theory of the Christian religion. . . . And we must be thankful not to their priests but to philosophy . . . and the milder light of our times for the fact that their grim quarrelsomeness, their intolerance, and their conceit have diminished. [Hegel 1793–1794]

According to Hegel, the Jewish people "*is without a soul and felt no need for freedom when it was emancipated*," isolates itself from other human groups, and is remarkable for its scorn and hatred for other human beings. He sees Jews as addicted to self-isolation, alienated from love, spirit, and life, and he considers "*the Sabbath characteristic of the slavish spirit.*" He also articulates the reproach that Jews are lowly, intellectually inferior beings and deniers of the true religion:

> (16) The spirit recognizes only the spirit; they saw in Jesus only the man, the Nazarene, the carpenter's son . . . as much as he was, he could not be more, he was only one like them, and they themselves felt that they were nothing. His attempt to give them awareness of something divine had to fail with them, for the belief in something divine, in something great, cannot reside in filth. [Hegel 1800]

After more than seventeen hundred years of defamation, hostility toward Jews was so deeply rooted in Western thought that even poets and thinkers who shook off the old church doctrine and paved the way for self-determination could not free themselves of that hostility, despite their reflections on the universal rights of man. This shows very clearly that hostility toward Jews was based not only on ideology but also on human systems of belief, supported by seemingly unshakable ethical principles or categories of thought. That these Manichaean thought categories had first found their way into the world through Christian church doctrine did not occur to these thinkers.

Until the late eighteenth or early nineteenth century hostility toward Jews was motivated primarily by religion and Christian anti-Judaism (see, e.g., Bauer 1992; Weinzierl 1995; Benz 2004). This anti-Judaism resulted concretely in exclusion, denial of citizenship, persecution, forced baptism, as well as sporadic pogroms, leading to the murder of Jews. The prevailing stereotypes that found expression in literature, in sermons, in the incitation of pogroms, and in anti-Jewish tracts characterized Jews as JESUS-MURDERERS, HOMELESS WANDERERS, MONEY-GRUBBERS, USURERS, HAGGLERS, and CONSPIRATORS (for thorough discussions, see the individual essays in Schoeps and Schlör 1999). No matter what Jews did or refrained from doing over the centuries, whether they had economic success and social prestige or not, from the resentment-skewed perspective they were always assessed negatively. Depending on the particular perspective, they might be labeled the enemy *de jour*—as *capitalists*, *socialists*, or *Bolshevists* (cf. Barkai 1999; Niedermüller 1999). In many texts they were portrayed as inferior creatures, often compared to animals and placed on a lower rung of being:

> (17) And despite all this influence, might, wealth, and freedom they were and are the bloodsuckers of the people . . . remained on the lowest level of civilization and spread filth and crudeness all about. [Fries 1816, 5]

Here the principle of demonization that forms part of Judeophobia becomes apparent, an element that extends beyond Jews' function as scapegoats: the hostility originally motivated by religion has become total hostility, directed as resentment not toward individual Jews but toward the Jews' very existence. In National Socialism this resentment formed the bedrock of antisemitism as salvation (cf. Bauer 2001; Friedländer 2006), the extirpation of Judaism in the name of "the good of mankind," in order to "preserve the German people from harm" (cf. Katz, 1980, 1990; see chapter 9, under Suggestions for Solving the "Jewish Problem").

Survival and Resistance of Judeophobic Stereotypes in Modern Times

An examination of the history of hostility toward Jews reveals that the most prevalent stereotypes result from discriminatory behavior of non-Jews toward Jews or, far more commonly, represent constructs that have nothing to do with reality, that are pure products of the imagination (e.g, JEWS AS CHILD-MURDERERS,[19] PLAGUE SPREADERS, OPINION MOLDERS, and WORLD CONSPIRATORS). Stereotypes transmitted over centuries through language, sometimes with conscious intent, sometimes unconsciously, came to form an encoding system or, as Volkov (1990, 29, 2006, 66) puts it, a "cultural and communicative code." From the perspective of cognitive linguistics, hostility toward Jews through the centuries can be described as the survival of a stable mental belief system whose ideological components are equated to ethical and moral values and whose units of knowledge are communicated institutionally. This hostility has become a conceptual construct based primarily on emotional resentment, never questioned but simply taken as a given and assumed to be valid. It forms a cognitive network of stereotyped concepts inscribed in collective memory and thus situated on a supraindividual level as an element of general knowledge.

These stereotype constructs had solidified in the minds of many into a system for making sense of the world. This system then gave rise to radical suggestions, for instance in Hartwig von Hundt-Radowsky's *Judenspiegel* [Jewish mirror] of 1819. To this hate-filled demagogue, Jews were "*subhumans*" and "*vermin*," "*malodorous hoopoes*." He categorically rejected any suggestion of conversion or assimilation; according to him, the Jews were terminally depraved and the males had to be eliminated, their women confined in brothels:

> (18) The best thing, however, would be to purge the land of this vermin, and there are two means by which to do this. Either to annihilate them altogether or, as Pharaoh, the Meiningen, Würzbergers, and Frankfurters have done, to chase them from the land. [Hundt-Radowsky 1819, 144]

One can, of course, see such tracts as the psychopathological products of individuals, but the fact that after this text appeared the author was not taken away to a municipal insane asylum indicates the broad acceptance or at least indifference with which such violent fantasies were received.[20]

Complex Judeophobic interpretive patterns were generally established that included all human characteristics (appearance, character, intelligence, and social conduct). As far as physical appearance was concerned, Jews were considered strikingly ugly, with specific demonic facial features, such as hooked noses, and dark hair and eyes.[21] Jews' character was associated with such epithets as *intellectual inferiority* or *destructiveness*, *hypocrisy*, *conspiratorial mendacity*, *slyness*, and *vengefulness*. To Jewish women, according to this pattern, was ascribed noxious beauty, along with sexual attractiveness and lasciviousness. Additional characteristics were stinginess, selfishness, mercilessness, emotional coldness, and cowardice. Allegedly Jews also practiced ritual murder, engaged in a blood cult, and were obstinate and blind toward the true faith and the ethical values of decent societies. The Jews' religious belief that they were the chosen people gave rise to the charge that they were arrogant:

> (19) They constitute the most arrogant and exclusive aristocracy. [Naudh 1861, 7, quoted in Hortzitz 1988, 161]

As social beings the Jews were alleged to harm society, functioning as parasites, spreaders of disease, exploiters, usurers, traitors, corrosive influences, and influential shapers of opinion:

> (20) Judaism is to be compared . . . to a gigantic freeloading tumor. [Holst 1821, 64]

The Jews reputedly aimed to take over the world and enslave all non-Jews (see *The Protocols of the Elders of Zion* and Hitler's concept of WORLD JEWRY):

> (21) The Jews want . . . to rule the world. [Scharff-Scharffenstein 1871, 50]

According to this racist ideology, all these negative qualities belong to the entire people, and the expression *eternal Jew* stands for the cliché of the immutably evil nature of Jews, along with the collective conceptualization of the entire Jewish people as depraved:[22]

> (22) I call this alien element a very scourge and bane. It should be called that all the more in that the Jews are a depraved and degenerate people. [Arndt 1814, 193]

(23) A closed society . . . which lives only from spying and lurking, cannot but become spiritually depraved. [Fries 1816, 16]

The religious dimension of hostility toward Jews was displaced or overlaid with a secular form: in the nineteenth century, religious anti-Judaism was joined by a racist antisemitism that emphasized Jews' fundamental differentness as a race or people:[23] the so-called Aryan ideal and the concept of human inequality moved into the foreground of the racial doctrine being promulgated as scientific and was used to justify the isolation and exclusion of Jews (cf., e.g., Gobineau 1853). Jews came to be described as an alien race, as foreign bodies, as parasites and corrosive elements within non-Jewish communities. Eugen Dühring (1881) and Houston Stewart Chamberlain (1899/1944) authored much-read and often reprinted texts that on the basis of racial laws allegedly derived from scientific principles divided the world's peoples into higher- and lower-order races, with the Jews classified as an inferior and non-Aryan people. The supposed fact that Jews could achieve positions of power because of their wily and scheming nature was likewise a common cliché. Stereotypes of Jews as parasitic exploiters and influential power-grabbers found particularly frequent verbal expression:

(24) They one and all shamelessly exploit peoples and governments. [Dühring 1881, 121]

(25) In Berlin, capital of the Reich, the Jewish race plays a dominant role in the city administration. . . . I shall not even mention other Jewified cities. [Dühring 1881, 123]

Terms such as *dejewification*, *half-breeds*, and *Jewish race character*, all attributable to the semantic network of racist ideology, were used to highlight the dangers emanating from the "*degenerate race*" (Dühring 1881, 158). Dühring also took up the "*Jewish problem*" and discussed in all seriousness "*solutions*" such as "*reduction measures*," "*agitation*," and "*legislation*" against "*Jewish hegemony*" and the "*proliferating power of Jews*," to serve as provisional "*aids*" and "*means of disposal*" (119 f.), and came to the conclusion that "*Shaking off the Jewish nightmare is a cause that must be embraced by all nations*" (154).

Similar passages can be found in the writings of Adolf Stoecker, the Berlin theologian and court chaplain, but also in political party platforms from the years 1884 to 1906 (see de Lagarde 1884; Friesel 2006).[24] Thus Paul de Lagarde

(1884) emphasized in the Prussian Conservative Party's program for 1884 "*that the Jews form not a religious community but a nation*" (88), noting that "*no nation has ever . . . been as worthless in every respect as the Jewish one*" (89) and that "*the Jews as Jews are a dire misfortune in every European people*" (91). These and others' comments posit a categorical separation of Germans from Jews, found in the nineteenth century on all institutional levels. In most texts that mentioned the "Jewish question" or the "Jewish problem" in Germany, the same solutions were put forward repeatedly, formulated as demands addressed to the allegedly non-German Jews, such as that "*the Jews cease to be Jews*" (de Lagarde 1884, 95). In his work *Jews and Indogermans*, he furthermore asserted:

> (26) One would have to have a heart as hard as a crocodile's skin not to feel pity for the poor Germans, who are being sucked dry, and—which amounts to the same thing—not to hate the Jews, not to hate and despise those who—out of humane forbearance—speak on behalf of these Jews or are too cowardly to crush this vermin. There is no negotiating with trichina worms and bacilli. Nor should trichina worms and bacilli be educated; they must be destroyed as quickly and thoroughly as possible. [de Lagarde 1887, 339]

This passage shows that classifying Jews as pests through the use of animal metaphors did not originate with the Nazis. The 1905 Leipzig platform of the German Socialist Party contained similar language:

> (27) The race-alien Jewish people has proved to be an element destructive to . . . our life as a nation. And thus we view the struggle against the power of Judaism as a moral, political, and economic necessity. [Salomon 1924, 155]

And in the 1892 Tivoli Platform of the large and influential German Conservative Party the following statement occurs:

(28) We combat the invasive and destructive Jewish influence on our life as a people. We demand Christian authorities for the Christian people and Christian teachers for Christian children. [Salomon 1924, 65]

These texts, whose semantics exhibit nothing but racism, extremism, and psychopathology, we read today, applying modern standards of judgment, with astonishment and revulsion, but readers of the time took for granted the ideas they expressed and considered them worthy of discussion. Traces of the widely and deeply rooted hostility toward Jews could be found everywhere: in words and in images on postcards bearing hateful caricatures,[25] in letters, novels, pamphlets, and prospectuses, in philosophical, theological, historical, economic, and political treatises, and on signs; Judeophobia thus constituted an integral part of communication on all levels of public life.

> (29) The Jew does not work but lets others work; he speculates and makes deals with the products of others' hands and intellectual work. The center of his activities is the stock exchange. . . . This alien tribe has installed itself surreptitiously in the midst of the German people in order to suck the very marrow from its bones. [Glagau 1878, 16f.]

Nor are the realms of art, music, and literature excluded: Richard Wagner's essay "Judaism in Music," with its sweeping generalizations, may be seen as symptomatic of antisemitic thinking in the nineteenth century (cf., e.g., Katz 1986).[26] This text combines racist devaluation with envy of the success of Jewish artists:

> (30) The Jew, congenitally incapable of speaking to us artistically, whether through his external appearance, his language, or least of all his song, has nonetheless managed to achieve dominance of public taste in the most widespread of the modern arts, in music. [Wagner 1850, 73]

Wagner viewed Judaism as inhuman and thus called for it to be jettisoned, a typical nineteenth-century demand directed at the Jews living in Germany:

> (31) To become a human being in association with us means for the Jew . . . ceasing to be a Jew. [Wagner 1850, 85]

Images of Jews as speculators and usurers, as evil and ugly shysters, as heartless, cold merchants or corrupting, immoral intellectuals also turn up in two widely read nineteenth-century novels written by authors who were otherwise liberal in their thinking, Gustav Freytag (*Soll und Haben* [Debit and credit], 1855) and Wilhelm Raabe (*Der Hungerpastor* [The hunger pastor], 1864).[27] These writers articulate in their novels, letters, and other writings traditional anti-Jewish stereotypes and feelings of distaste, although one would not be justified in characterizing them as filled with burning hatred of Jews. But it was part of the cultural communicative heritage to verbalize animosities toward Jews; as an element of the collective consciousness it was not unusual but, on the contrary, to be expected and seldom given any thought. Dehumanizing descriptions and metaphors occurred in conjunction with traditional stereotypes:

> (32) . . . and in the public square . . . the Jewish element wriggles through like a slimy eel. [Freytag 1855, 490]

Freytag describes the Jew Itzig Veitel in standard Judeophobic clichés:

> (33) It was the face of a devil . . . red hair standing up like bristles, the ugly features bespeaking hellish fear and malice. [Freytag 1855, 386]

Using personification, Freytag depicts the house of the Jew Ehrenthal as devoid of character and uses the simile of a gypsy woman to evoke the stereotype of the alien, the homeless wanderer. Furthermore, the tastelessness of the Jewish family is stressed:

> (34) There was no good character in the house; it looked like an old gypsy woman. [Freytag 1855, 175]
>
> (35) . . . and the numerous hideous oil paintings on the walls . . . [Freytag 1855, 175]

In Raabe's *Hungerpastor*, the protagonist, Hans Unwirsch, and his antagonist, Moses Freudenstein, are constantly contrasted by means of polarizing descriptions. In (36) and (37) we have typical examples:

> (36) It was touching to see the timid reverence with which Hans . . . but in truly diabolical fashion Mose . . . attempted to trip up this belief in authority. [Raabe 1864, 137]
>
> (37) For the first time in his life, Hans Unwirsch felt what hatred was; from this moment on, he hated with all his heart the slippery, constantly changing creature that had once called itself Moses Freudenstein. [Raabe 1864, 295]

In both novels similar descriptions turn up, drawing on the same semantic fields to focus on the demonic ("*face of a devil*" and "*diabolic*"), the unpredictable and dehumanized ("*like a slimy eel*" and "*slippery*"), the non-German (thus both Freytag and Raabe imitate the Yiddish spoken by the Jewish characters and stress their foreign appearance), and the anti-Christian elements (Freudenstein's conversion is invalidated as an opportunistic misstep).

Theodor Fontane, too, repeatedly revealed an attitude hostile toward Jews. In a letter written in 1882 from the holiday resort of Norderney he notes:

> (38) The Jews were a disaster: their impudent, unattractive, knavish faces (for all their greatness resides in knavishness) crowd around one everywhere. Anyone who has cheated people in Rawicz or Meseritz for a year, or if not cheated outright at least pulled off shady deals, has no right to prance around on Norderney among princesses and countesses. [Quoted in Fleischer 1995, 84]

In his private correspondence Fontane expressed negative views of Jews several times, using generic comments such as "Borkum is Jew-free" (see endnote 28; cf. Fleischer 1995, 84; see also Benz 2001, 9, 58f.). A letter from 1898 contains explicitly racist formulations:

> (39) Everywhere they are in the way (much more so than previously); they mess up everything, interfere with consideration of every question as such. Despite all its talents, it is a terrible people, not a "leavening" providing strength and freshness but a ferment in which the uglier forms of fermentation are active—a people to which from the very beginning something conceited and lowly has adhered, which the Aryan world cannot tolerate. What a difference between the Christian and Jewish criminal element. And all that ineradicable. [Quoted in Paulsen 1981, 310; see also Goldammer 1993, 54f.]

The term *antisemitism* was first employed in 1879 by the journalist Wilhelm Marr to distinguish a rejection of Jews understood to be scientifically motivated and secular from hostility based on religion (see also Berger Waldenegg and Christoph 2000; Bergmann 2006, 6ff.; Rensmann 2004, 71f.).[28] In Marr's text *The Victory of Judaism over Germanic Identity*, numerous conceptualizations find verbal expression that were dominant in the nineteenth century (JEWS AS INTELLECTUAL OPINION MOLDERS IN THE PRESS AND FINANCIAL POLICY, JEWS AS ALIENS AND FOREIGN ELEMENTS, JEWS AS DESTROYERS OF CHRISTIAN SOCIETIES) (see also Zimmermann 1986, 2005, 112ff.). The following examples all come from this work.

According to Marr, Jews are characterized by "*acting to harm Germanic identity, to break down the Germanic and destroy it.*" He describes Jews as "*aliens in our midst,*" "*Semitic aliens,*" "*this alien people,*" an "*alien tribe*" (Marr

1879, 14). We also encounter the traditional stereotypes of the USURER, DEMAGOGUE, REVENGE SEEKER, and the theory of a world conspiracy:

> (40) Money-grubbers . . . without a fatherland [14]; commit usury . . . are natural hagglers and usurers . . . shrink from regular work, . . . are highly gifted and talented [13]; hostile toward others . . . slippery . . . sly . . . resilient [14]; domineering, influential [23]; . . . Jewified daily press . . . vengeful [50]. [Marr 1879]

This text manifests a Judeophobia that does set itself apart from religiously motivated anti-Judaism and does not obviously draw on theological considerations or religious motifs, yet continues to cultivate the old resentments and the traditional dichotomization. In this work Marr reveals himself rhetorically and argumentatively to be a forerunner of those who express hostility toward Jews today in that he insists on the facticity of his defamatory statements and presents them as indubitable truths.[29] Marr contends that he has "*no evil intentions*" but relies rather "*on facts*," "*irrefutable and historical facts*" (1879, 33, 55).

An article by the historian Heinrich von Treitschke launched the so-called Berlin antisemitism debate among academics in 1879 (see Boehlich 1965; Volkov 2006, 22f.).[30] The respected historian had spoken out against what he feared would be a mass immigration of East European Jews, and he charged the German Jews with inadequate willingness to assimilate:

> (41) What we have to demand of our Jewish fellow citizens is simple: they should become Germans, see themselves simply and properly as Germans—without prejudice to their belief and their old sacred memories, which we all recognize as worthy of respect; for we do not want the millennia of Germanic customs to be followed by an era of German–Jewish hybrid culture. . . . But it remains equally undeniable that numerous and powerful circles among our Jewish population by no means harbor the good will simply to become Germans. [Treitschke 1879, 573, quoted in Boehlich 1965, 10]

Among members of the educated middle classes, racist concepts also joined forces with intolerance and a sense of Christian superiority:

> (42) . . . and thus the lukewarm agitation of the moment seems merely a brutal and hateful but natural reaction of the Germanic sensibility against

a foreign element that has come to occupy far too much space in our lives. . . . But the contrast can be mitigated if the Jews, who talk so much about tolerance, really become tolerant and show some reverence toward the beliefs, customs, and feelings of the German people, who long ago did penance for the old wrong and have given them the rights of man and the citizen. [Treitschke 1879, 575f., quoted in Boehlich 1965, 11f.]

In this work Treitschke produced the sentence that in the Nazi period was instrumentalized as the permanent headline in the *Stürmer*: "*The Jews are our misfortune!*"[31] This sentence, in which Treitschke expressed his conviction that the Jews were having a destructive influence on the cultural and economic life of the German state, mirrors the essential constants of hostility toward Jews: the unreal, hyperbolic, and demonizing fantasy of the Jews' negative role. The Jews accounted for barely 1 percent of the German population (cf. Friesel 1990, 104) and were hardly in a position to be Germany's misfortune. Today no historian doubts that they had no influence whatsoever on developments in the Reich. The history of hostility toward Jews does, however, reveal one thing distinctly: it was not actual factors that played a role in the defamation and discrimination visited upon the Jews, but exclusively the mental images, the intellectual constructs that were firmly fixed collectively in the minds of non-Jews. These conceptualizations in turn rested on a dichotomous value system that categorized Judaism as an illegitimate, inferior religion per se, in comparison, for instance, with Christianity. Thus even the liberal historian Theodor Mommsen, who turned vehemently against Treitschke and declared his complete commitment to equal rights and to the integration of Jewish citizens, could not refrain from viewing Judaism itself as standing in the way of Jews' full integration into Christian society:

(43) To be sure, the blame rests in part with the Jews. What the word "Christendom" once signified it no longer completely signifies; but it is still the only word that summarizes the character of today's international civilization and in which millions and millions feel themselves united in a world so rich in peoples. [Mommsen 1880, 114]

This expression of antisemitism, which today we would recognize as unintentional, shows how deeply inscribed in Western structures of thought and feeling is the conceptualization of the Christian model and the sense of its superiority. Rudolph Steiner, the founder of anthroposophy, was not an (active) antisemite either. He rejected antisemitism as representing "*a danger both for Jews and for non-Jews*" and as a "*cultural sickness*," and he criticized the *Protocols of the Elders of Zion* as a forgery (Steiner 1919). But his texts contain passages that illustrate how normal it was in the nineteenth and early twentieth centuries to verbalize pejorative attributions and assessments vis-à-vis Jews:

> (44) It can certainly not be denied that today Judaism still manifests itself as a closed entity and as such has intervened in the development of current conditions in many ways, and that in a manner that was in no sense favorable to Western cultural notions.
>
> Judaism as such, however, has long since outlived itself, has no justification within the modern lives of the peoples, and the fact that it has nonetheless survived is a mistake on the part of world history whose consequences will be felt. Jews who have adapted to the Western cultural process should be in the best position to recognize that mistake, which consists of transplanting an ethical ideal from gray antiquity into the modern age, where it is completely useless. The insight must come first to the Jews that all their separatist strivings must be swallowed up by the spirit of modern times. [Steiner 1888, 152]

When we contemplate the nineteenth century, it becomes apparent that nothing—not increasing secularism in Europe or technological progress, not far-reaching political shifts or reforms in education and social welfare, not such early forms of democratic expression as the press and socially critical literature—eliminated the reservations against Jews and Judaism (see Reinharz 1975). Hostility toward Jews had long since become part of the culture,[32] constituting the Zeitgeist as a habitualized communicative system, and was consequently felt to be normal, being transmitted through verbal expressions and idioms as well as through distorting images and caricatures. It formed part of everyday life and was taken so much for granted that even among the educated middle classes no critical reflection and questioning took place. Attitudes hostile toward Jews could be found at all levels of society and in almost all institutions and elites of the German Reich, and they had far-reaching consequences. German Jews in part experienced serious difficulties when it came to obtaining civil-service jobs, memberships, and positions. In many circles and realms of life an openly articulated rejection of Jews was considered to be perfectly normal (cf., e.g., Leschnitzer 1956, 170; Volkov 2006, 256f.).

Antisemitism as State Doctrine: The "Final Solution" as the Ultimate Consequence of Judeophobia

> Once it has established its premises, its starting point, ideological thinking is on principle immune to the influence of experience and to the teachings of reality. [Arendt 1955, 742]

During the Nazi period, racist antisemitism reached its pinnacle[33] and eventually produced the eliminatory brand of antisemitism posited as an answer to the "Jewish question" that Dühring (1881, 119f.) had already articulated in the nineteenth century; it was an answer that called for exterminating a people viewed as inferior and noxious (cf., e.g., Bauer 1982; Longerich 1998; Friedländer 2006). Eliminatory antisemitism under the Nazis can be explained only against the background of centuries of enmity toward Jews. Any attempt to examine German policy toward the Jews in the Third Reich without looking at the historical context is bound to fail. The Nazis' extreme hatred of Jews was not a temporary aberration during the years between 1933 and 1945, implemented by just a few deluded criminals; rather it had a two-thousand-year history of transformations behind it upon which Hitler and his henchmen could build.

At the very beginning of his political activities, Hitler, together with the other founding members of the National Socialist Party (see Adam 2003), enunciated an extreme version of antisemitism. The speech he gave in Munich in 1920, "Why We Are Antisemites," already revealed his hatred, nourished by prejudices and specifically antisemitic conceptualizations. He resorted to the racial antisemitic stereotypes characteristic of the nineteenth century and combined them to argue for his specific construct of the enemy:

> (45) And with all this we must see that there are no good and bad Jews here, but each of them works exactly according to the calling of his race, for the race, or let us rather say nation and what is linked to it, character, etc., resides, as the Jew himself explains, in the blood, and this blood compels

every individual to act according to these principles. [Hitler 1920, quoted in Phelps 1968, 415]

(46) For him there is no spiritual emotion, and as his forefather Abraham before him prostituted his wife, he sees nothing unusual in it when today he prostitutes girls . . . that all these pimps are only Hebrews. There's material that can be presented here that is hair-raising. To the Germanic sensibility there should be only one punishment here: the punishment would be death. [Hitler 1920, quoted in Phelps 1968, 414]

We see here a closed form of conceptualization according to which the naturally criminal Jew wants to rule the world and divide the capital accumulated through thievery among fellow Jews, using it to harm the German people. Here the extreme dualism characteristic of antisemitism[34] finds the expression that turns up repeatedly in *Mein Kampf*: human existence is viewed as a struggle for existence between Aryans and Jews, who stand for good and evil in the world (Hitler 1934, 317). Constructs of the enemy that combine racist and political elements give rise to fictional notions of conspiracies forged by the Jewish-Bolshevist "world enemy" to achieve universal hegemony:

(47) . . . the merciless universal Jew fights for his power over the peoples. [Hitler 1934, 738]

Hitler revealed as early as 1920 that he favored a particular "solution" for the Jewish problem, as indicated in (46). Thirteen years before his seizure of power, the platform of the National Socialist Workers' Party and all his other proclamations featured the "Jewish question" as the ideological basis. In 1931 he predicted to German Jewry that in case of a confrontation it would be "crushed under the wheel of history" (conversation between Hitler and Breiting, June 1931, quoted in Calic 1968, 94f.; cf. Adam 2003, 27ff.). In this connection the 1920 statement by Gottfried Feder, one of the founders of the Nazi Party, on the party's fundamental worldview is significant:

(48) Antisemitism is in a sense the emotional underpinning of our movement. [Feder 1927, 17]

Hatred for Jews amounted to an emotional dogma within the Nazi program. In the guise of racial theory, resentment was elevated to the status of a science, on the one hand, and to the main plank of the party platform, on the other. After 1933 antisemitism became official state doctrine. The hostility previously articulated in society by individuals now acquired an official legal basis and was institutionalized across the board as binding. To remove Jews from German society was not an idea that had economic, social, or political motivation; rather it followed from the resentment-driven ideology of the Nazi regime:[35]

> (49) Certainly the Jew is also a human being. None of us has ever cast doubt on that. But the flea is also an animal—just not a pleasant one. Since the flea is not a pleasant animal, we do not have the duty before ourselves and our conscience to protect and care for it and allow it to flourish, but rather to render it harmless. That is exactly how it is with the Jews. [Goebbels 1943, 89]

In accordance with these views, antisemitism found expression at all public communicative levels. Posters, newspapers, shops, kiosks, and the walls of buildings everywhere displayed verbally aggressive sayings with demands, warnings, curses, and threats such as "*Germans, defend yourselves, don't buy from Jews!*" (in Berlin, 1933; cf. Königseder 2011, 61), "*Death to Juda*" (in Berlin, 1933), "*None should hunger, none be cold, but Jews should perish, none grow old*" (in Germany, 1935; cf. Améry 1966/2008, 35). All the mass media spread anti-Jewish propaganda. Along with the unfettered verbal aggressions of Goebbels and the numerous vicious attacks by various *Gauleiter*s who indulged in threats of violence directed at Jews, from 1934 on it was principally the *Stürmer* that every week spewed crude, hate-filled, nakedly violent verbalisms in which animal and disease images predominated. Display cases were set up all through Germany where this antisemitic tabloid was posted. As early as 1933 the Nazis had begun to normalize slogans hostile toward Jews (e.g., in the form of exclusion from professions). Terror and violence were increasingly legalized by the state bureaucracy.

All verbalizations in the Nazi period mirror the conceptual and emotional devaluation of Jews and Judaism and reveal semantic constants present in all forms of defamation, discrimination, delegitimation, demonization, and dehumanization (see chapter 5).

The conceptualization of Jews as GLOBAL EVIL was the basis for the Nazis' eliminatory antisemitism, which led to the Final Solution within the framework of their closed ideological view of the world and an immanent "logic" that lacked any basis in reality. From the Nuremberg race laws, a straight unbroken line (cf., e.g., Longerich 1998; Browning 2003), ideologically homogeneous and bureaucratically perfected, led—by way of public stigmatization, exclusion from all realms of normal life, denial of all rights, and refusal to recognize Jews' humanity—to the gas chambers. The race laws "for the protection of German blood" laid out with painstaking exactitude who was a "full, three-quarter, half, or quarter Jew." Paragraphs stipulating the smallest details regulated the "sorting" of those thus classified, as well as their relatives and offspring. On the basis of this legislation Himmler demanded "*for 2nd-grade mixed-race persons*" a "*process . . . such as is used in animal husbandry*" and, "*in case of inferiority*," sterilization (Adam 2003, 328).

The minutes of the Wannsee Conference, called to arrange for implementation of the Final Solution, reads like the text of a pest-control company describing, bureaucratically and emotionlessly, the procedures for eliminating vermin and filth. In this case, the fact that those classified as pests and listed as "filth" are human beings is masked out. The radical approach of the Final Solution was consistent with the Nazis' closed worldview. The Final Solution corresponded to the "reason" given, namely to exterminate the Jews for the benefit of mankind, although the Jews were highly productive and fully integrated into German economic, scholarly, and artistic life, and far from representing a danger enriched German society by their presence. In October 1943, the SS-Reichsführer Heinrich Himmler offered a drastic example of the Nazis' peculiar "reality." In a secret speech to high officers of the SS, Himmler said:

> (50) I wish to mention a very difficult subject here, with complete frankness. . . . I mean the evacuation of Jews, the extermination of the Jewish people . . . This is a chapter of our history in which we can take great pride. . . . We had the moral right, we had the duty toward our people, to do away with this people that wanted to do away with us. [Himmler, 4 October 1943; see Smith and Peterson 1974, 203]

We make it too easy for ourselves if we decide, applying our modern sensibility, that Goebbels or Himmler was mentally disturbed. In the context of Nazi ideology they were not, and they were not seen as disturbed by those around them. They basked in a personal conviction that they were doing the right thing.[36]

(51) I believe, gentlemen, that you know me well enough to realize that I am not a bloodthirsty person and not a man who takes pleasure or enjoyment in anything harsh that he must do. On the other hand, I have such sound nerves and such a great sense of duty—if I do say so myself—that when I recognize something as necessary, I carry it out, uncompromisingly. [Himmler, 24 May 1944; see Smith and Peterson 1974, 206]

In this case Himmler was talking about the murder of Jewish women and children. As Himmler understood it, they had to be killed because otherwise "*the children would grow up to be the avengers . . . who would then do away with our children and grandchildren.*" Today we find it impossible to imagine such an absence of feeling, such absolute mercilessness and inhumanity, but it forms part and parcel of a closed anti-Jewish view of the world, a monstrous imaginative construct indebted to a long tradition and explicable only by reference to that tradition (see also Bauer 2001 and chapter 8, under Cruelty and Emotional Coldness). Here we can see the unique aspect of this phenomenon, that Jews were exterminated simply as Jews, without economic, social, or political justification. The "ideal of salvation" occupied the foreground of Nazi thinking: freeing the world of Jews. Hitler maintained his demented beliefs to the very end:

(52) Above all I pledge the leadership of the nation and its followers to strict observance of the racial laws and to ruthless resistance against the world-poisoners of all peoples, international Jewry. [Berlin, 29 April 1945 (Hitler's last will and testament, 1945, 10)]

We have become accustomed to using relatively abstract terms in scholarly and societal discourse about the Nazi period—expressions and phrases such as *brutality*, *inhumanity*, *Jewish victims of racist Nazi policies*, *Nazi atrocities*—but the loss of concreteness that such impersonal usage entails protects our consciousness and our feelings from the enormity of the caesura in civilization, the sheer horror of the Nazis' monstrous realpolitik. One must try to imagine vividly and specifically what happened between 1933 and 1945: a segment of the population in Germany was declared to be the enemy of the people and a pest, was robbed of all its rights, was officially and legislatively designated as inferior by the Nuremberg racial laws, and was finally loaded into cattle cars and sent to its death. All these activities were carried out painstakingly and precisely, with meticulous bureaucratic organization and record keeping, and with rational planning. The bureaucratic efficiency, involving all important organizational structures in Germany, ultimately resulted in the disappearance of 6 million human beings, who literally went up in smoke.

Hostility toward Jews after 1945: Minimization of the Caesura in Civilization and Withholding of Empathy

After 1945, once the dimensions of the crimes against the Jews became widely known and unmistakable, the transformation in the collective consciousness that this caesura in civilization should have brought about did not occur. To be sure, Judeophobic images and texts were officially banned, their reproduction publicly subjected to sanctions and taboos, but there was no truly probing reflection, no comprehensive critical analysis of the reasons and motives for the hatred and the extermination policy.[37] Instead the Holocaust was usually described as resulting from the obsessions of a few Nazis, an explanation that led to decisive misinterpretation and a failure to take into account the extent to which Jews were hated. Neither the institutional elites nor the general population sufficiently explored the hatred of Jews that had existed in almost all parts of society as an integral part of the much-invoked Western way of thinking and had belonged for centuries to the general culture.[38] Thus the opportunity was missed to initiate a thorough rethinking of this tradition. A few isolated and halfhearted attempts could not eliminate from the collective consciousness or from linguistic usage in a few years what had been passed down for centuries (on postwar antisemitism, cf. Stern 1991a, b, 1993).

Both Wolgast (2001) in his solid historical analyses and Kämper (2005, 2007) in her comprehensive discussions of language and discourse document, independently of one another, that no intensive and far-reaching processing of the Nazis' antisemitic actions took place in the institutions that bore responsibility for such work. Instead, as early as 1945–1946 members of universities, political parties, and churches launched efforts to relativize what had happened and to ward off guilt. Analyses of university speeches, pastoral letters, and political parties' policy statements reveal that although the Nazi regime and its violent tactics were unanimously condemned, at the same time no reckoning with antisemitism took place, and the significance of the Holocaust was minimized. In pastoral letters issued in the summer of 1945, the German bishops did not so much as mention the murder of Jews (Wolgast 2001, 188). In the "Fulda Pastoral Letter" of 23 August 1945 the crimes did receive mention, but the reference to the Jews adopted usage characteristic of racist ideology, calling them "*non-Aryans*" and "*members of a foreign tribe*" (Wolgast 2001, 191). The pastoral letters issued by Archbishop Gröber of Freiburg display the same tendency to minimize and cast doubt on the Holocaust that was typical of the Catholic Church in the immediate postwar period: the leading figures of the Nazi regime were characterized as outliers, referred to by phrases such as "*out of touch with reality*" and "*shortsighted nationalists*" (pastoral bulletin for Freiburg 1945, quoted in Wolgast 2001, 197). Gröber, like many others, described the victims as "*people of a foreign race.*" This usage reveals the unbroken power of racist and Germanophilic antisemitism and the way in which use of the phraseology that went with it had become habitual. The Protestant Church, too, hesitated to confront the extermination of the Jews. In 1933 the church had welcomed the Nazi takeover euphorically, and after the collapse it did not distance itself appropriately from antisemitism (Wolgast 2001, 226). Much the same problem manifested itself in the case of politicians and academics: the speeches university presidents delivered after 1945 offered no evidence that they had seen the light or engaged in self-criticism. The scholarly criteria of rationality, respect for truth, and objectivity were nowhere in evidence (Wolgast 2001, 328ff.); the speakers did not enter into any discussion of the causes of hatred of Jews or of the mass murder inflicted upon them. In sum, no comprehensive, serious, or jarring debate over the antisemitic Nazi ideology took place, and its deep roots in Western culture and the essential causes of the Holocaust remained untouched. Germany's elite institutions instead minimized their own culpability and responsibility while blaming the Nazi inner circle as they clung with unbroken certainty to their traditional values. Repressing, reinterpreting, and minimizing what had happened emerged as the dominant tendencies when it came to the extermination of the Jews.

Kämper (2005) has applied the methodology of discourse analysis to the ways in which Nazism and its crimes were spoken of after the war. Her findings confirm that no fundamental confrontation with the past took place, no critical assessment of the present and future. Instead of processing and rethinking, repression and minimization were the order of the day.[39] Kämper sees "refusal to accept culpability" and "rationalization" as characteristic of most postwar discourse and points to the repeated emphasis on "just following orders," fulfilling one's "duty," and having no knowledge of what was going on as a standard feature of the way Germans spoke of the recent past (496f.). Traditional Western values were repeatedly invoked, and integral to those values was the old hatred of Jews.

No attention was paid to the fact that antisemitism as a cultural and historical phenomenon, as part of the Western heritage, had been passed down for centuries collectively through all communicative structures (Volkov 1990, 2000, 2006). Instead, starting immediately after the war, the singularity of the persecution of Jews as specific to the Nazis' violent policies and racist ideology was emphasized.[40]

Correspondingly, the realpolitik of the day called for concentrating on the reconstruction of Germany and on the country's future. Despite the so-called denazification, former Nazi functionaries often managed almost effortlessly to obtain high and responsible positions in politics, the economy, and culture (see Frei 1997). Rebuilding the war-ravaged country took priority, and looking back suited neither the political leadership nor the general populace. The decisive line that should have been imposed after the Holocaust because of its unique monstrousness thus never got drawn, either cognitively or emotionally.

Horror, shame, guilt, compassion for the victims and the survivors of the extermination camps: these feelings did not come to the fore, but rather self-pity and hope for a better life in the future. Embarrassed silence and lack of interest, as well as defensiveness and indifference, marked the attitude toward the Jews, dead and alive. The following text exemplifies this attitude:

> No one suffering from a severe illness will occupy himself in his sickbed with studying fever charts, and it is entirely understandable that in the Germany of 1947, where hunger and cold have become our near neighbors, the concentration-camp literature cannot find a large receptive audience. Did the prisoners suffer hunger? So do we. Did the prisoners freeze? So do we. Did the dead pile up in front of the crematoria? If things continue this way, that will soon be happening again. Were the prisoners locked up? Thousands of prisoners of war were as well. [Borchert 1947/2009, 503]

The statements of the much-praised postwar writer Wolfgang Borchert, who in his plays and stories dwelled on Germans' sufferings in the war's aftermath and found not a shred of empathy for the Jewish victims of German mass murder, offer insight into the attitudes prevailing among Germans. The crimes against the Jews are relativized by means of silence, their suffering placed on the same plane as the deprivations suffered by the population in postwar Germany and thereby robbed of its true dimensions, which exceed all bounds of humanity.[41] Equating the consequences of war and violent exercise of power with systematic extermination reveals the absence of any critical awareness of or willingness to develop empathy. Viewing as equivalent two dimensions of suffering that were in no way comparable also made it possible for Germans to shake off the burden of guilt and moral responsibility (a tendency that can be observed to this day among some in Germany).

Between 1945 and the late 1960s one could often hear people in Germany say, "That wouldn't have happened under Hitler." The expression typifies the kind of linguistic utterance through which minimization tended to occur (in part unconsciously). By highlighting the positive aspects of the control the Nazi regime exerted over the populace, the speaker simultaneously blocks out the dimension of ethnic murder, downplaying its relevance. This expression, still in use decades after the collapse of the Nazi regime, epitomizes the way many Germans treat the Holocaust. It focuses on characteristics of the Nazis' policies that are recalled as positive (curbing crime—the conservative notion summed up in the expression *law and order*).[42] The enormity of the murder of the Jews takes a back seat to Hitler's success, for otherwise that success would not be worth mentioning.

On right-wing extremist and neo-Nazi websites this stock phrase can still be found (cf. the right-wing extremist platform thiazi.net, not shut down until 2012, under the heading "Sayings of Mama and Papa").

To feel grief and pain, to develop empathy, Germans would have had to realize that an integral and culturally vital segment of their society had been isolated and destroyed—not an external group that could be classified as foreign and non-German. But because this basis for identification was lacking and was also not invoked, what resulted was the "inability to mourn" (see Mitscherlich and Mitscherlich 1967) or to experience shame. Many Germans felt that the official morality of shame and responsibility had been imposed on them from without. Their emotional resistance in turn gave rise to a postwar form of antisemitism that the Jewish psychoanalyst Zvi Rex (quoted in Heinsohn 1988, 115) summed up in the telling formulation, "The Germans will never forgive us for Auschwitz!"

Constitutive elements of postwar antisemitism are the relativizing or denial of Germany's culpability for the ethnic murder as well as the projection of guilt onto the Jews: a modern version of perpetrator–victim reversal. This antisemitism born of resistance to culpability is often described in the scholarly literature as "not in spite of but precisely because of Auschwitz" (see Benz 2001, 55). In fact, however, both dimensions are important if one wants to understand postwar antisemitism. Despite the Auschwitz experience, many Germans did not fundamentally alter their attitude toward Jews (and accordingly the traditional clichés remained in use in everyday discourse), and because of Auschwitz additional stereotypes developed based on denial of responsibility and repression of shame. Among these the following stand out: JEWS AS DISTURBERS OF THE PEACE AND IRRITATING ADMONISHERS; JEWS AS EXPLOITERS OF THE HOLOCAUST AND (OPINION) BLACKMAILERS. Such concepts must not be considered secondary,[43] since they grow out of traditional Judeophobic conceptualizations and are simply applied to the current situation, and modified or elaborated accordingly (a procedure characteristic of centuries during which Judeophobic images and forms of articulation underwent repeated transformation).

The allegation that Jews exploit the memory of the Holocaust and act as leeches on society when they make financial demands on the Federal Republic of Germany matches the traditional conceptualization of Jews as GREEDY PARASITES AND HARMFUL PESTS. The stereotype of Jews as IRRITATING, IRRECONCILABLE, AND VENGEFUL ADMONISHERS is a modern version of the image of Jews, already current in the Middle Ages, as disturbers of the peace; it also rests on the conceptualization of Jews as not being Germans. Holocaust denial, paired with the notion of a conspiracy of Jews to invent their own extermination in order to put the world under moral pressure and extort money, goes with the characterization of Jews as liars and is linked with the stereotype of the GREEDY HAGGLER AND MONEY-GRUBBER. The anti-Jewish concepts remain, but the forms in which they are expressed undergo transformation and modification according to current social and political circumstances (cf. also Bergmann 2001, 38; Simmel 1946/2002a, 12; von Braun 2004, 11; Kreis 2005, 21).

One change very important for this study did take place after 1945, however: after the end of the war, the articulation of antisemitic thinking that had been practiced openly and publicly for centuries was formally prohibited. The communicability of verbal antisemitic expression thus experienced limitation; the latitude for expression of Judeophobia shrank, and the discourse moved from the public to the private realm.[44] This development did not mean, however, that representations of attitudes hostile toward Jews or stereotypes also disappeared.

> Rather, anti-Jewish stereotypes can be identified in the democratic, established public sphere across all political camps and are disseminated by all sorts of actors more widely than years ago. [Rensmann 2004, 487]

Legal and social taboos or sanctions imposed on explicit antisemitism gave rise to new forms of communication.[45] Judeophobic contents were, and still are, transmitted (except in right-wing-extremist circles) as indirect speech acts (and realized as "circumlocutions"; cf., e.g., Rensmann, 2004; Bergmann and Heitmeyer, 2005a; see chapter 2).[46]

While up to 1945 antisemites also described themselves openly and without embarrassment as such, this has not been the case since revelation of the crime of the Holocaust. Today people who hold views hostile toward Jews style themselves "*critical thinkers*" or "*peace activists*," speaking "*in the name of justice and human rights*" and out of "*concern for world peace*." Marin (1997, 2000) characterizes this seemingly nonfanatical and nonracist everyday antisemitism—in a phrase that is still accurate—as "antisemitism without antisemites" (see also Améry 1969, on "honorable antisemitism," and Schwarz-Friesel 2010a, on "legitimate antisemitism").

This phenomenon holds decisive significance for the following observations on current Judeophobic linguistic patterns and communication processes, insofar as the ways in which antisemitism finds expression nowadays, and more publicly, work primarily through implication and/or through anti-Israel views, presented as "criticism of Israel" (see chapter 6). This development enlarges the communicative space in society for verbal antisemitism.

Present-Day Hostility toward Jews: The "New" Antisemitism of the Twenty-First Century

For some years antisemitism researchers have been debating whether certain alterations in public communication, the increasing acts of violence against Jewish institutions and facilities worldwide, tendencies in mass-media reporting on Israel, as well as certain types of criticism of Israel make it imperative that one speak of a "new antisemitism" in the twenty-first century (cf., e.g., the discussion in Naumann 2002; Rabinovici et al. 2004; see also Kaufmann and Orlowski 2002; Nonn 2008, 101ff.; Schwarz-Friesel et al. 2010, 2ff.).[47] What gave rise to the debate was in part the discrepancy between the results obtained by certain opinion polls and the analyses of public discourses, as well as the increase in antisemitically motivated acts of violence.[48]

No doubt exists as to the changes that manifest themselves in contemporary hostility toward Jews, yet the classification and assessment of these phenomena and their effects occur in different ways: some scholars see the expressions of Judeophobia as adhering to the old patterns, with the semantics remaining constant, which makes the current phenomenon a variant of postwar antisemitism, while other scholars see a qualitatively (and quantitatively) new phenomenon of Judeophobia that represents (or might represent) the basis for its spread to the majority in society.

Rabinovici et al. (2004, 8) see an essential difference between the old and new antisemitism in the fact that previous patterns of coming to terms with the past, focused primarily on the Nazi era and the Holocaust, no longer have any hold over people.[49] According to them, the central element of the current hostility is the problematic existence of the conflict in the Middle East and the resulting challenge to the legitimacy of the state of Israel as the political form of Jewish sovereignty. At the same time, for Rabinovici (2006, 247), the global interlacing of European and Muslim antisemitism plays an essential role:[50]

> In addition to the old religious and racist hatred of Jews, a new form has arisen that operates on a global scale, that no longer sees the "Jew" as a "rootless cosmopolitan" but damns him as an incarnation of Israel. The murderous antisemitism of radical Islamism is new, as is the approval that this hatred and the suicide attacks receive from some intellectuals, who were less tolerant toward classic right-wing racism.

Goldhagen (2004, 93f., 97) likewise emphasizes this component as "globalized antisemitism" (cf. also Kreis 2005, 23; Wistrich 2005, 2, 2007, 2010). The fixation on Israel as the predominant characteristic of contemporary antisemitism induces Rensmann to categorize this phenomenon as anti-Zionism (Rensmann 2004, 87; see also Gessler 2004, 126). Here we have a form of communication that purports simply to criticize Israeli policies but in fact contests Israel's right to exist (see also Klug 2004, 227, who describes this as "new anti-Semitism"). Although Israel is criticized, what is actually meant is the state as a symbol of Jewish life. This form of communication gains acceptance as politically correct and can be openly articulated (see also Schapira and Hafner 2006).[51]

Because the current manifestations of antisemitism reveal traditional stereotypes, those who argue for the thesis of continuity see nothing new in them (cf. Bergmann 2001, 38; but see also endnote 51, this chapter);[52] on the basis of its high degree of adaptability, antisemitism today also appears as anti-Zionism or criticism of Israel (Benz 2004, 24; Bergmann 2006, 117f.; see also, e.g., Quadfasel 2005, 188). Holz (2005, 57, 59) characterizes the phenomenon of altered antisemitism after 1945 as "democratic antisemitism," meaning a hostility toward Jews that can be expressed in the democratic public and whose core consists of the process of coming to terms with the past by reversing perpetrator and victim.[53] For Holz, anti-Zionism and anti-Israelism, if they can be assigned to this core, thus represent nothing more than adapted variants of so-called secondary antisemitism. Like Bergmann, Holz rejects the term "new antisemitism" for current manifestations because he sees the term as positing changes to fundamental semantic patterns that would result in the creation of a new form of antisemitism (cf. Holz 2005, 11). Holz does recognize a new aspect in the strong focus on Israel within the most varied political currents and population groups. Typical of this "anti-Zionist antisemitism" is, according to him, the distinction between "Jewish" as a religious category and "Zionist" as a political category, such that only Zionists (ergo, the state of Israel) figure as a political enemy, but not Jews as a collective entity, race, or religion (cf. Holz 2005, 43).[54] Holz emphasizes at the same time that this anti-Zionist antisemitism is becoming increasingly acceptable among the majority of the democratic public (Holz 2005, 97; see also Müller 2006, 309). Thus adherents of the theory of continuity also recognize changes in the communicative use of antisemitism but do not consider them a significant innovation.

Among the most notable communicative events that have specifically shaped the political discourse in Germany and widened the scope of what is permissible to say must be counted the Goldhagen debate of 1996, the debate over Martin Walser's speech in 1998, the Bundestag debate over the Berlin Holocaust memorial in 1999, the 2001 debate over reparations for forced laborers from the Nazi period, and the role of Jewish organizations, as well as the 2002 Möllemann–Friedman debate and the controversy over anti-Jewish positions in the Free Democratic Party (see Rensmann 2004, 60, 2006, 44; Reinfrank and Ebbrecht 2004; Nonn 2008, 102ff.; Pallade 2008a, b; Reinfrank 2008). These public debates resulted in a shift in the areas considered taboo. In particular Martin Walser's speech when he accepted the Peace Prize of the German Publishing Industry represents a dividing line, because here antisemitic defensive aggression toward reminders of the Nazis' crimes could reveal and establish itself publicly for the first time without eliciting any unified public condemnation: "Here an intellectual moral figure had articulated openly and with pathos something that up to then had been largely taboo in mainstream discourse or at least considered inappropriate" (Pallade 2008a, 321f.). The new quality of the discourse since the debate over the Walser speech can be seen in the fact that antisemitic utterances encounter less and less resistance and are regarded as "normal." Furthermore, the ideological positions of political fringe groups have gained greater acceptance in the political and social mainstream (cf. Reinfrank 2008, 109; Pallade 2008a, 340). Inappropriate and historically insensitive verbal formulations like *antisemitism bludgeon* have become slogans that can be used in polite society. Jürgen W. Möllemann took advantage of these changed communicative conditions for his right-wing-populist election campaign in 2002; but a central feature of his public persona is the linking of resistance to memory with anti-Zionism, in the context of which the perpetrator–victim reversal as applied to the Nazi past receives justification from an invocation of Israel's misdeeds (cf. Holz 2005, 23).

In the research, two phenomena figure as the primary sources of motivation and the catalyst for current antisemitic tendencies: the outbreak of the Second Intifada and the escalation of the Middle East conflict (with the dimension of international terrorism since September 11, 2001, playing a role; cf. Beck 2003; Chesler 2004, 10; Reinfrank and Ebbrecht 2004, 50; Bergmann 2006, 118; Müller 2006, 309, Reinfrank 2008, 110; Wetzel 2008, 88; FRA 2009, 24).[55] Thus Beck (2003) speaks of the "spillover from the Intifada" and the "globalization of the Israeli–Palestinian conflict" because, as he sees it, hostility toward Israel in many places (locally) and all over the world (globally) explodes in aggression and violence against Jewish representatives and institutions and thus spreads from the Middle East.[56]

Independently of the debate over whether the current changes that can be observed should be considered new or old-new, traditional or innovative, the following can be established: As an object of hatred, Israel occupies the central position in current antisemitism. In the twenty-first century the Middle East conflict provides the overarching pretext for the expression of antisemitic opinions and serves as a catalyst for hostility toward Jews. Anti-Israelism is communicated not only by extremists on the right or left but also by academics and intellectuals, as well as representatives of the mainstream, since this attitude can pass for politically correct. This situation is not confined to one region but is globalized; that is, hostility toward Israel appears all over the world, disseminated through the mass media (cf. Chesler 2004, 76–86, Reinfrank 2008, 107f.).

Verbal violence in everyday and public discourse on Israel has taken on a new cast; increasingly prominent in the mainstream communication realm are virulent forms of denigration (see chapter 6, under Tools of Demonization). Another new feature is the willingness manifested by more and more people the world over to agree with drastically pejorative and derealizing statements about the Jewish state of Israel (see, e.g., EUMC reports of 2003 and 2004, the results of the 2009 ADL survey, and the 2012 Forsa survey [Weber 2012]). Yet another new feature is the unlimited access to and massive dissemination of verbal antisemitisms (as well as anti-Jewish cartoons) provided on the Internet, which as a virtual world and communication system has long since become an essential feature of the real world (see Marx and Schwarz-Friesel 2013) and contributes in a crucial way to transmitting explicitly Judeophobic utterances as well as anti-Israeli hate speech quickly and effectively to countless recipients. Yet antisemitic thinking is by no means restricted to right-wing-extremist, fundamentalist, or Islamist websites (see Wetzel 2005), but also appears in mainstream Internet forums and chat rooms, and on social network sites (see Schwarz-Friesel 2013a). As a result, anti-Jewish utterances in public communication can come to seem habitual and normal and become firmly established.

Thus antisemitism in Germany is clearly a contemporary phenomenon, by no means merely historical and not confined to the extreme fringes of society. Despite all attempts at education, it is firmly anchored in parts of the (educated and not radical) mainstream. Yet with the exception of research on antisemitism, this reality still receives far too little attention and is viewed too seldom as problematic or worrisome.

The discrepancy is striking between, on the one hand, the emotions of those affected (i.e., the Jewish communities and institutions; cf., e.g., Pallade 2008a, b) and the observations and analyses of researchers (for the most part coextensive) and, on the other hand, the viewpoint of large segments of the population:

> While Jews are affected by antisemitism, and with justification feel threatened as a minority by violent Judeophobia, as indicated, for instance, by safety measures still necessary for Jewish facilities and synagogues in Europe, today portions of the majority society view what they consider largely groundless charges of antisemitism as a serious social problem and antisemitism as a phenomenon belonging to European history. [Rensmann and Schoeps 2008, 11]

Despite decades during which antisemitism was officially rejected and discredited, despite intensive attempts at education and efforts on the part of governments to counter antisemitic violence and attitudes, large portions of the population are by no means sensitized to the dangers of stereotyped thinking and rhetoric that has the effect of creating prejudice and images of an enemy. The inhibition threshold for articulating verbal antisemitic sentiments even in public has become markedly lower in recent years (cf. Schwarz-Friesel 2009a, b, 2010a, b, 2013a), and receptivity to stereotypical Judeophobic and/or anti-Israeli comments has risen. In light of current research findings, the thesis of a "collective learning process" with respect to antisemitism that Bergmann (1997, 502) thought he discerned in Germany and in democratic discourse can no longer be confirmed without qualifications (see also Rensmann 2004, 490ff., 224ff.; Nonn 2008, 103).

The Bundestag's expert commission thus comes to the following conclusion in its 2011 report:

> The report was able to show that in the majority of German society antisemitic attitudes are present, with considerable variations in form and

content. These attitudes in turn are based on widespread prejudices and deeply rooted clichés, or in simple ignorance about Jews and Judaism. In view of modern forms of communication such as exist in particular on the Internet, dissemination of such thinking can hardly be prevented. The far-reaching taboo imposed on antisemitism in public discourse that was previously an important feature of the Federal Republic is thus in danger of losing much of its effectiveness. What seems particularly dangerous is the receptivity of right-wing extremists to antisemitic attitudes that reach far into the social mainstream and have not been sufficiently ostracized. Determined countermeasures must receive a high priority, not least in view of the devastating historical effects of Nazi antisemitism. [BMI 2011, 182]

Conclusion

Hostility toward Jews was and is an enduring component of Western patterns of thought and speech.[57] Centuries of defamation and stigmatization of Jews have left deep traces in the collective memory and in patterns of communicative language usage. If we look at history, we can discern not only the long tradition of thinking and feeling that is hostile toward Jews, but also certain patterns of verbal stigmatization and defamation mirroring semantic and conceptual constants that have been preserved and passed down through the ages. The stereotype of the Jew as the FOREIGNER, the OTHER, is a concept used for categorization and devaluation that has survived for two millennia in a number of variations. Depending on religious, ideological, or political perspectives, Jews are alien and different because, according to their critics, they do not represent the true faith or because they represent a race of their own or because their thinking is hostile, their behavior indecent and destructive. When taken together and connected to each other, the additional specific stereotypes that have arisen over the centuries constitute a cognitive system of beliefs that provides mental support to the emotional resentment against Jews. Language serves as an archive for components of collective consciousness and makes them transparent through forms that carry meaning. Utterances hostile toward Jews transport and transmit intellectual stereotypes that form the basis of fundamental antisemitic attitudes. Therefore, they contribute decisively to preserving templates of thinking and clichés. Thus patterns of linguistic usage activate and reactivate anti-Jewish attitudes. Correspondingly, the ways in which Jews and Judaism are named and described reveal an unbroken continuity in anti-Jewish concepts and patterns of mental devaluation, such as dehumanization, demonization, and derealization, through imaginary constructs and conspiracy theories.

On the one hand, the following chapter will show which traditional mental stereotypes expressing hostility toward Jews have survived through the ages in the Germans' cultural and communicative memory and are still used today, despite all efforts at education since the Holocaust. On the other hand, it will show the extent to which cognitive representations of antisemitism find expression in new formulations, but also to what extent old anti-Jewish conceptualizations are currently undergoing modification or elaboration.

4 PRESENT-DAY VERBALIZATION OF STEREOTYPES

Any examination of present-day verbal expressions of antisemitism must ask which anti-Jewish stereotypes occur most often in current usage, how these stereotypes take form in language, and to what extent new antisemitic stereotypes have emerged, for example through the fusion or expansion of concepts. But it is also critical to ask how stereotypes in particular function in current antisemitic usage, how they can best be described in scholarly terms, and how they relate to certain emotional attitudes.

Stereotypes, Mental Models, Prejudices, Clichés, and Stock Phrases: Terminological and Conceptual Clarifications

> But the *Idols of the Market Place* are the most troublesome of all—idols which have crept into the understanding through the alliances of words and names. For men believe that their reason governs words; but it is also true that words react on the understanding; and this it is that has rendered philosophy and the sciences sophistical and inactive. [Bacon 1620/1974, 59]

As a phenomenon, hostility toward Jews is tied inextricably to the existence of certain mental stereotypes. On this point scholars are unanimous, despite their otherwise very different approaches and positions (see, e.g., Schoeps and Schlör 1999; Pfahl-Traughber 2002; Benz 2004; Gessler 2004; Holz 2004; Rensmann 2004; Laqueur 2006; Nonn 2008; Wistrich 2010).

In the scholarly literature, however, definitions of stereotype and the concepts germane to it are both inconsistent and vague. Often concepts such as "stereotype," "prejudice," "resentment," "cliché," and "stock phrase" are used synonymously, which is both inaccurate and confusing.[1] Stock phrases are concrete verbal expressions, while the other items represent mental phenomena that cannot be observed directly. Although it is easy to make these distinctions, it must be conceded that the mental phenomena themselves can be very difficult to differentiate, since they often overlap or merge imperceptibly into one another. But using them synonymously obscures important differences, ignores interactive conceptual connections, and fails to explain such causal influences as language, cognition, and emotion. For an understanding of current antisemitism, knowledge of traditional stereotypes proves indispensable, but so is insight into the ways in which they are embedded in complex cognitive schemata, how they relate to emotional states, and how they are verbalized and transmitted.

Since Lippmann (1922) defined the "stereotype" for the social sciences as a "preformed opinion about social groups,"[2] the term has come to be used primarily in a sociopsychological sense to describe a widely held image of the characteristic features and behaviors of the members of social and ethnic groups. In this context, the social-functional component takes precedence (see in this sense Stangor 2000; Ewen and Ewen 2009). But for many years the most varied definitions, some more, some less precise, have circulated in the literature, definitions such as "stereotypes are mental compartments" (Nicklas and Ostermann 1976, 4), "unjustified generalizations with an emotionally subjective tendency" (Wenzel 1978, 16), and "recurring patterns of thought" (Ohde 1994, 41). That stereotypes are, on the one hand, long-lived and, on the other, remarkably changeable (and adaptable) becomes particularly evident in the case of hostility toward Jews (see also von Braun 2004, 11).

From the cognitive point of view, a stereotype is a mental representation in our long-term memory that captures what is considered to be characteristic of a person's or a group's features,[3] doing so by means of crude generalization or simplification in such a way as to present a reduced, distorted, and/or false representation of that which it represents.[4] For instance, a stereotype of the JEW can include such features as HAS A LARGE NOSE AND DARK HAIR, IS AVARICIOUS, POWER-MAD, AND INTELLECTUALLY CORROSIVE. Another stereotype represents the JEW as FOREIGN/UN-GERMAN, SLY, GRUDGE-BEARING, EXPLOITING THE HOLOCAUST, and so on. If judgments and verbalizations are based on stereotypes, the result from a linguistic perspective is a disproportion between the intellectual meaning and the extralinguistic referential level: the representations of meaning and the associated mental attributions do not do justice to the actual referents in the world. When stereotypes form, the multiplicity, the heterogeneity of a group goes largely unacknowledged, individuals' unique characteristics go unnoticed, and characteristics are freely invented.

Like stereotypes, prejudices rest on generalizations and unjustified overgeneralizations about single traits or behaviors.[5] Prejudices constitute a subset of stereotypes. Characteristic of both is a mental misrepresentation or simplified representation, with the caveat that prejudices always carry a negative judgment, whereas in the case of stereotypes the function of categorizing and providing orientation may be either positive or negative. Prejudices can theoretically form in reference to any group (see, e.g., Heitmeyer's concept of group-oriented misanthropy, 2005b, 2007; see also Pelinka et al. 2009). Systems of prejudice usually target certain groups; they are motivated by xenophobia and have specific social functions. The Judeophobic explanation of the world, based on traditional conceptualizations and resentments, however, targets primarily the existence of Jews and as such is unique (see chapter 2, under Conceptual and Verbal Antisemitism, and chapter 3, as well as Schwarz-Friesel and Friesel 2012).

The word *cliché* is often used synonymously with *prejudice* and *stereotype*. In many scholarly treatments and technical dictionaries one also finds an impermissible conflation of the intellectual and verbal realms; thus one encounters such definitions as "forms of speech and expression" or "thought schemata" (see, e.g., Erler 2004, 22), "formulaic figures of speech," "overused images, speech, and thought schemata," "handed-down image or unoriginal thought schema," "an outdated saying or fixed expression, an overused image," "also in the sense of stereotype, of stock phrase, or of formula" (cf. Burger 2007, 11; Bussmann 2008, 339; Kroucheva 2009, 130f.). Here the necessity of already differentiating at the level of language becomes apparent. For example, cliché and prejudice must be differentiated as follows: while one can say, *I have prejudices against Jews*, one cannot say, *I have clichés against Jews*. The only correct way to express the latter idea would be *There are clichés* or *He/she uses a cliché*. Viewed this way, prejudices, unlike clichés, should be understood as mental judgments, as individuals' mental attitudes toward specific situations, persons, or groups. Clichés, on the other hand, exist independently of persons; they are not personal attitudes but rather supraindividual components of a society's collective knowledge. That makes them a specific subtype of stereotype; clichés are specific, standardized conceptualizations, shaped by certain cultural experiences, that pertain to persons, things, or circumstances that can be assumed to be familiar to members of a given community. This definition fits the cliché of romantic love as well as that of the happy rich person or the Jew with financial acumen.[6] It is no coincidence that clichés are so often associated with figures of speech or phrases and are sometimes viewed as identical with them, for clichés belong to the subclass of stereotype that is linked to typical forms of expression. All clichés, but not all stereotypes, necessarily have a clear correlation between content and form. For a Judeophobic as well as anti-Israel stereotype such as ALL JEWS FEEL SOLIDARITY WITH THE ISRAELIS' EXCESSIVE USE OF FORCE, no standard expression exists (as yet), but there are numerous ways of expressing the same idea. In modern linguistic usage, however, a correlation exists between the cliché of WEALTHY, INFLUENTIAL JEWS and the stock phrase *East Coast bankers*, and between the cliché that JEWS SHOOT DOWN ANY CRITICISM BY CHARGING ANTISEMITISM and the stock phrase *antisemitism bludgeon*. The cliché according to which ISRAELIS ARE LIKE ALL JEWS; THEY HAVE ALWAYS BEEN VENGEFUL is used as a stock phrase, often in association with the ancient biblical saying *An eye for an eye, a tooth for a tooth*.

Clichés can arise from communicative practice: individually articulated prejudices can harden in a given community into clichés if people hear and read them over a longer period of time. Anti-Jewish clichés have become established as cultural commonplaces in the course of centuries by way of utterances and images that make use of stereotypes (see chapter 3). If one takes this context into consideration, it becomes clear what danger the acceptance of antisemitic formulations poses in the current communicative space: every verbal antisemitism not refuted or punished has the potential to contribute to the establishment and construction of a cliché. The passage from Bacon quoted at the beginning of this chapter offers a telling characterization of the influence language has on processes of thought and judgment. Acceptance of verbal antisemitism can lead to habituation and normalization. Language serves as a very effective instrument of power, capable of consciously or unconsciously manipulating consciousness by way of its semantic elements (see chapter 3). Existing clichés are "employed" (by individuals on the basis of a particular attitude); that is, people draw on generally familiar clichés in the form of illustrations or stock phrases. Stock phrases are formulaic, overused linguistic expressions, known because they occur so often and function semantically as placeholders. Typical stock phrases are *in the millions, Jewish haggling, Jewish hustle*, or sayings such as *An eye for an eye, a tooth for a tooth.* They resemble idioms—that is, combinations of two or more words that within a specific speech community are used in combination and associated with a specific meaning (cf. Burger 2007; Skirl and Schwarz-Friesel 2007). The fixed phrase *East Coast Jewish bankers* makes use of the cliché that WEALTHY JEWISH FINANCIERS IN AMERICA WIELD GREAT INFLUENCE and thus supports the prejudiced notion of the RICH JEW. The lexeme *Auschwitz bludgeon* has by now become a stock phrase that makes use of a cliché (as discussed later in the chapter).

A clear line must thus be drawn between the cognitive representational elements in a speaker's mind and the various linguistic manifestations of these elements[7] (as Quasthoff 1973, 1987, as well as many others, fail to do;[8] see Schwarz-Friesel 2007, 336f.). Stereotypes are mental images that can be expressed in a variety of verbal forms (e.g., with a lexeme such as *Jewish swine* or *Jewish greed*, a noun phrase such as *the sly usurer* or *Jewish corrosiveness*, or a generic statement such as *Jews are hagglers*). Verbalizations of stereotypical contents can be articulated consciously or unconsciously as antisemitisms (see chapter 2, under Conceptual and Verbal Antisemitism, on intentional and unintentional verbal antisemitism). Ordinary usage contains a range of expressions that for centuries have passed stereotypes from one generation to the next, sometimes without reflection.[9] The phrase "Jews and Germans," which posits a contrast, provides an example. In current discourse the phrase *Auschwitz bludgeon* or *antisemitism bludgeon* has become a common device for alluding efficiently to the stereotyped suggestion that Jews instrumentalize the Holocaust to their own benefit. Stereotypical contents can be verbalized explicitly or implicitly. Thus the stereotype of JEWS AS FOREIGNERS can take the explicit form of *You are not a German, Frau Knobloch!* or (addressed to the Central Council, where Ms. Knobloch served as president from 2006 to 2010) *your un-German association*, or it can be transmitted implicitly: *you as guests in our country* or *in your country, namely Israel.* As a general principle, one should take into consideration the difference between stereotypical antisemitic contents, the strategies employed to convey these contents argumentatively, and the concrete linguistic form chosen (at the level of words, sentences, and texts, e.g., in explicit or implicit comparisons with the Nazis; see chapter 10). Stereotypes can convey positive or negative value judgments.[10] The concept of JEWISH INTELLIGENCE, in itself positive, does not become an antisemitic stereotype until it is used in a negative context (e.g., in a sentence such as *Jews use their high intelligence to oppress and deceive others*) or when it is stored mentally in conjunction with the generally negative value judgment that JEWS USE THEIR INTELLIGENCE TO HARM OTHERS. Philosemitism, for example, draws on stereotypes that consistently generalize about Jews and Judaism in a positive manner.

Stereotypical conceptualizations of Jews have nothing to do with reality; they are in fact constructed images of an enemy, fictive categories,[11] yet for persons who have them stored in their long-term memory they possess the force of convictions. An essential characteristic of antisemitism is that it attributes to Jews traits and behaviors that spring from the imagination of antisemites. They project imagined negative attributes onto Jews that in turn give rise to anti-Jewish constructs (see chapter 3, under On the Genesis of Resentment toward Jews).

Cognitive science has established empirically that conceptual elements are not stored in the long-term memory as isolated mental representations (see, e.g., Schwarz 2008, 91ff.). Instead they form part of more complex conceptual schemata (i.e., mental models that represent certain referential aspects of the world in a specific way). Schemata consist of various linked categorical concepts that (presumably) represent realms of extralinguistic reality. As verbalized models they mirror the views and the belief systems of those who use them. In antisemitic texts one finds for the most part complex conceptual linkages of stereotypical representations. As the reader of such texts, one therefore usually confronts not isolated stereotypical concepts but entire mental models with structures all their own (as in the following message from a resident of Krefeld writing to the Israeli Embassy in Berlin):

> (1) I am beginning to understand why so many perfectly normal people view the Jews as avaricious, cowardly, sly and slimy types always lurking in the shadows who let others fight their battles for them and after things go wrong stage a worldwide outcry that continues for decades, bewailing the great injustice that was done "yet again" to the Jews, after which, with all means at their disposal and for decades, they "reap" as much financial benefit as possible! [IBD_01.02.2008_Woe_001]

This communication contains numerous stereotypes that taken together reveal a homogeneous conceptual net in which Jews are collectively devalued. Anti-semites' mental models generate a closed view of the world whose cognitive categorization and emotional evaluation function entirely within certain absolute parameters, such as 'good' and 'evil.' Every stereotype has its place value in the mental model, is linked quasi-logically with the other stereotypes, and thereby stabilizes an entire system by which the world is explained. Constellations of stereotypes can be formulated as generic statements of belief that conform to the pattern *X is Y*.[12] A chain of beliefs can take a form like this: *The Jews, who are avaricious by nature, have always exploited other peoples. Ever since the illegal establishment of the Israeli state, they have been oppressing and enslaving the Palestinians. On the basis of the Holocaust they shamelessly exploit Germans' guilt feelings and quash free expression of opinion.*

Individuals acquire stereotypes in the course of their socialization (cf. Banaji 2001; Raabe and Beelmann 2011), and these stereotypes become fixed in their minds. They pick up stereotypes in the family or from friends and/or as expressions of public opinion by way of communicative stock phrases. Many stereotypes referring to Jews are passed down unthinkingly through common patterns of expression. Pejorative comments in specific contexts can also have a powerful influence (such as *That's so typically Jewish*). Verbal habituation—that is, the frequent use of or exposure to certain linguistic forms—can result in conceptual normalization and thus lead to (conscious or unconscious) acceptance and internalization of that which is transmitted conceptually. The communicative coding of hostility toward Jews rests above all on such internalizations. We must also take into consideration the (unintended) effects of educational programs and memorialization with respect to the Holocaust, which collectively lend all Jews the nimbus of exceptionality. Emphasis on the dimension of suffering and sacrifice causes some people to react not with empathy, shame, or grief but rather defensively or uneasily (on defensiveness in the face of guilt and memory, see chapter 8, under The Mentality of "Being Fed Up"). Uneasiness in turn can result in reinforcement of existing stereotypes and affective resentments. German history then comes to be seen as threatening the person's own normality and desire for a positive self-image; pressure to face the past and preserve its memory into the future on moral grounds becomes a personal burden that generates resistance. This resistance transfers the resulting negative feelings onto those seen as responsible for causing the emotional distress—the Jews—who in any case have been suspect for centuries, viewed as peculiar and unusual. In this way individual aversions coincide with culturally transmitted resentments and acquire the desired legitimation. Resentments are (for the most part unconscious) feelings of aversion and hostility (see chapter 8). These negative feelings toward a specific group of people coincide with the emotional attitude of antipathy. Here the alter ego functions as the diametric opposite of the ego. The hostility and defensiveness derive from a global projection of negative qualities onto the opposite group. For those motivated by resentment, their own normality and integrity stem from their projection of negative qualities onto the Other (cf., e.g., Frindte 1999; Heil 2001; Holz 2004; Hegener 2006; Haubl and Caysa 2007). At issue here is a Manichaean view of the world. Those who think in stereotypes and base their value judgments on resentments spare themselves the critical and difficult task of coming to terms with reality. Strictly dichotomous distinctions according to clearly defined categories representing unshakable values make for a closed view of the world, one that refuses to acknowledge the multiplicity and complexity of phenomena, thereby avoiding the problem of making subtle distinctions. Instead, those who subscribe to such a view place their trust in simplistic solutions and unambiguous, precisely targeted interpretations. Antisemites order the world's confusing aspects clearly and rigidly, without any doubt as to the correctness of their beliefs, into an internally coherent system. The axiom reads as follows: 'The evil Others are the Jews.' All other beliefs derive from this unshakable principle, and those who question it are liars, those who affirm it friends.

The connection between the related phenomena can now be described again as follows (starting with that which can be perceived concretely and proceeding to the mental aspect): stock phrases are established linguistic formulations that are stored in the mental lexicon and often used to express clichés. Thus stock phrases are expressions and phrases that verbalize clichés. Clichés can be defined as commonly recognized, socially disseminated conceptualizations, in other words notions that are anchored in culture and familiar in the context of a given society. They belong to a society's collective knowledge, and generally recognized expressions exist within the language community to represent them. These clichés are a subgroup of stereotypes—that is, cognitive representations of groups of people that constitute prejudices when coupled with negative feelings. Many clichés, stereotypes, and prejudices are based on resentments, which are unconscious emotional aversions. Cognitive and emotional representations come together in the case of antisemitism to form a complex evaluative system that is conceptually closed and provides a grid for interpreting the world.

The antisemitic communications sent to the Central Council and the Embassy, but also the numerous Judeophobic statements and comments on the Internet (see Schwarz-Friesel 2013a), show how homogeneously this interpretive system is anchored in the minds of many, impervious to facts and education and not dislodged by knowledge of the horrors of the Holocaust and the sequelae of prejudicial thinking.

Current Stereotypes and Their Verbal Manifestations

What (traditional) anti-Jewish stereotypes appear explicitly and/or implicitly in our twenty-first-century texts, and in what combinations do they occur? Have decades of post-Holocaust educational efforts broken the continuity of mental hostility toward Jews or in any way altered it? Do signs exist (after intensive efforts devoted to uncovering the dangerous effects of demagogic rhetoric and language control during the Nazi era) of more responsible use of language as an instrument of power and of critical reflection on collective, culturally and communicatively transmitted clichés?

The Stereotype of Jews as Foreigners and Jews as Israelis

The mental basis for defining and segregating Jews as a group felt not to belong to one's own group and classified accordingly is the concept of the OTHER, the FOREIGNER (cf. chapter 3).[13] This fundamental categorization, which originated in antiquity, provides the foundation for all further stereotypes. Without this differentiation or discrimination, the negative attributions derived from it would not exist in such massive proportions. Only comprehensive exclusion of a certain social group makes it possible to focus on features deemed to set it apart. One generally ascribes positive characteristics to one's own group in order to reinforce one's identity and self-concept.[14] Excluded persons (groups) can be judged all the more harshly if one invokes the separation of one's own group from the other. That Jews are seen as foreign, nonbelonging, and fundamentally different is communicated strikingly often in the formulation JEWS AS NON-GERMANS in the messages (even those written by persons with advanced degrees). This feature can take an explicit form, as in (2), (3), and (4), where German Jews are declared to be non-Germans:

> (2) you should refrain from criticizing german activities abroad, which is interference in internal affairs of the german state that is none of your business as a non-European sect. [ZJD_29.05.2007_Sch_002]
>
> (3) you are a guest in this country, so behave yourself as such and stop your constant instigation against the host people. [ZJD_22.03.2007_ano_001][15]

The distinction expressed grammatically in such texts correlates in its argumentation to the lexical means employed: thus the Central Council and/or all German Jews are referred to as a *troupe*, *group*, *association*, *ethnic minority*, *(religious) sect*, or *guests*, and in extremists' messages as *non-German rabble*, *foreign riffraff*, or *degenerate non-Aryans*:

> (4) I hereby demand that you immediately withdraw from our country, together with your ethic group, which is not welcome either in Germany or in the Catholic church. [IBD_13.11.2010_Fis_001]

In (5) the use of the contrasting pronouns *you* versus *us* expresses the distinction between Jews and "genuine Germans" and thereby creates a semantic polarization (cf. also Scherr and Schäuble 2008). The addition of "*your country, by which I mean ISRAEL*" reveals the conceptualization JEWS AS ISRAELIS (for a more thorough treatment, see chapter 6). For some years now this stereotype has been the dominant variant of the conceptualization JEWS AS FOREIGNERS; it constitutes the current prototypical version of this old Judeophobic interpretive schema:[16]

> (5) Re: you are absolutely the last ones who have a right to give us advice! As regrettable as right-wing radical attacks in Germany may be, your country is absolutely the last one that has a right to criticize other countries, because your country, by which I mean ISRAEL constantly perpetrates actual state terrorism and has no concept of human rights [. . .] [ZJD_25.10.2006_Sch_001]

In this form of argumentation German Jews are denied the status of "German," and the words *Jew(s)* and *Israeli(s)* often appear as synonyms. This usage mirrors the conceptual conflation of the two different reference groups in the minds of the authors. At the same time, the old stereotype of the JEWISH FOREIGNER is perpetuated by communicative means, because Jews are conceptualized as GUESTS in Germany, loyal to their alleged homeland, Israel, not to their "host country."

The stereotype JEWS AS ISRAELIS is conveyed explicitly by messages addressing Jews directly as Israelis or categorizing Jews as Israeli citizens:

> (6) All this should be familiar to you Israelis. [ZJD_18.02.2006_Bri_001]
>
> (7) DOESN'T IT BOTHER YOU THAT YOUR COUNTRY CONSTANTLY COMMITS MURDER STAGES MASSACRES WITH IMPUNITY AND LIKE YESTERDAY AND THE DAY BEFORE YESTERDAY IN THE REFUGEE CAMP [ZDJ_03.08.2002_Sch_001]
>
> (8) Persuade your country to stop its attacks on Lebanon. [ZJD_26.07.2006_ano_001]

In messages such as (9) the authors also often provide information about themselves to emphasize the distinctions they are drawing with respect to nationality:

> (9) as a citizen of the Federal Republic of Germany I observe with great concern the escalation of violence on the part of your country and your government. [ZDJ_19.06.2006_Web_001]

Assumptions that the generalizations 'All Jews are Israelis' and 'All Israelis are Jews' are synonymous also appear frequently in the letters:

> (10) What irritates me above all is that precisely the Jews, who should have been sensitized by their experience with the Hitler regime, are becoming war criminals. [ZJD_31.07.2006_Gla_001]
>
> (11) I at any rate will not hold my tongue and will make public everywhere the crimes of the Israelis, that is, the Jews. [IBD_04.07.2007_Dro_001]

Conveyed implicitly and recognizable by way of conclusions based on universal knowledge is the stereotype in utterances like (12), where one must infer contextually from information in the subject line that the author of the e-mail sees a causal connection between events in the Middle East and the behavior of the Central Council:

> (12) Re: gaza strip. You are making the entire world your enemies. [ZJD_Gaza2009_349/816_Ado_001]

Rhetorical questions such as those as in (13) also present implicit forms of verbal discrimination, since they verbalize the intended reading not explicitly but as a possibility:

> (13) What are the members of the CENTRAL COUNCIL really: Jewish citizens in Germany ? German Jews ? Israeli Jews in Germany ? The last interpretation makes sense, seeing as how Frau Knobloch and Herr Korn—like their predecessors Herr Bubicz and Herr Spiegel—behave toward German politicians and citizens like the "5th column" of a foreign state? [ZJD_02.11.2006_Buh_001]

Not only the Israeli Embassy but also the Central Council receives massive and aggressive criticism, insults, and defamation for military operations in Israel, as in (14) and (15):

> (14) You sneaky people of Jews should be ashamed to play your wretchedgame with the people in Gaza. You're no better than the NAZIS. You Jews in Germany are jest as responsble as your kind in the cripple state of Israel, the way you make all Germans responsible for the deeds of the NAZIS 62 years ago. Because of you few "CHOSEN PEOPLE" so many have to die. [ZJD_20.09.2007_ano_001]

It is striking how many of the writers refer to reports in the media that apparently created the concrete pretext for their sending their e-mails (see chapter 6, under "*As I just read in my paper . . .*"):

> (15) The Tagespresse, 9 January 2009, Cardinal in the Curia Renato Martino of the Vatican in an interview: "Let us look at the living conditions in the Gaza Strip: it is more like gigantic concentration camp." One can only concur with this statement. [IBD_09.01.2009_Her_001]

The very fact that the Central Council receives messages referring to Israel shows the influence of the cliché (born of the conspiracy theory) that a universal Jewish community with shared values exists independently of spatial and national affinities and represents purely Jewish interests; furthermore, the stereotype is confirmed that Jews in Germany are not German; on this point many university-educated authors also fall prey to the stereotype. In numerous messages to the Central Council even writers with advanced degrees ascribe collective guilt and responsibility to Jews, as in (16), an e-mail from a social scientist from Göttingen with a PhD:

> (16) You people have contributed to the killing of sevral hundred thousands of people and the expulsion of 4 mill. people. By giving unlimited support to israel. [ZJD_Gaza2009_43/816_Mie_001]

The absurdity of such generic assignment of guilt becomes particularly striking if one uses analogies to show how nonsensical similar overgeneralizations would be if applied to non-Jews, for instance if one said, 'All Catholics in Germany and in the world are guilty of and responsible for sexual abuse by Catholic priests' or 'All Muslims are responsible for 9/11.' It is significant that such collective attributions of guilt across societies do not occur in conjunction with other religious groups.[17]

In addition to direct assignment of guilt based on the notion that JEWS ARE BY DEFINITION (CO)RESPONSIBLE FOR ALL CRISES AND WARS IN THE WORLD BECAUSE THEY ARE JEWS, there are indirect and more specific variants along the lines of 'German Jews become (partly) responsible for Israeli military actions and political developments in Israel because they do not criticize Israel harshly but instead defend the country out of solidarity.'

> (17) Dear Ladies and Gentlemen: Your declaration of 30 December 2008 gives a perverse, mendacious, and completely naive picture of the Israeli war of extermination in the Gaza Strip. [. . .] You know the worldwide antipathy to the Jews—through this war boundless hatred is inevitably created. Israel is engaging so to speak in self-destruction. INCOMPREHENSIBLE. [ZJD_Gaza2009_660/816_ano_001]

This version rests on two premises (constructed by the authors): first, that Israel is guilty and in the wrong and, second, that Jews in Germany defend this injustice only because it was committed by Jews. If the authors additionally establish the pseudo-causal connection that for this very reason antisemitism will increase, they are validating one antisemitic stereotype by means of another (see also the examples in chapter 8).

Even when the pretext for writing has nothing to do with Israel (but rather, e.g., with comments by the Central Council on antisemitism or coming to grips with the Holocaust), almost all the authors of letters or e-mails mention Israeli policies in their argumentation and apply their (extremely) negative views and strong emotional judgments to the Central Council or to all Jews. Thus Israel merely serves as a hook, brought into focus by current media reporting on the Middle East, and as a pseudo-causal reference point that allows the writers to articulate anti-Jewish opinions. In the linguistic form these notions take, antisemitic, anti-Zionist, and anti-Israeli referentializations merge almost seamlessly, as can be seen, among other things, in the synonymous use of *Israel*, *Judaism*, and *Zionism*.[18] The Central Council and the Embassy (two completely different institutions, after all) receive reproachful communications from highly educated persons in prominent positions to the effect that in supporting Israel they are advocating for *an unjust apartheid regime*, *state terrorism*, *violent excesses*, or *a second Nazi state*, and are not showing *solidarity with* or *loyalty to Germany*. A professor of jurisprudence begins his long, polemical, cliché-ridden e-mail to the Central Council with the following observation:

> (18) since these days you are uncritically taking the side of Israel, at least any claim that a distinction must be made between the Central Council and Israel has been eliminated from the world. You consider yourselves one team, you are one team. [ZJD_27.07.2006_Rau_001][19]

This author sees the Central Council's call for solidarity as confirmation of the belief that Jews are Israelis, loyal only to Israel. The wording "*a distinction must be made*" suggests that any previous distinction between Jews and Israelis was merely a social imperative or demand. Here the stereotype of an imposed opinion is implied. For the professor, the Central Council's solidarity with Israel, viewed by him as an unjust state "*dedicated to terror*" "*in others' territory*," constitutes a commitment to unfathomable evil: he portrays Israel as a cruel, lawbreaking, morally bankrupt entity. He charges the Central Council with exploiting a "*painstakingly cultivated role as victim*" and with behaving "*with an unheard-of degree of irresponsibility.*" Segregation of German Jews as an alien group identified with Israel from the in-group of non-Jewish Germans finds expression in the contrasting pronouns *you* and *we*: "*you and the state of Israel*" and "*we Germans.*" The Judeophobic notion that Judaism as a religion serves as the basis for moral degeneracy also finds expression in the following message from another university-educated person who conflates religious and political/ideological aspects:

(19) In the background is most likely the Zionist idea of being a chosen people. [ZJD_27.07.2006_Rau_001]

The way this correspondent links several Judeophobic clichés to form a coherent text reveals his closed anti-Jewish worldview. Contrary to all reason, contrary to all facts, and contrary to any knowledge of the dangers of resentment-driven condemnation, this representative of a social elite communicates the very stereotypes that were typical of the virulent antisemitism of the nineteenth and twentieth centuries and previously turned up in such concentrated form only in right-wing-extremist pamphlets. Altogether, in this communication and in thousands of others, the conceptualization of ISRAEL AS A COLLECTIVE JEW becomes unmistakable (see chapter 6).

The indirect speech acts in which Jews are implicitly excluded from the we-group of Germans include (rhetorical) questions, as in (20) and (23), and statements, as in (21) and (22), in which either improper conflations occur ('Jews are Israelis,' 'Jews are foreigners') or unjustified distinctions are made ('Jews have no place among Germans'):[20]

(20) what are Jews in this world or what are the Jews in Germany (Jews, german, german-Jews or simply just Jews again?)!!! [ZJD_27.12.2008_Wel_001]

(21) Yes, if the Jews and foreigners behave in a human way, I have no objection. [ZJD_06.04.2002_Klo_001]

(22) that you want to deny the Germans the right to demonstrate and express their opinions freely I find intolerable. This is a purely German concern. [ZJD_11.07.2007_Glo_001]

By means of a statement couched as a question, the author of (23) expresses the stereotype JEWS ARE NO GERMANS:

(23) I wonder what business this eulogy is of theirs. [ZJD_16.04.2007_Moh_001]

Here the writer implies that (German) Jews do not belong to the German people and therefore also have no right to comment on a speech by a "real German" (in this case the speech in question is Günther Oettinger's eulogy for Hans Filbinger). A similar variant can be found in (24), where the addition of "only us Germans" makes the exclusionary impulse even clearer:

(24) My friends and I wonder why they always meddle in matters that concern only us Germans. [ZJD_08.01.2008_Hei_001]

In many of these messages (including those that voice Judeophobic stereotypes explicitly), the authors attempt to justify their judgments as neutral, objective, and/or not in the slightest antisemitic, as in (25):

(25) In case word has not reached the Jews yet, we in Germany have free speech. [. . .] We Germans also do not call for the murderous ministers in Israel to be fired. So you should keep your nose out of our business. [. . .] And leave us in peace. We don't dictate anything to Israel either. P.S. I'm not anti-Jewish, but this kind of thing really gets to me! [IBD_09.10.2007_Gro_001]

Such attempts at legitimation, which mention the authors' motives for articulating critical views and at the same time deny antipathy toward Jews (see chapter 10), are the only indication that an awareness exists that in the post-Holocaust era such statements are inflammatory. This consciousness comes into play cognitively[21] and communicatively but does not prevent the articulation of verbal antisemitisms or cause their producer to reflect critically on what he or she is saying. The antipathy (in conjunction with the culturally rooted stereotypes) determines the speaker's attitude and buries any conscious component. Thus no metacognitive reflection occurs.

Jews as Murderers of Christ

Since the nineteenth century, religiously oriented hostility toward Jews has been replaced by secular, racist, nationalist-ideological, or social and economic criteria, yet the concept of JEWS AS MURDERERS OF CHRIST still plays a role in current linguistic practices when it comes to arguing against and discrediting Jews (see also Scherr 2011):[22]

> (26) Bavarian Broadcasting wrote in its program, "The Romans crucified Jesus!" That is not true. They were only the ones who carried it out! . . . The Jews nailed Jesus to the Cross and to this day do not recognize our Savior! [ZDJ_17.06.2002_unl_001][23]
>
> (27) We Christians have long since forgiven the Jews for betraying Jesus Christ and having him crucified, thereby incurring incalculable guilt. The Lord Himself forgave them on the Cross. Can mercy and forgiveness be greater? [. . .] So why are some Jews so against our Lord? Why does their hatred for us Christians persist? For my part, I bear no grudge against any Jews; the Lord forgave them, and I am glad of that. I at least will pray that the heart of Frau Knobloch may also be illuminated by the light of our Lord and that she may overcome her obvious dislike for us Christians. [. . .] May the Lord forgive Frau Knobloch. [ZJD_22.03.2008_Rog_001]

To be sure, only very few of the texts that contain the phrase *murderers of Christ* as a term of condemnation and defamation actually invoke religious convictions or theological considerations or use the attribution of guilt that was current in the Middle Ages and recurs today in fundamentalist discourse, as in (26) and (27).[24] Instead the phrase is used primarily for purposes of general devaluation. Most such usages either occur as part of collective negative attributions, as in (28) and (29), or link to several other stereotypes that conflate the historical with the contemporary and at the same time engage in the reversal of perpetrator and victim.

> (28) To me the Jews are the most disagreeable people in the world. To me as a Christian they remain the murderers of God. [IBD_30.06.2006_Son_001]
>
> (29) But as a people of Christ-murderers of course they always have to distract attention from themselves. [IBD_28.10.2006_ano_002]
>
> (30) Christ-murderers—desecrators of humanity!! [IBD_22.07.2006_ano_007][25]
>
> (31) Go to hell, you vermin! You're the lowest race God unleashed on

this world. Christ-murderers was just the beginning. [IBD_24.05.2010_ano_003]

(32) You gang of murderers!!!!!!!!!!!!!!!!!!!!!!!!!!!!! You filthy Jews!!!!!!!!!!!!! !!!!!!!!!!!!!!!!!!!!. There are still too many of you. Child-murderers!!!!!!!!!!!!!!!!! Christ-murderers!!!!!!!!!!!!!!!!!!!!!!!!!!!! Perfidious!!!!!!!!!!!!!!!!!!!!!! Dishonest, as Jews are known to be!!!!!!!!!!!!!!!! I hope lots more Jew children die that's the only way you crooks will learn. [ZJD_Gaza2009_301/816_ano_001]

Messages that explicitly call into question Israel's right to exist are especially likely to contain references to the historical murder of Christ, which is deemed particularly shameful and presented as a historical fact:

(33) Israel has no right to exist there. Just because some Christ-murderers were going about their nefarious business there two thousand years ago doesn't mean by a long shot that they have any right to be there today. [ZJD_Gaza2009_488/816_May_001]

(34) Christ-murderers! Your current provocations in Lebanon and toward the Germans have only one goal. And this goal shows your base character and your scheming nature. [IBD_31.10.2006_ano_001]

(35) That's what you've known how to do for 2008 years!!!!!!!!!!!!!!!!!!!!!!!!! You're the NAZIS of today [ZJD_Gaza2009_301/816_ano_001]

These messages portray the entire history of the Jewish people as characterized by murder and violence. Authors who give their names and addresses and present themselves as educated tend to encode implicitly this defamatory catchphrase, once religiously motivated and today functioning as a stigma, as in (36); one can infer from the allusion to universal knowledge that from the author's perspective Jews murdered Christ and to this day operate in this bloody tradition:

(36) Jerusalem deciphered means consciousness of Christ. Jesus made this consciousness incarnate for us. What your people did to him, you know. So leave us in Germany in peace at long last. That will also bring you peace. [ZJD_03.06.2007_Her_001]

Jews as Child-Murderers and Practitioners of Blood Cult

In these texts, the CHRIST-MURDERER concept appears strikingly often in conjunction with the stereotype JEWS AS CHILD-MURDERERS ENGAGING IN BLOOD RITUALS, as in the following messages:[26]

(37) What the hell! The "chosen" people is showing the world its religiously/ideologically distorted true face and revealing itself as an immoral gang of bloodthirsty child-murderers. [ZJD_Gaza2009_632/816_ano_001]

(38) You child-devourers. [ZJD_Gaza2009_9/816_Hai_001]

(39) Child-slaughterers! [ZJD_09.01.2009_Hel_001]

The phrase *child-murdering Jews* already occurs frequently in the Middle Ages; in English literature the lexeme *bloudie* turns up (see Trachtenberg 1943, 125). This old Judeophobic stereotype is constantly projected onto the state of Israel in particular, revealing, on the one hand, the continuity of the old clichés and, on the other, the conceptual blending of old and new (anti-Israeli) stereotypes:

(40) The way the state of Israel behaves, one can only describe these people as murderers, child-murderers. What is your position on this appalling phenomenon? [ZJD_Gaza2009_811/816_Kil_001]

(41) To me Olmert is a child-murdering pig, I hope he kicks the bucket soon, lowly and painfully! And to me Israel is a child-murdering criminal people who learned absolutely nothing after the 2nd World War! [ZJD_Gaza2009_383/816_Kol_001]

By ascribing intentional murderous activity to them, these writers justify their hostility toward Jews, since according to this interpretation the Jews draw hatred to themselves though their acts of murder and violence:

(42) I never knew why Jews were hated so much. Now I know. They are CHILD-MURDERERS [...] [ZJD_Gaza2009_320/816_Ado_001]

The collective anti-Jewish characterization of JEWS AS PERPETRATORS has been passed down through the centuries and is now applied to Israel and its population; thus Jewish and Israeli matters are commingled in one concept:

(43) Your history is dripping with blood. You are perpetrators, not victims. [IBD_20.07.2006_ano_008]

Explicit references to the blood-cult legend and attribution of it to the Jews,[27] however, occur exclusively in extremist and Islamic fundamentalist texts:[28]

(44) Does a more hypocritical state even exist than the terrorist state of the Jews, which nourishes itself on the blood of the Palestinian civilians. [IBD_11.06.2006_Oez_001]

(45) You stink! You look like shit! You fuck your own children in the butt and commit ritual murder. Just go away, so humanity can finally live in peace again. [ZJD_Gaza2009_577/816_ano_001]

Yet in messages from mainstream authors, references to Israel are often accompanied by words and metaphors drawn from the semantic fields of murder and violence, words like *murder lust*, *blood frenzy*, *violence-obsessed*, *violent excess*, *murderous*, *bloody-minded*, *bloodthirsty*, and *bloody violence*, whose meanings suggest a close association with the BLOOD-CULT stereotype:

(46) Have you ever asked yourself why no country in the world can stand you Jews? Because you don't hesitate to walk over dead bodies. [ZJD_08.01.2008_Hei_001]

Educated authors tend to invoke the MURDERER and CHILD-MURDERER cliché implicitly by referring to conclusions that can be drawn:

(47) Again, no one has the right to murder children, and that includes Jews! [ZJD_Gaza2009_647/816_Pet_001]

Jews as Antichrists

Religious motifs (often in conjunction with intertextual references to passages in the Bible and apocalyptic threats) also play a role in the mental image of JEWS AS ANTICHRISTS AND BLASPHEMERS:[29]

(48) Of course you remain silent as collaborators in this Jewish crime against humanity! May the blood of all the innocents killed there in the Gaza Strip be on the head of all Jews who have remained silent the world

over! For every innocent person killed in this war a hundred Jews should die—Lord, let these blasphemers not get away with their infernal crime!" [ZJD_Gaza2009_233/816_Kra_001]

(49) These "Jews" belong to the sect which falsified the Holy Writ of God and they obey Satan. The Satanists have had enough time to become civilized. But their goal is the destruction of civilization, the destruction of justice and order. [IBD_18.01.2009_ano_001; according to his own information, a Palestinian in exile]

Expressions like *devil, spawn of Satan, children of Satan, pact with the devil* dominate in the encoding of this stereotype:

(50) Devil's spawn! Anti-Christs. [IBD_07.05.2010_ano_003]

(51) you are proud of gaza?? what human being can be proud of murder? an antichrist. jesus already said 'you have the devil for a father.' thats in the bible! you can recognize arihmans children by their deeds.... im looking forward to that day. that day will go down in cosmic history as the day when EVIL was beaten. [ZJD_Gaza2009_84/816_Dar_001]

Here we also see, presented as an article of faith, the conviction that the Jews are the source of evil in the world, a conceptualization established by the church fathers two thousand years ago (see chapter 3, under On the Genesis of Resentment toward Jews). The intertextual reference to the Bible, supposedly to a saying of Jesus's, is intended to legitimate the devaluation of Jews as children of the devil.[30] The textual allusion, however, is decontextualized—that is, ripped out of its original context and given an inappropriate reading (which does conform precisely to the author's meaning but not to the original).[31]

The notion of JEWS AS THE EPITOME OF EVIL IN THE WORLD can also be activated without any religious context when it entails demonization of Jews and/or Israelis on principle (usually the two are conceptually conflated). For further discussion, see chapter 6, under Tools of Demonization.

The Stereotype of the Jewish Physiognomy

Although anti-Jewish caricatures are well known and have been subjected to serious critique, many of those writing to the Central Council or the Embassy mention specific physical characteristics traditionally regarded as typically

Jewish.[32] They intend thereby to stigmatize Jews purely on the basis of their appearance:

(52) And the Israelis (Jews): crooked noses, grasping businessmen [...] [IBD_24.01.2009_Kut_001]

The stereotype of the HOOKED NOSE recurs especially often in messages from right-wing extremists, but is always accompanied by further Judeophobic clichés such as JEWISH POLITICAL CORRECTNESS and RAPACIOUS MERCENARIES:

(53) ARD [German Public Broadcasting] and the Tageschau [*Daily Show*] has finally revealed itself as demagogic infotainment serving the interests of hooked-nosed lobbyists! [ZJD_Gaza2009_487/816_ano_001]

(54) Re: lotte knoblauch. dear charlotte should pay more attention to her matzos and her sabbath grub and keep her smart alec nose out of the german press. [ZJD_23.10.2007_Sch_001]

In (55) the reference to physiognomy is associated with ancient Jewish character traits, conveying a classic racist attitude:

(55) Certainly there were always a few exceptional minds who transcended the Jewish mentality and Jewish thinking, like for instance Sigmund Freud or Karl Marx, but the critical thought of such people never resulted in freeing the Jewish circles of black sheep and rabble rousers of the Jewish negative traits or having the Jews take in with their hooked nose what was perhaps right and justified about the charges leveled against the character traits ascribed to them. [ZJD_30.11.2006_Gel_001]

In general, however, the physiognomic stereotype is seldom used in a concrete sense. Instead a conceptual dislocation has occurred: the image of the UGLY JEW has been transformed into a metaphor and now turns up primarily with a figurative meaning as the stereotype of the MORALLY UGLY ISRAELI as in (56), an e-mail from a Protestant minister who uses quotation marks to signal that he is conscious of the cliché but is using it on purpose to defame the Central Council, which he charges with furthering antisemitic proclivities:

(56) If at the present time antisemitic resentments should surface in Germany, you are personally not without blame. [. . .] Why must you drag in that "ugly Jew" Ariel Scharon to demonstrate solidarity? [ZJD_06.04.2002_Sch_002]

Jews as Money-Grubbers and Usurers

The concept of the Jew as someone wedded to finance and money matters who unscrupulously enriches him- or herself at others' expense occurs particularly often in the corpus, and by no means only in messages from right-wing extremists:[33]

(57) [. . .] a small tribe that happens to have a talent for dealing with dough! [ZJD_08.01.2008_Bal_001]

(58) just squeezing money out of others [. . .] that's all you care about! [ZJD_12.03.2008_ano_001]

(59) My own experiences and contact with rich Jews coincide with the reservations always expressed. Jews are said to be greedy Jews are said to be power-mad yes, I think there's something to that. The occupation of Palestinian territory shows the whole world how arrogantly Jews behave even toward the UN. [ZJD_Gaza2009_20/816_ano_001]

In examples like (59) comments often occur that reveal the authors' awareness that their views would be generally considered prejudices or resentments, despite which they remain convinced of their truth.

In conjunction with constructs based on the conspiracy theory that Jews control world finance (of which Wall Street is cited as a prototype), this stereotype is elaborated with descriptors such as CHEATING, EXPLOITATIVE, and NOMADIC to produce a complex conceptualization of the ETERNAL JEW, into which the alleged crimes of the Israelis are also integrated:

(60) The Jewish Talmud contains a wealth of passages that permit cheating of non-Jews by Jews. That's precisely the basis of Jews' international domination of finance. And that is what makes the Jew hated so much internationally. And then the Jew has the gall to claim that his Talmud was given to him directly by God. [ZJD_Gaza2009_536/816_ano_001]

(61) According to the exegesis of the Jewish Bible and after thorough examination of the rabulistic Talmudic doctrine, the Jews are actually nothing but a psychopathological sect of mentally ill people who have the temerity to claim they possess the only measure of what society and the way of the world should be, according to the formula: "The Lord spoke, let the world and its fruits be yours, seat yourselves at the table, no matter who has spread and prepared it . . ." For this reason the Jews love the nomadic and vagabondish networks of speculative money markets for that's where their constitutive identity resides, to sneak into others' houses, take up residence there, and plunder their hosts, and for that first the appropriate parasitical communication has to be smuggled in so a people's natural reflexes to resist parasitic pests are paralyzed. With good reason the peoples of the world have known for centuries why that sect of child-murderers, money-changers, and land-grabbers from Egypt was ostracized and shunned. [ZJD_04.11.2006_Tur_001]

In texts of this sort historical and contemporary references always occur in tandem with collective devaluations and conspiracy theories. The linguistic patterns bear a striking resemblance, even down to the vocabulary used, to manifestly Judeophobic texts from the nineteenth and early twentieth centuries.

To Jews are ascribed the exclusive responsibility and blame for both the international financial crisis and the general misery in the world:

(62) That you still have the gall to take a position on the financial crisis, knowing perfectly well that the Zionists of Wall Street are behind this greatest financial fraud in world history. Paulson, Bernanke and other Zionist players are Jews or Semites. [ZJD_Gaza2009_624/816_ano_001]

(63) With what moral claim do the Jews justify the misery that Jews bring into the world (crimes day in, day out in Palestine); the recent financial crisis caused by America has its origins, after all, on Wallstreet (which is controlled by Jews) ? The worldwide misery its causing should certainly get alot more attention in your central council. [ZJD_21.03.2008_Bie_001]

Applied to the conflict in the Middle East, the stereotype undergoes considerable elaboration: according to this notion, the allegedly money-grubbing

Jews, always focused on profit, extend their greed to include others' territory. At the same time a direct connection is established to Jews' alleged desire for world domination:

(64) [. . .] in plain German: the Jewish riffraff wants to STEAL the Palestinians' gas and oil resources. Oil and gas are once more the sole reason for this bloody and murderous Jew-war! [ZJD_Gaza2009_549/816_Grä_001]

(65) That the Jews have the say in the investment banks in New York and now want to unleash a economic holocaust on 6.7 billion people is something only a complete greenhorn can question. Basis: boundless greed, money obsession, . . . Israelism . . . [ZJD_Gaza2009_16/816_Del_001]

Thus the conflict in the Middle East is interpreted on the basis of an ancient anti-Jewish stereotype as resulting directly from Jews' alleged greed for wealth, power, and land, with all the blame placed on them. Traditional and current stereotypes merge. In addition to the Middle East conflict, which serves primarily as a pretext for the articulation of anti-Jewish statements, the second prominent theme in all the communications is the question of the Germans' Nazi past. Thus many combinations of conceptual markers turn up, as in (66) and (67), where the ancient cliché of the USURER joins the postwar concept of JEWS AS GRUDGE-BEARING EXPLOITERS OF THE HOLOCAUST (see further discussion later in this chapter):[34]

(66) You can't engage in eternal usury with the crimes of my ancestors, at some point that's going to land you in the ditch. [ZJD_08.01.2008_Sch_001]

(67) So why does Jewry always act as though all Germans were involved in the Nazis' crimes and are supposed to be reminded of that and forced to pay forever? [. . .] is it because of the money? [ZJD_22.05.2004_Poh_001]

Starting in 2005, the reproach that Jewish immigration to Germany imposes an unjustified burden disappears almost entirely from the messages (whereas it still turns up often in 2002–2003). Instead, the stereotype JEWS ARE FREELOADERS undergoes a shift from the postwar forms—'Jews exploit Germany/the Holocaust' and 'we pay for Jewish immigrants'—to a form referring to

Israel, such as 'it's us who have to pay for Israel' or 'the EU/the world has to make up for all the damage inflicted by Israel.' Analogously, many shifts in traditional stereotypes take place in light of current headline-grabbing events, demonstrating how quickly verbal manifestations of antisemitism adapt to situational changes.

Often many of the classic stereotypes appear in quick succession in a given text, as in (68), an e-mail from a high-school student who expresses her anti-semitic notions of Jews by means of a series of adjectives, all descriptive of negative characteristics, and at the same time supports her assumptions by referring to a majority from the mainstream:

> (68) now I understand why Jews are considered nasty, brutal, untruthful, greedy, and ruthless. Many of my classmates and friends see it the same way! [IBD_11.03.2010_Bel_001]

The author of (69) likewise reveals a radically Judeophobic view of the world, according to which Jews, as non-German, vengeful, mendacious, exploitative, morally degenerate beings and pests harmful to the German people, should be driven out. It is impossible to miss the linguistic parallels to the aggressive pamphlets and diatribes produced by eliminatory antisemitism (see chapter 3, under Anti-Semitism as State Doctrine).

> (69) You god-damned murderous brood! Don't you dare to shake your moral finger ever again at us Germans [...] you blood-dripping child-slaughterers. [...] Spare us your parasitical, greedy demands for money and get out of our country. A plague and all things bad on your vengeful heads! [ZJD_09.01.2009_ano_001]

Jews as Animals

Collective negative judgments predominate in the emotional hate speech of right-wing but also left-wing radicals, in which the dehumanization of Jews always occupies the foreground. Jews are denied human qualities across the board, being characterized as *animals*, *Jewish swine*, *pests*, *criminal vermin*, *devils*, or *subhumans*. Thus a January 2004 e-mail addressed to the Central Council begins with the salutation "*SUBHUMAN RIFFRAFF!*" and ends with "*You can't croak a day too soon!!*" These communications present a fixed image of the enemy in which the object of hatred is represented as a figure of inhuman evil, not deserving to live. This demonization of Jews usually goes hand in hand with dehumanizing language that makes its point through allusions to animals:

(70) You're all miserable cowardly pigs! You don't belong to the human race, that's what your deeds prove! You damned cheats who siphon off taxpayers' money! [ZJD_Gaza2009_730/816_Pan_001]

By preference Jews are described as *pigs*, *rats*, *bacilli*, and *parasites* (cf. examples [10]–[29] in chapter 9), evidence of the long tradition of such characterizations:

(71) One rat helps the other. [IBD_22.07.2006_ano_007]

Often such references occur in combination with the stereotype of JEWS AS EXPLOITERS OF OTHER PERSONS AND PEOPLES:

(72) withdraw from palestine you stinking parasites [ZJD_22.05.2007_Lan_001]

(73) You're living at others' expense, it's well known that the Jews live that way! [ZJD_Gaza2009_92/816_ano_001]

(74) Freeloaders. [ZJD_Gaza2009_530/816_Jüt_001]

Similarly, old motifs such as that of the biblical plague of locusts are projected onto the Jews and currently also the Israelis, making use of personification:

(75) The fat, aggressive locusts are chomping away! [. . .] just terrible, what those Israelis are up to over there [. . .]! [ZJD_27.07.2006_Ren_001]

Terms such as *freaks*, *monsters*, *nonhumans*, and *subhumans* also come into play. Jews' status as human beings is explicitly negated, as in (76), or called into question, as in (77). Wishful thinking about eliminating Jews altogether derives from such images:

(76) YOU'RE NOT EVEN HUMAN ANYMORE! UNFEELING MONSTERS! [. . .] You all have to be WIPed out! [IBD_07.05.2010_ano_024]

In texts such as (77) and (78) it is striking that even after articulating manifest hostility toward Jews, the writer denies his or her own hate-filled and/or stereotypical attitude (often with a legitimizing self-characterization) as in (78):[35]

> (77) Sometimes I wonder whether you all have even a whiff of conscience and humanity or are simply like animals following their instincts. I am no antisemite, but I take a clear stand against Israel's right to exist. [ZJD_Gaza2009_43/816_ano_001]
>
> (78) Fewer and fewer people believe you no, your the ones shooting the little children bringing down lasting psychoterror on the civilian population. What kind of people are you the only thing to do is ignore you. But I do have a question why is it always worse where a Jew is [signature] (no right-winger, a person who loves children) [ZJD_Gaza2009_646/816_Kra_001]

In the case of such texts one has to ask oneself whether the authors really believe what they are writing and whether their skewed perspective results from ignorance as to what antisemitism is and how it can be recognized, or whether they want to protect themselves from possible sanctions by relativizing what they have just expressed (see chapter 10).

The propensity for dehumanizing Jews can also be found among "educated antisemites," but it takes less drastic verbal forms:

> (79) Does the community of Jews in Germany really not include any wise, self-critical, and humane fellow human beings? [ZJD_Gaza2009_502/816_Cri_001]

This question was sent by a woman from Celle to the Central Council during the Gaza crisis in 2009. By implication, Jews are categorized and denigrated in this text as stupid, war-obsessed, inhumane beings.

Jews as a Race and the Concept of the Eternal Jew

Dehumanization of Jews often occurs in combination with racist notions linked in particular to Nazi ideology, with its differentiation between congenitally superior and inferior human types:[36]

(80) YOU ARE A DISEASED RACE [IBD_07.05.2010_ano_004]

(81) A person is a Jew, goy, American, Arab by birth. So Michael Wolffsohn is a Jew. [25.06.04-m-S1][37]

(82) Along with the dumb Yankees you think you're the chosen people. What idiocy and what a mockery of God. How can he have chosen such a lowly race? [IBD_31.10.2006_ano_001]

Belief in the existence of a Jewish race that is genetically determined and displays certain unchanging physical, mental, and spiritual traits is inextricably coupled with the concept of the ETERNAL JEW, according to which the Jewish people have wandered through the world spreading harm for thousands of years, unimpressed and uninfluenced by their changing surroundings:

(83) That all of you just create unrest, bringing war and death, and never able to fit in anywhere. [...] What a repulsive people [...] [ZDJ_Gaza2009_401/816_Jar_001]

(84) Typical Jewish, that's how you've been known for 2000 years, your incoridgible creatures. [...] Unteachible as Jews always are!!!!!!!!!!!!!!!!!!! [ZJD_Gaza2009_301/816_ano_001]

This conceptualization finds explicit expression in (85) and (86), where the authors link the current delegitimization of Israel to the traditional stereotypes of Jews as HOMELESS WANDERERS and/or IMMORAL HUMAN BEINGS:

(85) Then you can all go vagabonding around again, as you've always had the habit of doing. [IBD_25.10.2006_ano_001]

(86) When I demand such an exodus of the Jews from Israel because of their immoral conduct and a scattering to the winds, I'm actually not doing anything unusual and the Jews have been used to this for millennia. Even in Old Testament times the Jews were a nomadic people that emigrated at one point to Egypt, at one point to Babylon, the latter, by the way, because of moral degeneracy, after which they moved back to Israel. [ZJD_30.11.2006_Gel_001]

The implicit variant in (87) verbalizes this stereotype vaguely and with less specific information as a question–response sequence, with the answer, intended to be taken as ironic, also minimizing the centuries-long hostility toward Jews:

(87) Why don't they ask themselves why Israel has been constantly involved in conflict, in wars persecution expulsion for 4000 years. Because they're such a peace-loving people- and the rest of humanity has conspired against them. [IBD_20.07.2006_Die_001]

By equating Jewry and the state of Israel, this comment additionally defines violence as a constant in Jewish history.

In such comments racist notions manifest themselves in part through the use of specific words, as in examples (88), (89), and (90), where *rape*, *half-Jew*, and *descent* reveal that the authors believe in congenital character traits:

(88) Re: Katsav's brother accused of sexual abuse. [. . .] Maybe the Jews have a rape gene—should be tracked down! All pigs, that family! [ZJD_12.03.2007_Kli_001]

(89) Does Gregor Gysi do such things, or Reich-Ranicki? They're also a half-Jew or Jew, and no one seems to mind!!!!!! [ZJD_28.05.2008_Wil_001]

(90) in the meantime I've spent a lot of time looking into German-Jewish history and have come up with many questions. One of the first questions would be: "...why haven't I met any co-worker who is a company electrician, for instance?" ...whereas I know many whose heritage is Jewish and engage in speculation, for instance in Frankfurt. [ZJD_17.07.2007_Sch_001]

Now and then Judeophobic clichés also merge with general racist and naive-sounding xenophobic considerations, as in (91):

(91) Is it actually true, as I heard recently, that M. Friedmann (the coke fiend) is also a gypsy ? From his appearance that would not actually surprise me. I could imagine that, although I hadn't thought of it earlier. Please give me a straight answer. [ZJD_20.11.2008_Ang_001]

Altogether, however, explicit racism turns up quite rarely in the corpus (and exclusively in messages from right-wing extremists). The majority of mainstream authors and also left-wing extremists emphasize in their messages that they reject racism and xenophobia. The demonizations and negative value judgments in their letters appear in a different sort of verbal manifestation, which, however, is not any less motivated by resentment and based on clichés (see chapters 6 and 10). Thus university-educated writers always present themselves as humane, peace-loving people, giving advice to Jews and/or Israelis out of a sense of responsibility (see also chapter 9, under Hostility toward Jews as a Missionary Urge). From their position of assumed moral superiority, these correspondents reveal, explicitly or implicitly, that they consider those to whom they write at the Central Council and the Israeli Embassy incapable of engaging in independent thought and human empathy, as three e-mails from persons with advanced degrees, (92), (93), and (94), show. Example (92) comes from a member of a church governing board:

> (92) You would certainly do much for the positive perception of citizens in this country of the commonality between Jews and the "others" if you did not embrace the principle of "an eye for an eye" but more Jesus' saying, "forgive them, for they know not what they do" as a standard for judging them. One need not always lash out immediately when another person makes a mistake. Usually it is worth asking questions first! [ZJD_25.06_2002_Chr_001]
>
> (93) As a Christian, I am at a loss to understand. Violence produces worse violence. That is what I sense from what is reported about conditions in Israel. It seems to be rooted in the people there and is palpable. [ZJD_26.07.2006_Gue_001]
>
> (94) All the world works for peace, but you have nothing better to do than not to use your heads but to lash out like a raging Goliath stung by a tarantula thoughtlessly and with crazed fury against your neighbors and Davids. Above all—and you know that perfectly well—it will not do any good. You should be ashamed of yourselves. [IBD_14.07.2006_Kus_001]

Intertextual references also turn up frequently in messages from educated people; by quoting the Old Testament (especially *an eye for an eye*, but also several variations on the David–Goliath motif, as in [94]), these writers aim to confront the Jewish recipients with the long tradition of Jewish aggression and brutality and denounce their behavior as atavistic.

> (95) The reason for my writing is the inhumane behavior of the Israeli defense forces in Gaza and especially in Lebanon. [. . .] It is pointless to

> ask who cast the first stone; thousands of years of Jewish history are full of the Hebrews' violent, bloody actions against their neighbors, or, when need be, against their own uncooperative tribes. Thus the feast of Passover recalls a terrible massacre in which all the firstborn Egyptians were slain, not by Yahwe but by his violence-prone people. "There was a great cry in Egypt; for there was not a house where there was not one dead." (Moses 2, 12:30). During the conquest of Jericho everything living was killed, men, women, children, and also animals, as you can read in the Bible. This thread of violence runs through the millennia and has not broken off even today. [ZJD_29.07.2006_Gru_001]

The intertextual references to the Bible are intended to provide "proof" of the tradition of the BRUTAL JEW while at the same time demonstrating how well read the letter writer is.[38]

> (96) I think Sharon and his comrades must be classified as Zionists who adhere strictly to the recommendation from the Old Testament, 'an eye for an eye, a tooth for a tooth,' which today can no longer be tolerated. As long as the Jews are not willing to give up the idea of vengeance and do not submit completely to the commandments of peace (see Moses' 10 commandments, among others "Thou shalt not kill," "thou shalt love thy neighbor as thyself," "thou shalt not covet any thing that is thy neighbor's"), there will be no peace in the Middle East. As an intelligent nation Israel should take the first step, even if it would be a painful and difficult road. [ZJD_22.06.2002_Luc_001]
>
> (97) The old Zionist law, an eye for an eye, a tooth for a tooth, was abandoned by the Israelis a long time ago, when the proportion was magnified many times over. [. . .] That was the essence of my letter to the editor. [IBD_17.07.2006_Rue_001]

The implicit variant, which conveys the stereotype of the CRUEL JEW simply by citing intertextual evidence, offers the author the communicative advantage of getting his meaning across while allowing him to rely on a quotation.[39] Educated speakers also seem to believe that in this way they can avoid revealing themselves unmistakably as antisemites who have the cliché of the ETERNAL JEW in their heads.

Often the Old and the New Testament are juxtaposed through the noncommittal technique of asking questions, which presents options in the guise of thought experiments; in this way a conceptual opposition between the teachings of "obsolete, misleading Judaism" and "good, valuable Christianity" is established, as in the following e-mail from a consultant with an advanced degree in economics:

> (98) And permit me to address a question to official Israel: can it seriously consider it right to guide its actions, whether politically or personally motivated, by the Old Testament maxim 'an eye for an eye, a tooth for a tooth'? Isn't it better for our actions—and also and especially those of a state—to be guided by the values of the New Testament, such as love of one's neighbors and tolerance, forgiveness, and reconciliation? [ZJD_18.06.2002_Klo_001]

Jews as Arrogant and Impudent Troublemakers

Among negative characterizations of Jews, it is striking how often stereotypical traits are described in words and phrases that have been used uninterruptedly since the nineteenth century to defame Jews, expressions that also turned up in the Nazi period, especially in Hitler's and Goebbels's speeches or in the *Stürmer* (see chapter 5). The lexemes *impudent* and *incitement* in such combinations as *Jewish incitement* and *Jewish impudence* are used with special frequency to discredit the morality of the messages' recipients.

> (99) What you [Paul Spiegel] practice as a Jewish fellow citizen is—to put it mildly—sheer impudence. Your arrogance and shamelessness are exceeded only by your moronic deputy. When are you going to stop hurling incitatory slogans and accusations at the German generation now alive? [ZJD_24.06.2002_Pin_001; signatures of friends and acquaintances appended]

This combination of the lexemes *incitement* and *impudent* occurs far more often in messages to the Central Council than in those addressed to the Israeli Embassy. This frequency apparently correlates to word combinations stored in the writers' mental lexicon or to associative patterns of connection and collocation along the lines of *impudent Jews*.[40] At the same time, the concept of the CORROSIVE JEWISH INTELLECTUAL is activated. When traits such as arrogance and impudence are verbalized in messages to the Embassy, the terms appear with noticeable frequency in combination with the noun *Jews*, not *Israelis*:

(100) Yet another example of the Jews' arrogance. [IBD_21.04.2009_ano_002]

(101) Impudent, arrogant, and ruthless, as you Jews always are [. . .] [IBD_015_14_April_2010]

It is significant that one finds this linguistic practice (common in the Nazi period) not only in messages from right-wing extremists but also in those from writers who clearly belong to the mainstream. Educated writers, the majority of whom characterize themselves as *humanists*, *peace activists*, or *highly responsible citizens*, complain that they feel provoked or disturbed by *arrogant, impudent Jews*. Thus a surgeon writes to the Central Council:

(102) I would like to ask you emphatically, Herr Paul Spiegel, to shake off your damn arrogance. You were and are arrogant and superficial. [. . .] I am from the generation of 46. Went to Jerusalem and planted a peace tree there. You're wrecking everything again. How am I supposed to explain your unfortunate behavior to my children? [ZJD_01.03.2005_Sch_001]

Paul Spiegel, the Central Council's chair at the time, is discredited morally because he advocated solidarity with Israel, while the letter's author legitimizes himself by portraying himself in positive terms (on strategies of self-legitimation, see chapter 10). In typical Judeophobic fashion, he ascribes destructive behavior to Spiegel. The author of example (103), a woman with a PhD from Hamburg, argues in a similar vein:

(103) As this letter shows, I feel constantly patronized and provoked as a citizen. I fear that other educated Germans feel the same way. [ZJD_20.09.2006_Fis_001]

That positions taken by the Central Council are viewed as a disruption and a provocation often finds expression in the letters:

(104) When I read the paper today, all I could do was shake my head again. Don't you have anything better (or any work) to do than to check every opinion expressed by a German for its antisemitic content and to warn us constantly not to use this word or that. [ZJD_13.11.2008_Hub_001]

At the same time the message contains the insinuation, conveyed by the reference in parentheses, that the Central Council does no real work but merely engages in agitation, issuing admonitions and disturbing the peace. This cliché also turns up as follows:

(105) Can't you ever do anything but wail, moan, and complain? You're such a pain! [ZJD_27.09.2007_Sch_001]

The concept of JEWS AS DISRUPTIVE ELEMENTS IN NON-JEWISH SOCIETIES appears in messages to the Embassy about the situation in the Middle East or in the world. In the process, the traditional stereotype merges with the modern conceptualization of ISRAEL AS A COLLECTIVE JEW:

(106) Israel is the disturber of the peace in the Middle East. [IBD_02.08.2006_Sch_001]

(107) Israel is disturbing world peace! [IBD_03.06.2007_Ko_001]

Comments by the Central Council on the German past, on Middle East policy, or on current antisemitism are very often branded in the letters as *interference* and as *un-German*, *impudent*, and *unacceptable*, judgments that disparage the Central Council's function in general:

(108) The constant interference and chiming in on German affairs by your religious group, which is living it up in Germany, supported by Germ. taxes paid by the working population, should be squelched as illegitimate and inappropriate. [ZJD_17.05.2007_Zie_001]

(109) Will we in Germany ever be allowed to act politically without you people always interfering? [ZJD_08.01.2008_Bal_001]

At the same time, many of the writers point to the activities of the Central Council as the cause of antisemitic sentiment, thereby transferring the blame for hostility toward Jews onto the Jews themselves (see also example [114]):

(110) The Central Council of the Jews should cease this interference from now on, since it gives rise to antisemitism. [ZJD_07.05.2007_Zie_001]

Announcements by the Central Council of the Jews in Germany undergo delegitimation through further comments that encode stereotypical contents such as BLACKMAIL, EXPLOITATION, and POLITICAL CORRECTNESS. At the same time, many of the authors also exclude German Jews from the community of Germans:

(111) So your Central Council, which by now has cost all those born after 1945 far more than 100 billion euros and presumably will cost another 100 billion as a result of your blackmail, will keep meddling in matters that are strictly the business of us Germans? [ZJD_08.01.2008_Hei_001]

(112) What in the world is wrong in this fatherland of mine???? Jews are calling the shots, determining who has a SAY, and what, when, where, and how, if anything, can be said. [ZJD_28.09.2007_Sch_001]

(113) The Federal Republic is an independent sovereign state and don't need any interference from the Jews. What "right" do the Jews in Germany have to poke their noses in every little thing? [ZJD_15.04.2007_Sie_001]

The generic reference to *Jews*, *the Jewish people*, *Jewry*, or *the Jews* indicates among other things a conceptualization of JEWS AS A FOREIGN AND MONOLITHIC GROUP.[41]

(114) The Jewish people does itself no favors when it lets itself be represented by this arrogance and exaggerated notion of its own abilities. [ZJD_08.06.2002)_Her_001]

In (114) Jews in Germany are conceptualized in general terms as TROUBLEMAKERS and ANNOYING NAGS. The pejoratively connotative lexeme *moralizer* turns up in many of these communications as a stock phrase. The repudiation and criticism of the Central Council articulated in these texts usually goes hand in hand with a desire to put an end to the culture of commemoration in Germany (see chapter 8, under The Mentality of "Being Fed Up" and Refusal of Empathy). This desire applies to the Nazi period, felt to be an annoying and uncomfortable burden that should be shaken off:

(115) By that I mean to say that more than 50 years have passed by now and it's about time we finally stopped feeling guilty. We Germans in particular, because of our past, learn so much in school about the Nazis and their crimes that these atrocities stick in our minds without the constant bleating of the Central Council. [ZJD_24.01.2008_ano_001]

(116) you can get just as indignant in Israel!!!! That may be a better place for you with your arrogant bitching!!! Yrs truly, Fed Up! [ZJD_07.12.2008_Blu_001]

Jews as Intellectually and Morally Inferior Beings: The Stereotypes of Jewish Slyness, Hypocrisy, Deviousness, Lies, and Corrosion

In many communications Jews are portrayed explicitly or implicitly as particularly bad, degenerate, morally inferior people. In this connection the stereotypes of DEVIOUSNESS and HYPOCRISY, which have persisted since the Middle Ages, are verbalized with particular frequency:

(117) You are hypocrites and murderers. Any further commentary is superfluous. [ZJD_Gaza2009_504/816_Ron_001]

(118) Never trust a Jew. [. . .] The fact that in this country you stir the pot in such a way and also amass real estate, art, and money makes you so very likeable. Is that really all you care about? [ZJD_01.09.2006_Len_001]

A political scientist from Berlin credits the Central Council with engaging in "*propaganda that poisons Germany's internal peace*" (ZJD_31.08.2006_Ros_001), thereby expressing the stereotype of the JEWISH CORROSIVE INFLUENCE.[42] In this connection the cliché of JEWS AS LIARS often invoked by the Nazis also finds frequent expression:

(119) Every word from your mouths is a lie. Your thoughts are lies. You breathe lies. [ZJD_Gaza2009_144/816_ano_001]

(120) What can one believe these days of what a Jew says? Probably little or nothing. [IBD_28.10.06_ano_002]

(121) Anyone who traffics as a regular thing in lies and conscious misrepresentation (referred to officially as "engaging in politics" or

"maintaining diplomatic relations") is unable to tolerate the truth and thus immediately resorts hypersensitively to the tried-and-true technique of turning the tables with raw, brute force. [ZJD_Gaza2009_169/816_Len_001]

There is a long tradition of employing Jewish-sounding names as a means of stigmatization (see Bering 2002, 2010), which in modern discourse occurs in a particular form of stereotyping expression:[43]

(122) the HR [Hessian Broadcasting] assigns an ESTHER SHAPIRO, obviously a Jew, to sow doubt [Sch_18.03.2002_Vog_001][44]

(123) At the very least the name of the author, 'Esther S . . .' (I didn't catch the last name and couldn't find it in the TV guide) suggests that the reporting was not objective [Sch_19.03.2002_Mei_001]

These e-mails convey a twofold implicature along the lines of "a Jewish name suggests that a Jewish person is involved; and Jews lie."

Frequent comments such as *Israelis do not want peace and are deceiving the international community* encode the stereotype of the JEWISH LIAR. We also see here the development of public views of the Middle East conflict. After the Lebanon/Gaza conflict the conceptualization that ISRAEL DOES NOT WANT PEACE also makes frequent appearances as a cliché in the German press.[45] The prejudiced notion that the Israelis are not really interested in peace seems to become solidified as the consensus of an entire society, a consensus in which media reports and expressions of private opinions coincide.

It is denied with particular frequency that Jews are capable of feeling sympathy and compassion for others. By means of questions and statements such as (124) and (125), Jews are dehumanized and discredited in conformity with old patterns and are thereby placed outside the bounds of a humanistically oriented community:

(124) is this the form the desire for peace and mutual striving for respect take among you? Are you even capable of human feelings? [ZJD_Gaza2009_34/816_Zon_001]

(125) What you people are doing can only be called genocide. You have no respect for life. [ZJD_Gaza2009_210/816_ano_001]

Such texts also often display the stereotype of the COMBATIVE, IRRECONCILABLE, and RESENTFUL JEW that is either invoked directly in reference to Jews, as in (126) and (127), or finds expression in the variant referring to Israel, as in (128):[46]

(126) For people like you life is nothing but a struggle. If you were to achieve reconciliation, you wouldn't know what to do with yourself. I feel sorry for you. [ZJD_18.05.2005_Ben_001]

(127) One gets the impression that the more enemies they find themselves surrounded with the better the Jews feel. [ZJD_24.03.2005_Dei_001]

(128) That the Israelis are not peace-loving can be seen in something as obvious as their regular violation of Libyan and Syrian air space. [IBD_07.05.2006_Dro_001]

These e-mails also reveal the assumption that reconciliation represents the polar opposite of the Jewish way of life. Judaism is thus interpreted as an atavistic doctrine, and Israel as the Jewish state is delegitimized.

In many communications the Central Council is accused of *complicity* and *pro-Israel propaganda* (as discussed earlier), but in equally many texts the Central Council is accused of *irresponsibility* and *indifference* because it allegedly remains *silent in the face of the crimes in Israel*:

(129) so long as you do not understand that your terror and worse (phosphorus bombs!) cannot produce any reconciliation, you will continue to be despised by humanistically oriented people, and justifiably so. [. . .] It's obvious: [. . .] with your permanent silence you declare solidarity with terrorism and have no right to be surprised that you are rejected in Germany. Your behavior disgusts me. [ZJD_Gaza2009_27/816_Stü_001]

An old feature of the Judeophobic worldview thus becomes clear: no matter what Jews do or do not do, say or do not say, it is always used against them. Jews are rejected by antisemites simply on the basis of being Jews:

(130) You should therefore not be surprised when the Jewish people still has enemies today or does not make any friends! [ZJD_Gaza2009_46/816_Bau_001]

Conspiracy Theories: The Stereotype of Jewish (Plans for) World Domination

(131) Why do you insist with all your might on ruling the entire world? [ZJD_28.09.2007_Sch_001]

The stereotype of the WORLDWIDE JEWISH CONSPIRACY appears most obviously, as in (131), when references are made to the supposed excessive influence that Jews/Israelis wield over the U.S. government. The letters to this effect, most of which emanate from extremist circles, also prominently display anti-Americanism (see also Jaecker 2004).

(132) Israel controls America and surely the whole world tomorrow. [ZJD_Gaza2009_522/816_ano_001]

(133) [. . .] I suspect more and more that there is a world Zionism that has posts everywhere, presumably also in the orbit of the U.S. government. [IBD_28.07.2006_Kun_001]

These writers believe in the existence of a sinister Jewish lobby. When classic conspiracy stereotypes are expressed in reference to an allegedly omnipotent Jewish power, this occurs explicitly and is embraced by persons who go to little trouble to conceal their antisemitic attitude. Such communications often deploy the morphological blend *USrael* to indicate the inseparable symbiosis of the United States and Israel:

(134) USrael [IBD_10.08.2006_Kra_001]

The conspiracy-theory-driven concept of Jewish influence, however, also appears in the context of charges that Jews benefit from the political correctness they impose on Germans by invoking their special status, as in (135):

(135) I know, a person mustn't say anything against Jews or Israelis, it's forbidden, and even if I'm risking being accused or denounced, or I'm blamed for something I didn't do, or your Mossad even sets fire to the roof over my head, poisons my pets, or whatever, I'm going to send this letter [ZJD_Gaza2009_497/816_Wün_001]

A specific variation on the conspiracy theory is the fantasy that criticizing Israel is taboo, a fantasy that by now circulates in everyday discourse as well as in the mass media:[47]

(136) So is Israel untouchable for Germany on the basis of Germany's past? [ZJD_08.04.2002_Nie_001]

(137) all war crimes go unmentioned...for Israelis are permitted to do anything! [IBD_12.12.2006_Rie_001]

The metaphor of the *Auschwitz or antisemitism bludgeon* is a compressed verbal expression often used to encode this stereotype.

The Stereotype of Jewish Vengefulness

Both Jews and Israelis are often accused of an *obsession with revenge*, and all sorts of actions or utterances are classified homogeneously as *revenge*, *act of revenge*, *revenge operation*, and the like. Thus a plumbing specialist who is outraged that German soldiers were wounded in the Lebanon conflict poses a question that connects the conflict in the Middle East with the German Nazi past, making use of the conceptualization that EVEN JEWS IN FAR-OFF LEBANON KILL GERMANS AS REVENGE FOR THE HOLOCAUST:

(138) I also find it sad and its very bad that your also killing Germans now. Is that revenge for things we did? [IBD_20.07.2006_Stu_001]

A similar pseudo-causal connection is established in (139), which interprets the involvement of Jews in Israel in the Middle East conflict exclusively as an expression of a base desire for revenge, projected onto others:

(139) Re: WG: Auschwitz Jews in Gaza. That the filthy business with Auschwitz cannot be denied is obvious, and the same goes for Ahmadinejad, but this doesn't give the stupid Jews the right to take revenge on the Arabs instead of on Germany. [ZJD_Gaza2009_16/816_Del_001]

(140) How can one accept the death of innocent children so cold-bloodedly, just in order to get revenge? Does a democratic contry do such a thing? [IBD_16.07.2006_San_001]

Thus the entire conflict is represented one-sidedly and monocausally, with the actual causative factors being omitted and replaced by an ancient Judeophobic explanatory system. In reference to the Middle East conflict, the

Central Council of the Jews in Germany is not only saddled collectively with the blame for violence and death (in thousands of e-mails), but also portrayed as unfeeling and morally despicable:

(141) Apparently the Central Council doesn't give a damn that women and children in Lebanon/the Gaza Strip are being killed by Israel. [ZJD_08.08.2006_Kre_001]

In communications from educated correspondents the stereotype of JEWISH VENGEFULNESS primarily appears in the variant of JEWS AS NAGS WHO CANNOT FORGIVE THE HOLOCAUST:

(142) Do you really want to take that away from us ? thinking independently and observing Israel's actions critically ? still because of the Holocaust ? [ZJD_01.09.2006_Roc_001]

Jews as the Epitome of Evil For many centuries, from antisemites' static perspective, Jews have represented THE EPITOME OF EVIL, a perspective that results in a dichotomous (Manichaean) view of the world.

(143) the whole world must bleed because of Jewish filth, which has robbed and terrorized us all for at least 3000 years, but now oil is also getting more expensive because of the pissed-off criminal Jews, that plague of mankind. !!! Jewish filth must leave God's earth!!! We'll get you all, it's only a matter of time. God's on our side. [ZJD_Gaza2009_788/816_ano_001]

During the Nazi period this particular conceptualization gave rise to the so-called Final Solution. In many contemporary texts, too, Jews are described collectively in hyperbolic terms such as *a profoundly evil people*, *the most degenerate subjects*, *the greatest filth of mankind*, the *worst pestilential boil on the world*, as well as *foul international criminal swine*, and thus as the antithesis of the rest of the world community. The conceptualization based on this polarization, that Jews are the incarnation of everything evil and responsible for all the misery in the world, all atrocities, wars, and crises, and that they should therefore be eradicated, also expresses itself literally, as in (144) and (145), almost exclusively in right-wing-extremist and fundamentalist messages:

(144) SOON ISRAEL WILL BE DESTROYED ALL JEWS MUST DIE SO THIS WORLD CAN FIND PEACE [IBD_03.11.2006_ano_001]

(145) You filthy Jew deserve a smack in the kisser. You're to blame for the misery in this world! [IBD_19.08.2008_Bau_001]

Yet the Judeophobic resentment underlying this stereotype also produces many structures in the thinking and communication of educated authors from the middle of the political spectrum, who project these beliefs onto Israel and articulate them through hyperbolic and derealizing references (especially through comparisons with the Nazis). In such texts one finds statements such as *Israel threatens world peace* or the claim that Israel *constantly (i.e., since the founding of the state) commits Nazi-style crimes against humanity*, that Israel is *the worst warmonger on earth* and must be *reprimanded*, *condemned*, or *dissolved as a Jewish state* (see chapter 6 and chapter 9, under Suggestions for Solving the "Jewish Problem," for more thorough discussions of this notion). Messages from people with advanced degrees to the Central Council, reproaching it for the policies of the Israeli government, prefer to encode the stereotype by means of implicit strategies of devaluation, as can be seen in (146) and (147), where Jews are collectively classified as inhumane:

(146) I can only hope that the Jews come to their senses as quickly as possible and that humane values return to their thinking and actions! [ZJD_Gaza2009_214/816_Sch_001]

(147) So don't they have a single spark of compassion, a single human reacton to the misery in Palestine? [ZJD_2009_Gaza767_Loh_001]

The form that verbal dehumanization takes is different here, but the semantics remain the same: Jews are positioned outside the community of the humanely thinking and feeling in-group. Implicitly Jews are again conceptualized as a conspiratorial, encapsulated group that thinks and acts exclusively in its own interests. But to preserve the appearance of not being antisemites, the educated mainstream writers make a distinction between "good" and "bad" Jews. "Good" Jews are either dead or exceptional in their hatred of Israel. "Bad" Jews defend Israel and are therefore subjected to semantic devaluation with all the tools at the writers' disposal.

(148) I want to respect and honor the generation of blameless Jews who were despised and murdered. But the Jews today parade themselves as a master race(probably following others' example) and to satisfy their megalomania conduct barbaric wars and are murderers. and belong on the list of terrorists. [ZJD_30.07.2006_Sur_001]

The writers apparently believe that by adopting this strategy they can ward off charges that they defame Jews collectively. These writers fail to realize that in addressing such messages to the Central Council they are imputing to it collective guilt and responsibility (as well as conflating Jews and Israelis), and thereby revealing an antisemitic view of the world.

Jews as Exploiters of the Holocaust and Enforcers of Political Correctness

The notion that Jews deliberately exploit the Holocaust and their special status as victims of the Nazi state in order to obtain material and/or general societal advantages forms the basis of all the updated stereotypes in postwar antisemitism and constitutes the main topic in the overwhelming majority of messages to the Central Council and the Embassy:

(149) when will you finally stop your constant, unspeakable blackmailing of German politicians! You would do better to pay attention to the violations of human rights in occupied Palestine and the wretched humanitarian situation there [. . .] [ZJD_14.04.2007_Pon_001]

(150) After more than sixty years there can't be a free pass anymore to bludgeon us in brutal pursuit of your own interests. [ZJD_12.03.2008_Til_001]

More than 85 percent of the authors refer explicitly or implicitly to the cliché, formed after 1945 and perpetuated to this day in stock phrases, of the HOLOCAUST EXPLOITER and the related ENFORCER OF POLITICAL CORRECTNESS.[48] This stereotype applies to the memory of the Shoah, the so-called reparations payments,[49] the question of German responsibility, and the culture of remembrance and commemoration. The notion that Jews exert pressure on Germany morally and financially and would instrumentalize the Holocaust for that purpose may be a variant specific to the postwar period, but it is by no means a new stereotype.[50] It is obviously based on the old cliché of the FREELOADER and EXPLOITER, as many of the messages, such as (151) and (152), also reveal in their choice of words:

> (151) Or to put it more clearly, go out and learn something instead of just freeloading all the time. [ZJD_14.04.2007_Wen_001]
>
> (152) If your ancestors only knew [. . .] that their fate was being "leached off'" and "sold" to put money in the pockets of their descendants [. . .] [ZJD_04.06.2005_K_001]

The fact that patterns of linguistic usage handed down over the centuries appear in combination with the verbalization of current topics is an unmistakable indicator of the conceptual elaboration and adaption of the old exploiter stereotype. The medieval *greedy usurer* and the nineteenth-century *parasitic freeloader* have become the contemporary *Holocaust exploiter*. That this stereotype could establish itself so quickly in the post-Holocaust era, despite all the revelations of Nazi era atrocities, and has remained so prevalent and persistent shows how deeply rooted and how durable Judeophobic thinking is in the collective memory. For that reason the oft-repeated assertion in the scholarly literature on antisemitism that after 1945 "antisemitism existed not in spite of but because of Auschwitz"[51] (see, e.g., Benz 2004, 19) cannot be defended. Antisemitism after the Holocaust merely found a new, contemporary conceptualization for the traditional resentment of Jews. That the two-thousand-year-old hostility toward Jews in fact did not lose its underpinnings once and for all, in spite of the caesura in civilization that Auschwitz represented, can be attributed among other things to the absence, in the immediate aftermath of the collapse of the Nazi regime, of any systematic, society-wide examination of the attitudinal and ideological foundations of the Holocaust, as well as the absence of any empathy for its victims (see chapter 3, under Hostility Toward Jews after 1945).

The wave of hate-filled, irrational anti-Israeli sentiment set in motion by the Middle East conflict and whipped up by the media has persisted for more than ten years, joined by increasing acceptance of certain manifestly antisemitic views (especially on the Internet). This phenomenon indicates the willingness of many people to believe unquestioningly that Jews and the Jewish state are fundamentally bad and guilty.[52] The potential for actualizing Judeophobic patterns of thought and feeling at any moment and on any occasion is correspondingly great.

(153) Yes, I believe that back before the Second World War the Jews probably pushed the German population around the same way as they do today with the Palestinians. The Jews were past masters at exploiting the Germans in those days and abusing their trust (nasty wheeler-dealers) [ZJD_Gaza2009_20/816_ano_001]

(154) This you can be sure of: Germans' rejection and hatred when it comes to your institution is certain. Forever and ever. Never forget: One and one makes two is taught in every elementary school! And not the "Holocaust"!; -)) The Germans feel solidarity with the Palestinian people [. . .] in this great, beautiful world where there is no place for diehard parasites and freeloaders. With cold regards [ZJD_Gaza2009_530/816_Jüt_001]

The sometimes obsessive preoccupation many Germans display when it comes to the Middle East conflict and their supposed sympathy for the Palestinians, who are characterized as the *victims of brutal Jewish pursuit of power*, ultimately amounts only to an expression of solidarity with themselves and their in-group and thus to nothing more than a situationally conditioned transfer of anti-Jewish feelings to Israel. The Middle East conflict thus functions only as a catalyst for global antisemitic resentment.

The notion that Jews would instrumentalize centuries-old persecution, and the Holocaust in particular, provides a conceptual template for reinterpreting or formulating anew the existing stereotypes, adapting them to current events. Thus a dentist from Cologne opines:

(155) Official Germany's kowtowing to the Jews is becoming intolerable. We have no reason to do this. The Holocaust they keep bringing up was a bad crime, but it doesn't give them a right to demand humility almost daily, decades later, while they commit almost the same crimes against other peoples. That account has long since been cleared [. . .] [ZJD_01.09.2006_Nor_001]

The ability of antisemitic concepts to adapt quickly to new situations reveals itself with special clarity in the corpus: if until 2003 references to alleged exploitation and blackmail by the Central Council with respect to internal German affairs predominate, after that time a striking increase manifests itself in charges that (German) Jews are using the Holocaust to pressure the German government into supporting Israeli policies.

(156) apparently nothing was learned from the 2nd world war. making germany responsible over and over for the holocaust and thereby extorting government money so it can be used for buying more and more new weapons for israel and its war machine. is somehow grotesque! [ZJD_29.07.2006_Now_001]

(157) The Jews exploit the Germans' ancestral guilt to enrich themselves more and more. They also expoit this ancestral guilt by demanding that the Germans show unwavering loyalty to the Israelis' shameful actions. [ZJD_30.11.2006_Gel_001]

The writers often argue that the culture of commemoration is battened on for the sole purpose of extorting money through moral pressure.[53] In so doing, as in (158), they verbalize and employ several stereotypes:

(158) Over generations the German people has had to do more than enough penance—in the form of oppressive tax burdens for the Jews. So what grounds are there for complaints? You're all doing just fine—at the expense of the state, at the expense of me and my husband, for instance, as taxpayers! Are you still not satisfied? [ZJD_04.05.2005_Kar_001]

The reference to Finkelstein's book (2001) on the so-called Holocaust industry is the most common intertextual citation the writers use to legitimate their own contentions:

(159) In spite of a past fraught with suffering, they seem to have no capacity for sympathizing with the pain endured by other peoples, and Jewish organizations seem to see the Holocaust primarily as an opportunity for blackmail. 'The Holocaust Industry' by Norman G. Finkelstein sends its regards. [ZJD_12.12.2006_Oeh_001]

(160) Again: the victims of the Shoah all deserve our respect, and should be honored. But they died in vain if their sufferings are instrumentalized as a

means for accumulating unjustificated political capital. You should read the books by Norman J. Finkelstein! [IBD_12.12.2006_Glo_001]

Alleged instrumentalization of the Holocaust is also cited as the (primary) cause of antisemitism in Germany, which places the blame on the Jews themselves.

(161) The frequent abuse of the Holocaust for current purposes is counterproductive to a normal coexistence between Jews and non-Jews. [ZJD_11.03.2008_Zen_001]

Almost all the texts reveal a sense of satiation that may find expression explicitly through direct speech acts that take the form of challenges or threats:

(162) It's time to let the past . . . be!!! Anything else only casts a wrong (and by no means favorable) image on the Jews! [ZJD_04.05.2005_Kar_001]

Alternatively the encoding may occur implicitly, in the form of a rejection of responsibility that calls for a halt to memorializing and nagging, as in this e-mail from a woman from Heidelberg:

(163) I myself am 42 years old, so belong to the generation that cannot be connected to the terrible crimes of the National Socialists. During the Third Reich my parents were children and likewise bore no responsibility for those crimes. [ZJD_10.04.2002_Sch_006]

The phrases *it's time to draw a line* or *this has to stop* occur frequently, either not differentiating between Jewish and Israeli issues or making the assumption that they are identical:

(164) Germany don't owe Isreal and the Jews anything that's what Israel and the Jews have got to understand by now . Germanys done enough for Israel and the Jews and this has to stop. Best [ZJD_13.05.2007_Lud_001]

Calculations and assumptions of guilt are also typical of these communications, as in (165), where an implicit comparison with the Nazis serves to relativize the crimes that took place in the German past and thereby also to exonerate the writer (see also [155]):

> (165) Dear Frau Knobloch, What was done to your people cannot be forgiven. But now all this whole business has to stop. What your fellow countrymen are doing to the Palestinians is not much better. Maybe they should consider this before they set out on another a tour of tears. [ZJD_25.11.2008_Rei_001]

This so-called exonerative antisemitism (see Schapira and Hafner 2006), based primarily on a reversal of perpetrators and victims, also activates and updates the ancient stereotype that Jews bear sole responsibility for the existence of hostility toward Jews.

The Stereotype JEWS THEMSELVES ARE TO BLAME FOR ANTISEMITISM

In centuries past, Jews were charged, depending on the period and current societal structure, with *false beliefs*, *blood rituals*, *usury*, *conspiring to conquer the world*, and/or *racial inferiority*, all of which were invoked as the basis for the hostility to which they were subjected. In the twenty-first century contemporary perpetrator images are constructed to portray Jews as the instigators of the antipathy they experience. This conceptualization takes three verbal forms, each with its own semantic emphases. The first form is based on the argument that 'Jews provoke antisemitism by their behavior' (HOLOCAUST BLACKMAIL and ENFORCERS OF POLITICAL CORRECTNESS; see also [158] with respect to the Nazi past):

> (166) If things keep going this way, you should not be surprised to see a rise in antisemitism. In that case, you will share the blame. [ZJD_07.11.2008_Bla_001]
>
> (167) You and your community have accused the Germans recently of an antisemitic attitude and tendencies. That's not how I see it [...] and the charge can also not be made in such a way. [...] Unfortunately I must tell you that with such accusations and notions you only promote antisemitism, and thereby encourage the antisemite. [ZJD_01.09.2006_Tef_001]

In this fashion Jews are stylized, on the one hand, as material perpetrators, since they 'extort monies from the German state and harm it financially,' and, on the other hand, as intellectual perpetrators, since they 'work against the inner tranquility and national pride of the Germans' and also interfere with a return to the often-invoked 'normalcy.' While right-wing-radical and -extremist correspondents make monolithic judgments such as *All Jews exploit us* and add collective comments such as *Freeloaders, that's what you have always been*, authors from the mainstream express their condemnation in a more reserved manner—although the semantics are not appreciably different—and rely more on indirect speech acts such as questions and conditional constructions, as in (168) and (169), or on admonishing or threatening predictions, as in (170), an e-mail from a lawyer from Munich:

> (168) Could it be that the moral bludgeon you people keep wielding is responsible for generating antisemtic feelings among germans? [ZJD_04.03.2002_Moe_001]
>
> (169) since the Central Council of Jews in Germany sees an increase in hatred of Jews, that could also be a result of the "behavior" of those making the complaint. [ZJD_Gaza2009_49/816_Kle_001]
>
> (170) I simply can't understand such authoritarian and intolerant behavior. You shouldn't be surprised if no normality returns to our country and prejudices against your faith community arise or become solidified. [ZJD_08.11.2008_Mad_001]

The second variant contains the assertion that Jews in Germany promote antisemitism by showing solidarity with Israel (cf. also [56] and the use of the 'antisemitism bludgeon' in conjunction with criticism of Israel):

> (171) No wonder antisemitism is also increasing in Germany. You share the blame for this development because you function as a propaganda department for the Israeli government. [ZJD_03.09.2006_Ack_001]
>
> (172) Your [...] behavior in no way promotes the mutual understanding of Jews and non-Jews; on the contrary, you do more to create aversions than to serve Jewish interests and garner sympathy. [ZJD_20.04.2007_Hil_001]
>
> (173) This behavior does not promote the coexistence of Jews and German Christians but rather produces in the population silent subliminal resentment against the Jews. [ZJD_12.03.2008_Til_001]

That the Central Council speaks out against the groundswell of animosity and one-sided condemnation of Israel is criticized by many of the correspondents as *complicity*, being an *accessory*, and *disloyalty to Germany*, and often also as *typically Jewish, this sticking together*. Accordingly, the blame and responsibility are often attributed jointly to the Central Council and the state of Israel:

> (174) If you want to remain trustworthy, you should appeal to your state of Israel and demand an immediate halt to the unrestrained violence. Otherwise you are contributing to the rise in antisemitism—and that can't be in your own interest! [ZJD_Gaza2009_785/816_Tho_001]

Ultimately all the authors critical of Israel who send their messages to the Central Council and not to the Israeli Embassy are thereby signaling indirectly that they also see German Jews as collectively responsible for matters concerning Israel. Thus simply by addressing the Central Council they encode the stereotype JEWS AND ISRAELIS ARE ONE PEOPLE WITH A SHARED POLITICAL POSTURE, and they employ the cliché of the WORLDWIDE JEWISH ALLIANCE, which they consider collectively to blame for what is taking place in the world.

The third variant blames Israel or Israeli policies for the increase in or the existence of antisemitism (in Germany and the rest of the world) (see also chapter 10, examples [116]– [118]):

> (175) Today Israel, more than any other country on earth, is number one as the source and supporter of antisemitism. [IBD_29.02.2008_Gel_003]
>
> (176) The result: thanks to its brutality Israel will see its reputation continue to decline, and afterward you will bemoan the increasing antisemitism. [ZJD_05.01.2009_Kra_001]

That even the most violent action in Israel cannot justify the increase in antisemitism, since it rests on an inappropriate equating of Jews and Israelis, as well as on a Judeophobic attribution of collective guilt, is not acknowledged even by educated correspondents, as the following e-mail from a sociologist with two PhDs makes clear:

(177) If Jews throughout the world should feel that the international criticism of this behavior discriminates against them, as I see it, they should address

their complaints to Israel and not to those who report it. [ZJD_11.08.2006_Bla_001]

Some of the correspondents also mention an attitudinal shift or a change in awareness they have experienced ("*recognized the truth*," "*had my eyes opened*") that ultimately serves to confirm old prejudices (see also [108], [109], and [127] in chapter 6):

> (178) I also know NOW why people have persecuted you for over 2000 years. [IBD_09.01.2009_Rud_001]
>
> (179) Only now do I know why the whole world hates you so. [ZJD_Gaza2009_792/816_ano_001]

Similarly, the sentiments expressed in (180) and (181) imply that there are good reasons for rejecting and combatting Jews:

> (180) And I am annoyed with myself for believing all my life that the Jewish people was persecuted unjustly. [ZJD_01.08.2006_Sch_003]
>
> (181) In the past I didn't understand how antisemitism arose but your instructive examples of murderers and war criminals give this madness a face. [ZJD_01.08.2006_Sch_003]

These admissions confirm the thesis that antisemitism in an individual need not be viewed as a biographical constant; rather it can be viewed dynamically as an evolutionary process (on this phenomenon, see Zimmermann 2005, 14). Even antisemites like Marr, Streicher, and Hitler verbalized an attitudinal shift much like that of modern antisemites ("*suddenly become a person with eyes to see*," "*the scales fell from* my *eyes*," etc.) (see Zimmermann 2005, 13f.).

All these variants display a psychological dimension that is typical of hatred and intolerance: the object of the hatred always bears the blame for being hated, for the hater locates hatred in the character or behavior of its object (see chapters 6 and 8 on internal attribution): "The victim . . . is always responsible for everything and is also responsible for the allegations against him, no matter whether they correspond to actual facts or not" (Haubl and Caysa 2007, 96).

Another feature of this attitude is that the actual antisemitism manifested by non-Jews is either denied or minimized.

Denial and Relativizing of Hostility toward Jews

Many of the correspondents deny or relativize genuine antisemitic proclivities, thereby also denying their own responsibility or projecting it onto others. Trivializing current hostility toward Jews always takes the form of the assertion that there is no antisemitism in German society, or none that need be taken seriously. The denial of antisemitism can appear in statements claiming to establish evidence, as in (182), where the writer's subjective opinion is presented as an assertion of fact (strengthened by the use of the phrase *in general*):

> (182) You, too, are whipping up such fears of an antisemitism that in general does not exist in Germany. [ZJD_11.06.2002_Esc_001]

The authors of similar messages that accuse the Central Council of *whipping up panic* and displaying *sheer hostility toward Germans* express this idea more as a doubt and subjective perception, as does a professor from Düsseldorf, born in 1979, who characterizes his own e-mail (183) as a "*view from the mainstream of society*," or the author of (184):

> (183) In my personal circles I at least do not see any antisemitism; that may be a function of my education (I hope!). [ZJD_Gaza2009_66/816_Her_001]
>
> (184) As I see it, your "average consumer" in Germany is not antisemitic. [ZJD_30.01.2005_Hof_001]

After the author of (185) explicitly articulates several antisemitic stereotypes and verbal attacks directed at the Central Council, which she chides, among other things, for "*pervasive, petty ranting*," she goes on:

> (185) Take a good look: so far as I can judge, the German population doesn't have anything against our Jewish fellow citizens. [ZJD_07.11.2008_Ber_001]

Her assertion stands in contradiction to the clichés and hostile verbal attacks she has previously communicated, something of which she is apparently not aware. Altogether, it can certainly be recognized as typical of antisemitic "argumentation" that it bristles with contradictions and paradoxes (for more on this subject, see chapter 8, under Contradictions and Paradoxes). One also finds semantic redefinitions: attitudes hostile toward Jews and anti-Israel expressions in modern society are reclassified, for instance, as *critical thinking* and *free expression*, and thus subjectively legitimated and justified:

> (186) Dear Frau Knobloch, What you consider an antisemitic atmosphere in Germany is nothing more than the Germans' emancipation and liberation from a way of thinking imposed dictatorially by the Central Council. [ZJD_14.09.2006_Bel_001]

The imaginary CRITICISM TABOO is another verbalized stereotype that finds frequent expression in modern antisemitic discourse. It turns up not only in many private e-mails and letters to the Central Council and the Embassy but also in public letters to the editor, comments on the Internet, and newspaper articles.

The Stereotype of Political Correctness and the Image of the Antisemitism Bludgeon

The cliché of JEWS AS (INTELLECTUALLY) INFLUENTIAL OPINION MOLDERS did not originate after 1945 but came into usage much earlier, in nineteenth-century antisemitic tracts. In Marr's *The Victory of Judaism over Germanic Identity*, we find the concept that Jews control the press in Germany and thereby play a major role in forming public opinion. Marr (1879, 23) portrays Jews in Germany as "*dominant*" and "*influential*," and the stock phrase *the Jewified daily press*, later adopted by the Nazis, appears here for the first time. Hitler and Goebbels employed this stereotype in numerous speeches even before their seizure of power. Thus in his 1920 speech, "Why We Are Antisemites," Hitler points to the sinister power of "*a Jewish press organized down to the last iota*" (Hitler 1920, quoted in Phelps 1968, 405).

In describing this imaginary influence, the writers in our corpus use such terms as *omnipresent opinion control*, *Jewish lobby*, *Zionist propaganda*, *Jewish blackmail*, *muzzling technique*, *forcible alignment*,[54] and *Israeli opinion terrorism*. If up to 2004, the writers focus largely on internal German matters, from 2004–2005 on, the variant TABOO AGAINST CRITICISM OF ISRAEL becomes the most frequent manifestation of this cliché in the corpus. The metaphors of the AUSCHWITZ and ANTISEMITISM GUILT TRIP serve as compressed codes for this notion and (since the Walser debate) have also come to be the most frequently written and voiced expressions in the public communicative space.

> (187) So long as criticism of German Jews/Jews in Germany is promptly countered with the so-called Auschwitz guilt trip, we remain far removed from a normal relationship. [ZJD_30.05.2007_Gir_001]
>
> (188) Dear Frau Knobloch: The Auschwitz guilt trip is working. No German politician has raised his voice against the murderous war that Israel is conducting in Gaza. [...] That is how hatred is sown. [...] By the way: many of my patients think and feel the same. With best regards, [signature], MD [ZJD_Gaza2009_160/816_Dös_001]

Several variants exist for verbalizing the widespread cliché of JEWISH POLITICAL CORRECTNESS. The taboo against criticism, which in fact does not exist, is portrayed as a social prohibition and as a fact, and at the same time is assessed in extremely negative terms:[55]

> (189) Unfortunately I do not dare to give my name and address, for when it comes to freedom of the press and speech relating to Jews in Germany there is no longer any such thing. [ZJD_29.12.2007_ano_001][56]
>
> (190) It's starting to make me sick that Jews in Germany can force us to keep silent. [ZJD_07.11.2008_Bla_001]

In (191) we also find the implicature that there are 'Jewish criminal elements from the Nazi period' about which Germans must keep silent because of the taboo:

> (191) The Germans from that time could tell us all sorts of things today if it were not for the fact that the Jews have muzzled us all. (also in Switzerland) [ZJD_Gaza2009_20/816_ano_001]

In another variant either the Central Council or all Jews are accused of blocking free expression of opinions and wanting to impose a criticism taboo (and this aspiration is mentioned as the basis for anti-Jewish sentiments):

(192) By accusing us of antisemitism you want to silence everyone immediately. [ZJD_16.04.2007_Don_001]

(193) And now you want to muzzle a man as worthy as Herr N. Blüm, just because he speaks the truth. [ZJD_18.06.2002_Mar_001]

This stereotype turns up implicitly in statements such as (194), an e-mail from a thirty-seven-year-old woman from Gelsenkirchen, whose conclusions are based on the notion that in Germany critical views cannot be expressed or are subject to sanctions, because of the Nazi past:

(194) I feel it is wrong that a person isn't allowed to express reservations on this subject only because we presumbly can't afford it for historical reasons. [...] It's my great hope that some day my three-year-old son, when he's as old as I am, will act as a mature citizen and be able to write openly without having the feeling he has to start out by asserting his integrity and honesty. [ZJD_20.06.2002_Kam_001]

These fantasies always appear accompanied by the cliché, as in (195) and (196), that Jews occupy a special status that they exploit to stifle any and all criticism by labeling it antisemitic (see also [197]):

(195) How long do you miserable Jews want to keep on pushing the world around thinking you're allowed to do whatever you want. A good German [ZJD_31.07_2006_ano_005]

(196) No one gives me an Auschwitz bonus [ZJD_03.06.2007_Sch_001]

These comments imply that the suspicion of antisemitism is used as an unfair and oppressive weapon with which people can be beaten over the head on any occasion to enforce a "muzzling policy":

(197) I must say, it's sad that the Central Council of Jews, of all organizations, pushes any and every criticism of Israel stemming from the political realm, the press, or any other area of public life into the category of antisemitism or at least brands it hostile to Israel, sparking violent, incomprehensible reactions. To this observer it therefore seems clear that as a German one is generally muzzled in all matters pertaining to Israel. [ZJD_14.09.2006_Man_001]

Since the alleged "political correctness" presumes that Jews occupy particular positions of power and exercise a high degree of societal influence, the traditional stereotype of JEWISH DOMINATION CONSPIRACY is activated implicitly. Correspondingly, massive derealizations sometimes result—that is, subjective representations of reality that are claimed to be facts but do not correspond to actual reality:

(198) It was certainly striking that no criticism of Israel found expression in the press (so much for freedom of the press). [ZJD_17.09.2006_Ros_001]

This message not only obscures the fact that all the media have published quantitatively and qualitatively intensive reports and commentaries on the Middle East conflict; it also casts general doubt on freedom of the press by way of the cynical parenthesis. The criticism taboo in relation to Israel, often invoked and bemoaned, does not exist de facto; it is pure fiction. It can be demonstrated that no other state receives as frequent or as sharp criticism as Israel.[57] Nonetheless, the correspondents repeatedly articulate this stereotype,[58] especially in conjunction with the stock phrase *This must be said*, which implies that such a thing is not allowed to be said or has not yet been said:

(199) There, I've finally got that off my chest; it had to be said at some point! [ZJD_08.08.2006_Kre_001]

(200) but the way many people of my generation think about this matter had to be said [. . .] [IBD_20.02.2009_Wei_001]

Educated correspondents from the mainstream, who always portray themselves as anti-antisemites, use this cliché especially often, as in (201) and (202), written by PhDs from Berlin and Hanover:

(201) Many other Germans and I are sick and tired, and it infuriates us to see the attempt being made to shut us up with the completely unjustified charge of antisemitism. [ZJD_01.09.2006_Sto_001]

(202) This must and should be said, above all by people who feel ashamed of the Germans' history with the Jews and are anything but antisemites. [IBD_02.06.2010_Fra_001]

What is declared to be *criticism of Israel* and defended as *free expression* but actually grows out of the deeply rooted but unacknowledged antipathy toward Jews is justified by means of this argument, which goes on the offensive. The self-image of a mature and humane citizen remains intact, while the blame is projected onto the Other.

Quite a few of these correspondents manifest the obsessiveness so typical of conceptual antisemitism: it reveals itself, for instance, in very long, detailed communications in which the authors engage in historical excurses and draw on numerous quotations in an attempt to prove that Jews are a "morally despicable people" and Israel is a "criminal state that endangers world peace." At the end of his twenty-two-page, single-spaced typed letter, the author, a PhD from Berlin, sums up his concern in a stock phrase typical of this discourse:

> (203) I felt I finally had to say what must be said. [ZJD_30.11.2006_Gel_001]

What Günter Grass portrays in the title of his tract disguised as a poem, "What must be said," as urgent, necessary, and exceptional had thus been expressed long before him by thousands of antisemites from a number of political camps; it turns out to be a not very original contribution by the well-known writer and Nobel Prize recipient. The implication that it would otherwise not be said because it is taboo is false and reveals an unwillingness to face facts. But why do antisemites cling so persistently to the idea of an alleged criticism as taboo, when the reality is entirely different? For one thing, accepting that no such taboo or prohibition exists would shake their Judeophobic view of the world and leave them communicatively bereft of arguments with which to convince themselves and others. The postwar stereotype that Jews wield influence over Germans as a result of what happened in the Holocaust forms the basis of and justification for the activation of Judeophobic resentment. If one could unmask the alleged political correctness as an age-old antisemitic and imaginary construct, contemporary enemies of Jews would see the essential basis for their accusations and charges crumble. If no political correctness imposed by Jews exists, there is also no basis for charges and complaints against them. First, this would shake the conceptual system in which one stereotype builds on the other, and then it would strip away the possibility of complaining "honorably" about Jews. It would also confront the educated citizens who consider themselves anti-antisemites with their own emotional economy, which in the post-Auschwitz era must be viewed as unacceptable, prejudiced, and dangerous. Last but not least, it would deprive the correspondents of the opportunity to present themselves as courageous defenders of critical opinions who speak out in defiance of the risk of incurring sanctions.

Conclusion

Despite all political, educational, and scholarly exertions, the stereotypes and clichés passed down from generation to generation, often without reflection and often conveyed by stock phrases, have remained intact and can be detected even now, in the twenty-first century, in current patterns of speech. In part they persist in words and phrases used frequently in the Middle Ages and integrated during the Nazi period into the standard repertory employed for verbal stigmatization of Jews; in part antisemitic constructs take on contemporary forms. These show, on the one hand, how traditional and contemporary conceptions merge and mingle to form new concepts and, on the other hand, how old, traditional stereotypes can be separated from their original context but applied with the same or similar meaning to current situations. It is striking that the basic conceptual type (JEWS AS FOREIGNERS, AS OTHERS) persists. By way of the semantics of delimitation, stereotyping, and devaluation, this is realized in language. In the texts under discussion the classic anti-Jewish stereotypes are conveyed either explicitly or implicitly. Their instantiation, however, is undertaken in accord with the temporal context, the process entailing elaborations and abstractions, but also concretizations.

The stereotype of the FOREIGNER appears in two variants: German Jews are conceptualized as NON-GERMANS and/or (depending on context) as ISRAELIS. The originally religiously motivated stereotypes of the TRAITOR, CHRIST-MURDERER, and INFIDEL have solidified into the concept of EMBODIMENT OF EVIL. The AGITATOR and DISTURBER OF THE PEACE have now become, on the one hand, the DISRUPTER OF GERMAN NORMALCY, THE ANNOYING NAG or, on the other hand, the THREAT TO WORLD PEACE. The DECEIVER, USURER, PARASITE, and MONEY-GRUBBER have likewise become the HOLOCAUST EXPLOITER and the (ISRAELI) LAND-GRABBER. The myth of the BLOOD CULT and RITUAL

MURDER is reactivated in a modern version with such descriptors as BARBAROUS AND ATAVISTIC, and turns up in conceptualizations like that of the ISRAELI CHILD-MURDERER and the JEWISH CHILD-MUTILATOR. The stereotype of the UGLY JEW, originally linked to the Jew's physiognomy, now takes an abstract form: UGLY has come to be understood primarily in a figurative sense, as referring to moral and intellectual depravity, with the prototype being the UGLY, INHUMANE ISRAELI. But in relation to Germany other variants occur: the GRUDGE-BEARING JEW and the POLITICAL-CORRECTNESS POLICE. These variants often appear in conjunction with the stereotype of the COLLECTIVE, ETERNAL JEW.

Thus to a great extent the stereotypes have, on the one hand, been decontextualized, generalized, and elaborated and, on the other, specified and referentially transferred.

The state of Israel often occupies a central position in the stereotype encodings. Since its founding, it has become the most important and weighty symbol worldwide of Jewish life and survival, for which reason it serves as the preferred target for anti-Jewish attacks. Hardly a single message in the entire large corpus fails to refer to Israel and to make this reference the pretext for defamatory and delegitimizing hostile comments. But at the same time, the arguments hostile toward Israel in most of the texts (also those alluding to the past) are pressed into service to devalue all Jews.

These verbal formulations reveal a conceptual network of Judeophobic contents that is communicated time and again, and by all the correspondents, regardless of their political, religious, or ideological orientation.

If one looks at the arguments that repeatedly (and particularly often, when examined quantitatively) turn up in the texts in various formal and semantic but only slightly deviating versions, the following picture emerges: present-day verbal antisemitism rests cognitively on a largely homogeneous mental model consisting of traditional Judeophobic stereotypes, some of which have been expanded and/or modified in reference to the contemporary world. The antisemitic conceptualization model can be characterized as follows:

> 'Jews are different. They always are and remain foreigners, oddballs, who constitute worldwide a people or a race that sticks together in solidarity and also supports and defends misdeeds committed in their ranks. As a people the Jews have traits that are shared by the entire community. These traits

pertain in particular to their social, cognitive, and emotional abilities as well as their behaviors: Jews are restless, homeless, eternal wanderers who do not fit in anywhere and do not develop solidarity with peoples that host them. In their tradition as murderers of God, Jews commit ritual murders and other criminal, violent, and usually bloody deeds. Jews are greedy, deceptive, and sly; they rob other peoples of their land and property, Jews are power-hungry and aim to control the entire world by accumulating wealth and occupying positions of power, for instance in the media. They also promote their own interests by means of lies and deception. On the basis of their wiliness and business acumen they exert great influence on governments. Jews are irreconcilable, grudge-bearing, and vengeful: they are not prepared to forgive or forget the Holocaust. Instead they avenge themselves by taking on the role of social freeloaders and parasites: they shamelessly exploit the memory of the Holocaust financially and morally and enforce political correctness. This prevents criticism of Jews and of the policies pursued by the state of Israel. This state is the fundamental evil in the world and embodies everything that is typical of Jews.'

This mental model possesses a logic all its own: the stereotypes are (pseudo-) causally connected and mutually reinforcing; that is, the inner consistency of the model is supported by every individual concept. This explains the "closed" worldview of persons who subscribe to such a construct: for them, these conceptual representations possess the status of an unshakable belief system.

5 ECHO OF THE PAST

"The insolent Jew is harassing Germans once again!"

Components of Nazi Speech in Contemporary Discourse Hostile toward Jews

We have shown that present-day antisemitic discourse often reveals a tendency to deny guilt and resist reminders of Germany's history.[1] Many messages in the corpus explicitly or implicitly invoke the same anti-Jewish stereotypes that were common currency during the Nazi period. Furthermore, the style of argumentation, which melds elements from the past with present-day themes, reveals how important the process of coming to terms with the past remains more than sixty years after the collapse of the Nazi regime. In this chapter we will provide evidence of the extent to which certain words and phrases used frequently in the Nazi period still turn up in anti-Jewish texts,[2] and we will examine the role these patterns of usage play in contemporary verbal antisemitism. This phenomenon raises the following question: Does the reproduction of linguistic components drawn from Nazi ideology mean that the semantically and conceptually related arguments and justifications are also adopted?

The linguistic markers and communicative functions of antisemitism during the Nazi period have been subjected to intensive philological and linguistic study and description (cf. Victor Klemperer's *LTI* 1947/2010, as well as, e.g., Ehlich 1989, Bering 1991a, b; Kinne and Schwitalla 1994; Schmitz-Berning 1998; Hortzitz 1999; Hutton 1999; von Braun 2007).

The essential features of this usage are as follows:[3] stigmatization through imposition of names (*Sarah*, *Israel*, *Cohen*, *Itzig*); alteration of titles—that is, use of professional designations as insults (*law twister*, *dental Jew*); racist metaphors drawn from biology (*bacilli*, *bloodsuckers*, *parasites*); combinations with animal references (*Jewish sow*, *Jewish swine*); emphasis on race by means of generic noun phrases that use the typifying singular (*the Jew, the insolent Jew*); repetition of clichéd stock phrases whose semantics derive from conspiracy theories (*world Jewry, Jewification, Jewish financial machinations*); referential reduction of all Jews to attributes such as *money-grubber, huckster, arrogant intellectual, schemer*, and *Bolshevik*; and generic description and collective denigration in the form of phrases (*Jewish atrocity propaganda, typical Jewish insolence, Jewified press, Jewish troublemakers, the Jews are our misfortune*). All these verbalizations express the Nazi ideology, which was based on nationalist and racist concepts.

Aggressive sayings containing anti-Jewish admonitions, warnings, curses, and threats such as "*Germans, defend yourselves: don't buy from Jews!*" (Berlin, 1933; cf. Königseder 2011, 61), "Croak, Juda" (Berlin, 1933), and "None should go hungry, none lack a cloak, but the Jews should one and all croak" (Germany, 1935, cf. Améry 1966/2008, 135) were in everyday use between 1933 and 1945. All the mass media spread anti-Jewish propaganda that established the standard official and public linguistic usage, which could expand its influence accordingly.[4]

In our corpus analysis we focused on lexemes (and typical abbreviations) such as *Aryan, extirpation, Final Solution, degenerate/degeneration, Führer, gas chambers, Gestapo (methods), forcibly align, master race, Jewish question/problem, concentration camp, propaganda, race, Night of Broken Glass/Reich Pogrom Night, SA, special treatment, SS, inferior race, pests, world Jewry*, and *corrode*. We also looked for references to prominent Nazis such as Hitler and Goebbels. After noticing that keyword analysis of the corpus often turned up the phrases *insolent Jew(s)* and *Jewish agitating*, frequently used in speeches and in writing by Hitler and Goebbels, we checked to see the extent to which such collocations typical of Nazi ideology also appear in current discourse.[5]

It is not surprising that correspondents identified as neo-Nazis and right-wing radicals resort to verbal methods and structures from the Nazi period, since these persons concur with the ideology of that period and identify with it. Thus the use of Nazi vocabulary is a typical marker of the right-wing-extremist pattern of communication. Among the e-mails and letters from right-wing circles, 98 percent use words, phrases, or sentences employed in the Nazi period either for defamation of Jews or for general propaganda purposes and identity affirmation.

Clear indicators of right-wing-extremist origins are formulaic greetings from the Nazi period (such as *Sieg, Heil!* or *With a Germanic/German salute*):

(1) Heil Olmert the Fuehrer and murderer of the criminal Israeli state. [ZJD_12.04.2007_Mon_001]

Correspondents from the right-wing scene also use striking e-mail usernames that contain intertextual references to prominent Nazis or scraps of ideology (*karinhall... @web.de*,[6] *wotan... @web.de*) or Nazi comparisons (*holocaust-gaza@ . . . com*), or they sign their messages with phrases such as *a decent German* or *a true Aryan*. They also shorten the German word for Jew, *Jude*, by dropping the *e*, in analogy to the Nazi era film *Jud Süss* (as in *der Jud Scharon*). Individual lexemes such as *capital of the Reich* or ironic allusions such as *the so-called FRG* (Federal Republic of Germany), Nazi buzzwords (*Volk*, *Reich*, etc.), extensive use of the adjective *German* (as in *German interests*, *German suffering*), as well as obviously racist vocabulary (such as *swarm of parasites*, *race*, *miscegenation*, *subhumans*, and *subhuman riffraff*) occur often. Especially frequent in the corpus are dehumanizing phrases employed during the Nazi era in everyday discourse, such as *Jewish sow* and *Jewish swine*. The use of verbal components from Nazi propaganda matches the ideology of these authors.

Accordingly, e-mails from writers located at the right end of the spectrum characteristically cite Hitler and other prominent Nazis as "authorities on the Jewish problem," and elements from Nazi discourse (lexemes, phrases, sentences) are reproduced verbatim to express antisemitic thinking. In particular, many references to the Nazis' racist pseudo-theory occur:

(2) Filthy german non-Aryan horde of illuminati, not Christian [ZJD_24.05.2007_ano_001]

(3) Heil Hitler! you subhumans! [IBD_07.09.2005_ano_Postcard]

Lexemes drawn from nineteenth-century works on race theory, such as *Aryan*, *race*, *inferior*, and *subhumans*, and frequently employed during the Nazi period turn up in nearly all e-mails from right-wing extremists, along with linguistic patterns borrowed from the Nuremberg racial laws, such as the term *half-Jew*:

(4) Does Gregor Gysi do such things, or Reich-Ranicki? They're also a half-Jew or Jew, and no one seems to mind!!!!!! [ZJD_28.05.2008_Wil_001]

Yet the notion that Jews constitute "a race unto themselves" also appears in messages from writers who do not display any right-wing-extremist views, as in (5), an e-mail from "*a simple German citizen from Cologne*," who positions himself "*in the mainstream of society*" and "*absolutely condemns the Nazis' crimes*":

(5) My shame as a German with regard to my people's crimes against your race [...] [IBD_24.03_2009_Wah_001]

In verbalizations such as these, the salient feature is not the writer's ideological orientation but rather the lack of knowledge and education. In the memory of such writers Jews continue to be conceptualized as a RACE (see examples [80]–[82] in chapter 4).

Among educated correspondents, Nazi lexemes from the vocabulary of racism also occur,[7] especially in comparisons to the Nazis that stigmatize Israel, but these phrases almost never serve to express a conceptually racist argument or worldview. On the contrary, racist thinking is strictly rejected, although the use of components drawn from Nazi linguistic usage is inconsistent with such a stance (see chapter 4).

Right-wing correspondents usually refer to Hitler as "*a great leader*" and "*farsighted*" and comment that he "*knew why he wanted to eradicate the Jews*" (in which connection they often express regret that "*the eradication was not fully carried out*"). With reference to the present, Jews and/or Israelis alive today are often dehumanized and demonized by means of Nazi terms and metaphors (with animal, pest, and disease metaphors predominating; see also chapter 9):

(6) Swarm of parasites, filthy Jewish swine. [ZJD_29.03.2009_Zel_002]

(7) Pests! Devil's spawn! Antichrists, cancerous tumor on the Middle East. [IBD_07.05.2010_ano_003]

In similar fashion, the authors voice threats, wishes, and prophecies to predict the "completion of the Final Solution" (see also chapter 9, under Abuse, Insults, Threats, Curses):

(8) Its time again for propper Aryans to turn on the gas! [...] HEIL HITLER! [IBD_19.01.2004_ano_001]

(9) Off to the gas chambers! [ZJD_Gaza2009_664/816_Pan_001]

Combinations of anti-Israeli demonization and Judeophobic conspiracy theories turn up especially often in such argumentation.

> (10) You Palestinian-killers! [...] at the next "Night of Broken Glass" we won't break any glass but only your stupid skulls crammed full of genocidal shit. . The "Night of Broken Glass" will be a worldwide event! We want to free ourselves at long last from the yoke and entanglement of Zionist financial interests, as well as their sickening genocidal actions. [ZJD_Gaza2009_624/816_ano_001]

It is striking how often rationales to justify the Holocaust are constructed by portraying Jews as a global threat and misfortune in both past and present:

> (11) Yes, I believe that back before the Second World War the Jews probably pushed the German population around the same way as they do today with the Palestinians. The Jews were past masters at exploiting the Germans in those days and abusing their trust (nasty wheeler-dealers) [ZJD_Gaza2009_20/816_ano_001]

Hitler is described in a number of messages as "*far too humane in his treatment of you Jewish criminals.*" For the Middle East conflict, he is invoked as an authority and visionary:

> (12) The Führer wouldn't have allowed such a thing to take place; the looters, vandals, and other pests preying on the Volk would have been shot immediately, precisely because he was a humanist. [ZJD_Gaza2009_423/816_ano_001]
>
> (13) You'll receive the same treatment you are dishing out to the Palestinians, no way around it. [...] One of these days Hitler will receive the Nobel Peace Prize posthumously, seeing the way all of you are carrying on. [ZJD_Gaza2009_730/816_Pan_001]

Consistent with the Nazi conceptualization of Jews as PESTS PREYING ON THE VOLK, all Jews are collectively belittled and their death by murder is portrayed as desirable:

> (14) Anyone who kills a Jew is doing a good deed and is actually acting as God would wish. Jews are simply criminal evildoers... [ZJD_Gaza2009_577/816_ano_001]

What figured in the antisemitic discourse of the nineteenth and early twentieth centuries as the "*Jewish problem*" and the "*Jewish question*" turns up verbatim in current discourse (see also the examples in chapter 9, under Suggestions for Solving the "Jewish Problem"):

> (15) P.S. I think I could contribute something to the Jewish question! Not the "dissolution" of the Jewish question will liberate us from the slavery and power hunger of this world but the Final Solution: who actually is a Jew and who isn't! [ZJD_15.04.2002_Fal_001]

Breakdowns of coherence and semantically contradictory arguments are typical: on the one hand these writers describe the Holocaust as "*not yet finished*," while on the other hand they deny that it ever occurred:

> (16) The way it looks, our grandfathers didn't do their job thoroughly enough! The day of reckoning will come Sieg Heil and then you'll get your Holocaust which has never happened up to NOW... what hasn't happened can still come to pass!HEIL HITLER! [IBD_19.01.2004_ano_001]

All in all, however, the messages contain remarkably few denials of the Holocaust, although for years just such denials were considered typical of right-wing extremists and neo-Nazis (cf. Lichtenstein 1999; BfV 2005). Considerably more often we find either regret that Jews are still alive or pride in the fact that at any rate 6 million were killed:

> (17) [. . .] am proud of having spared the world 6M Jewish parasites[.] Too bad we couldn't wipe out all the vermin and now it's still gnawing at our grandchildren's health[.]Soon Jews will be shipped off to Auschwitz again! [IBD_06.04.2012_ano_004]

References in this context to *world Jewry* and *international Jewish financial control* turn up, along with generic references to all Jews by means of the typifying singular:

> (18) But what is the "Jew" doing with the Palestinians now? ...didn't the "Jew" learn anything from the past? [ZJD_Gaza2009_271/816_ano_001]

Legitimation of the Holocaust takes the form of evocation of the "criminal and evil activities of the Israelis" in the Middle East conflict. Instances of conflated references to the past and the present predominate:

(19) you all are and remain worldclasscriminalswine ..murder of adolf eichmann. Your filthy murderous swine of a mossad abducted adolf eichmann and condemned him to death by a filthy jewishcriminalriffraffcourt,just for that you jewish swine deserve to be wiped out.insulting adolf Hitler You filthy worldclasscriminalswine insult our dear adolf and are allowed to run around with impunity that's an insolence. I demand the death penalty for every filthy pig that insulted adolf. Adolf Hitler treated you jewish worldclasscriminalsmuch too humanely. **For the attack on Lebanon you jewish worldclasscriminalswine deserve to be Wiped out.** [ZJD_13.08.2006_Kam_001]

Interesting in this connection are (numerous) messages in which Jews are, on the one hand, classified as an inferior race, consistent with Nazi ideology, and on the other, declared to be new Nazis. This way of thinking results in a contradiction typical of antisemitic discourse: the Nazis saw themselves as a master race and the Jews as subhuman. The right-wing writers share this ideological point of view. In their interpretation of the world, Nazis have the status of heroes and role models. But then when they equate "the non-Aryan Jews" with the "Aryan German Nazis," they create a striking semantic contradiction:

(20) You're the new NAZIS, ...simply an inferior race!!!!!!!!!!!!!!!!!!!!!!!!!!!!!!!!!!! [IBD_25.10.2006_ano_001]

(21) You filthy degenerate Jew-Nazis just make us sick! [ZJD_11.03.2007_Mon_001]

These contradictory and senseless statements can be explained by reference to the persuasive potential of comparisons with the Nazis: no event in German history is as vivid and emotionally fraught in the collective German consciousness as the Nazi period. No other era stands as clearly for inhumanity and monstrosity. In the postwar era the Nazis represent the greatest possible crime against humanity. This assessment, anchored in social consciousness and transmitted officially and publicly, is therefore applied to Jews and Israelis in order to discredit them as thoroughly as possible. That in the process a conceptual clash with the writers' antisemitic ideology occurs either goes unnoticed or is simply accepted. Contradictions, tautologies, and false conclusions are not confined, however, to the messages of neo-Nazis and right-wing extremists, but rather constitute a characteristic feature of antisemitic texts in general (see chapter 8, under Contradictions and Paradoxes).

In many communications *Hitler* is evoked by way of pseudo-causal justification for the condemnation of Jews:

> (22) Hitler was right after all!!! [ZJD_20.09.2007_ano_001]
>
> (23) I am deeply shaken to read today that the Israeli army, after the war, dropped cluster bombs on South Lebanon. In the past few weeks I have come to understand Hitler why he wanted to exterminate the Jews! From today on the Jews are my enemies, too, the best thing is for you to get out of Germany first.Such war criminals are not welcome here. [ZJD_01.09.2006_Sch_002]

The author of (23), who describes himself as "*not racist*" and "*no neo-Nazi*" but rather as a "*left-leaning liberal citizen*," sees the violence in the Middle East as a reason to condemn all Jews collectively as war criminals and at the same time to justify Hitler's policy of murder. Such justifications, however, occur seldom in the messages from educated and left-leaning liberal authors. Most of the writers from the middle of the political spectrum expressly disassociate themselves from the Nazis' actions and ideology. Yet many of them engage in comparisons to the Nazis when they comment on the Middle East conflict, using crude rhetoric to discredit those they consider responsible and to create an extreme image of the enemy, as in (24) and (25), e-mails from two educated senders who characterize themselves as "left-wing voters" or "left-leaning."[8] The author of (24) comes from Munich and has a PhD:

> (24) The Israel of 2006 is the fascist guard dog for US-american raw-material interests: as brutal, as inhumane, and as ferocious as Hitler's Germany. [ZJD_01.09.2006_Haf_001]
>
> (25) The deformed and illegitimate state of Israel is the continuation of the sick thinking of NAZI Germany...! [IBD_15.06.2009_ano_001]

As many as 32 percent of the correspondents from the mainstream of society (and 8 percent of all those with higher education and those with advanced degrees) explicitly (as in [26] and [27]) or implicitly (as in [28]) use comparisons to the Nazis:[9]

(26) Israel isn't doing anything HITLER didn't do! [ZJD_04.05.2007_Hof_001]

(27) YOU PEOPLE ARE ALMOST WORSE THAN THE NAZIS IN THE OLD DAYS! [IBD_29.06.2006_Mue_001]

(28) Esteemed Central Council, I ask you to convey my warmest combat greetings to your Israeli brothers and sisters for the murder of Palestinian children, women, and old people—now Israel has succeeded after all in attaining the level of fascist Germany. [ZJD_Gaza2009_672/816_Nie_001]

While comparisons to the Nazis in the public communicative space are used primarily for purposes of persuasion, for highlighting a given utterance and intensifying criticism of certain situations, in antisemitic discourse they are deployed for defamatory purposes:[10]

(29) Nowadays by far the greatest and bloodiest share of the violence comes from Israel, and it is certain that what we have here is the greatest crime of the present era. In addition, where this violence is largely intended to ensure the creation of <u>new Lebensraum</u> for the chosen people, in violation of international law. (<u>Here, too, ominous parallels cannot be ignored!</u>) [ZJD_09.11.2006_Mei_001]

Educated correspondents, especially those who characterize themselves as "*peace activists*" and identify with left-of-center views,[11] posit an analogy between leading Nazis and not only Israelis but also directors of the Central Council:

(30) Those in power in Germany, like Hitler, Göbbels, etc., would look up admiringly to you and your methods. [IBD_03.03.2006_Bur_001]

(31) We also had a Herr Dr. G... in our history and can therefore recognize demagoguery when we see it. Tone down your rhetoric—that will serve your cause better! [ZJD_18.07.2006_Mue_001]

Israeli military operations are likened to the state-ordered mass murder of the Jews, with Ramallah being referred to, for instance, as a *second Warsaw Ghetto* and Gaza as a *concentration camp*. These comparisons relativize the Holocaust, denying the uniqueness of the Nazis' atrocities and at the same time drastically demonizing the state of Israel. At times the intertextual references to Nazi precedents are marked explicitly as such by means of quotation marks, an indicator that the authors are deliberately and consciously drawing on such usage:

(32) I am certain that Israel will come up with a "Final Solution" for the Palestinians, right? [IBD_28.06.2006_Hop_001]

(33) The Israeli policy of building settlements in occupied territories comes very close to the policy of a "Volk ohne Raum" [people without land], and now in the military confrontation there have been overtones of something like "till the final victory." [ZJD_Gaza2009_186/816_Sta_001]

Nonverbal elements come into play as well; in addition to caricatures (which often strikingly resemble the images in the *Stürmer*), graphics that meld the Star of David with the swastika turn up. Even educated correspondents seem unaware of the inflammatory potential and inappropriateness of such equivalences, or they see nothing wrong with them:[12]

(34) I find Israel's behavior incomprehensible.On television I saw shots of a demonstration against the war (Malmö, Sweden) and a Star of David–swastika poster. It seems to me this comparison really deserves careful consideration. [ZJD_29.07.2006_Pet_001]

Voicing demands for a boycott of Israel (and sometimes of all Jews)—coming rather infrequently from right-wing-extremist but significantly often from leftist and left-wing-extremist writers and usually displaying a structure identical to those of the Nazis—the authors resort to strategies that they call "*punitive measures*" or "*necessary operations*," but that affect Jews or Israelis collectively and thus correspond exactly to the Nazis' ideological positions.

(35) Germans, don't buy fruit from Israel. [ZJD_10.08.2006_Neu_001]

(36) Boycott of Zionist products! [ZJD_07.05.2007_Nom_001]

(37) I plan to boycott everything Jewish from now on! That's how I'm registering my opposition to Israel's unjust policies. [IBD_03.07.2008_Lam_001]

The call from the Nazi period to "*take arms against Jews*"[13] also occurs frequently in this context, either in the lexical variation that refers to Israel, as in (37), or in exactly the same words, as in (38), from a letter written by a prominent Berlin academic:

(38) Yet another reason to take arms against Jews, at least verbally. [ZJD_30.11.2006_Gel_001]

In the corpus the inflationary use of the lexemes *Holocaust*, *Final Solution*, and *concentration camp* results in an additional expansion of meaning in texts expressing hostility toward Jews:[14] the original meanings of these words undergo a referential shift when the words are used in a decontextualized and ahistorical fashion. In these texts they no longer allude to the unique historical events and stages of the Nazi genocide but are employed as defamatory tools directed against Jews or Israelis. Thus the communicative strategy of perpetrator–victim reversal is mirrored on the verbal microstructural level with a derealizing effect.

Lexical Analyses of Insolence/Insolent and Harass/Harassment

Analysis of a sample taken from a partial corpus available in digital form, comprising 1,034 messages to the Central Council and 2,000 messages to the Israeli Embassy,[15] revealed that the lexemes *insolent* and *insolence* appeared significantly often in conjunction with the lexeme *Jew* or *Jewish*.[16] This phenomenon raises the question of whether we are dealing here merely with the reproduction of stock phrases from the Nazi period,[17] or whether the texts in which these phrases occur also display semantic and conceptual correlations with Nazi thinking. In many Nazi speeches and written texts, the negative characterization of Jews and Jewish conduct by means of the lexeme *insolent* turns up in several variations, as in the phrases "*true Jewish insolence*" (Hitler 1934, 314) and "*an example of genuinely Jewish insolence*" (Hitler 1934, 248), or in charges directed against a Jew such as that "*his usurious levels of interest are finally arousing resistance, his increasing insolence outrage*" (Hitler 1934, 339). Jews are conceptualized as UNABASHED, COCKY, REFUSING TO ADAPT TO SOCIETY, WORKING AGAINST THE GENERAL WELFARE, as manifested in the stereotypes JEWS ARE IMMORAL, JEWS ARE DISTURBERS OF THE PEACE, JEWS HAVE A CORROSIVE INFLUENCE.[18]

In the messages to the Central Council the lexemes *insolent* and *insolence* appear far more frequently than in the messages to the Israeli Embassy. This difference in frequency suggests that even today negative evaluation and moral disapproval of Jews and their behavior are more habitual and more likely to be stored in the speakers' mental lexicon than the collocation *insolent Israelis*. To be sure, a change is already making itself felt: if verbalizations such as "*the insolent Israelis*" (ZJD_24.06.2002_Mau_001) occur only sporadically in the texts up to 2005, starting in 2006 a clear increase can be noted in the frequency with which they appear. Here we see conceptual merging of Jews and Israelis taking place, with antisemitic stereotypes being transferred to the concept ISRAELIS.

Contrary to expectation, this specific form of verbal antisemitism turns up less commonly in messages to the Central Council and the Embassy from the right-wing or right-wing-extremist sector than in those sent by writers from the social mainstream.[19] Thus a person complains as follows about Michel Friedman, a Jewish activist and former vice-president of the Central Council of Jews, in a lengthy e-mail to the Central Council:

> (39) You see, that is precisely [. . .] the height of Jewish insolence and shamelessness. [. . .] Friends, acquaintances, and business associates from all over, even as far away as Austria and Switzerland, keep complaining to me on the telephone and on the Internet about that man's incredibly insolent behavior. [ZJD_30.07.2006_Ren_001]

The semantic generalization conveyed by the noun phrase "*Jewish insolence*" shows that the denigration does not apply only to Michel Friedman and his behavior as a talk show host; rather, it ascribes morally disreputable behavior to all Jews in general. In the case of such a generalization, the use of 'insolent' as a pejorative descriptor is inherently linked to the category JEWISH. In the e-mails we analyzed, the behavior of the Central Council is predicated as an expression of Jews' immoral characteristics, in combination either with the stereotype JEWS EXPLOIT THE PAST TO THEIR FINANCIAL ADVANTAGE or with the stereotype of POLITICAL CORRECTNESS.

> (40) It is sheer insolence the way you try to blackmail the FRG with the past, 60 years after the end of the Third Reich. Even in these tough times you keep insolently making greater demands for financial support. [ZJD_12.08.2006_Gru_001]
>
> (41) I always feel that pronouncements by the central council of the Jews are insolent intervention and malicious provocation, but maybe in the

eyes of the Jews I'm just another Nazi (because I speak my mind !!) [ZJD_Gaza2009_302/816_Wel_001]

When the writers specify what they consider insolent, they reveal the stereotypical conceptions of Jews that they consider to be personified, *pars pro toto*, by the members of the Central Council. The authors use the cliché that Jews exploit, financially and intellectually, the German responsibility for the past; they thereby adopt a dominant postwar stereotype. At the same time, the traditional stereotype of the VENGEFUL AND IRRECONCILABLE JEW is encoded.

The behavior of representatives of the Central Council is also described as *insolent* or *insolence* when these representatives express critical views of antisemitic or anti-Israeli incidents. Thus a letter reproaches Paul Spiegel, president of the Central Council, for improper interference:

(42) That's unacceptable, and it won't happen that you meddle in the German party landscape. And it's pure insolence on your part to accuse a Herr Möllemann, even if he is a populist, of antisemitism. [...] May I remind you of how they always act, the Jews? [ZJD_18.06.2002_Ser_001]

The argumentation in (42) builds on the antisemitic stereotype JEWS ARE NO GERMANS. Paul Spiegel is explicitly and specifically denied the right to express his opinion freely. The fact that Spiegel—a Jew—speaks critically about a German politician, Jürgen Möllemann, is characterized as inappropriate and inacceptable insolence. This invalidation goes hand in hand with a general devaluation of Jews that emerges particularly from the rhetorical question that follows. Through the use of the particle *always* and the collective generalization by means of the generic reference to *the Jews*, Paul Spiegel's conduct is declared to be Jewish across the board.

A conceptual conflation of Judeophobic and anti-Israel stereotypes manifests itself in a message from a man from Aschaffenburg:

(43) What Scharon is up to these days, in concert with his entourage, is Jewish insolence that cries to high Heaven. [ZJD_06.04.2002_Klo_001]

Here the phrase *Jewish insolence*, as applied to Ariel Sharon, on the one hand equates ISRAELI and JEWISH and on the other hand asserts the moral shamelessness of all Jews.

Another distinctive lexical feature in the corpus is the frequent use of the lexemes *harass* and *harassment*, or composite words containing those concepts.[20] The writers apply these terms to everything, from what they view as hatemongering propaganda to alleged racist agitation. When Jews and/or Israelis are described as harassers,[21] the stereotypes CRITICISM TABOO and JEWISH INFLUENCE often appear as well, referring to suppression of freedom of expression in German society. Example (44) shows how the antisemitic concept of JEWS, which is closely linked with the *hetz-* lexemes, can combine with negative evaluation and emotional denigration:

> (44) Why, dear Frau Knobloch, are you whipping up hostility in their typical fashion against the German bishops? Do you lack sufficient education? No? So it's simply blind Zionist hatred of Germans? [ZJD_11.03.2007_Ise_001]

To the authors of the messages in the corpus, the concept JEWS is inherently linked to the stereotype already current in the Nazi period of JEWS AS AGITATORS; the chair of the Central Council, Charlotte Knobloch, is described as agitating "*in typical fashion*," with the possessive "*their*" referring to all Jews. Although the writer poses a question as to the reason for Frau Knobloch's position on statements German bishops made during a visit to Ramallah, she clearly assumes that it was Jews' hated for Germans that motivated Frau Knobloch's criticism. This conceptualization rests on the stereotype JEWS ARE IRRECONCILABLE, which yields the pseudo-causal argument "Jews harass Germans because they are irreconcilable." Implied is the reproach that Jews cannot let go of the past and thus refuse to indulge the fervent wish of the perpetrators' descendants that the Nazi period be put behind them.

In the messages in which the lexemes *Hetze/hetzen* appear in conjunction with antisemitic conceptualizations, Nazi linguistic usage often occurs in combination with charges of collective guilt:

> (45) You saw to it that we in Europe had to experience the revolution and the world wars. Worldwide 200,000 million deaths as a result of war, revolution, and civil wars can be charged to the account of your harassers and your Communist, capitalist, misanthropic mendacious ideology. Your racism masquerading as religion is revolting! [IBD_19.07.2006_Bec_001]

Argumentative patterns drawn from Nazism[22] are applied to occurrences in the current Middle East conflict: Jews allegedly bear responsibility for social and economic developments in modern times, as well as for the atrocities of the world wars. Building on this notion of the fundamental evil and power of the Jews, Israel's conduct in the present is conceptualized as devious and contemptible (see chapter 6).

The phrase *harassment campaign* is combined in many texts with the stereotype of the CRITICISM TABOO, as in the following e-mail from a self-styled "devout Catholic and good person":

> (46) A few have tried, and [. . .] been subjected to a veritable onslaught of harassment, like the late politician Möllemann, who certainly did not always do the right thing but found the courage to speak out! Or are we condemned to silence? [ZJD_27.07.2006_Stu_001]

A statement like this one also implicitly fends off charges that the author is antisemitic, or it denies and minimizes any hostility toward Jews that others might impute to him. With particular frequency any expressions of solidarity with Israel voiced by the Central Council are characterized as "*insolent propaganda*," "*harassment*," and "*shamelessness*," and categorized as criminal:

> (47) If I have to hear 'yet another' press release, I'm going to spend the next few years putting my X on the line for the NPD [German Nationalist Party]. Whether they win won't matter to me. So there, and now I wish you lots more fun with harassing the German people. [ZJD_30.07.2006_Ren_001]

The writer's threat to vote for a right-wing-extremist party, whose antisemitic positions are widely known, if the Central Council does not change its posture implies that a causal connection exists between the behavior of Jews and antisemitism.

Conclusion

Analysis of the texts reveals the extent to which current linguistic usage harks back in form and content to Nazi ideology and how "coming to terms with the past" figures in discourse hostile toward Jews. When words, phrases, and sentences from Nazi era antisemitic writings and speeches occur, this usage usually goes hand in hand with verbalization of anti-Jewish thinking. Therefore, the reproduction of elements of Nazi language generally also goes hand in hand with the coding of anti-Jewish stereotypes. What manifests itself here is thus not unconscious recourse to stock phrases stored in the memory that are activated quickly because they are so well known. Rather, the use of this particular ideological vocabulary expresses an attitude hostile toward Jews. While right-wing-extremist authors express concepts of racist and exterminatory antisemitism almost identical to the Nazis', thereby demonstrating how a particular worldview and a certain linguistic usage are intertwined in right-wing extremism, mainstream authors eschew the expression of overt racist antisemitism while transferring their antisemitism to Israel. As in the case of the articulation of stereotypes, the texts convey very similar arguments relating to past and present. Authors from the mainstream, however, tend to project both traditional and newer postwar stereotypes of hostility toward Jews onto Israel.

The cognitive and emotional effects of the Nazi regime, and the resulting programmatic efforts to come to terms with the past, leave their mark in anti-Jewish language no matter what the correspondent's political, social, and ideological persuasion. Yet clear group-specific differences can be discerned: right-wing extremists invoke conceptual categories and patterns of degradation almost identical to those of the Nazis in form and content. They do not differentiate between Jews and Israelis. Denial of the Holocaust, for decades a characteristic feature of arguments put forward by right-wing extremists and neo-Nazis, now seldom occurs. Instead these writers express regret that the Nazis failed to be sufficiently thorough, with the result that there are still Jews on earth. Or the Holocaust is cited for purposes of comparison to defame the Jews living in Israel today: Israel's military operations are presented as no different from the purposeful mass murder carried out by the Nazis.

Both leftist and left-wing-extremist writers use many comparisons to the Nazis in reference to Israel, changing the linguistic patterns of Nazism to fit their own political ideology. Conspiracy-theoretical constructs find expression in extreme anti-Zionism. In resisting admonitions to remember and fending off imputations of guilt, mainstream authors call primarily upon stereotypes expressing classic hostility toward Jews, in combination with clichés from the postwar era. They use the strategy of perpetrator–victim reversal, projected onto Israel through largely implicit comparisons to the Nazis.

A feature shared by all the writers who reproduce Nazi linguistic patterns (identical or modified) can be recognized in the way they resort to Judeophobic conceptualizations and attempt to reduce their responsibility to come to terms with the past by assigning blame to the victims or launching verbal attacks.

6 ANTI-ISRAELISM AS A MODERN VARIANT OF VERBAL ANTISEMITISM
The Modern Conceptualization of the Collective Jew

Why the black answer of hatred to your existence, O Israel?
[Sachs 1961, 100]

Criticism of Israel versus Anti-Israelism: Two Different Speech Acts

Framing the Problem

To antisemites, Israel, the most important symbol of Jewish life and survival, constitutes an immense provocation. For that reason it has been the focus since its founding of (right- and left-wing) extremist defamation campaigns and hatemongering propaganda. But for several years now the public communication space has increasingly witnessed violent verbal attacks on Israel that, regardless of the attackers' political or ideological orientation, exceed the bounds of legitimate criticism, ignore complexities, and bring Judeophobic thinking (sometimes consciously and calculatingly, but sometimes also thoughtlessly and unintentionally) into the midst of society and expand the range of antisemitic ideas that can be expressed without anyone's raising telling objections.[1] For instance, references occur often (also in the mass media) that employ comparisons to Nazism in phrases such as *Nazi methods*, *state-sponsored terror as in the Third Reich*, *racist apartheid state*, and *illegitimate terror regime*. How powerfully such expressions shape public opinion and the collective consciousness can be seen from a variety of surveys that reveal how widespread negative views of the state of Israel have become in the public at large. Thus 65 percent of those surveyed in Germany in 2003 saw Israel as "the greatest danger to world peace" (EC 2003). In January 2007, three out of ten

Germans surveyed by the Bertelsmann Foundation expressed their belief that Israel was "conducting a war of extermination against the Palestinians" and that "what the state of Israel is doing to the Palestinians" was no different from "what the Nazis in the Third Reich did to the Jews" (Bertelsmann 2009). In 2012 a Forsa survey commissioned by *Stern* magazine found that 70 percent of the subjects thought that "Israel pursues its interests without regard for other peoples." Fifty-nine percent considered the country "aggressive," and 13 percent even denied the country's right to exist (Weber 2012). These results clearly show the direct effects of decades-long defamation campaigns directed against Israel, as well as the often one-sided, emotional reporting by the media of the conflict in the Middle East.

A related question has to do with the distinction between legitimate criticism of Israel and anti-Israelism as a current variant of hostility toward Jews. For years this question has arisen in reference to certain events,[2] occasioning vigorous discussion and creating controversy not only among antisemitism researchers but above all in society at large, but it has yet to be answered with sufficient precision or reproducible conclusions. In the twenty-first century, circumlocutions presented as criticism of Israel but actually grounded in antisemitic thinking and aimed at Jews in general have become the dominant verbal form in which Judeophobic ideas are articulated and disseminated.[3] Through language Israel is demonized and pilloried, and in recent years the revival of old Judeophobic stereotypes has established an anti-Israeli caricature. This state of affairs is problematic from a societal point of view primarily because no distinct awareness exists of the risks such language entails, with its capacity for conveying stereotypes and intensifying resentments. But this language also triggers defense mechanisms that block any society-wide critique and rejection of such ideas. Attempts by researchers to call attention to the inflammatory nature of certain forms of communication and patterns of linguistic usage with regard to this topic often encounter an immediate, automatic, and emotional defensive attitude among many Germans. The forms of defensive communication range from statements such as *That is a policy of forcible alignment!* to *They want us all to be muzzled!* And one hears these statements even from representatives of the so-called elite institutions. The absolute refusal by many people to enter into a serious discussion based on facts or at least to admit to doubts about the appropriateness of certain speech acts makes it extremely difficult to conduct any rational debate. Even educated people seem completely oblivious to the maxims "Never again!" and "Beware the slippery slope!" formulated after the Nazi period with reference to the acceptance of stereotypes. These people also seem deaf to the possible negative effects of a rhetoric that constructs drastic images of an adversary; they describe such language as "freedom of expression" (cf. also Bergmann and Heitmeyer 2005b, 229f.) and "simple expression of one's own opinion" to trivialize or even defend it.

In this connection two further questions arise that have come up repeatedly over the past few years (including in the mass media, which often falls short when it comes to engaging in critical reflection and educating the public):[4] first, whether criticism of Israel or of Israeli policies always and per se must be categorized as hostile toward Jews or at least inflammatory and, second, under what conditions a statement critical of Israel is actually only a veiled form of antisemitism. The first question has been asked countless times in the public discussion space and has become superfluous, having been answered long since: of course, criticism (including harsh criticism) of decisions made by representatives of the Israeli government or extreme nationalist groups or of actions by the Israeli military is not necessarily antisemitism; such criticism can play a legitimate role in political debate and problem-oriented communication. Accordingly there is much that can be addressed critically from an internal or external perspective, as with any other country.[5] This happens repeatedly in the German (and Western) mass media, especially in relation to the still unresolved conflict with the Palestinians, and up to now no serious critic of the Israeli settlement policy or military operations has been accused of antisemitism. Such an accusation is justified only in the case of anti-Israel statements that contain antisemitic stereotypes and/or expressions of verbal violence that convey false information[6] and/or have the potential to create an atmosphere hostile toward Jews. Yet the cliché persists stubbornly, almost obsessively, in the face of a far different reality and all factual refutation, that criticism of Israel is taboo in Germany because of the Nazi past (this stereotype was discussed in chapter 4). The assertion that criticism is taboo also makes use of a traditional Judeophobic cliché that has existed since the nineteenth century and rests on the notion that a Jewish-dominated press sets the tone in Germany. Its articulation supports the position, dictated by conspiracy theories, of the speakers, who accordingly present themselves as defenders of free expression (cf. the variants of "What must be said" in chapter 4, as well as chapter 10, under Strategies of Legitimation and Self-Aggrandizement and Strategies of Justification).

> (1) with no other state would that be necessary, but if one criticizes israel in germany one pretty much has to add: I'm no antisemite, no right-wing radical, yes, among my acquaintances I have jews and am an admirer of the european jews but since in israel the cynical equation has developed that criticism of israel = antisemitism, it will probably make little impression on you. now to the topic at hand: i view israel's treatment of the palestinians with dismay and disgust. [IBD_11.07.2006_Sch_001]

The fact that, on the contrary, no country in the world receives such disproportionately frequent and harsh criticism as Israel (cf., e.g., Behrens 2003; Jäger et al. 2003; Schapira and Hafner (2010) is ignored in messages such as (1) or denied.[7] What is striking and significant in this connection is that the alleged political correctness is always ascribed exclusively to persons whose statements must be categorized not as critical of Israel but as verbally antisemitic. That brings us to the second question mentioned earlier concerning the distinction between speech acts that can be defined as criticism of Israel and those that express anti-Israelism.[8] Despite all the doubts and negative considerations raised to date in the public discussion, a clear distinction can be made here: the two communicative phenomena can be precisely differentiated by means of scientific cognitive and linguistic criteria. Denial of the possibility of making such distinctions merely reveals antisemites' fear that they might be prevented from publicly articulating Judeophobia. The more arguments and facts research turns up to reveal the antisemitic dimension of anti-Israelism, the greater and more obstinate is the resistance on the part of self-declared Israel critics. Even unmistakable verbal expressions of antisemitism are declared to be "anti-antisemitic." At the same time, politicians and journalists often defend persons who find themselves accused of antisemitism, arguing that they are "just being critical" or merely "expressed themselves clumsily." These skewed interpretations and trivializations arise in part from a lack of knowledge when it comes to the traditional and current verbal forms through which antisemitism expresses itself and in part from underestimation of the damage that the rhetoric of demonization can cause.

Decisive for this discussion is not the fact that criticism is voiced but the way in which this criticism is justified and the language in which it is formulated. When Israel serves as the surface onto which antisemitic resentments are projected and traditional anti-Jewish stereotypes and arguments are deployed to discredit the state of Israel in general, when its Jewish citizens are collectively demonized and Israel's right to exist as a Jewish state is called into question, that is not criticism of Israel but verbal antisemitism taking the form of anti-Israelism. Different types of Judeophobic verbalizations, explicit and implicit, can be distinguished; we will now examine their formal and semantic characteristics.

Criticism of Israel as a Communicative Act

It is helpful to begin by establishing what kind of communicative act criticism is, what function criticism fulfills, and on what conditions it rests. A person who criticizes is offering a judgment on behavior and/or actions. Criticism entails a negative assessment. The critic must believe that the person being criticized is not aware of any inadequacy (for otherwise the communicative act would be superfluous) and that the thing criticized can be improved or eliminated in the future (otherwise the speech act would be meaningless; cf. absurd and irrational criticism such as *#I criticize you for being mortal* or *#I criticize you for having been born*).[9] The speaker must also possess sufficient knowledge to be convinced that the thing or situation being criticized actually exists (for otherwise the criticism amounts to pure speculation, libel, or a lie). The speech act we call criticizing functions, on the one hand, to assert the truth of what is said (which makes criticizing representative) and, on the other, to influence the recipient in such a way that he or she will recognize the aspect evaluated as negative and will undertake to change it (which makes criticizing also a directive with appellative function). The critic intends to alert the addressee to a problem and to persuade the addressee to change his or her thinking or to adopt a different course of action. To achieve these goals, the critic must convey reproducible judgments that can be supported by arguments and related to facts and have the power to persuade the recipient of the validity of the criticism. Criticism differs markedly from other communicative acts such as cursing, insulting, disparaging, libeling, and making discriminatory comments, all of which have in common that they attack the honor of the addressee, impair his or her dignity, and/or demean his or her person altogether (see chapter 9). Accordingly, a speech act such as *I am* *criticizing the fact that a revolting creature like you exists* cannot be categorized as criticism; rather, it is a (drastic) personal insult that impugns the recipient's honor. If one subsumes criticism under the persuasive speech acts, intended to influence the addressee, one condition for its potential success is that the negative assessment (as well as its alternative) be presented to the addressee as reproducible, factually grounded, and capable of being acted upon (cf. Schwarz-Friesel et al. 2012). That makes criticism a communicative act that conveys value judgments in a fashion that is based on reality and oriented toward establishing truth and solving problems, the point being to suggest (the possibility) of change in the interest of improving a state of affairs.

That criticism in this precise sense can also be employed in political crisis situations, and that, of course, not every criticism of the state of Israel is antisemitic per se, can best be demonstrated by specific texts. Although in the e-mails and letters to the Central Council and the Embassy Judeophobic messages and those hostile toward Israel predominate, messages that in both form and content can be categorized as verbally antisemitic, the corpus also contains texts that simply articulate criticism or concern without engaging in antisemitic argumentation or making radical, destructive suggestions and without resorting to inflammatory Nazi vocabulary and pejorative lexemes. Drawing on two such texts from the corpus, we will demonstrate the conditions under which a message can be assigned to the category of "criticism of Israel."

When criticism pertains to individual political, military, or social subjects (such as the building of settlements, procedures at border checkpoints, deployment of objectionable weapons, or the influence of the Orthodox on civil institutions), such criticism represents legitimate exercise of freedom of speech and articulation of a sense of responsibility. Such criticism appears in (2), an e-mail from a couple from Bad Driburg:

> (2) this morning my wife and I heard on West German Radio 5 about the use of 4 million cluster bombs during the Lebanon conflict by your country during the past year. It became clear that they are still injuring people and will continue to do so for an indeterminate time. We are amazed and disturbed that Israel is refusing to give the drop coordinates to the mine clearers working there. We implore your Excellency to use your influence to urge your government to release the information. [IBD_14.08.2007_Rie_001]

In (2) a specific situation (the deployment of cluster bombs) provides the occasion for the writers' articulating a critical position and formulating an appeal to the ambassador, as Israel's representative in Germany. Nothing in this e-mail is either explicitly or implicitly hostile toward Jews or anti-Israeli. The negative judgment ("*that they are still injuring people and will continue to do so for an indeterminate time*") focuses on facts, has ethical underpinnings, and can be reproduced cognitively and emotionally. The criticism was sent to the Israeli Embassy as the official representative of the country of Israel; the message does not question the right of Israel to exist or to defend itself. By announcing their position by means of the adjectives "*amazed*" and "*disturbed*," the authors reveal that they do not conceptualize ISRAEL AS AN AGGRESSOR. On the sentence and textual level, the message contains no verbal expressions that would point to such a conception or would lead one to suspect a collective negative evaluation and/or demonization of Israel. The message displays coherence and is free of contradictions; the occasion for writing and the content are consistent with one another, and the argument is clearly and logically constructed. The information that occasions the criticism appears in conjunction with a clear designation of the source (the radio broadcast). The facts provide the basis for the criticism of Israel's behavior, and a directive speech act transmits the request that the ambassador contribute to ameliorating a circumstance that merits criticism.

In other e-mails to the Embassy, the construction of settlements and targeted killings, among other things, are characterized as "*counterproductive for the peace process*," as "*disturbing*," or "*harmful to coexistence*." Critics conscious of how problematic it is, in view of the Nazi past, for Germans to dispense advice to Jewish Israelis use so-called hedges, expressions such as *of course I am not sure whether* or *somehow* or *you can certainly judge better than I, yet . . .* (cf. example [3]).[10]

Messages that do not concentrate on only one aspect but speak critically of the Israeli government's general role in the Middle East conflict are likewise not necessarily antisemitic:

> (3) It is very hard for people here in Germany to interpret the situation in the Middle East accurately, especially since the reporting is one-sided and portrays things in a false light because they are taken out of context. Please allow me nonetheless to express a few thoughts on the aforementioned

> conflict. [. . .] The conditions of life in Israel must call for particular measures; and it is possible that I cannot possibly imagine how difficult and unsafe life in your country is. Even so, I cannot support Israel's policies. And I beg you to intercede with your government to find an alternative to war and to continue the peace talks or pursue them more vigorously and enter into discussions with the autonomous authority in the Gaza Strip. I thank you for giving my comments your attention. [IBD_01.09.2006_Die_001]

Although the author of this message, a woman from Frankfurt, apparently considers the Israeli government, not the Palestinian Authority, primarily responsible for the hostilities in the Middle East conflict and in so doing assumes a one-sided perspective, she refrains from verbal aggression and/or extreme assignation of blame and generalized discreditation. Her message does not rest on any Judeophobic stereotypes. In a spirit of self-criticism and one critical of the media, she also makes a point of mentioning her lack of knowledge based on personal experience, and thereby acknowledges that as a critic she has a limited view and capacity for judgment.[11]

Criticism of Israel's policies in (2) and (3) clearly focuses on problem solving. We see no traces of an antisemitic or anti-Israel attitude. Nor do the authors stress that they are not antisemitic. Such strategies of denial are adopted almost exclusively by writers who communicate antisemitic notions.[12] Aware of the inflammatory power of their own utterances, such writers hasten to counteract the reproach they anticipate. That the authors of (2) and (3) address their messages only to the Embassy, and not, as many others do, (also) to the Central Council, is likewise an important indicator: only correspondents who conceptually conflate Jewish and Israeli concerns and impute collective blame and responsibility to all Jews when it comes to the Middle East conflict send messages critical of Israel to the Central Council as well. These two messages also address the Israeli ambassador in his actual function and make a specific request without resorting to personally demeaning or discriminatory comments. Observance of the linguistic conventions of courtesy further demonstrates a desire to preserve a form of communication based on social acceptance of all parties and intended to further cooperation.[13]

In contrast, the bulk of the messages come from authors who may characterize themselves as critical of Israel and anti-antisemitic but in fact express antisemitic thinking. The methodology of cognitive linguistics can uncover the specific features of such utterances and thereby clearly distinguish patterns of usage critical of Israel from those that are antisemitic.[14]

Anti-Israelism as an "Ism" and Verbal Expression of Violence

A number of studies have already been conducted on antisemitic utterances cloaked as criticism of Israel.[15] These studies have identified characteristics (without undertaking detailed analyses) that are typical of anti-Israeli antisemitism. Most frequently mentioned are the three Ds (see, e.g., Neugebauer 2003; Markovits 2004; Rensmann 2004, 88f.; Pfahl-Traughber 2007a): demonization (semantic devaluation), delegitimization (denying Israel's right to exist), and double standard (applying a special standard to Israel). These keywords, however, are semantically fairly vague and must be concretized in order that sharp, reproducible, and comprehensible distinctions can be made. Thus the European Monitoring Center on Racism and Xenophobia (EUMC) has established the five following indicators that can be used to determine when criticism of Israel is antisemitic (on these indicators, cf. EUMC 2004, 229; Gessler 2004, 10, 15; Bunzl 2005, 278; Heyder et al. 2005, 146f.; Kloke 2005, 22; Schapira and Hafner 2006):

1. When Israel's right to exist and/or its right to defend itself is denied
2. When a double standard is applied to Israel, by contrast with other countries
3. When antisemitic stock phrases, symbols, or images are used in reference to Israel or Israelis
4. When Israeli policies or Israelis are equated with Nazism or persons from the Nazi period
5. When Jews worldwide are held responsible for Israel's policies

This catalog, as we shall show, must be expanded and rendered more precise. The listing of criteria does not make clear the extent to which a specific criterion or several indicators must be present for an utterance or a text to be classified as antisemitic; nor does it stipulate whether the indicators have reciprocal effects or are interdependent, or whether it makes a difference how explicitly or implicitly indicators manifest themselves.[16] Missing above all are concrete examples to illustrate how and in what variations antisemitism is or can be expressed as anti-Israelism. The following examples demonstrate how important answering these questions and examining a wide range of specific manifestations can be.

> (4) The state's criminal actions on stolen land—Israhell—will be punished, of that you Jewish swine can be sure. [. . .] Do you really believe that your concentration camp in Gaza has not already been recognized as such? You swine will hang, burn, be gassed, and that according to the strict law of nations. To guarantee freedom in the world, the Jew must disappear. You make us sick to our stomachs! Especially when you think you can preach to us about morality and human rights. Your U.S. Jews have destroyed the world financial system. It's high time Buchenwald, Auschwitz, and Dachau were reopened to take care of the stinking remains of you people. We have no fear of any laws or dumb Jewish propaganda. A Jewish graveyard is just good enough to serve as a garbage dump. We don't want you in Europe anymore! Get lost or go gas yourselves! [ZJD_Gaza2009_300/816_Mon_001]

The Gaza crisis served as a pretext for sending this Judeophobic e-mail, dripping with hate, to the Central Council of Jews in Germany. Israelis are explicitly equated with Jews (and Jews with Israel) by means of direct address and reference, and they are collectively dehumanized, insulted, and threatened in traditional Judeophobic stock phrases. Numerous racist stereotypes are deployed in rapid succession to dehumanize and demonize Jews and Israelis semantically (e.g., Jews as animals, Israel as hell), along with images of the adversary inspired by conspiracy theories (destructive domination of world finance, exploitation of power over the media, assignment to foreign groups, etc.). Various comparisons to Nazis are made; Israel is delegitimized as a state; its founding is called contrary to international law; and it is excluded from the company of nations as an embodiment of evil, and thereby consigned to damnation. Negative collective attributions and monocausal assignments of guilt that distort reality are coupled with fantasies based on conspiracy theories. What becomes visible is a conceptually and emotionally closed antisemitic view of the world.

Example (5), on the other hand, can be categorized as antisemitic on the basis of a single indicator: the old antisemitic stereotype of the BLOOD CULT (namely that their religion compels Jews to drink blood) is explicitly applied to Israel:[17]

(5) What's the story with the Israeli fascists and murderers running around loose who not only have "blood on their hands" but nourish themselves from human blood [. . .] [IBD_28.06.2007_Ard_001]

As we have already shown in conjunction with verbalizations of current Judeophobic stereotypes, there also exist considerably more subtle forms of expression that cannot always be identified as antisemitic at first glance. In example (6) an indicator of antisemitism is present; it takes the form of application of the classic antisemitic stereotype JEWS ARE DISTURBERS OF THE PEACE to Israel, but it can be discovered only by means of an implicature:

(6) Israelis are disturbers of the peace. [. . .] You should have learned from history and not rely on the assumption that Israelis are allowed to do whatever they please [IBD_07.05.2006_Dro_001]

The formulation "You should have learned from history" carries an implicit allusion to the Holocaust that equates Israelis with Jews. This implicit equation, activated by general knowledge, in turn gives rise to a second pejorative judgment that attributes to Jews a particular degree of alleged moral failure (implicature: 'Anyone who suffered in the Holocaust should now behave decently and peacefully'). Finally, the statement presented as factual, that "*Israelis are allowed to do whatever they please*," implicitly communicates the existence and exploitation of a Jewish exceptional status, likewise a traditional Judeophobic stereotype.[18]

Example (7) portrays denial of an Israeli nation-state's right to exist as politically justified without displaying further indicators of antisemitism. The author, a PhD, manifests an anti-Zionist attitude. His anti-Zionism (which, from a historical perspective, can be characterized as a skeptical and defensive attitude toward the Jewish national movement) shows itself in his strict refusal to accept the idea of a Jewish national state:

(7) Dear Ambassador Stein: The best solution for a lasting peace in the Middle East is the dissolution of the state of Israel [. . .] [IBD_23.03.2007_Hof_001]

In this connection it is important to remember that anti-Zionism, which one finds represented especially among leftists and left-wing extremists, nowadays takes only the form of denying that Jews have a right to the nation-state already in existence (see Kloke 1994, 19). This attitude goes far beyond merely theoretical rejection of the political idea of Zionism, since this anti-Zionist position has the practical consequence of calling for abolition of the Jewish state. Thus contemporary anti-Zionism reveals itself as an expression of the anti-Jewish concept generated by intolerance and hostility, a concept that does not accept Jewish existence and collectively denies Jews their right to exist. The demand that Israel as the Jewish state be dissolved thereby fits into the spectrum of various "proposals for solution of the Jewish problem" that have been put forward over the centuries (see chapter 9, under Suggestions for Solving the "Jewish Problem").

> Contemporary anti-Zionism, which rejects or delegitimizes the existence of the Jewish state, functions to a great extent "as a ticket for the traditional hostility toward Jews, and its ultima ratio is the annihilation of Israel" (Weiss 2005). [Rensmann and Schoeps 2008, 17]

As described earlier, honest criticism of Israel presents a pattern of argumentation based on rational principles and socially accepted values. It aims for truthfulness and purposefulness and observes the conventions of linguistic propriety. By contrast, anti-Israelism represents aggressive behavior based on irreal Judeophobic images, as well as irrational wishes and aims.[19] This aggressive behavior finds expression in statements that can only be characterized as verbal violence; altogether it manifests an absolute refusal of respect and denial of the right to exist, as we find explicitly articulated in (8) and implicitly in (9):

> (8) Are Jews really human? In light of the crimes in Gaza and Lebanon, one can answer this question only with a decisive No. Maybe we should try using the Jewish books on you again! We know what's in them—racist rubbish, yet you yourselves are the filthiest racists. Off to the gas chambers! Heil Zion! [ZJD_Gaza2009_677/816_Pan_001]
>
> (9) Israel is a historical mistake. A solution must be found. [ZJD_2009_Gaza_87/816_Her_001]

Despite all the variations, underlying the verbal aggressions against Israel is a hostile attitude engendered by powerful repulsion and mental stereotypes. This attitude represents an extreme form of bias.[20] In the minds of those who harbor such a bias, the classification and evaluation of people, situations, and processes is therefore already mentally completed, without reference to what actually takes place in the world. Bias interferes with a realistic assessment of extralinguistic events and results in blanket prejudgments as well as one-sided assignment of blame. Anti-Israelism, like every other "ism," has no empirical basis, and thus does not correspond to existing structures. It functions as an interpretive schema for those who embrace it. Israel is seen as bad, evil, and degenerate, and accordingly its existence is felt to be a provocation and annoyance, or a threat.

(10) We are outraged at Israel's political aggression. This state is a great danger to world peace. [IBD_22.03.2004_Sch_001]

(11) Get lost! Remove yourselves from the world, you lowdown murderers! [IBD_04.07_2006_Postcard]

(12) you jews are a stain on the map of the world. [IBD_16.07.2006_Man_001]

The "anti" in anti-Israelism indicates a totally negative evaluation. The "ism" indicates that everything categorized as Israeli is by definition collectively and with overgeneralization determined by the "anti." Onto the complexity and heterogeneity of the external world is imposed a rigid, conceptually impervious pattern of orientation and categorization that leaves no room for alternative points of view. The individual makes his or her own perspective absolute, with the result that any cognitive or communicative sharing or exchange of opinions with the Other, already dismissed as inferior because it is considered morally degenerate, is categorically rejected. Whereas legitimate and serious criticism offers options for improvement without excluding the object of the criticism,[21] anti-Israelism aims only to stigmatize and ultimately to radically alter or dissolve the Jewish state.

Characteristics of Antisemitic Anti-Israelism

Derealization: False Statements, Concealment, Distortion, Biased Perspective

As a result of the mental and emotional prejudice against Israel, the processes of perception, consciousness, and classification in those with such an orientation are strictly limited or confined to a single interpretation. In this sense persons with an anti-Israel attitude succumb to a distorted view of reality that expresses itself communicatively in verbal patterns that generate a mismatch between language and the real world.[22] The referentializations—that is, the linguistic representations of extralinguistic situations—that these persons produce display specific markers of incongruence (such as collective attributions of blame, blanket negative categorizations, hyperbolic exaggerations, monoperspectivizations, and skewed analogies). These can be assigned semantically and conceptually to the previously mentioned phenomena of demonization, delegitimation, and application of a double standard. The three Ds thus turn out to be a direct consequence of the derealized position and to a great extent build on each other or mutually support each other in pseudo-rational "argumentation."

As we explained in chapter 2, language not only portrays reality; it can also produce, by way of semantic structures, realities that do not necessarily bear any resemblance to what actually exists. Verbal derealization involves the relationship between language and the world. Derealizing linguistic utterances do not portray reality as it is (and can be intersubjectively experienced), but rather constitute, on the basis of their semantic contents, the language generators' own subjective realities. In this case, the representational function of language, which depends largely on the criterion of truth (and the possibility of testing a thing's truth value), is instrumentalized by the language generators to verbalize aspects of the world as they view them. The following examples show how language can draw a distorted image of Israel:

> (13) It's a crying shame what your country feels it can get away with! The figures are out of proportion: 1 Israel-eye for 500 others. One war and genocide for a couple of abducted Israelis. Cluster bombs dropped on residential districts. One war crime after the other. Don't tell me I'm a neo-Nazi. I'm a humanist. The real fascists (Nazis) rule in Israel. [IBD_31.07.2006_Pop_001]
>
> (14) Israel is a bloodthirsty, brutal, and aggressive apartheid state. [IBD_06_05_2009_Kre_001]

Since derealizations are formulated as representative speech acts,[23] however, the claim to truthfulness remains intact, a reflection of the closed nature of the speaker's belief system (see the discussion of strategies of justification and legitimation in chapter 10).

In the thousands of e-mails and letters received by the Central Council and the Embassy, but also publicly all over the Internet (see Schwarz-Friesel 2013a), so many derealizing claims are made about Israel—all portraying the Jewish state and its citizens as aggressors, sometimes citing grotesque conspiracy theories—that we must confine ourselves here to discussing several representative and particularly frequent types.

Because some readers of this book may have become habituated to a number of the derealizing linguistic usages applied to Israel in the public communication space, we would like to introduce here a reading experiment that can serve to disrupt possible effects of that habituation and illustrate by analogy the phenomenon of derealization with particular clarity:

> (15) With disgust and dismay we have learned from the press that the German GSG9 [Border Protection Group 9 of the German Federal Police] has again, in SS style, used disproportionate force against decent young people of upstanding character who are merely engaged in a desperate struggle for freedom in the face of Germany's state-sponsored terror. Allegedly it was a question of a 'counterterrorism operation.' The German Federal Republic is a fascist criminal regime that in the spirit of the primitive Germanic tribes brutalizes and willfully destroys those who think differently, and, just as under Hitler, behaves with appalling aggression toward its European neighbors. Its racist and incredibly self-serving economic policy is a disgrace to the entire civilized world, but perfectly reflects the thinking of this cruel nation of evildoers. What Germans are doing at present to the poor, unfortunate Greeks is infuriating and threatens world peace! Germany should be dissolved as quickly as possible and placed under UN mandate. For our part, we plan to boycott all products from Germany from now on. P.S. We really do not hate Germany, but our conscience will not allow us to remain silent in the face of the crimes being committed by this illegitimate state.

This text, which we constructed specifically for illustrative purposes,[24] offers an image of Germany that can immediately be recognized as false, distorted, hyperbolic, and irreal. That Israel has been the target for years of just such derealizing representations and charges is not, however, consciously reflected on and acknowledged.[25] The distorted image of Israel created through language is already widely accepted.

Typical of the derealized image of Israel is the portrayal of the country as the sole aggressor in the Middle East conflict:

> (16) It's absolutely clear to me that Israel's policy of using force will fan increasing hatred in the Arab states, and that Israel will never find peace. But that's something Israel, and Israel alone, must own and take responsibility for. There, I've finally got that off my chest; it had to be said at some point! [ZJD_08.08.2006_Kre_001]

In the interest of maintaining this one-sided image of Israel as the aggressor, elaborate claims are constructed on the basis of false statements. The falsification of facts can entail reversals, omissions, or twisted information. The linguistic structures create the image of an enemy called ISRAEL that does not correspond to reality yet perfectly fits the Judeophobic view of the world and thus fulfills the function assigned to it (see chapter 8).

A reversal based on falsification of history would involve, for instance, the claim that Israel from the outset actively launched wars against its Arab neighbors and bears the sole responsibility for the unstable situation in the Middle East (the aggressive role is attributed collectively to the "Jewish mentality"):

> (17) Even you must be aware,that Israel is a very aggresive state. You certainly know how many wars the Jewish state has started. [ZJD_Gaza2009_61/816_Sch_001]
>
> (18) From the beginning your state was born a monster, deceitfully imposed on the Arabs by certain powers. You should all see yourselves as guests in the region and cultivate normal relations with your neighbors. Obviously your mentality makes that impossible. [IBD_16.07.2006_ano_011]

The omission of information, on the other hand, reinforces the argument that Israeli behavior toward the "*defenseless and peaceable Palestinians*" (to the Embassy in 2006) is purely arbitrary (which supports the variant 'Israelis are by nature stubbornly mean and degenerate'):

> (19) You harass the poor P. without reason and hold them captive behind walls. Yuck! [IBD_10.03.2001_Lar_001]

What these messages fail to mention is that Israel has had to take measures to protect its civilian population from terrorist attacks. Nor is there any recognition that rocket attacks by the Israeli military on Hamas targets constitute responses or counterattacks to rockets fired at Israeli territory (cf. also example [37]). "*Groundless*," "*intentional*," and "*completely disproportionate*" are terms these writers consistently use to describe all actions by the Israeli military that result in deaths, even when they obviously occurred in dire situations.

If aggressive moves on the part of the Palestinians are mentioned at all, they are either relativized, in a manner that distorts the reality, and/or justified: terrorists are transformed into "*children and youths*," rockets become "*rubber bullets*," "*rocks*," or "*blanks*." Bombings become "*desperate defensive acts*" or "*legitimate freedom struggles*":

> (20) The army of the murderous, torturing, landgrabbing state of Israel has once more proved victorious over rock-throwing Palestinian children and youths. [IBD_28.03.2004_Wul_001, Letter]
>
> (21) What you Jews have done in the Gaza strip today is no more and no less than brutal murder. People fired a few blanks over the border, and you zoom in with jet fighters and copters, commit murder, and swoop away. You're beasts. I will do everything to incite my fellow human beings against Israel. [ZJD_27.12.2008_ano_001]

Military actions by Israel are allegedly "*massacres of the defenseless*," "*war on civilians*," "*bloody deeds*," "*murderous bloodshed*," "*ethnic cleansing*," and "*state-sponsored terrorism*." Other terms include "*merciless atrocities*," "*irresponsible inhumanity*," and "*unacceptable brutality*." The lexical permutations all support a comprehensive negative assessment of Israel.

One semantic principle pervades the verbal derealization of Israel, regardless of the writer's political orientation or level of education: the violence and concomitant danger brought to the conflict by the non-Israeli parties are minimized while the aggression and culpability on the Israeli side are maximized:

> (22) I completely understand why Hamas—Hisbollah—Jihad—Fatah defend themselves against Israel's ceaseless terrorism. They are the terrorists ,they steal and occupy land they constantly discriminate against Arabs, not the other way round.Why don't you ask yourselves why Israel has been constantly involved in conflict, in wars persecution expulsion for 4000 years. [IBD_20.07.2006_Die_001]
>
> (23) Hello from Munich, it's high time that Israel dismantles the atom

> bombs Israel has pointing at Iran and other peaceful nations, before Israel makes demands on Iran for example and wants to forbid it to produce atomic energy. [IBD_30.10.2007_ano_001]

The aggressive behavior imputed to Israel and labeled genuinely Israeli is often substantiated pseudo-causally and in racist fashion by reference to characteristics that have been attributed to Jews collectively for centuries; the stereotype of the ETERNAL JEW is thereby activated:

> (24) You Jews just can't leave well enough alone. You should focus on your own atrocities. ... Your state is an abomination, as you know yourselves. You need to fix your relationship with your neighbors. But then you see yourselves as the chosen people. [IBD_12.06.2006_ano_001]
>
> (25) Jews! Dropping phosphorus bombs on civilians. MURDERERS! Is there any more despicable people than you? [IBD_27.10.2006_ano_001]

Implicit racist argumentation turns up even in messages from self-described humanists and peace activists when they identify Israelis in terms of their Jewishness and insinuate that the individual suffering of Jews during the Holocaust must have been passed on as collective experience to Israelis and should have made them particularly sensitive to violence and injustice. The fact that they do not show such sensitivity makes them even more despicable in the eyes of the (mostly educated) correspondents.

> (26) [. . .] that the Holocaust was often only a means to an end—to this day. How would it be possible otherwise that Jews of all people can inflict so much suffering on other innocent people. [ZJD_30.07.2006_Ans_001]

Due to the suffering endured by the Jewish people, the state of Israel is asked to meet expectations imposed on no other country (see the double standard):

> (27) Unbelivable, such cruelty—and that with your history, too! [IBD_25.4.2010_Erl_001]

Israel and its entire Jewish population are reduced one-sidedly to the infliction of military force. In addition, a homogeneous conceptualization is established according to which there is no distinction between the government and the people:

(28) I hereby challenge you to apologize publicly for the following verifiable crimes committed by what I see as your still cowardly and bloodthirsty Israeli soldiers and what I see as your still cowardly and bloodthirsty Israeli population against the Palestinian population in the period from 1967 to the present [. . .] [IBD_07.01.2011_Urb_001]]

Even among educated writers the derealized perception of Israel turns up, characterized by a one-sided view of the Middle East conflict. These writers charge Israel with perpetrating state-sponsored terrorism against the Palestinians and thereby failing to live up to democratic or social/ethical standards:

(29) Anyone with even a shred of education knows that the current violent acts against the Palestinian people are NOT acts of self-defense. Israel is committing crimes against humanity. Its goal is annihilation, erasure, and extirpation. Israel is waging the Holocaust against the residents of Palestine. Obviously Israel does not belong to the circle of enlightened humanistic peoples but has remained stuck culturally and spiritually/morally in a barbarous condition. [ZJD_Gaza2009_552_Mer_001]

(30) I despise everyone in your congregation who supports the Israeli terror in Palestine. What you (and by that I mean the Israeli people participating in democratic elections) are doing is at least as reprehensible as the Holocaust. I despise everyone who under these circumstances demands even a single monument to the victims of the Holocaust. [ZJD_01.09.2006_Sal_001]

In these messages one repeatedly finds conflation and equating of Jewish and Israeli concerns, as in (30) and (31):

(31) so long as you fail to grasp that your terror [. . .] can never achieve a meeting of the minds, you will be despised by humanistically oriented people, and rightfully so. [ZJD_Gaza2009_27/816_Stü_001]

According to the *pars pro toto* principle, the entire state of Israel is seen through the lens of its military activities.[26] Negative characteristics receive the sole focus and are employed to define the Jewish state and its population. This limited perspective and the resulting narrow concept of ISRAEL then makes possible a mental transference that supports a conceptual elaboration: Israel, the "aggressive illegitimate state," comes to symbolize what it means to be Jewish. The conceptualization of the COLLECTIVE JEW ISRAEL then provides the basis for identifying and evaluating all Jews. Accordingly, the accusatory and blame-assigning messages are addressed to the Central Council in Germany.

Decontextualization and the Analogy to Apartheid The term *apartheid state* shows that the use of a single lexeme can give rise to a specific derealizing conceptualization:

(32) At issue here is a brutal, racist apartheid state. [ZJD_27.10.2006_Kna_001]

Writers often characterize Israel as an *apartheid state*, *apartheid regime*, or (with semantic overdetermination) a *racist apartheid state*, and we find such usage among many educated authors and politicians, who should know what the term actually signifies.

Apartheid refers to the state-imposed, institutionalized racial separation practiced in South Africa; the policy imposed legal and social disadvantages on certain ethnic groups. If Israel were de facto an apartheid state, harsh international criticism would be not only justified but necessary. But Israel is as little an apartheid state as the Federal Republic of Germany. Non-Jewish citizens, whether Arab Christians, Druze, or Muslims, enjoy the very same rights and educational, developmental, and advancement opportunities as Jewish citizens.[27] Accordingly, Arab Israelis are represented in all sectors of society, as business people, doctors, police officers, soldiers, lawyers, and parliamentary deputies. Nonetheless, referring to Israel as an apartheid regime creates a false analogy to the former South Africa, ruled by an unjust government.[28] The word *apartheid* is ripped out of its historical context and decontextualized. Decontextualization in linguistics means separating a word or phrase from its original context and transplanting (recontextualizing) it into an entirely different setting. In the process, the original meaning undergoes a semantic contraction or expansion or a thorough transformation (e.g., through processes of marker transfer). *Apartheid* as applied to Israel functions as a doubly stigmatizing term: for one thing, it libels the democratic state, and for another, it portrays Israel's security policy in a pejoratively distorting light. Many also apply the concept of *apartheid* to the measures Israel has had to adopt after excessive terrorist attacks within its borders to secure those borders and stiffen controls affecting non-citizen Palestinians. This policy, which in any other country would be viewed and accepted as legitimate self-defense and counterterrorism measures,[29] is interpreted in the case of Israel as "state-sponsored terrorism," "racism," and "arbitrary action."

> (33) Through brutal exercise of power you have turned Palestine into a prison, because you apply ruthlessly the right of the mighty. [IBD_02.05.2008_Zu_001]

The fact that all Palestinians, including those who are not radical and who desire peace, have to suffer from the security walls and the sometimes drastic border-control procedures gave rise by way of decontextualization to conceptual expansion and referential overgeneralization;[30] features of the border policy were applied to the state of Israel as a whole, giving rise to the stereotype OPPRESSIVE AND ILLEGITIMATE STATE. This concept in turn was applied out of context, and now the term *illegitimate state* is used to defame Israel. The power of words resides in part in their capacity to activate specific mental images that can exert a powerful emotional effect. The word *apartheid* creates a scenario in a person's consciousness (in analogy to the former South Africa) in which certain people suffer disadvantages and exclusion as citizens. From this conceptualization many deduce an inhumane "Jewish ethos." The result is activation of the traditional stereotype of Jews as a united community that acts only out of self-interest and feels no empathy for others. Judaism thus comes to be equated with Israel's Middle East policy.

> (34) But unfortunately a Jewish life is valued by you far above an Arab one. [ZJD_31.07.2006_Omi_001]

Since such discrimination is disapproved of and rejected by civilized and modern states as obsolete and inhumane, the attribution *apartheid* stigmatizes Israel as a backward *illegitimate state* that does not belong among the modern community of nations. In constructions in which this word occurs, many equivalent semantic lexemes, such as *primitive*, *inhumane*, *uncivilized*, *racist*, *brutal*, *bloodthirsty*, *murderous*, and especially often *Old-Testament-style*, are employed to intensify this (Judeophobic) conceptualization.

(35) By now it exceeds everything one can expect of civilized people. This is no longer self-defense; it is bloodthirsty, Old-Testament-style vengeance [. . .] [ZJD_18.04.2002_Eck_001]

In this connection one finds especially often total moral condemnation: Israel is a disgrace to the civilized world and should be ashamed of itself:[31]

(36) Israel is a disgrace to the entire world! [IBD_01_09_2006_ano_001]

(37) You should be ashamed to belong to a terrorist state that liquidates its opponents and the innocent with rocket attacks. [IBD_22.03.2004_Kis_001]

The apartheid argument, invented and communicated for purposes of defamation by those who hate Jews and Israel, has gained broad currency, even in the social mainstream, where it can develop its persuasive potential.[32] The "*apartheid state of Israel*," a derealizing and stigmatizing imaginary construct, has become common parlance whose truth value no one questions or examines anymore. Nazi comparisons in reference to Israel and/or Jews represent a further form of extreme decontextualization. In the next chapter we will describe this form of derealizing defamation as a specific variant of demonization.

Approximately as frequent as its portrayal as an apartheid state is Israel's characterization as a terrorist state that has allegedly shown great brutality in waging war on its Arab neighbors ever since its founding and bears all the blame in the conflict with the Palestinians. This interpretation assigns to Israel the role of provocateur and disturber of the peace not only in the Middle East but in the rest of the world.

(38) And now ships headed to Lebanon are being provoked. Perhaps the Iranian president has the right idea after all when he wants to drive you out of the region. [IBD_25.10.2006_ano_001]

(39) Stop terrorizing the entire world. It's high time you stopped playing the role of eternal victims and faced up to your own crimes.You illegally occupy areas promised to others, conduct active, brutal, and disproportionate wars of aggression, think you have a right to do all this, and don't realize you're completely isolating yourselves on the one hand and

on the other causing a practically insoluble conflict with states that were previously well disposed toward you. [. . .] Israel is causing a rift in the world again. [ZJD_31.07.2006_Wol_001]

By way of the mental process of elaboration already described, which rests on the concept of the COLLECTIVE JEW, the role of global terrorists is assigned to the Central Council of the Jews in Germany.

Extreme derealizations manifest themselves not only in the thinking of extremists on the right and left but also in that of (highly educated) correspondents from the social and political center. The semantics of denigration, arising from omission, distortion, and falsification of information, characterizes the language of all antisemites who argue against Israel (even when they declare themselves to be anti-antisemites). Example (40), an e-mail from a social scientist with a PhD, denigrates Israel by means of demonization, calling the country a "monster armed to the teeth," and refers to the Old Testament as an atavistic document rooted in a morally obsolete and degenerate Judaism:

(40) That is very shameful for the state of Israel, which is not strong enough for any real peace but instead acts like a monster armed to the teeth, to which everything else and all others don't matter. Hatred sows hatred, and today's Israel is stuck in the bloody muck of the Old Testament. I fear for its future. [IBD_01.06.2010_Göl_001]

But while derealizing linguistic patterns are found primarily among extremists who indulge in crude insults and invective as well as explicit expressions of Judeophobic stereotypes, educated enemies of Israel tend to communicate their distaste through implicatures cloaked as moral appeals, advice, and admonitions. The writers thereby assume a paternalistic attitude toward Israelis (and Jews) (see chapter 9, under Suggestions for Solving the "Jewish Problem"). A typical example of this sort of implicit condemnation is the much-used stock phrase *disproportionate force*, which implies that there is no compelling reason for the deployment of the Israeli military.[33] The writers thus arrogate to themselves, despite being at a distance of more than four thousand kilometers from the crisis area that they claim to be judging in strategic terms, a position as omniscient observers and experts. If there is no plausible reason for the use of force, the most obvious implication would be that the Israeli army uses force because that is what it is accustomed to doing, because it considers excessive military strikes necessary even when no provocation exists, and/or because it is by nature prone to violence. These assumptions yield possible variations with distinct potential for antisemitic associations and effects. Phrases like *systematic annihilation*, *brutal treatment*, and *war on the civilian population* imply that Israel's (military) posture is needlessly destructive on purpose and could be easily altered if only goodwill were present. The dominant word field in characterizations of Israeli military operations, especially in the Lebanon and Gaza deployments of 2006 and 2009, has at its core the semantic feature of 'not appropriate to the circumstances.' Accordingly, along with the word *disproportionate*, the messages contain above all lexemes such as *inappropriate*, *exaggerated*, *excessive*, *unjustified*, *unjust*, *unfair*, and *indecent*, as well as *murderous*, *ruthless*, *brutal*, *barbarous*, and *merciless*. Military operations tend to be referred to as *murderous* (*acts*). The second dominant semantic field in the e-mails has to do with the theme of victims. Along with *victim* (often paired with *of Israeli force*), lexemes such as *sufferers*, *innocents*, and *bystanders* are used to point out and emphasize the alleged disproportionality of Israel's military policy.[34] The conceptual fields of MURDER, DISPROPORTIONALITY, and CIVILIANS/INNOCENTS are thus situated in an argumentative relationship to one another.

The typical criteria for antisemitic utterances—demonization, delegitimation, and double standard (as a unique measure of assessment)—and the resulting arguments can now be designated, against the background of the preceding analysis, as specific forms of derealization. All three rest on a Judeophobic conceptualization that consists of a distorted image of Israel, and their aim is to devalue Israel as a Jewish state. Therefore, they usually occur in combination, linked semantically and conceptually by pseudo-causal relations.

Tools of Demonization: "*Israel is the devil!*"

For two thousand years Judeophobia has found expression in the demonization of Jews (see chapter 3). In its current guise, anti-Israelism, Israel has become the focus of this devaluative process. Judeophobic demonization represents a process of extreme exclusion and segregation of Jews by means of irrational negative judgments. The objects of this demonization are viewed as the personification of evil or as the quintessential evil in the world that afflicts human beings, frightens them, threatens them, and/or harms them:

(41) a totally awful people, that's what they are. Israel is the devil. sorry, but that's how it is. [ZJD_Gaza2009_60/816_Ste_001]

(42) The Israelis are and remain, no matter what a show they put on, the greatest racists, war criminals, warmongers, murderers, child-murderers, violators of international law, torturers, robbers and thieves, Nazis, liars, terrorists, nothing and no one can convince me otherwise.[35] And that won't happen in the future either because the Israelis never change. In other words they are and remain lying swine. ...the world hates them. [IBD_04.12.2007_Dro_001]

According to this perspective, the iniquity ascribed to the Jews emanates solely from their innate character or nature; they are seen as innately and unalterably bad. The concept of the ETERNAL JEW is projected onto Israel, as in examples (50), (56), and (57) and in the following e-mail from a family in Berlin:

(43) With disgust and profound contempt we are following in the media Israel's massacre in Gaza and Lebanon. The flimsy rationales for the massive attacks on civilian targets are more than pathetic. If one looks back through the centuries, it was always Israel that took land away from others, destroyed cities, and leveled villages. [. . .] In the entire world the Jews have lost respect and trust. [ZJD_30.07.2006_Ans_001]

That which is demonized is always located outside of the social values and ethical norms that provide the basis for the (positive) self-assessment of the in-group (cf. Befu 1999, 22f.):

(44) You are beasts, devils, monsters! [ZJD_27.12.2008_ano_003]

(45) And we will be against Israel until Israel has returned to the path of humankind. [IBD_08.07.2011_Wac_001]

The use of contrast and absolute devaluation makes it possible to condemn the persons or things that are demonized as (presumed) destroyers of the community and to negate their right to exist:

(46) Hello you Jewish swine dripping with blood! I challenge Israel's right to exist and the Jewish pestilence's right to live. [IBD_26.04.2009_Kru_001]

(47) The Jew state of Israel resembles right now a stinking boil that must be lanced. [IBD_10.08.2006_Mue_001]

The salient verbal indicators of demonization are the use of pejorative lexemes that usually dehumanize the object referred to; of negative hyperboles and metaphors; and of analogies with the Nazis.[36]

Pejorative Terminology and Dehumanization That the use of pejorative lexemes like *swine*, *butchers*, *criminals*, *murderers*, *monsters*, and *terrorists* has a long tradition as a feature of verbal hostility toward Jews has already been demonstrated by reference to various aggressive speech acts directed against Jews in the past and present (see chapter 9).

(48) You're showing yet again that Israelis are swine. They break the cease-fire to provoke the Lebanese and Hisbollah so they can go on slaughtering people. [IBD_20.08.2006_Dro_001]

(49) The state of Israel is behaving in Gaza like a nation of swine. [ZJD_09.01.2009_Wol_001]

Anti-Israelism often involves a reference to membership in a group; terms like *Jewish swine* and *Jewish criminals* reveal that the speech act aims to defame not only Israel but all Jews. Explicit semantic devices show that the insults and threats express hostility toward Jews collectively. But the notion of group membership can also be conveyed implicitly, as in (50):

(50) You Israeli butchers, for 2000 years you've brought nothing but violence and war into the world. [IBD_30.3.2006_Sur_001]

Here the history of the Jewish people is cited as "evidence" of the degeneracy of the Israelis, invoking a homogeneous category of JEWS. In (51) the Jewish people and Israelis are conflated:

(51) It seems the Jews have learned nothing from history, and are now doing the same thing they reproach us germans for (3rd Reich) to the Palestinians, harassing, bombarding, punishing them with water shortages, and so on. [IBD_05.06.2009_Jou_001]

Dehumanizing descriptors are the most common form that collective negation takes: Israel and its citizens are described as *a pestilent ulcer*, *filth*, *devil's handiwork*, *monster*, *thalidomide freak*, and so on.

(52) You're nothing more than human garbage. [IBD_20.02.2009_Wei_001]

(53) Disgusting Israeli rabble, [. . .] you rat pack. [IBD_05.05.2007_Kol_001]

Dehumanization always entails demonization as well, for denying a person human qualities constitutes an extreme form of devaluation. Demonization, however, does not necessarily include dehumanization. People can be excluded, as particularly bad or degenerate, from the community of values without being labeled NOT HUMAN:

(54) You Israelis are all just pathetic, disgusting victim wannabes!!! You behave inhumanly and cruelly to aid ships.....you mercilessly kill Innocent people [. . .] [IBD_01.06.2010_Rei_001]

Every verbal demonization semantically performs an extreme negative evaluation and exclusion. It involves a bilateral conceptualization—a Manichaean worldview—that distinguishes sharply between good and evil, a process in which the concept of the TOTAL OTHER plays a decisive part.

Judeophobic fantasies are projected onto Israel as the "collective Jew." The messages contain several references to the Israelis ("*Jewish butchers in Palestine*") as "*bloodthirsty*" (IBD_22.07.2006_Ble_002); in this metaphor one can discern an updated application of the traditional BLOOD-CULT stereotype to Israel. Numerous other ancient stereotypes (JEWS AS LIARS, as WILY SWINDLERS, as EXPLOITERS AND PESTS) are projected onto the modern state (see the examples in chapter 3). Political discreditation for the most part occurs through imputation of character traits alleged to be typically Jewish:

(55) Your current provocations [. . .] have only one purpose. And this purpose shows your base character and your deceitful nature. [IBD_3.10.2006_ano_001]

The mental image of the COLLECTIVE JEW ISRAEL is explicitly articulated by means of generic references, either singular or plural (see also chapter 5):[37]

(56) But what is the 'Jew' doing now to the Palestinians? [...] didn't the 'Jew' learn anything from the past? [ZJD_Gaza2009_271/816_ano_001]

(57) Here's one in the kisser for you, you filthy Jew. You're to blame for the misery in the world! [IBD_19.08.2008_Bau_001]

While in (56) and (57) the conceptualization of a homogeneous being, Jewish in nature, is activated by means of the typifying singular, the same thing takes place in (58) and (59) through a plural reference, which can be rendered personal or more formal by the mode of address:

(58) The Jews in Israel are behaving with unimaginable brutality. [ZJD_24.07.09_Har_002]

(59) You filthy Jews and GANGS OF MURDERERS. [IBD_05.08.2010_ano_001]

Both forms result in a semantic reduction to the categorical version 'typical of Jews.'

That Israeli concerns and actions are categorized as Jewish can also be seen from the conceptual conflation of *Jews* and *Israelis*, as in (60); the assignment of Israeli citizenship, as in (61); as well as the preference for addressing messages to the Central Council when the author wishes to object to Israel's policies.

(60) Alls that should be real familiar to you Israelis. [ZJD_18.02.2006_Bri_001]

(61) [...] genocide, which your government and the heads of your religion are committing in Gaza [...] [ZJD_Gaza2009_14/816_ano_001]

Using hyperbole, the authors describe Israel's activities as "*the most terrible massacres*," the "*most awful atrocities*," the "*greatest injustices*" and emphasize the uniqueness of the viciousness they attribute to the "*state of criminals and injustice*" and to the moral degeneracy of its citizens:

(62) You're absolutely the basest thing God could do to humanity. [IBD_22.07.2006_ano_007]

These writers prefer to characterize Israel itself with hyperbolic expressions and metaphors, thus stigmatizing it as the essence of evil:

(63) Israel is the greatest evil that humanity has ever produced. It's high time Iran developed its atomic bomb, something Israel has had for a long time, to deployment readiness and that Israel, that hydra-headed monster, at long last disapeared from the face of the earth, once and for all, never to be seen again! [IBD_03.06.2010_Spe_001]

(64) Israel, the only racist apartheid regime in the world, is the sole danger to world peace. [IBD_06.05.2009_Hai_002]

Underlying the metaphorical construct in (65) is the conceptual notion of ISRAEL AS A BOIL (see also example [47], which uses the same metaphor):

(65) Israel is the boil in the Middle East! [ZJD_Gaza2009_87/816_May_001]

These images characterize Israel as a 'malignant, disgusting growth.' One can conclude that the author of (65) would like to cast doubt on Israel's right to exist, since boils are customarily eliminated by means of an appropriate medical treatment or even excised operatively.

Some authors know no bounds when it comes to demonizing exaggeration. In such instances, the extreme irrationality that accompanies any kind of derealization becomes evident:

(66) To situate Israel there was the greatest mistake of modern times, even including the First and Second World War! [ZJD_Gaza2009_498/816_May_001]

(67) Israel [...] Worse than the Holocaust, if in fact that even happened. [ZJD_Gaza2009_153/816_Rie_001]

Right–Left–Center Despite all the homogeneity that exists, regardless of political orientation and disagreements, when it comes to demonizing semantics and discrediting argumentation, a quantitative and qualitative difference can be discerned in anti-Israeli messages: right-leaning and right-wing-extremist writers leave no doubt when they name their "enemies" that they mean not only the Israelis but all Jews. Hardly one of their messages fails to describe Israelis as *Jews* or *Jewish*.[38] Leftist and left-wing-extremist authors by contrast prefer to use the lexeme *Zionists* (to make clear that they oppose the idea of a Jewish national state), often in combination with the adjective *fascist*. Mainstream writers, who represent themselves as honorable anti-antisemites and wish to avoid displaying a Judeophobic attitude, for the most part use the lexeme *Israelis*, thus refraining from making a direct connection with religion. Yet they implicitly encode numerous Judeophobic stereotypes and address their messages more often to the Central Council than to the Embassy. Additionally, these writers usually include an explicit demand that the Central Council do more for the peace process and that it criticize Israel:

(68) Speak unmistakably and dissociate yourselves from this senseless murdering. [ZJD_Gaza2009_582/816_Bac_001]

Or they express implicitly, through moral appeals, the reproach that the Jews in Germany display a lack of moral insight (see also the examples in chapter 4):

(69) What is called for is the courage to be truthful and show some genuine human emotions. [ZJD_29.12.2006_Glo_002]

Such appeals assign responsibility collectively, not only to the Israelis but also to the German Jews, for the conflict in the region and suggest that the latter could influence the choices made by the Israeli government.[39] The writers then offer concrete suggestions for solving the Middle East conflict not only to the Embassy but also to the Central Council:

(70) It's time you finally started acting like a religious community and put into practice the supreme principle of all religions: peace! [ZJD_01.09.2006_Haf_001]

(71) It's time to make peace and give back the land you took seized illegally. [ZJD_13.04.2007_ano_001]

Many of the messages convey a polarized view of Germans and Jews: German Jews are segregated (according to the well-known tradition) and characterized as a monolithic uncritical group loyal to and operating out of solidarity with Israel, not Germany (see especially examples [13], [18], and [25] in chapter 4).

The conflict in the Middle East furnishes the occasion to activate long-held resentments and to assert their legitimacy.[40]

(72) Hatred and contempt for all Jews in the world is sure to result. [IBD_23.07.06_Hud_001, Postcard]

(73) The only real reason for the war waged by the apartheid regime in Israel against the Palestinian civilian population is the Israeli racists' lust for murder. [ZJD_Gaza2009_32/816_Hai_001]

(74) The Jewish question must be solved. [IBD_18.01.2009_ano_001]

It is clear that the Middle East conflict serves as a catalyst for anti-Israeli and antisemitic sentiments. If one looks at the long history of hostility toward Jews, one can see that over time various crises and conflicts have played a role in intensifying these sentiments. If the Middle East conflict were resolved peacefully, other reasons for blaming Israel would likely be constructed, such as responsibility for environmental catastrophes, global warming, and the risks of global nuclear proliferation.

The author of (75), a student, sees the Israeli army's use of cluster bombs as confirmation of the degeneracy of all Jews and deduces from that the "causal necessity" of the Holocaust:

(75) I am deeply shaken to read today that the Israeli army, after the war, dropped cluster bombs on southern Lebanon. In the past few weeks I have come to understand Hitler why he wanted to exterminate the Jews! From today on the Jews are my enemies, too, the best thing is for you to get out of Germany first. Such war criminals are not welcome here. [ZJD_01.09.2006_Sch_002]

This writer invokes the past, while commenting on the current Middle East conflict, to come up with a traditional Judeophobic explanation for the crimes of the Nazis, and he combines past and present to justify his personal hatred of Jews. A similar form of argumentation can be found in (76):

(76) You have all shown your true face at last ! Now I can understand A.H. For you are no better. [IBD_01.06.2010_ano_042]

The author of (76) finds in the actions of the Israelis a reason for rejecting responsibility for the crimes Germans committed against the Jews and to dissociate himself from Germany's culture of memorialization. This strategy of reversing victim and perpetrator, which enables the writer to deny guilt and exonerate himself, turns up in numerous e-mails.

(77) Someone who after 57 years of peace and freedom in our country continues to poke around looking for bad things he can pin on us would be

more than well advised to see to it that order and peace are restored in his own country. [ZJD_07.06.2002_Bre_001]

(78) As long as the Israeli people (or part of it) lets Scharon go on pursuing his bulldozer/butcher policies, I never want to hear accusing speeches about the Holocaust again, including that architecturally super-hideous monument. [IBD_19.07.2006_Sch_003]

Even educated correspondents who use arguments of this sort fail to realize that the analogy in these examples that places Israel's military strikes on the same level as the mass murder of European Jews results in a derealizing minimization of the Holocaust.

"You Jewish Nazis": Nazi Comparisons as a Demonization Technique By means of comparisons to the Nazis, irreal contrasts are established that are intended to magnify to the utmost the verbal characterization of Israelis' use of force. These comparisons constitute absolute perpetrator–victim oppositions.

(79) Today the defenseless and blameless Palestinians are the victims of the Nazi-Jews! [IBD_15.03.2007, Postcard]

Nearly all the correspondents use Nazi comparisons (demonizing Jews and Israelis and minimizing the Holocaust) in a variety of formal and semantic variations (see also Schwarz-Friesel 2007, 195–199; Eitz and Stötzel 2009).

Representatives of the Israeli government are compared to Nazis or equated with them:

(80) The Israeli government speaks like the Nazis, acts like the Nazis—they are the Nazis of the 21st century. [IBD_02.05_L_001, Postcard]

(81) The murderous gang under the Star of David would do the SS under the swastika proud. A prime minister Olmert and a female foreign minister with the mentality of a concentration-camp guard reject any ceasefire. [ZJD_01.08.2006_ano_009]

All Israeli citizens are reviled as Nazis and charged with employing Nazi methods; they are accused of having a (Jewish) Nazi mentality:

(82) YOU NAZIS AND CONCENTRATION CAMP GUARDS OF THE PALESTINIANS. FILTHY JEWS!!! [IBD_14.05.2010_ano_001]

(83) You're the new Nazis, killing and provoking that you know how to do! [IBD_25.10.2006_ano_002]

Even when making comparisons to Nazis, some of the writers see fit to escalate the invective further:

(84) You're even worse than the Nazis! [IBD_16.01.2009_Mar_002]

Either the entire state of Israel is directly equated with the Nazi regime or the names of well-known Nazi criminals are cited in order to construct an analogy (see chapter 5):

(85) Israel = Nazi state ; Nasrallahgrad. [ZJD_19.10.2006_Bor_001]

(86) We put Hitler behind us—unfortunately not Israel yet. [IBD_18.07.2006_Sta_001]

(87) Adolf Hitler would have been thrilled by his fascist comrades in Israel! [ZJD_25.07.2006_Wag_001]

(88) The expropriation and extermination of the Palestinians couldn't have been planned and executed more effectively and contemptuously by Eichmann & Co. [IBD_05.07.2006_Pue_001]

But German Jews, as whose representatives the members of the Central Council are primarily seen, are also described as Nazis—because the violence in the Middle East is ascribed collectively to them. Thus a publicist from Munich, a member of the party known as Die Linke, comments:

(89) So: quit perpetrating targeted genocide, you're the spitting image of the criminals of Auschwitz and Buchenwald. [ZJD_Gaza2009_776/816_Sch_001]

The policy toward the Palestinians is described as "*Israeli Holocaust*" or "*genocide.*"

(90) Now you're engaging in the Holocaust!!! [IBD_04.08.2006_Pun_001]

The analogy to the Nazi period appears implicitly, in the form of statements and questions, in e-mails from two university-educated correspondents from Halle and Berlin:

(91) Here terrible memories are awakened for us Germans. [IBD_07.04.2007_Lie_001][41]

(92) Doesn't that remind you of the terrible time in Germany when you yourselves were the victims? [ZJD_18.02.2006_Bri_001]

Jews appear in this reversal as a perpetrator people. Along with their discrediting function, these inappropriate comparisons always serve to impute guilt as well (as described earlier).

Targeting, Unique Standard, and Delegitimation

When examining anti-Israelism, one cannot avoid a question that goes beyond the kind of text-oriented analysis one undertakes in cognitive linguistics: Why would a small democratic country be labeled the source of all evil in the world? It is a country with a critical press, an independent judicial system, a freely elected government, and a multicultural population, a country in which women enjoy equal rights, and all opportunities in society are open to them. It is a country that treats homosexuals tolerantly and affirmingly, a country that makes corrupt and criminal politicians answer in court for their misdeeds. Why not countries in which women are oppressed, humiliated, and stoned, and homosexuals are killed; countries in which criticism is brutally suppressed; countries in which elections are manipulated or not allowed at all, that regularly test weapons of mass destruction to intimidate their neighbors, while the population goes hungry, that allow criminal and corrupt politicians to have their way, while critics of the regime are threatened, incarcerated, abused, or killed, that make children into soldiers and allow women to be gang-raped? Why is Israel the only country on earth for which an "ism" has been developed (no anti-Chinaism, no anti-Koreaism, no anti-Sudanism) that has assumed massive proportions? Why is a distinction made between the government and the people for all other countries, while Israel is discredited as an entire country for the actions of a few individuals? Why does no other country in the world find its right to exist challenged?

In comparison with other regions embroiled in crises and conflict, Israel finds itself subjected quantitatively as well as qualitatively to criticism characterized to a striking degree by extreme emotionality. No topic occasions such overwhelming hatred, rage, and indignation as debates and controversies involving the Israeli–Palestinian Middle East conflict. In no other situation do people feel so great a need to propose "solutions," dispense "good advice," and impose "sanctions." If, however, there can be no doubt that violence, human-rights violations, and conflict are markedly more prominent in other countries than in Israel, another reason must exist for the excessive condemnation and prejudice inflicted on Israel. Our analyses suggest the explanation that Israel is Jewish, and Jews have been victims of massive campaigns of defamation for millennia, and still are.

All modern antisemites focus squarely on Israel, as the Jewish state. As a result of this singling-out, a unique form of targeting and evaluation occurs. Persons with an anti-Israel attitude direct their attention and criticism solely and with particular ferociousness toward Israel, not toward other crises and conflicts in the world that would certainly merit criticism. The hyperbole discussed previously is symptomatic of this unique perspective:

> (93) Your country is [. . .] by far the worst evil in the world [. . .] [IBD_25.10.2006_Sch_002]

The Middle East conflict is viewed as the most significant regional crisis, with absolute priority in world politics, posing a particular danger to the rest of humankind. Other regional or global conflicts are either ignored or not subjected to the same degree of criticism. Scholars refer to this phenomenon as a double standard:[42] Israel is judged by different criteria, measured by another standard.[43] When it comes to Israel, what would count in the case of any other country as legitimate self-defense, as the struggle against terrorism, or as unavoidable collateral damage in a state of war is viewed as "proof" of the country's "cruelty and nefariousness." Accordingly, the Israeli army is accused of intentionally targeting civilians in its operations:

> (94) Dropping bombs with that kind of explosive power in the middle of a densely settled city has absolutely nothing to do with legitimate self-defense. Civilian victims are being consciously targeted. ... This state of Israel is a disgrace to the entire civilized world and to all who still have a teeny-tiny spark of decency. AND I AM NO ANTISEMITE! [ZJD_Gaza2009_330/816_Gün_001]

Every actual or putative mistake on the part of Israel comes in for immediate identification and dramatic derealization, every use of force is interpreted as particularly despicable and willfully evil. Thus military actions undertaken in the interest of self-defense become "cold-blooded murders":

> (95) Your government's brutal measures against the women peace activists in the Gaza solidarity fleet fill me with horror. It shocks me that your country, which portrays itself as civilized, would capsize these ships in a way that violates international law and cold-bloodedly murder people on board. It shakes me to the core that people have to die because they are want to bring help to the population of Gaza and give them hope. [IBD_02.06.2010_Rat_001]

Things are expected of Israel, some of them impossible to fulfill, that are expected of no other country on earth (e.g., the demand that Israel renounce self-defense). The "particular responsibility" consists for many primarily in the demand that Israel accept the violence perpetrated against its own people:

> (96) The solution would be [. . .] withdrawing the army. That would certainly be followed by suicide attacks. But then the crucial thing would be not to retaliate. [ZJD_10.04.2002_Kut_001]

Even though, viewed objectively, the military activities, armaments buildups, and violations of human rights in many (dictatorial) countries are far more serious than in democratic Israel (and would thus far more deserve the attention of "peace activists and humanists"), all the attention is focused on Israel.

> (97) I protest [. . .] against the continued and intentional flouting of human rights and the numerous violations of UN resolutions that the state of Israel [. . .] commits in Palestine and intends to continue to commit. [IBD_29.03.2004_Sta_001]

This unique targeting and evaluation results directly from the derealizing demonization: Israel becomes something like the "Jew among the states in the world" (see also Grigat 2009), and accordingly the object of precisely the same mechanisms of discrimination and defamation that Jews have known for hundreds of years. Just as Jews in the eyes of antisemites constitute the quintessence of evil, Israel is the worst of all states per se, regardless of what it does or does not do (see example [93] for a representative expression of this mechanism).

(98) The founding of the state of Israel is the greatest mistake human beings ever made. [IBD_03.03.2008_Moe_001]

(99) The 3rd World War will probably be started by Israel. [IBD_02.06.2010_Bra_001]

We see the different standard at work when, as in (100), (101), and (102), e-mails from university-educated correspondents present the explicit or implicit argument that "the state of Holocaust victims," of all countries, must not become a "perpetrator" itself.

(100) the Jewish people has had much to endure and to suffer in the last decades and centuries.Expulsion, terror, defamation, genocide. So wouldn't it make sense for precisely the Jewish people to become role models and inspirations to others in neighborly love, goodness generosity and tolerance? [ZJD_07.04.2002_Pek_001]

(101) After your own terrible experiences actually inconceivable. [IBD_30.11.2007_Rat_001]

(102) Isn't it the specific duty of the Israeli people, after all its experiences, to use methods other than force or killing to coexist with its neighbors? [IBD_17.07.2006_Ley_001]

Up to now history has not shown that the experience of suffering has made an entire people collectively more sensitive and better (or worse) and has handed this effect down to future generations. Nevertheless, this very effect is expected of Israel as something to be taken for granted, on the basis of the homogeneous concept of the COLLECTIVE JEW. Here pseudo-psychological connections are constructed to support the double moral condemnation of Israelis and Jews: 'They are despicable because they use force. And this although their painful history should have educated and purified them. That in turn makes them especially nefarious beings.'

(103) The descendants of the victims become themselves indescribable perpetrators. [ZJD_01.08.2006_Bah_001]

(104) Your declaration of solidarity with the warlike offensive launched by your fellow countrymen in Israel is an expression of scorn for the victims of your bombs in Lebanon. Hasn't your people learned anything from the Second World War? [ZJD_29.07.2006_Boe_001]

The lack of sensitivity toward earlier suffering that the writers perceive must be a result of the inability to learn that they ascribe to the "Jewish people" and of the transfer of this "moral failure" to the state of Israel. This interpretation derives from the assumption that Jews' character remains constant: 'Jews are by nature incorrigibly bad.' The contrasting assumption that 'we Germans have definitely learned from history' lends additional emphasis to this negative evaluation.[44]

Persons with anti-Israeli attitudes often do not stop at personal verbal aggression but seek public attention, try to engage in "convincing others," and accordingly send copies of their messages to the Central Council and the Embassy to journalists, politicians, and/or the federal government, as well as post them on the Internet. They also demand nonverbal actions; in particular they often call for protests and boycotts against Israel, which they characterize as "necessary sanctions":

> (105) Germans, don't buy fruit from Israel. [IBD_10.08.2006_Neu_001]
>
> (106) You are a wretched, wretched country. For the rest of my life I am going to boycott everything that comes from Israel. [IBD_31.07.2006_Sch_2008, Postcard]
>
> (107) I hope Germans will boycott Israel's products and not buy any products from this country until Israel acts sensibly for a change. We plan to do this and have also canceled our vacation trip to Israel. [IBD_14.07.2006_Beh_001]

No mention is made of the fact that such actions against Jews were common during the Nazi period (and were called for in nearly identical words). Nor are the consequences of those measures discussed, or else they are defended as "legitimate." Calls for boycotts appear mostly in messages sent to the Central Council and the Embassy by left-wing self-styled peace activists. The texts contain a prototypical argument that turns up in the same form, down to the smallest linguistic detail, in messages from all mainstream boycott advocates: if anyone criticizes them for their inappropriate suggestions and their petition drives, they complain of being "*maliciously libeled as antisemites*" and inveigh against the political correctness being imposed by means of the "*antisemitism bludgeon*." They stress that they "*have Jewish friends*" and feel "*an affinity for Judaism*," that they "*love Kishon*" and "*go to klezmer concerts*," that they receive "*support from prominent Jewish circles*." They claim to be "*unable to recognize*" the obvious parallels to Nazi antisemitic boycott calls; rather, they insist that their "*conscience does not permit*" them to "*remain silent*."[45]

It is striking that some of the writers highlight a transformation in their view of Israel that "*opened*" their "*eyes*" after they had been indoctrinated for years by the "*forcibly aligned press*" and the "*cowardly self-censorship of official government circles*" (see also examples [178] through [181] in chapter 4). Typical of this phenomenon are (108), an e-mail from a professor from Saxony, and (109), an e-mail from a left-leaning Berliner:

> (108) Up to a few years ago I held the standard German opinion of Israel, but since the wars in Lebanon and Gaza, in which the Israelis behaved with unimaginable cruelty, I have thought a good deal about Israel. I believe many people in Germany are rethinking the situation, and soon the mood will undergo a radical change. [ZJD_24.07.2009_Har_001]
>
> (109) Fortunately every Israeli aggression produces more anti-Zionists especially in Germany and it remains to be hoped that as a result a more critical attitude toward Jews in Germany will generally prevail. [ZJD_15.08.2006_Moe_001]

Some of the writers maintain that the "*taboo subject*" has to "*be discussed,*" the "*facts laid on the table,*" the "*grip of political correctness broken,*" the "*silence ended.*"[46]

A distinct missionary fervor on the part of anti-Israeli activists forms part of their obsessive intolerance: antisemites declare their anti-Israeli statements to be "*freedom of expression*" and demand a right to speak out without constraint. *I demand, I insist, I assert my right*, and the like are phrases that occur often in this context. Yet they deny the same right to people who represent a contrary opinion, calling it "*manipulation*" and a "*hateful anti-German attitude.*" They stridently maintain that they have a monopoly on the truth, rejecting any other point of view:

> (110) That is the reality in Palestine. That is the truth! [ZJD_11.03.2007_Mon_001]

Accordingly many of these writers end their messages to the Central Council and the Embassy with an appeal to these institutions to rethink their "*false consciousness*" and an expression of "*hope for a change in their orientation and values*" [ZJD_01.09.2006_Tef_001].[47]

The authors of these messages reject vehemently and with fierce polemics any counterargument and any factual information:

(111) I refuse to let myself be sent to the antisemitic corner, that is intellectual fascism. [ZJD_04.03.2007_Mar_001]

This attitude is reflected in the e-mails and letters (but also on the Internet); the findings of antisemitism research are dismissed ("*bought and paid for*," "*unscientific*," "*methodologically suspect*," "*commissioned by Jewish donors*," "*bad science*"), as are reports in the mass media that offer a realistic, balanced view of the Middle East conflict ("*not objective*," "*prejudiced*," etc.):[48]

(112) What's up with this antisemitism. The minute someone criticizes the Jews a bit, he's called an anti-Semite. . . . But what's up with the Jews who day in, day out commit crimes against the Palestinian people. . . . Of course one's not allowed to say anything about that. Jews are allowed to do everything they please and the rest of us have to keep our mouths shut, otherwise we're scolded for being antisemites. Man, when I read that kind of thing, I want to throw up. [Response from a reader on the Internet to the expert commission's 2012 report on antisemitism, shortnews-kommentare.de]

Emphatic and emotional comments such as "alarming!" are not, as one might expect, an expression of dismay at right-wing-extremist violence or the disturbing research findings on the proliferation of antisemitism in the mainstream, but rather melodramatic expressions of indignation at the revelation that apparent criticism of Israel is actually antisemitism. All strategies used to defame Jews also come into play when it is a question of discrediting research and researchers: overgeneralization, falsification, decontextualization of research results turn up on the Internet especially, in response to postings and on home pages.

Delegitimation From the unique evaluation or devaluation of Israel stems (following the pseudo-causal logic of antisemites) the veritably obligatory delegitimation of the entire state of Israel. A state that is so abysmally evil and dangerous, so the argument goes, has no right to exist in the civilized world community. When doubt is cast on Israel's right to exist (which often occurs in combination with the demand that this state be dissolved) and when its right to defend itself is denied, what results is delegitimation.

(113) Since the proclamation of a Jewish state 50 years ago, Israel has not yet developed into a tolerant democracy. [. . .] In any case you have lost your right to exist. [ZJD_12.04.2002_Ana_004]

Most of the writers lack any sort of personal, reliable, direct experience; by their own admission they have never been to Israel (which means they have formed their opinions solely on the basis of secondhand information), but they insist on their position as vehemently and emotionally as if they had been victims or had witnessed in person unimaginable brutality on the part of Israel (see chapter 8, under The Emotional Potential of Antisemitic Texts). The felt need and the willingness to believe in Israel's degeneracy, to accept as true any nefariousness ascribed to that country, must be very great indeed. Persons with an anti-Israeli orientation are thus not intent on conflict resolution or mediation but want to see the Jewish state dissolved or radically altered. This attitude can be expressed drastically and crudely, as in the messages from right-wing extremists, who almost always couple their demand for the annihilation of the Jewish state with negation of all Jews' right to exist (see examples [46] and [47]) or in verbally aggressive and demonizing (left-wing-extremist) anti-Zionism, as in (114):

> (114) The establishment of the Zionist entity in Palestine is one of the great crimes in human history, and the Zionist entity does not enjoy the slightest moral right to exist. I at least agree completely and totally with the Iranian president when he says Zionism is a disease and the Zionist entity an illegitimate entity. [IBD_16.07.2006_Tsc_001]

Typical of educated mainstream writers who characterize Israel as an *anachronism*, *anomaly*, or *apartheid state*, on the other hand, is their claim to be offering global "*proposals for a solution*" "*for the good of mankind*," in the "*spirit of justice*," or "*in the interest of world peace*." These solutions often boil down to the suggestion that the Jewish state be dissolved or altered, and some are downright ludicrous:

> (115) The best thing would be moving Israel to German soil. That way penance would have been done for the (German, not the current Israeli) Holocaust, and peace would finally come to the Middle East. [ZJD_Gaza2009_498/816_May_001]

Arguments calculated to delegitimize Israel's existence as a state rely on a series of prior assumptions and pseudo-causal connections (see the relevant examples in the present chapter, under Anti-Israelism as an "Ism" and Verbal Expression of Violence, and Derealization).

Racist delegitimation draws on the enemy image of the ETERNAL JEW (combined with the stereotypes of the EXPLOITERS, PARASITES, and HOMELESS NOMADS):

(116) Only dissolution of the Israeli state can counter the Jews' solidarityand thereby also their highly aggressive tendencies as a united people that ruthlessly indulges its congenital aggression and frustration. The Jews who move away from Israel will then have the possibility of settling elsewhere. In Old Testament times the Jews were already a nomadic people that emigrated at one point to Egypt, at another to Babylon, the latter, by the way, because of moral turpitude, after which they moved back to Israel. [ZJD_30.11.2006_Gel_001]

Moral delegitimation invokes alleged violence perpetrated on Arab states ("*atrocities by the Israeli military leadership*") and the Palestinians ("*uncivilized behavior,*" "*disproportionate force,*" "*state-sponsored terrorism*"):

(117) But I don't accept that Israel's policy makers in the years of its existence have not figured out how to assimilate in a foreign region in such a way that this could have taken place without systematic extermination (especially in most recent times). [ZJD_15.08.2006_Ran_001]

(118) It becomes increasingly clear that Israel is the sole aggressor in the Middle East—it's time to implement a Final Solution to this problem! Israel has already lost its right to exist! [ZJD_15.08.2006_Moe_001]

Historical and political delegitimation involves the assertions that Israel is an illegitimate state (see the comparisons to apartheid) whose founding violated the law of nations and that Israel poses a global threat to world peace ("*as a result of continuing aggressions*") and engages in an imperialist policy of occupation ("*theft of land and unlawful occupation*"):

(119) Today I assert: the founding of the state of Israel [. . .] could not be prevented, given the Nazi atrocities that had just been overcome. But it is indisputable that this founding [. . .] was an action that violated the law of nations. [ZJD_08.11.2007_Wen_001]

(120) [. . .] policy in Israel. [. . .] But this is just as unlawful as apartheid in South Africa in its day, and I assume it will prove equally short-lived. [ZJD_20.12.2009_Has_003]

In many texts the three types of delegitimation merge, and in the process its inseparable connection with demonization becomes visible:

(121) On stolen land a historical monster was begotten, born, and fattened: Israel, the only military "democracy" in the world! [IBD_15.05.2006_Bec_001]

What results is the demand that the state of Israel be strictly controlled or, in the worst case, dissolved (on the various suggestions for "solutions," see chapter 9, under, Suggestions for Solving the "Jewish Problem"). In these demands a position of supposed cognitive, emotional, and moral superiority finds expression, along with the paternalistic notion that Israel needs to be taught a lesson. These proposals are calculated to disempower Israel and deprive it of its right to make its own decisions and determine its own fate.

Delegitimation and withholding of respect also articulate themselves communicatively through the refusal to utter the name of the state thus rejected. While right-wing extremists like to use neologisms like *Israhell* and *USrael*, as well as metaphorical invective such as *Thalidomide State* and *Cripple-Israel*, leftists prefer descriptions such as *occupied territory*, *territory*, and *Zioniststate*, and mainstream authors employ paraphrases like *Holy Land*, *the land of the Palestinians*, and the customary name for the region before the founding of Israel, *Palestine*, in order to indicate linguistically that they do not accept Israel. Since names have an important function in establishing identity and, as symbols, represent the person or country in question (see Bering 2010), the stigmatization of names always takes aim at the very existence of that which is criticized.

"*As I just read in my paper . . .*"—Intertextual Allusions and Verbal Convergences: On the Potential Effects of One-Sided Reports on the Middle East Conflict

With striking frequency the writers refer to reports on the Middle East conflict that they have received from the media:

(122) Mr. Ambassador, I was just listening to the radio, and I ask you: Why are you still surprised that so many people hate the Israelis when these

occupiers humiliate and torment the Palestinians day in, day out and destroy the basis of their lives? [IBD_23.12.2005_Sch_001, Letter]

Such intertextual references to information conveyed by the mass media show that many people use certain crisis reports as a pretext for articulating anti-Israel opinions.[49] Whether and to what extent they have been influenced by these often one-sided reports and commentaries cannot always be established unambiguously through linguistic analysis. One can only guess, given the extremely emotional reactions that move the writers to express their rage and indignation, that the conflict reports in question are those that strive to evoke a strong emotional response. But some of the authors also offer detailed information on their sources:

(123) Friday, 3 April 11PM, German Television 2, Aspects: long report on your war crimes in Gaza. It sends chills down one's spine! You miserable wretches, you war criminals! [ZJD_27.12.2008_ano_001]

Many writers copy entire texts or passages into their e-mails to support and provide cover for their own argumentation. Thus the author of (124) legitimizes his statements with a *Spiegel* news ticker reporting the death of twenty Lebanese civilians. The news ticker is quoted in full without commentary, along with its source in the form of a hyperlink:

(124) [. . .]Why must innocent people also die? ... Killing innocent civilians? that goes too far! If that continues, the state of Israel will be showing itself to be no better than the attackers from Hezbollah!
http://www.spiegel.de/politik/ausland/0,1518,42688,00.html

Israel's air force fires on mini-bus—20 dead

Israel's air force is flying heavy attack missions over Lebanon: in the south of the country 20 people were killed, according to Lebanese security circles. The headquarters of Hezbollah in Beirut was destroyed. Rockets also landed in Israeli Tiberias on the Sea of Galilee. [IBD_15.07.2006_Koh_001]

The author of (125) adds to his anti-Israel e-mail an attachment consisting of five complete anti-Israel quotations along with their sources. He describes these quotations as "food for thought." He thereby indicates that he shares the anti-Israel position of the texts he quotes. The quotations are intended to provide factual support for the author's hostile statements:

(125) Sinceourfederalpresidentregardlessofallfacts,includingUNfindings supports the criminal zionist waging of war, the reputation of our German people is suffering considerable damage internationally. [. . .] Appendix: A different kind of food for thought!" [The five anti-Israel texts that follow are taken from the Internet sites www.medico.de and www.kommunisten-online.de, and texts identified as "Shoot First, Ask Later (*Junge Welt*) by Rüdiger Göbel" and "White Phosphorus: Is Gaza a Testing Ground for Experimental Weapons? by Jonathan Cook 14 January 2009—ZNet."] [IBD_16.01.2009_ano_001]

As factual legitimation for his accusation, "*You are the real terrorists*," the author of (126) quotes in full a German Press Agency report, which he introduces by writing "*as the following report clearly proves*":

(126) Dear Ladies and Gentlemen, You are the real terrorists, as the following report clearly proves. [. . .] Tel Aviv (dpa)—Israeli soldiers have shocked the public with statements about random shooting of civilians and wanton destruction during the most recent Gaza war. [IBD_19.03.2009_See_001]

But in most cases the authors do not quote the reports in full but only the passages they consider relevant, or only the parts that support their own position; what we have are thus partial and often decontextualized quotations. Whether the often-mentioned change of heart is or was actually (and exclusively) caused by reports in the media, as the author of (127) claims, we cannot ascertain:

(127) [. . .] the terrible shots of your violence on television. [. . .] You should be ashamed; to me—once a friend of Israel—this country is dead. [IBD_05.02.2009_Kel_001]

For some years now scholars (and journalists) have been studying the extent to which trends in the German media's reporting have contributed significantly to creating an emotionally and cognitively distorted image of Israel and helping to promote antisemitic thinking (see, e.g., Dichanz and Breidenbach 2001; Faber 2002; Jäger and Jäger 2002; Behrens 2003; Sahm 2006; Langenbucher and Yasin 2009; Schapira and Hafner 2010; Schwarz-Friesel 2013b; Beyer 2013; see also Beyer's exhaustive study [2015]). A comparative analysis of texts in our e-mail corpus and texts from the media has shown that in these two discursive types one can find numerous convergences in the way conceptualizations hostile toward Israel are expressed (see Beyer and Leuschner 2010). For instance, the frequency with which the lexeme *disproportionate* appears in the corpus obviously reflects the powerful influence that media reporting has had on the authors. In the English-speaking realm, Kalb and Saivetz (2007, 49–52) have already called attention to the way the reproach of disproportionality dominates the discussion:[50]

> There appears to be little doubt that the media everywhere emphasized the theme of "disproportionality" from the opening day of the conflict, as though nothing else measured up to it in importance. [Kalb and Saivetz 2007, 49]

As a representative example of the proliferation of clichés that can result from careless use of language by the mass media, let us look at excerpts from a talk show titled "Tough but Fair: Bloody Ruins in Gaza—How Far Does Our Solidarity with Israel Go?" Broadcast on 21 January 2009, the show focused on the Middle East conflict. The reporter, Ulrich Kienzle, first equated Israelis with Jews, obscuring the necessary differentiation and ascribing to them an unwillingness to seek peace. He reinforced this cliché by speaking to Michael Friedman, a German citizen, as if he were to blame for the situation, thereby invoking the classic Judeophobic stereotype of GERMAN JEWS AS NON-GERMAN or AS ISRAELIS.

> (128) Kienzle: Unfortunately it's true: we really have to go back to the conflict. Its origin was very simple. The Israelis or the Jews, or whatever we want to call them, drove out the Palestinians. [. . .] It's a matter of the source of the conflict in 1947, and at the time they were driven out and you [to Friedman] won't let them come back.

The sources of the Middle East conflict were thus distorted historically and portrayed monocausally, with responsibility for the conflict assigned one-sidedly. Instead of checking himself when Friedman pointed out that he was a German citizen, Kienzle merely reiterated his cliché-ridden argument, even more emphatically. Rather than admit his mistake, he forged ahead, "but sometimes you sound like an Israeli propagandist." When Friedman pointed out the absurdity of this reproach, as well as of the previous one, the journalist persisted in pressing the widespread Judeophobic interpretation: "*Now you're bringing out the old antisemitism bludgeon.*"

The persuasive, opinion-molding, and opinion-guiding potential of linguistic structures and their capacity for creating prejudices and reinforcing resentments are ignored or minimized in such statements, perhaps also deemed acceptable for populist journalistic purposes. Employing Israel-hating and derealizing patterns of verbal usage, such utterances activate and reactivate traditional stereotypes for Judeophobic discourse, even in the public communication space of society as a whole.[51] "The turn . . . toward evident events, publicly visible through the media, opens the door to the political mainstream" (Bergmann and Heitmeyer 2005b, 234; see also Schwarz-Friesel 2009b).

For years now, many media treatments of the Middle East conflict have presented extreme contrasts and polarizing portrayals of Palestinians and Israelis, calculated to awaken intense emotions; the Palestinians are often pictured as weak, subjugated, suffering, and helpless. Idyllic landscape descriptions predominate. By way of contrast, the Israelis, almost exclusively represented by members of the armed forces or the National Religious Party (Mafdal), appear as superior and strong, and as a high-tech power with absolute control. Lexemic analyses reveal that in the portrayal of the Israelis the verbs *control*, *destroy*, *attack*, *dispatch*, *order*, and *confiscate* figure prominently, while descriptions of the Palestinians stress verbs such as *suffer*, *dream*, *endure expulsion*, and *die*.[52] Nouns connected with the Palestinians derive particularly from the word fields for *family*, *fields*, and *farmers*, and emotion-laden adjectives are *sad*, *powerless*, *enraged*, *intolerable*, *hopeless*, and *weak*.

When the Palestinians' misery and despair are emphasized but not the Israelis' sorrow and fear, when army operations are portrayed as arbitrary, without mention of the reasons for them, and comprehensive perpetrator–victim structures are created, when Israel appears as an overwhelmingly powerful aggressor, what results is a one-sided image with high emotional potential that can evoke intense reactions when coupled with anti-Israel evaluations (see Schwarz-Friesel 2007, 222–230).[53] The possible effects of such reporting manifest themselves in utterances like (129), (130), and (131), as well as in the responses to the surveys of Germans' views on Israel cited earlier:

(129) To my surprise I must recognize that I have experienced a change of heart, from being a friend of the Jews to being an adversary. I cannot

be assigned to the brown mob but rather belong to the liberal part of our German population, and this state of affairs is what distresses me most. A few weeks ago I couldn't have imagined undergoing such a change. The pictures of all the innocent children, old folks, and sick people killed by the Israeli military have contributed to this change. [ZJD_01.08.2006_Wei_001]

(130) Re: The Spiegel 25/08, page 132[54]

Am just reading in the current Spiegel about your repulsive actions in Palestine. Shame on all Jews! [. . .] What I can do: everything Jewish will be boycotted from now on, without exception! [ZJD_26.08.2008_ano_001]

(131) The terrible pictures confirm yet again that the Jewish state was born out of and with terror and is therefore apparently condemned to keep giving birth to new terror in perpetuity. [ZJD_Gaza2009_5/816_Stö_001]

Conclusion: The Israelization of Antisemitic Discourse

As a result of the social ostracism and sanctions imposed in Germany on explicitly antisemitic utterances, indirect ways of verbalizing and disseminating Judeophobic thinking have developed. They can take the form of "criticism" of Israel and are legitimized as "freedom of expression" (and can be detected on all levels of public discourse). Analysis of the contents and the verbal devices used in these utterances reveals that these forms of linguistic defamation have nothing to do with legitimate criticism of Israel. Authentic criticism and anti-Israelism can be clearly and precisely distinguished from one another in linguistic and cognitive science terms as two entirely different types of texts or communicative acts.

In the case of anti-Israel texts, the most striking feature is derealization—that is, a distorted portrayal of Israel, disconnected from reality, in the form of false statements and/or omission of facts, as well as hyperbolic demonizations. The pejorative lexemes, hyperboles, and metaphors in the anti-Israel texts collectively defame not only its citizens, but usually all Jews as well, by means of general imputations of guilt and responsibility. From the demonization of the Jewish state arise patterns of unique assessment and delegitimation. When Israel, the Jewish state, is pilloried as uniquely evil and degenerate (while considerably worse offenses, mistakes, and crimes committed by other countries receive hardly any mention or none at all), the conceptual circle of hostility toward Jews closes: Israel becomes the target of aggressive attacks because it is a genuine symbol of contemporary Jewish life. The patterns of verbal usage used to stigmatize Israel correspond exactly to the devices and strategies that have been employed for centuries to discriminate against Jews. Both argumentatively and grammatically/lexicographically antisemitic and anti-Israel communicative acts are identical. Thus text-based empirical analyses confirm that anti-Israelism should be viewed as a modern variant of the old hostility toward Jews. Hatred and rage are directed toward the Jewish state, conceptualized as a collective Jew. Only the strategies of denial, justification, and legitimation used by antisemites from the middle-class and educated mainstream mark a difference vis-à-vis the manifest antisemitism of right-wing radicals. The authors' explanation that they are speaking to express moral indignation and concern cannot conceal the fact that they are verbalizing a deeply felt resentment. Accordingly, their protestations that they are "by no means antisemitic but only critical toward Israel" can be seen as nothing but communicative diversionary tactics intended to fend off sanctions and avoid loss of face, as well as provide legitimation. Regardless of the fact that anti-Israel statements (even when they are in part not intended to be antisemitic) are inappropriate, linguistically insensitive, and irresponsible, since they have the potential to activate or reactivate antisemitic resentment by way of inferences, generalizations, and associations[55] they create an irreal, distorted image that stylizes Israel into an aggressor, contrary to reality. To defame Israel, the most important symbol of Jewish life, with comparisons to the Nazis and to stigmatize it argumentatively by means of adversarial rhetoric and anti-Jewish topoi creates an additional danger: through such linguistic usage, the basis for exacerbated antisemitic resentments is established and intensified in an entire population.[56]

7 A COMPARISON WITH OTHER COUNTRIES IN EUROPE

Results of a Contrastive Analysis

Contrastive textual analyses can reveal whether the features typical of verbal expressions of antisemitism in Germany also occur in the rest of Europe or whether significant differences can be discerned.[1] Such analyses also provide insight into the extent to which the specific influence of Germany's Nazi past may account for any differences. A subcorpus of 1,002 e-mails and letters sent to the Israeli embassies in Vienna, Berne, The Hague, Madrid, Brussels, London, Dublin, and Stockholm between 2010 and 2011 has been assessed both qualitatively and quantitatively.[2] From the quantitative standpoint, one can ascertain first that far fewer communications belong to the right-wing-extremist category. While more than 10 percent of the German authors can be assigned without hesitation to right-wing-extremist and neo-Nazi groupings, the percentage in the other European countries is distinctly smaller. Barely 3 percent of the writers are extremists; in Austria, however, the number exceeds 10 percent. The vast majority of authors either occupy the center or have a pronounced leftist orientation. Quantitatively and qualitatively, the most significant trait is that almost all the authors (i.e., 97 percent) subscribe to the anti-Israelism variant, which is to say that the Middle East conflict provides them with a platform onto which they project thoughts and feelings hostile toward Jews.

Austria

The greatest overlap in the expression of stereotypes and Judeophobic argumentation occurs between German and Austrian correspondents.[3] Here the tendency to reject guilt and memorialization turns up in almost identical form, whereas such a proclivity is hardly present in the other countries; the similarity can be attributed to the close relationship between the two countries during the Nazi period, and perhaps also to Hitler's Austrian origins:

> (1) If Israel's policies continue (Golan this weekend) and that of the Jews (with their incessant bleating and waving around Auschwitz as the elixir of life), Israel and Judaism mustn't be surprised if it's held responsible itself for producing more and more Nazis—maybe I'll be one, too, in the not-too-distant future, because I'm getting fed up myself! [IB_Wien_07.06.2011_Kun_001]

A powerful sense of surfeit with respect to the Nazi past finds expression in many Austrian e-mails, as in (1). This attitude usually occurs in conjunction with a perpetrator–victim reversal and the cliché that Jews themselves cause antisemitism by employing alleged Nazi methods in Israel and exploiting the Holocaust in Austria. Accordingly, the lexemes *Jewish* and *Israeli* often appear as synonyms. Furthermore, as in (1) and (2), blends of many traditional and current stereotypes predominate:

> (2) I find it regrettable that yesterday on the Golan Heights the Israeli-Jewish snipers, like a hunter in a blind, shot down four, maybe even twenty Palestinians like wild animals, barbarically and mercilessly, following the Nazi ideological playbook. The particular brand of Israeli-Jewish courage, which the rest of the world would call utter cowardice, manifested itself in the way they managed to slaughter a twelve-year-old unarmed child with heavy military weaponry and armed to the teeth. But the ideological basis is apparently the Torah, which preaches such ritual murders. Downright pitiful! [IB_Wien_06.06.2011_Kat_001]

Israel is morally discredited through the reactivation and projection onto the Jewish state of Judeophobic stereotypes that serve primarily to demonize it.

Switzerland

Swiss correspondents, on the other hand, focus almost exclusively on current events in the Middle East, displaying an extremely negative attitude toward the state of Israel, whose actions they characterize as *illegal*, *violations of international law*, and *criminal*. Derealized portrayals of the situation and monocausal attributions of guilt predominate. The following e-mail from a

Basel resident with a PhD, who serves on the board of a business organization, offers a prime example:

> (3) After the most recent massacres of 23 unarmed civilians trying to cross the border to the Golan Heights, illegally occupied by Israel, I shall refrain from lecturing you on international and human rights, [. . .] in Switzerland [. . .] live many refugees from state-sponsored terrorism of the sort that Israel in particular practices. [. . .] Rather the language of the Israeli government reveals xenophobia and racism.......you can expect from us citizens neither support nor understanding. [IB_Bern_23.05.2011_Die_001]

Conceptual conflation of Israelis and Jews also turns up in some of these texts:

> (4) It's time to give back to the Palestinian people their stolen land. The entire world knows how disgracefully the Jews treat their neighbors!!!! We wish the Palestinian people much success in establishing their own state. [IB_Bern_24.09.2011_Por_001]

Although many Swiss aver in their verbally aggressive e-mails that they are not antisemites, they verbalize Judeophobic stereotypes and conspiracy theories and call for boycotts in a manner reminiscent of the Nazi era:

> (5) I have nothing against the Jews in general, but I do have something against the few extremist Jews and part of the Israeli government, which hold the entire world in checkmate and are the basis of all evil in the world. it's you who provoke hatred of Jews, which of course the great majority of Jews living in the world don't deserve. But if you can't keep that small other part under control, with the powerful lobby, of course..., then you're also to blame. [IB_Bern_16.10.2011_Wil_001]

The contradictions typical of hostility toward Jews turn up in these messages: on the one hand, they articulate highly aggressive accusations and threats, while on the other hand, they deny and minimize antisemitism as a motive for the verbal violence to which they resort:[4]

> (6) This modest instrument that I possess I intend to use as long as the situation in the Palestinian areas does not improve, and I also challenge my circle of friends to refrain likewise from using products from your country.

This boycott is not an expression of antisemitic feelings. It is supposed to express my views on a circumstance that I view as unjust and profoundly despicable. [IB_Bern_28.07.2011_Sto_001]

Altogether, all the writers are notable for their use of inflammatory and inappropriate linguistic patterns that construct irreal scenarios with respect to Israel. Military operations, for example, are almost without exception described as *unnecessary massacres* and as *an expression of racism*.

The Netherlands

Although the majority of the Dutch authors communicate a virulent hatred of Israel grounded in the present, occasionally references to the past occur as well, as in (7):

(7) I can put this very concisely: back in the day the wrong 6 million were killed. With sincere contempt. [IB_Den Haag_12.07.2011_Cou_001]

This corresponds to the conceptual contrast often discerned in the German texts between GOOD JEWS and BAD JEWS (see chapters 4 and 10), with the "good Jews" being either dead or harsh critics of Israel, while the "bad Jews" live in Israel and/or allegedly behave in a morally reprehensible fashion. The implication in (7) is, however, not only that it would be better to kill the citizens currently living in Israel. The allusion to the Holocaust also implies that the Jewishness of the 6 million is decisive for the author's contempt and his desire to see them exterminated.

Dominant in almost all the texts from the Netherlands is the stereotype of Israelis as LAND-GRABBERS and UNSCRUPULOUS MURDERERS, as are the characteristic features of antisemitic anti-Israelism, namely derealization and delegitimation:

(8) When do you filthy murderers give the stolen land back to the rightfull people, the Palestinians! I despice all of Israël, this land has been stolen and now you are going to get on with murdering people who rightfully want THEIR land back, fuck all Israeli! [in English in the original] [IB_Den_Haag_16.05.2011_Kpu_001]

Spain

In the Spanish communications one finds especially often the stereotypes of Jews as the murderers of God[5] and of the eternal Jew, reactivated and projected collectively onto Israel:[6]

> (9) Re: 'Peace' Activist from the Marmara region. This photo was shown on Turkish television. Are you ever! going to stop being the ruthless and criminal country you were back when you crucified Christ? I doubt it. You will always be committing JEWISHNESSES. The only possibility for stopping you would be to ship you all—with the exception of the few decent Jews, who would stay—off to such hospitable places as treblinka and Auschwitz, because sending you to the Nevada desert would be like taking you to a candy store. When your so eagerly awaited Messiah appears, a new one, who could be a new Christ, what would you do to him? You'd probably crucify him again, because you don't trust even your mother. [IB_Madrid_03.06.2010_Fer_001]

Nazi comparisons appear often in these messages; the elimination of the Jewish people is mentioned as the only solution for world peace:

> (10) I must add that you surpass the Nazis in maliciousness and vileness, and in addition that you are as vicious as they were. You manipulate EVERYTHING to the most unbelievable extremes. You should be driven out of ALL honorable places, for you are THE [unrecognizable word] NEGATION OF EVERYTHING WORTHY AND you must be treated at least the way you treat the Palestinians, whom you treat like scum. One must, one should reopen the camps at Auschwitz and Treblinka to send you back there, because you are the EYESORE OF HUMANITY. God will not forgive you. AND THE USA, COMPANION OF THE WRETCHED, who has always protected you from being punished by humanity, must go with you to the disgraceful extermination camps. YOU'RE THE ABSOLUTE EYESORE OF THE WORLD. [IB_Madrid_03.06.2010_Jul_001]

Belgium

Along with a few brief, crudely antisemitic messages like (11), in which typical anti-Jewish profanities are verbalized with dehumanizing semantics,

> (11) The Jews are shit! [IB_Brüssel_01.07.2010_Tri_001]

the Belgian messages consist primarily of anti-Israel e-mails that portray themselves as "*humanistic*" and "*written out of concern*," and see in Israel, with its "*revolting crimes*" and "*massacres*," a threat to world peace:

> (12) [. . .] they are a threat to world peace [. . .] [IB_Brüssel_02.06.2010_Sam_001)

Here Jews and Israelis are conflated, and traditional stereotypes (JEWS DO NOT HAVE NORMAL HUMAN FEELINGS) are verbalized. Reasons are cited to legitimize past and present antisemitic notions of extermination:

> (13) If you were human, you would never subject others to the Calvary your parents endured! Is that Judaism? Does it mean inflicting pain on others, killing women and children? Is it bombarding humanitarian ships? If so, I understand better why people have wanted to exterminate you yesterday and today!!! [IB_Brüssel_31.05.2010_Sab_001]

England

Striking in the texts from England are the numerous monocausal attributions of guilt and the extreme demonizations of Israel, as in (14), an e-mail from a Birmingham resident who confirms that his views on Israel rest solely on secondhand information—that is, on hearsay and reports in the mass media:

> (14) I am listening on the radio to the ambassador. I am 60 years old and have been watching Israel over the past 50 year. My views have been informed by reading the history, talking to British soldiers who defended Palestine, and watching the activities of Israel. Israel does not have a right to exist. Its establishment after the 2nd world war was a major mistake, and rode roughshod over the human rights of the residents of Palestine.

People do not have the right to walk in and appropriate other people's land. The fact that some Hebrews lived there 2000 years ago is not relevant to the present. Until the current state of Israel accepts that it needs to return the land to the true owners of Palestine and abandons racial and religious cleansing, it will be considered a pariah. The human cost has been and will be massive. Zionism has transformed from religious philosophy to an evil world view. [IB_London_03.06.2011_Hoe_001]

The author of (14) is so unshakably convinced of the truth of his beliefs that he unhesitatingly articulates collective condemnations, anti-Zionist accusations, and total pejorative delegitimization. The conflation of Jewish and Israeli matters is indicated by the historical reference to "*some Hebrews*" and the denigration of Zionism as an "*evil world view.*" We find very similar argumentation in the following message from an educated repeat correspondent from London, who views all Israeli military operations on principle as "*criminal*" and "*unfathomably evil*":

(15) All Israel achieves by these actions is to increase hatred against it and to further delegitimize itself as a civilised member of the international community. [IB_London_27.07.2001_Ale_001]

Israel is collectively discredited and excluded from the community of civilized peoples, described as a "*corrupt apartheid system*" and a "*bankrupt Zionist regime*" that is ruled by "*cheats, thieves and murderers.*" The Embassy staff, who had written back to the correspondent, are accused of being notorious liars (the writer thereby invokes the traditional cliché of JEWS AS LIARS AND SWINDLERS):

(16) I don't believe one word of your response. You lie as always...... It isn't difficult for an army of occupation, operating under a corrupt apartheid legal sysem, to imprison whomever they like whenever they like for as long as they like. [. . .] unfortunately for the Palestinian People it has had to wait some 44 years for a Godot to come and rescue it from the deadly grip of the morally bankrupt Zionist regime. In acting as an apologist for that gang of cheats, thieves and murderers you make yourself just as guilty as the worst racist settler in Hebron, throwing her garbage and worse onto the innocent men, women and children below. [IB_London_01.07.2011_Ale_001]

Example (17) comes from an Oxford resident with a PhD who characterizes himself as a pacifist and humanist and who, "disgusted by Israel's actions," makes drastic and explicit comparisons to the Nazis ("*Israelis as Nazi scum*") to devalue and defame all Israelis collectively:

> (17) It is with disgust and horror that I watch the actions of Israel. You behave like the Nazis, persecuting another race, committing atrocities. As a pacifist it is hard to say this but I hope you pay the price according to your cred, namely an eye for an eye, I hope you suffer as much as the Palestinians (which would mean many many more Isrealis need to die to bring the justice you believe in). Disgusted human being who now sees Isrealis as Nazi scum. May your future pain bring humility. [IB_London_15.09.2011_C00_001]

Lexemes expressing intense emotions ("*with disgust and horror*") and threats and curses inconsistent with a pacifist attitude characterize the extremely aggressive verbal acts of this author, who despite his high level of education makes use of traditional Judeophobic clichés ("*according to your cred, namely an eye for an eye*") and seems unaware of the atavistic and inhumane nature of his arguments, in which generic wishes for suffering and humiliation predominate: "*I hope you suffer*" and "*May your future pain bring humility.*" The author does allude to the fact that his cognitive posture and his emotional attitude are miles apart; when he says, "*As a pacifist it is hard to say this but* . . . ," he does suggest the contradiction, yet his intense disgust and hatred are greater than any reasoned reflection. Thus the text's semantics reveal his overwhelming anti-Jewish resentment, and his cognitively oriented pacifism does not extend to Jewish Israel.

Ireland

One of the few anonymous messages, crudely antisemitic, very brief, and consisting entirely of demonizing invective and curses, comes from Ireland:

> (18) When I think of ISREAL I think of <u>EVIL.</u> I Hope you all Burn in Hell. Murdering SCUM you are <u>Hated</u> [underlined three times in the original] all over the world. Stolen any IRISH PASSPORTS Lately?? [IB_Dublin_10.06.2011_ano_001]

Most of the correspondents, however, like those in Germany supply their names and addresses, and some of them demand a response and compose rather lengthy texts in which they offer pseudo-arguments for despising and hating the Israelis or the Jews. In (19), a letter from an Irishman from Westbury, Judeophobic stereotypes are mixed with defamation of Israel:

> (19) It is with great anger that I put pen to paper so-as-to-speak to express my horror and utter disgust at the disgraceful behaviour of Israel [. . .] flotilla of Aid vessels bringing relief to an impoverished people, impoverished at the hands of a people which, I now see as the filth of the world. Israel has given the 'two fingers' to the decent and law abiding countries of the world and their peoples, effectively saying that as jews we can do what we like, we can murder who we like, we can abuse international laws, we can abuse passport systems, we can commit crimes 'when and where we like' and be answerable to nobody. There is little I can do. But, I can boycott all jewish products and businesses. ...It is now my considered opinion that the jews are in reality, an utterly despicable, vile (and a most horrid race of people). [IB_Dublin_02.06_2010_Fit_001]

Traditional, racially based stereotypes (JEWS AS A RACE, JEWS AS EXPLOITERS AND USERS, JEWS HAVE SPECIAL STATUS) are incorporated argumentatively into current anti-Israel considerations bearing on the Middle East conflict and cited as justification for the author's conclusion that Jews are the scum of the earth.

Sweden

All the messages from Swedes analyzed in the subcorpus are characterized by an extremely negative attitude toward Israel.[7] Israel is consistently referred to and delegitimized as a "*murderous state*" and an "*unjust system.*" These negative feelings are transferred to the Embassy staff, who are often urged, as undesirables, to leave the country, as in (20):

> (20) Still here? Get out or respect international laws. I will not go to Israel, please do not come here to my home country you killers. Bye asap. [In English in the original] [IB_Stockholm_20.07.2001_Tho_001]

The material in this corpus also displays an anti-Israel communicative practice found all over Europe, regardless of national boundaries, that the Internet makes possible: a number of identical messages, all bearing the same date, are sent to several Israeli embassies and to government offices and key press outlets in the countries where those embassies are located. Sometimes it is individuals who send the messages, sometimes networked groups hostile toward Israel that coordinate their defamatory campaigns. For instance, on 9 November 2011 the same text, beginning with the line in (21), was sent to almost all the Israeli embassies in Europe. Only the address and the name of the sender varied:

> (21) I am writing to you to register my disgust at the actions of the Israeli state and military in its treatment of the activists on board the MV Saoirse and Tahrir. [In English in the original]

Similar communication practices can be observed on the Internet's social media. Globalization by means of technology is strategically instrumentalized by antisemites.

Conclusion

The characteristics and trends to be found in Judeophobic discourse in Germany do not represent an isolated phenomenon. All across Europe similar features turn up in verbal manifestations. Along with the articulation of antisemitic stereotypes,[8] in particular increasing communication of inflammatory anti-Israeli sentiments can be observed. This comparative corpus-based analysis reveals a high degree of unanimity across national borders. The markers typical of anti-Israelism, a variant of antisemitism, namely derealization, demonization, and delegitimation, appear in all the texts. While Judeophobic argumentation in current German discourse combines rejection of blame for the past with attribution of blame to Jews with respect to the present (through perpetrator–victim reversal), as well as the projection of traditional Judeophobic stereotypes onto Israel, in the antisemitic texts from other European countries the hostility is clearly directed toward Israel. As in the German messages, one often finds Israeli and Jewish aspects linked or equated conceptually and verbally. Either the extremely negative conception of Israel is applied to all Jews, or, on the contrary, traditional Judeophobic stereotypes are projected onto Israel.[9] Just as Jews were negatively conceptualized and excluded for centuries as the counterimage of the observer's view of the world, so Israel today is precondemned across the board as a collective Jew, as well as drastically devalued and excluded from the community of peoples or nations.

In messages from educated persons, too, one finds stereotypes embedded in patterns of argument. As in the German texts, a form of argumentation predominates in which irrational radical views and emotional aggression go hand in hand. The most prominent conceptual conflations are JEWS/ISRAELIS = PERPETRATORS and ISRAEL AS A CRIMINAL STATE = JEWS ARE CRIMINALS. The distinctive rhetoric that casts Israel as the enemy assigns to the Jewish state the role of global criminal. The Middle East conflict is not seen as a multilayered and complicated phenomenon; rather, it is portrayed monocausally and to Israel's disadvantage, as a simple, irreal perpetrator–victim situation.

While the texts in the corpus from Germany sometimes manifest offensive aggression, and sometimes defensively reveal implicit resistance to guilt and to reminders of the past, in the messages from other Europeans the offensive component clearly predominates. For that reason the strategies of attenuation, legitimation, denial, and justification—intended to provide moral extenuation for the authors and appearing often in the texts of mainstream German writers, where they are employed to soften the radical semantics and maintain a positive self-image—occur far less frequently in messages from other countries. The emotionally based sense of surfeit that is typical of many German writers and finds articulation in refusal to accept shame and be reminded of the past plays little or no role in the messages from other European countries, with the exception of those from Austria.

8 THE EMOTIONAL BASIS OF MODERN HOSTILITY TOWARD JEWS

On the Relevance of Emotions to the Analysis of Antisemitism

> Hatred of the Jew is not the result of a rational process. . . . Underneath . . . lies the powder keg of emotional predisposition, of a conception of the Jew which has nothing to do with facts or logic. [Trachtenberg 1943, p. 2f.]

Hostility toward Jews presents many dimensions, causes, and facets and, in its concrete realization, must always be seen as embedded in its respective historical phases, where it appears as a religious, political, economic, and/or ideological interpretive pattern. Up to now, antisemitism research has concentrated primarily on the socioeconomic and political-ideological aspects of hostility toward Jews. But this hostility also has an important emotional dimension, whose critical role must be taken into consideration when one is trying to explain Judeophobic attitudes and activities. Two books by the antisemitism researcher Robert Wistrich characterize antisemitism tellingly in their titles as the "oldest hatred in the world" (1991) and the "deadly obsession" (2010). These titles pinpoint two essential emotional aspects of hostility toward Jews (expressed in 1986 by Henryk Broder in the phrase "the eternal anti-Semite"). This deeply irrational resistance and rejection, which exists independently of experience and logic, can be called antisemitic resentment (see chapter 3); up to now it has not been sufficiently taken into consideration or analyzed in detail, although as early as 1948 Sartre had already observed, and clearly named in his phenomenological treatise on antisemitism, several crucial characteristics of its emotional basis and irrational character (see also Trachtenberg 1943; Adorno 1950/1973).[1] Of course, there are psychoanalytic and social-psychological approaches that look at the causes of antisemitism.

Ernst Simmel (1946/2002b, 60), for instance, calls antisemitism "an individual's psychological symptomology," which can become the societal explanatory variable or "pattern for explaining the world" (see also Berliner 1946/2002; Hacker 1990; Staub 1995; Wahl et al. 2001; Glucksmann 2005; Hegener 2006). Whether antisemitism should be categorized as a "defect of perception," "paranoia," "collective mania," or "mental illness" is a matter for the individual disciplines to determine (on this subject see, e.g., Pohl 2010). Yet the collective emotional dimension of hostility toward Jews is so fundamental to and constitutive of this phenomenon that historical, sociological, political, and cognitive research on antisemitism must attend to this factor (see initial efforts in this direction by Rensmann 2004, 129ff.; Botsch et al. 2010; Salzborn 2010a). In this connection it must be made very clear that antisemitism is by no means only a pathological obsession found in extremists and narcissists; it also appears in educated, sensitive, and thoughtful individuals (cf. also Glucksmann 2005, 85).

For a long time scholars considered emotions irrelevant to an understanding of cognitive and social processes;[2] they thought that emotions merely interfered with cognition and therefore did not deserve their attention. In cognitive science in particular, emotional factors were deemed to be irrelevant or trivial, or highly problematic from a methodological standpoint. The very attempt to define emotions with precision was long held to be difficult. But emotions are not something diffuse, nebulous, or immune to scholarly definition; rather, they can be described, in analogy to the models of cognition, as mental systems of knowing. Since the emotive turn initially occasioned largely by the findings of neuroscience, feelings are now taken into consideration as important determinants of our social and cognitive experience (see Schwarz-Friesel 2007, 15). Human cognition is no longer understood as a completely autonomous system controlled exclusively by reason and intellect (see also Damasio 2000; Kahneman 2011). Mental and social activities are decisively steered and accompanied by emotional processes (see, e.g., Salovey et al. 2004 and, on "socio-emotional orientations," Wahl et al. 2001, 54).[3] The effect that emotions have on thoughts and behavior stems from their characteristics and definition as systems of knowing and evaluating. Emotions are multidimensional and internally represented categories or syndromes that can be subjectively experienced and registered both mentally and physically by the individual. Their most important function consists in transmitting either positive or negative evaluations. These value judgments can be conveyed to others in perceptible variants of expression. The evaluation processes have to do with the assessments with which individuals judge themselves, their physical perceptions, their impulses to act, or their thinking, or other people's behavior and situations in the world around them (in the broadest sense).[4] Emotions can be perceived and expressed as feelings (see Schwarz-Friesel 2007, 77ff.).

Emotions are evaluations that determine attitudes toward the world. On the other hand, cognitive attitudes in turn form part of the system of knowledge that is stored in long-term memory. They participate in the general system of evaluation by means of which we judge the world, our fellow human beings, their actions, and so on. The emotional system also stores socially transmitted feelings that represent collective knowledge. These feelings can play a decisive role in shaping individual attitudes. The phenomenon of emotional attitudes also reveals the inevitable interaction of emotional and cognitive systems of knowing. Emotional attitudes are based on cognitive representations and on the resulting judgments. A prejudice toward a certain group of people is thus a complex stereotyped representation stored in long-term memory that is accompanied by a negative emotional attitude. If a stereotyped representation, for instance one that is ideologically determined, incorporates extremely negative features, if it contrasts starkly with a person's own self-concept, and if it constitutes an image of an enemy, this cognitive representation can cause basic feelings such as compassion and empathy, as well as moral feelings, to be completely turned off. This explains how human beings can treat other human beings cruelly without experiencing any twinge of conscience and have no empathy for others' sufferings (see also Welzer 2005; Haubl and Caysa 2007).

Since attitudes and emotional systems of evaluation are inner states that cannot be observed but are reflected in linguistic utterances, analysis of language makes it methodologically possible to gain insight into the underlying evaluative patterns. In what follows we will therefore concentrate on the empirically demonstrable manifestations of emotional states and processes that can be reconstructed from verbal expression and the style of argumentation.

We are thus examining the emotional potential of antisemitic texts that reveals itself in numerous verbal forms, indicative of the emotional state of the language producer.[5] Feelings such as hate, rage, fear, discomfort, and distaste are explicitly named and expressed. Textual analysis also reveals the influence of emotions, as irrational sources of interference that run counter to reason and logic, on structures of argument as well as on semantic coherence: antisemitic texts often display striking contradictions, mistaken assumptions, and false conclusions.

The Emotional Potential of Antisemitic Texts: Expression of Emotions and Description of Feelings

The emotional potential of the messages communicating Judeophobic content is very high.[6] The texts contain an above-average number of lexemes descriptive or expressive of emotion. The authors utilize numerous verbal forms to express their "*helpless rage and indignation*," their "*great anger*" and "*boundless fury*" when it comes to discussing the "*Israelis' criminal actions*" or the "*impudent complicity of the Central Council*."[7] The authors often mention a diffuse sense of agitation and indignation, and emphasize how upset they are as they write:

(1) A totally disorganized e-mail I know but I am simply too upset. [IBD_12.07.2006_Fra_001]

Many of the correspondents provide explicit indications, as in (2) and (3), that their emotional situation leaves them no choice and that the need to criticize Jews sharply and to verbalize everything they are feeling in the way of hate, rage, and disgust is so overwhelming that no rational reflection can dissuade them (see also example [23]):

(2) I have written what had to be written. I felt an inner compulsion to do so. [ZJD_Gaza2009_169/816_Len_001]

(3) In the rage I am feeling at present it even makes sense to me to write this way, because I hope that this way you will not be so stubborn and obstinate, and my appeal will reach you! [ZJD_27.07.2006_Stu_001]

Emotions are generally determined by three fundamental parameters: valence (positive or negative emotion), duration (the time an emotional state lasts), and intensity (cf. Schwarz-Friesel 2007, 69ff.). In the case of verbally antisemitic texts, these parameters display extremely high values.

There are many verbal indications, such as the emphatic phrases in (4) and (5), that the level of intensity in the authors' emotional processes is very high:

(4) I am speechless and deeply shaken!!!! [ZJD_23.11.2007_Wer_001)

(5) it shakes me to the core to have to read such a thing. [ZJD_26.07.2006_ano_001]

The degree of intensity is also revealed by the use of graphemic signals of emphasis (above all an excessive number of exclamation points), font size, capitalization, and boldface. Interjections used to express disgust, revulsion, and the like are inserted at the beginning or end of evaluative statements:

(6) Shame on you, Israel, shame on you! [IBD_18.05.2006_Oss_001]

In this connection the authors often mention being thunderstruck or speechless in the face of what they describe as the "*ominous*," "*appalling*," "*unimaginable*," and "*dreadful*" happenings in the Middle East (which is also blamed on the Jews in Germany, as in [8]):

(7) with disbelief I have followed on the news your completely over-the-top reaction to the abduction of your soldiers. I am appalled at your violence , what right did you have to destroy bridges and streets and Kill innocents? [IBD_12.07.2006_Fle_001]

(8) I'm speechless, you should be ashamed for your country ! my family and I are appalled.revolting.disgusting. [ZJD_29.07.2006_Gol_001]

Such intense feelings normally occur only when individuals are personally affected—that is, when their own existential or familial concerns are involved. The correspondents thus display an emotional involvement disproportionate to a form of discourse that consists of "taking a position on political situations" and to the occasion and the writer's personal situation. They produce texts with such a large emotional quotient that one might think they had suffered immeasurable harm—had lost a close relative or were in grave personal need or danger:

(9) These words come from my soul, which is torn apart. [. . .] Even now, when the weapons have fallen silent, I am not feeling much better. [IBD_19.01.2009_Man_001]

The correlation of inner agitation or pain with wordlessness or difficulty verbalizing feelings manifests itself when individuals find themselves in extreme situations (see Schwarz-Friesel 2007, 234ff., 311ff., 2011a), but it is not characteristic of political discourse. There critical reflection and rational argumentation (in spite of occasional great indignation) tend to dominate. The powerful affective involvement indicates that instead of taking a critical position the authors are facing a situation they perceive as threatening and highly emotional.

The lexeme *hate*, along with *fury*, occurs most frequently in the messages. More than 49 percent of the texts offer related concepts, such as *hate*, *hate-filled*, and *hating*. *Hate* serves as an umbrella term for particularly aggressive hostility. Hate, which signifies a powerful revulsion to a person or group, often appears in tandem with bitterness, fury, and fear that takes the form of helplessness. Hate is obsessive, based on a rigid, conceptually closed attitude that compulsively reinterprets everything about the hated object negatively and blocks the formation of any empathy. Hate can manifest itself linguistically in an eruptive manner and unencumbered by rational thought, but it can also be expressed, like any emotion, consciously and strategically as feeling.[8] One can thus distinguish in the messages between affective hate and rational hate (for a more thorough discussion of these modalities of hate in antisemitic hate e-mails, see Schwarz-Friesel, 2012).

Right-wing-extremist writers articulate their feeling directly and personally, as in (10) and (11), coupling it with invective and curses (see chapter 9):

(10) May you all suffer—I hate you all—!!!!!!!!!!!!!" [ZJD_Gaza2009_754/816_ano_001]

(11) We hate you Jewish swine! [IBD_09.04.2006_ano_026]

(12) I can't describe the hate I feel for your country. [IBD_13.07.2006_ano_003]

Authors from the mainstream, usually educated, express their aggression as *concern*, *sorrow*, *disappointment*, and *indignation*, although in their messages one can plainly see that they are motivated by Judeophobic sentiments (see also chapter 10, under Strategies of Legitimation and Self-Aggrandizement):

(13) I am writing out of concern for the civilians, especially the children, in the south of Lebanon. [IBD_26.09.2006_Fra_001]

(14) I am very disappointed and indignant [. . .] [ZJD_Gaza2009_63/816_Wil_001]

Such authors articulate hate not crudely and emotionally but with apparent rationality. It often manifests itself as cold fury and contempt, in the form of paternalistic self-righteousness and didacticism (see also the examples in chapter 9, under Hostility toward Jews as a Missionary Urge).

(15) You should view this message not as an attack but as friendly advice. [ZJD_07.08.2006_Hön_001]

One often recognizes aggression that is barely kept in check, held back only by the desire to maintain social proprieties (see also ZJD_27.07.2006_Rau_001 in the appendix):

(16) As German Jews you should advise your brethren in faith in israel. [ZJD_Gaza2009_98/816_Pet_001]

(17) Where is your sense of justice when it comes to Israel and Palestine??? So you should not be surprised if the Jewish people still has enemies today or is not making any friends. [ZJD_Gaza2009_46/816_Bau_001]

Formulas describing emotions often turn up at the end of e-mails, in a closing such as "*with concerned regards*," "*a disappointed friend of Israel*," or "*without solidarity*." The mainstream correspondents avoid messages couched in the first person, such as *I/we hate*. They prefer to communicate feelings of hate as generic, impersonal assertions, such as "*The world hates Israel!*" (IBD_04.12.2007_Dro_001) or "*That is how hatred is sown*" (ZJD_Gaza2009_Dös_001). Often emotions are projected onto third parties; thus the authors are apparently not writing about themselves but about others' emotions ("*My friends are filled with real hate*") and thereby avoid identifying themselves as feeling hate or fury. Often extreme feelings are also presented as well-founded reactions of "legitimate indignation or contempt" to reports in the media or announcements by the Central Council:

(18) Your announcements occasion in me as a social scientist more and more negative feelings about your organization. Consider what consequences your know-it-all statements produce in the long run! (ZJD_16.04.2007_Sch_004]

(19) The things one hears every day on the radio, sees on TV, and must read in the papers create real feelings of hate. This morning there was a

commentary on the radio that reported on conditions in the occupied West Jordan land… [IBD_21.09.2011_Kub_001]

Performance of Emotionalism?

To what extent the emotions mentioned in the messages are authentic cannot be established unambiguously; perhaps the authors are merely performing in order to preserve a positive self-image, or to give greater emphasis to the sentiments they express. Here we encounter the problem of differentiating between actual and feigned emotion. For the majority of the e-mails and letters it is safe to assume, however, that genuine feelings are being verbalized, since the authors have addressed themselves spontaneously to the Central Council or the Israeli Embassy, not anticipating that their communications will be made public.

It is significant that in their hostile messages the mainstream authors use strategies that serve to legitimate their hate, which is always recoded as "*concern for world peace*," "*fear of global war*," or "*a humanistically informed sense of responsibility*." These strategies include denial of their own hate, even when that hate has been articulated through intensely emotional and stereotyped lexemes; the denial takes a metacommunicative form:

> (20) You are incorrigible, miserable, self-serving creatures! This is no hate mail—just my own opinion of you! [ZJD_Gaza2009_20/816_ano_001]

The writers often anticipate the effect of these enraged and hate-filled verbal attacks, but without being able to accept it:

> (21) Oh, yes, I know what's coming: the inevitable antisemitism bludgeon. Be my guest. [ZJD_24.07.2006_Sch_001]

Although some authors address the specific communicative situation, they are incapable of separating themselves from their conceptually closed view of the world and reflecting critically on what they are writing. The need to express their intense feeling remains too great:

> (22) I finally did have to say what I think! [ZJD_24.06.2002_Mau_001]

A repeat correspondent from Berlin, a man with a PhD, addresses the conflict between societal expectations and subjective feelings:

> (23) What has been happening in the conflict between Lebanon and Israel, especially in the past few days, has left me speechless and made me really furious at Jews. I know one's not allowed to express such feelings of fury and hate toward Jews in this country, and it took a lot for me to reach the point where I couldn't stand it any longer. [ZJD_30.11.2006_Gel_001]

The writer justifies his hostility by citing pseudo-objective factors and arguments. First he transfers his hate from the Jews to the state of Israel, as a stand-in for all Jews stigmatized accordingly (see chapter 6). He soon follows up, however, with a generic reference to all Jews. This reveals, on the one hand, how the present-day self-image of such correspondents collides with the image of a person motivated by prejudices and, on the other hand, the deep roots of their anti-Jewish resentment in the emotions, which makes it immune to reflection (on this subject, see also Contradictions and Paradoxes in the present chapter).

> (24) Dear Ladies and Gentlemen, I would like to express my indignation and disgust at the inhumane and criminal policies of the Israeli government. [ZJD_31.07.2006.Sch_003]

Fury, likewise, almost always occurs in the context of alleged Israeli crimes (and of the exploitation of the Holocaust imputed to German Jews), usually in the phrasing *makes* or *has made me/us furious*:

> (25) I would like to express my astonishment and my fury at the current war the Jews are waging against the Muslims! [ZJD_28.07.2006_Ren_001]

A sense of disappointment likewise appears frequently in the messages. It always implies blame attributed to the addressee. On the one hand the messages stress that the authors are reacting to an alleged atrocity ('Israelis/Jews behave so wickedly that one cannot help being shocked and disappointed'), and on the other hand the writers' own emotionality is rationalized ('a reason or occasion exists for these powerful feelings') and legitimated ('one has no choice'). Thus the emotional expressions of disappointment, indignation, and fury very often appear in conjunction with the explicit or implicit stereotype that JEWS HAVE ONLY THEMSELVES TO BLAME IF PEOPLE DISLIKE THEM.

> (26) Yet you fail to recognize that this provocative attitude on your part is precisely what makes more and more people furious—which causes me only disappointment and profound concern. [ZJD_27.07.2006_Stu_001]

Of the numerous adjectives referring to emotional states, *horrible* and *terrible* appear with particular frequency when it comes to Israeli policies:

> (27) For my part, I am disappointed, saddened, and ashamed that the Israelis, of all people, who really should know better than anyone how terrible injustice, tyranny, and murder are, let themselves be drawn into and engage in such barbarous behavior. [ZJD_26.07.2006_Kra_001]

More than 90 percent of the e-mails referring to Israel contain inflammatory verbal forms of evaluation and devaluation: words such as *massacre*, *unimaginable cruelty*, *indiscriminate slaughter*, *mass murder*, and *disproportionate force* are used to characterize Israeli military operations, conveying through their semantics drastic perspectives and evaluations. They all furthermore imply internal attributions with respect to the way Jews and/or Israelis behave.[9]

> (28) I have come in the meantime to understand those who hate Jews. What the Jews are doing in the Gaza Strip is mass murder. [ZJD_Gaza2009_211/816_Eku_001]

According to these versions, hate stems not from the authors' mental state and attitude but from external causes such as the Jews' and/or Israelis' behavior. Accordingly Jews are viewed as responsible not only for suffering and violence in the world but also for the authors' personal emotional pain:[10]

> (29) You alone are to blame for the entire misery. Robbing others of their living space is simply not done. I hate you all. [IBD_02.12.2006_ano_022]
>
> (30) The way this monster behaves can only fill one with rage and hate

towardIsrael. And under the circumstances I find it only justified that the Palestinians defend themselves with suicide attacks, for they don't have the kinds of weapons the impertinent Israelis have. [ZJD_24.06.2002_Mau_001]

Such encodings of emotion constitute a particular variant of the Germans' self-stylization as victims: 'the suffering incurred by the Israelis' crimes and the irresponsible failure of the Jewish Central Council that the Germans must endure, never finding peace' and being 'forced to experience' disgust, hate, and fury.

It is striking how often mention of these feelings (most of them pseudo-religious) includes an appeal to a metaphysical power:

(31) How could God allow us to have to put up with you. [ZJD_23.10.2007_ano_001]

(32) Oh, please, God, pass judgment also on the murderous state ISRAEL. [IBD_12.07.2006_ano_002]

Envy

In contrast to hate, fury, anger, and repulsion/disgust, the feeling of envy seldom finds expression; in the thousands of e-mails the lexeme *envy* occurs only twelve times, and only in messages from right-wing conservatives or extremists. Implicit expressions of envy, as in (33), also appear seldom:

(33) You are always talking about antisemitism in Germany. What enormous advantages you derive from it—you have only to lift a finger and immediately the German state heaps money on you. [ZJD_27.07.2006_ano_008]

It is significant that in these texts feelings of envy always appear in conjunction with the stereotypes of JEWS AS EXPLOITERS/PARASITES/POWERFUL BENEFICIARIES:

(34) It was also Jews who were the first to take shameless advantage of the perfidious strategies of enrichment that spread through our world with the advent of capitalism, and extended it to the rest of the world. So it is no accident that many of them have achieved great wealth and also

> much influence in the economy and managed to get their grubby hands on the nicest places to live (in this connection, let me just remind you of Liebermann's villa in Berlin Wannsee). [ZJD_30.11.2006_Gel_001]
>
> (35) That's taking advantage of the Holocaust bonus, which you abuse. [ZJD_31.08.2006_Ros_001]

But the significantly infrequent expression of feelings of envy and jealousy provides an indication of the small role this feeling (or a "mixture of destructive feelings of envy" [Hegener 2006, 19f.]) plays in present-day antisemitism. And from a historical perspective as well, an attempt such as that of Aly (2011) to trace eliminatory hatred of Jews, with its pseudo-religious and ideologically grounded salvation components, to material tensions and economic interests is unproductive (see also chapter 3, under Survival and Resistance of Judeophobic Stereotypes in Modern Times).

Altogether, the emotional potential of the texts not only provides insight into the authors' individual feelings but also reveals much about the collective feelings that go into creating hostility toward Jews.

The Obsessive Dimension

Cruelty and Emotional Coldness

The emotions of hate, anger, rage, and fury, all of which belong to the destructive emotions and can be assigned to the phenomenon of human aggression, give rise, on the one hand, to a merciless emotional coldness and, on the other, to a cruel brutality toward Jews, who are conceptualized as ENEMIES, DISTURBERS OF THE PEACE, and MONSTERS. Aggressive hostility finds articulation in utterances such as (36) and (37):

> (36) I hope many more Jewish children die—that's the only way you criminals will learn. [ZJD_27.12_2008_Did_001]
>
> (37) And as long as Scharon blocks the Palestinians' right to a state of their own, may Israel find no peace and live in fear of the next attacks. [ZJD_24.06.2002_Mau_001]

In many of the messages we encounter a striking emotional coldness, coupled with aggressive curses directed at Jews and Israelis that sound downright reactionary for a civilized community. Thus a man from Baden-Württemberg faxes the following:

(38) The Jewish symbol of the star has blood smeared all over it, and I feel no pity for the victims in Israel. [IBD_12.08.2006_Sch_003]

The emotional self-portrayals, which show all the signs of intensely felt states and processes, contrast starkly with an ostentatious indifference to Jewish or Israeli victims.[11] Often this indifference goes hand in hand with a hostile aggression that consists in explicitly wishing pain, injuries, or death on Jews and/or Israelis (for a more thorough discussion, see chapter 9).

(39) Re: Jewish crimes in Hebron. May someone storm your house, put you out on the street, etc. [ZJD_05.12.2008_ano_001]

(40) I hope and wish that [...] many, many Israelis die and their families have to suffer. [IBD_22.03.2004_Sei_001]

The author of (41) articulates his fantasies of violence very emphatically:

(41) I pray to God—who the Jews seem not to know—that the same number of Israelis may perish wretchedly, like the women and children of the Palestinians who have a right to their land that was partially stolen from them by war criminals. [IBD_20.02.2009_Wei_001]

In their messages the majority of the correspondents charge Jews and Israelis with "*moral failure*," "*unbelievable cruelty*," and "*pitilessness*." But in the process they verbalize the very emotions they themselves are feeling. Through language they project, with astonishing precision and accuracy, their own emotional deficits onto the mental construct of the JEW.[12]

Verbal acts of violence like this, which invoke visions of horrific destructive power, can be articulated only in the complete absence of empathy for those on whom the violence is wished. Empathy is the capacity to visualize oneself in someone else's position and to share that person's feelings. A person who feels empathy for others is incapable of wishing pain and suffering on them. If a basis for identification were present, such cruel curses could hardly be articulated. Since the hostile and dehumanizing conceptualization of the JEW blocks any kind of sympathy, intimacy, or identification,[13] the only possible emotion in response to this absolute devaluation must be radical.

The refusal to feel empathy for Jews and Israelis contrasts strikingly with the strong feelings the authors attribute to themselves; they claim to "*suffer intensely*," to "*be deeply troubled*," and to feel "*outraged*," but they also project such feelings onto the putative victims of the "*Jewish perpetrators*" (on this subject, see Schwarz-Friesel 2010a, 47; 2012b):

> (42) I feel only disgust and revulsion, and after more than 30 years during which I defended Israel, I am no longer prepared to support this country and its discriminatory policies, which have kept an entire people under its heel for decades and not allowed it to live under conditions worthy of human beings........I've had it! [ZJD_26.07.2006_ano_005]
>
> (43) I am shaken to the core by the Zionists' mendacity. [ZJD_26.07.2006_Koe_002]

They are "*full of sympathy*" and "*impotent rage*," their "*hearts break*" when they think of the "*misery of the Palestinians*," and they are "*stunned at the Jews' heartlessness*," as the author of (44), a doctor, indicates:

> (44) My sympathy and my solidarity go out to the Palestinian people . By the way, many of my patients think and feel the same. [ZJD_Gaza2009_160/816_Dös_001]

An engineer from Nuremberg expresses similar sentiments in his e-mail to the Central Council:

> (45) I myself feel simultaneous sorrow and impotent rage at your blindness. Your greeting means "peace." Why don't you live according to that? Shalom! [ZJD_03.08.2006_Stu_001]

A correspondent from Bochum with an MBA articulates his feelings in a similarly drastic manner:

> (46) It disgusts me to see what Israel is up to these days in Lebanon. I'd love to puke in front of your Embassy to show what I think of your aggressive policies ... [IBD_11.08.2006_Loe_001]

These writers clearly have a double standard when it comes to feeling or expressing empathy: on the one hand they refuse empathy to Jews and Israelis, while on the other they express ostentatious and intense sympathy for the "*victims of Zionist-Jewish terrorism*." But this emphatically expressed identification in all likelihood merely translates their own self-pity into a socially acceptable form, that of sympathy. As "sympathy," their destructive feelings of hate and rage are legitimated, and at the same time their self-pity is channeled outward. Thus identification with the "Jews' victims" ultimately facilitates empathy with themselves. And it helps the writers repress the sometimes uncomfortable and emotionally burdensome recognition that their intense feelings emanate from a profound hostility toward Jews.

The Mentality of "Being Fed Up" and Refusal of Empathy

The refusal of empathy by many writers can be interpreted as a form of emotional cruelty, for instance when they reproach Jews for "*talking too much about the Holocaust*" (an opinion also expressed in a variety of surveys) or when they demand "*an end to the eternal memory-and-pity trip*."

> (47) Would you please just shut up. The 2nd World war ended over 60 years ago. [ZJD_19.04.2007_Mue_001]

The writers employ drastic expressions of emotion, such as "*it makes me want to puke*," "*pitiful*," and "*there goes the pity train again*," to express how they react when Jews raise the subject of the Nazi atrocities and want the victims remembered:

> (48) I can't stand hearing about the Holocaust anymore. Or see the Central Council of Jews wagging its finger. That's enough! [ZJD_13.06.2002_Mau_001]
>
> (49) I've had it up to here with your endless yammering—and the majority of citizens feel the same! [ZJD_23.11.2007_ano_001]

Rejection of the culture of memorialization is connected to the refusal of empathy: no understanding is shown for the victims' need, and that of their descendants, to keep the memory of the Holocaust alive:

(50) I can't stand it anymore to see Messrs. Spiegel and Friedmann constantly wagging their finger at the Germans and setting themselves up as the apostles of morality. [ZJF_08.06.2002_Her_001]

On the contrary, this need is held against Jews as "*disturbance of the peace*" as a "*cause of antisemitism*" (see chapter 4):

(51) But of course we have to be reminded of our collective guilt yet again. Again and again—until every last one of us has had it up to here, and antisemitic feelings develop. [ZJD_01.05.2006_ano_001]

Writers, including those from the mainstream, justify their demand for an end to reminders of the Holocaust by arguing that the obligation to remember and commemorate has held sway long enough and that sufficient reparations have been paid (see also example [164] in chapter 4).

Resistance to memorialization often occurs in tandem with resistance to guilt and responsibility (see the early recognition of this mechanism by Adorno 1962/1971, 115; see also Rensmann 2004; Bergmann 2006) and with the demand that "*a line be drawn under the past*" and Germans left in peace (often in combination with reversal of perpetrator and victim):

(52) stop trying to tell me a German citizen born in 1961 that I have collective guilt for the Holocaust, because it's sheer impertinence to make me responsible for something I couldn't have any influence on! And furthermore you should look in the mirror yourselves and see what Nazi methods the state of Israel has used and is still using today! [IBD_19.07.2011_Fre_001]

Connected with this demand for an end to the discussion is the feeling of being pilloried by Jews' moral appeals and of therefore being unable to develop national pride:

(53) In my opinion we don't need those constant reminders from the likes of Knobloch or Friedmann—constant ceremonies where our politicians have to go down on their knees and that cost the taxpayer a bundle. Anyone who's still terrified of the new germans should really consider whether Germany is the right country for him , everyone's free to leave and spare us his constant memory and pity trip (We can't and won't put up with hearing about it anymore). [ZJD_10.11.2008_Hub_001]

The attitude of being fed up is reflected in the refusal to entertain feelings of shame, dismay, and sorrow (on this subject, see the seminal work of Mitscherlich and Mitscherlich 1967). The victims and their families are admonished to stop bothering the public with their pain. Often implied is the stereotyped reproach that the Jews in Germany use reminders of the Holocaust to secure advantages for themselves, as the following e-mail from a man from the Sauerland illustrates:

> (54) With your "German guilt" you've managed to obtain advantages from so many German politicians (for instance J. Rau) that we can't stand listening to your preaching anymore. [ZJD_27.07.2006_Bar_001]

What many, including many highly educated Germans, fail to consider is that in view of the extent of suffering, destruction, and unprecedented inhumanity, the traumatized victims, their families, and their descendants desperately need the memory to be kept alive.[14] In addition, any civilized society that deals responsibly with its own history cannot, and must not, dispense with a culture of memorialization focused on the greatest caesura in civilization that the human race has known. The events of the Nazi period are interpreted by many of the correspondents not as a moral burden that would impose existential sorrow, sympathy, and reflection but rather as an imposition by the Jews that they are determined to shake off. Here a contradiction becomes glaringly apparent: on the one hand the culture of memorialization is felt to be exaggerated and burdensome, while on the other the authors' massive use of verbal antisemitisms reveals the urgent necessity of a thorough processing of the factors behind the traditional hostility toward Jews. So many Germans chafe at what they perceive as "too much" focus on memorialization and complain about the "flood" of studies devoted to the Nazi period, yet, as recent surveys have shown, many young Germans no longer even know what Auschwitz was and what it stands for.[15] This contradiction reveals the discrepancy between subjective opinions and feelings and the objective situation. As the texts in the corpus and a variety of polls administered in recent years demonstrate, in the consciousness of many Germans, including highly educated ones, the notion exists that after 1945 a continuous, comprehensive, and intensive processing of the past took place, reaching everyone and sensitizing all German citizens collectively. Yet studies of postwar discourse have shown that no such thorough processing took place and that after the Nazi regime's collapse its atrocities were largely ignored for more than twenty years, with the result that Germans missed the opportunity to establish the Holocaust as a caesura in the collective consciousness (see chapter 3, under Hostility toward Jews after 1945). The authors of the messages in the corpus reveal the absurdity of the way they picture the situation when they load their messages with stereotypes and resentment, displaying the absence of any tolerance, understanding, and empathy, and their failure to have drawn any lessons from a history whose presence they claim overshadows everything.

Contrary to Reason: On the Dominance of the Irrational Dimension in Antisemitic Texts

Fallacies and Self-Fulfilling Prophecies

> How is it that men believe of the Jews what common sense would forbid them to believe of anything else? Why? There can be but one answer: people believe such things because they want to believe them. [Trachtenberg 1943, 1f.]

The influence of negative emotions as irrational sources of disturbance that run counter to reason and logic also manifests itself very distinctly in the illogical and paradoxical arguments presented in the texts and in their semantic and conceptual incoherence.

Hardly a single message sent to the Central Council or the Israeli Embassy in Germany dispenses entirely with justifications or arguments (see chapter 10).[16] Except in the case of pure declarations of solidarity and a few very terse hate messages, the authors of the texts feel a powerful need to support the positions they take and the demands that often follow from those positions by citing what they consider rational arguments. This obsession with justification shows up in numerous "logical lines of argument," some of them as lengthy as academic papers, complete with appendixes, citations, and footnotes:

> (55) Dear Herr Spiegel, I am enclosing an outline of historical facts and would ask that you give these facts your careful attention. [ZJD_08.04.2002_Lud_001]

Yet fallacies and false conclusions appear often in these arguments, generated especially by the writers' intense emotional involvement.[17] As a result, they put forward whole chains of pseudo-rational arguments, which on the surface seem to follow the rules of reason but in fact contain semantic and conceptual errors.

Such invalid and counterlogical arguments are classified as fallacies or false conclusions.[18] They result from the faulty inner structure of an argument, from the act of drawing false conclusions from an argument's premises, or through questionable support or absence of veracity. In the Judeophobic messages the majority of the fallacies can be attributed to the writers' resorting to false premises, ignoring facts, and invoking unacceptable stereotypes. Rigid cognitive stereotypes and sometimes the authors' extreme agitation cause them to disregard or violate the laws of logical argumentation, a characteristic of antisemitic thinking.

Fallacies on the Basis of False Premises False conclusions often result from false premises—that is, false theses or presumptions of fact.

> (56) Our German people is struggling for economic survival because it is being strangled more and more by the taxes imposed by our politicians. In Berlin a Holocaust memorial is being built for 60 million. That's a crime against the German people. [ZJD_04.06.2002_Ric_001]

This writer, from Monheim, starts with the premise that the German people or the German state is fighting for its "*economic survival*" because of public debt (a derealizing exaggeration). Since the first premise is false, the conclusion that the Berlin Holocaust memorial is a crime is also false. Using Toulmin's (1958) model, one can easily portray the process by which this false conclusion was reached. This model makes use of the classic syllogism, a form of argumentation in which two premises yield a conclusion. Toulmin expands this model by bringing in a "backing" that explains from which argumentatory field one of the two premises was derived.

Analysis of example (56) according to the Toulmin model looks as shown in the table on page 224.

A striking feature of many of these fallacies is the invocation of irrelevant facts or clearly false facts to justify the author's own position or attitude. These 'facts' are then woven into the argument as if they spoke for themselves (in

THESIS (first premise)		**CONCLUSION**
The German people are fighting for their economic survival ▶	therefore ▶ ▼	The expensive Holocaust memorial was a crime
	Conclusion (second premise) ▼	
	Anyone fighting for survival cannot build expensive monuments	
▼ First premise false	▲ Backing	▼ Conclusion false

this case a large national debt has never prevented a government from making unnecessary investments). One can assume that the construction of the Holocaust memorial caused the author of (56) annoyance or struck him as a provocation, clashing with his rejection of the culture of memorialization. Lest he have to express his disapproval as merely one individual's opinion, he cites seemingly plausible counterarguments, reproducible and acceptable to people in general, arguments he finds in the thematic realm of government finances or economic consolidation:

> (57) Palestinian children are treated by the Israelis with ever-increasing brutality and murdered. The numbers keep growing. The world is better off without the Israelis. So the conclusion is that exterminating the Israelis is the only solution. [IBD_15.10.2007_Dro_001]

From the premise constructed on the basis of the author's derealized view of the world, which is backed by the apparently factual but likewise imagined 'fact' of increasing numbers, the Judeophobic author concludes that all Israelis must be eliminated. Such conclusions take on the character of self-fulfilling prophecies.[19] They exist as unshakable articles of faith (e.g., 'All Israelis are Jewish murderers [of children] and criminals') in the minds of the language producers, are expressed as facts, and are then established by means of 'arguments' that confirm the article of faith. Applied to the phenomenon of hostility toward Jews, this mechanism can be described as follows: in the mental framework of antisemites, the concept of JEWS is linked with certain stereotyped notions that predict Jews' behavior, for example 'Jews are cruel and devious.' Everything Jews do is then by definition bad,[20] and all pseudo-causal judgments and motives cited consist of rationalizations of this resentment. Here the generalized suspicion of Jews, a concatenation of suspicion, mistrust, ignorance, and stereotypes, finds verbal expression. Every opportunity and every piece of information, no matter how implausible and vague, is used to support and confirm this generalized suspicion.

Israeli military operations are assessed according to this belief system as cruel and devious. A different reading is categorically rejected or not even entertained. Thus the authors systematically produce the very confirmations that they expect. In a formal sense, consistency is established, which, however, is merely apparent conceptual consistency (see also Hacker 1990, 119).

Fallacies through Stereotypes

Numerous texts simulate (apparent) plausibility, in the sense of causally determined connections that depend on anti-Jewish stereotypes to back up the chosen premises. This backing, however, is fundamentally false because it is based on unjustified generalizations or fictions (cf. chapter 4):

> (58) Germans no longer want to work because they must pay so many taxes and pensions. Pensions are cut and the increase becomes less every year. If this continues, the foreigners in Germany will have all the say. In business and industry the Jews and Americans are the major warmongers and the most bloodthirsty people in the world. [ZJD_13.09.2002_ano_004]

In example (58) coherence within the text is created only by means of a stereotype-based inference. Not until one draws the conclusion that for the author the concepts FOREIGNERS and JEWS largely overlap (meaning that he conceives of German Jews as NON-GERMAN and has thus internalized the antisemitic stereotype of JEWS AS ALIENS), and combines the information node ARE RESPONSIBLE FOR REDUCTIONS IN PENSIONS with the concept FOREIGNER, does this utterance have any kind of coherence.

Invoking Inappropriate Topoi

Topoi, or conceptual categories with thematic emphases and sometimes a large visual component, are mental sources for arguments. With their assistance, one can generate arguments both for and against a specific point, but one cannot argue with them alone. Examples of such topoi are freedom, the economy, and also conclusions drawn from comparisons.

> (59) The occasion for my writing is the inhumane behavior of the Israeli armed forces in Gaza and especially in Lebanon. [...] It is pointless to ask who cast the first stone, thousands of years of Jewish history are full of the Hebrews' violent, bloody conduct toward their neighbors or if necessary also against uncooperative tribes of their own. Thus the feast of Passover commemorates a terrible massacre in which all the first-born Egyptians were slaughtered, not by Yahwe but by his violence-prone people. [...] [quotation from the Bible] During the conquest of Jericho everything living was killed, men, women, children, and also animals, as you can read in the Bible. This thread of violence runs through the millennia and has not broken to this day. [ZJD_29.07.2006_Gru_001]

In example (59), the topos 'religious (texts)' or the conclusion from comparison—'as in the Bible so also in the present'—serves to support arguments against the conduct of the Israeli military, arguments that, however, are applied collectively to all Jews. This would be at least rhetorically legitimate in a religious dispute, although this sort of argumentation is morally problematic and logically false; the author of this text, however, is not operating in that sort of communicative situation. He is writing to the Central Council of Jews in Germany and intervening in a contemporary political/military discourse. In this connection his topos, religious and oriented toward the past, is not appropriate and furthermore reinforces the Judeophobic cliché of the eternal Jew as a disturber of the peace. The final argument, that using violence has been an inherent trait of Jews through the millennia, and the inference to be drawn, that the behavior of the Israeli armed forces conforms to this bloody tradition, results exclusively from the stereotyped mental notion of JEWS stored in the mind of the writer.

Ignoring, Excluding, and Reinterpreting Facts In example (60) an academic from Munich likewise formulates arguments that lead to a conclusion that is inappropriate because he omits relevant historical and current facts. He argues purely in terms of military strategy and, in the process, ignores the fact that a state and its guarantee of existence depend on more than its military budget, as well as the fact that Israel has already been involved numerous times in wars initiated by the surrounding Arab states. He also overlooks the hostile, threatening rhetoric directed against Israel by many nearby countries, as well as the terrorist attacks within its borders. The writer's reduction of his argument to the status quo of Israel's armaments therefore leads to an erroneous conclusion. This conclusion matches, however, his image of Israel.

> (60) You argue that Israel is fighting for its 'existence.' Granted, life in Israel under these conditions is almost unacceptable. But please consider that Israel has several thousand tanks and armored vehicles, the second-strongest air force in the world, in extreme situations two and a half million soldiers, and atomic weapons as well, which it—I have no doubt—would also use. What country could risk a war against Israel? Mr. President, that Israel is fighting for its existence is sheer nonsense. [ZJD_05.04.2002_Stu_001]

The authors of such messages often base their judgments on pure speculation and belief, which they however reinterpret and present as "factual arguments."

> (61) Experience shows, however, that for every 'terrorist' killed, two new ones are born!! [. . .] but in that case you are engaged in state terrorism and are lowering yourselves to the same level as the terrorists you are fighting. [IBD_23.03.2003_Sch_001]

Drawing on the topos of 'experience' for backing, the writer puts forward the thesis that every terrorist killed creates two new ones. No empirical experience confirms this thesis, created out of the belief system of this writer from Hersbruck and presumably based on the stock expression *Violence breeds violence*. But the author sees this notion as providing support for his negative attitude toward Israeli military power (even when that power is used for responding to violence or engaging in self-defense). The conclusion drawn from this argument, that Israel is committing state-sponsored terrorism because it is defending itself militarily against terrorism and thereby increasing the use of force, contradicts all rules of reason (and of international law) and makes sense only if a unique status is assigned to Israel.[21] Apparently it sounds perfectly plausible and convincing to its author. Similarly, many of the authors simulate, according to their Judeophobic and anti-Israel conceptualizations, a plausibility and rationality that de facto do not exist but maintain consistency in the authors' convictions.

The irrationality of these mental constructs contrasts with their communicative use—that is, their verbalization and embedding in texts.[22] The authors go to considerable lengths to portray their opinion of Jews as empirically based and argumentatively convincing. Thus stereotypes and alleged facts, arguments, and evidence that are conditioned on or support each other form a complex argumentative fabric of Judeophobic pseudo-logic.

Altogether, it can be established that in these messages, including those from highly educated writers, the explicit support or conclusions presented are inadequate or questionable, in part because the authors argue emotionally and irrationally, drawing on closed-minded views of the world, and in part because they cite inadmissible premises to support their arguments. Anti-Jewish stereotypes often form the mental basis for premises or backing. Breaches in logic and erroneous conclusions appear when conclusions are drawn from such premises, confirming the conclusions the authors wish to reach. Thus these resemble self-fulfilling prophecies; that is, they correspond exactly to the authors' expectations because from their perspective they were constructed as plausible and real. Thus antisemitic language producers, following the internal "logic" of their evaluative system, produce confirmation of their Judeophobic resentment.

Contradictions and Paradoxes: Statements in Collision

Along with invalid argumentative chains and false assertions within the constructed justifications, the messages also often present absurd contradictions in content or logic. A contradiction occurs if a language producer articulates that something is the case when it is not actually the case. From this situation result paradoxes that run counter to the laws of reason. Irreconcilable statements turn up particularly often after self-attributions and self-legitimations such as "*I am a humanist*" or "*I am no antisemite*," which stand in dramatic contrast to the authors' further (antisemitic) utterances.[23] In (62) the author first declares himself to be no antisemite and then proceeds to ostentatiously refute this statement by means of dehumanizing comments that denigrate Jews and Israelis:

> (62) I am a German citizen and no antisemite [. . .] creatures from Israel who call themselves human beings slaughter innocent women and children. [. . .] You are all simply human garbage. [IBD_20.02.2009_Wei_001]

Contradictions like these often appear in the corpus, highlighting a striking discrepancy between the authors' self-image and their image of others. They are often based on the conceptualization that Jews must not be judged by the same standards that apply to all others.

> (63) [. . .] that calls for tolerance and respect for foreigners as well as advocating for peace and human rights in the world. [. . .] what the cannibals in the israeli government [. . .] are engaged in is terrorism against humanity. [ZJD_12.04.2002_Wie_001]

Similar semantic oppositions and incompatibilities turn up as well in statements such as (64) and (65):

> (64) A friend of mankind who hates the Jews from the bottom of his heart! [ZJD_Gaza2009_792/816_ano_001]
>
> (65) I am no racist and respect human beings. [. . .] Do you consider yourselves something special other than that you are mass murderers? I pray to God that no JEW turns up in my family. [ZJD_Gaza2009_295/816_Ado_001]

In one and the same sentence the author of (64) refutes his self-stylization as a friend of humankind. Because of his belief that Jews are not human beings, he sees no contradiction in his exclamation. The author of (65) first denies that she has a racist attitude and legitimates herself as someone who respects human beings, but then reduces both of these claims to nonsense by expressing, with powerful emotional emphasis, her racist collective rejection of Jews.

In (66) the author, an academic, first flaunts his lack of prejudice and denies any inclination to reject or harbor negative feelings toward Jews:

> (66) I am a German, and proud of it. I was born in 1951, and I had nothing to do with Nazism. My generation never did do anything

> to the Jews and never will. We have nothing against Jews. [. . .] Your behavior merely creates more hate between my generation and the Jews. [ZJD_09.11.2008_Det_001]

The opening statements are contradicted by the (stereotype-laden) assertion that the Central Council is responsible for the hate between Jews and Germans, a hate the author has just declared does not exist.

The author of (67) first announces her opinion that the Middle East conflict does not concern Germans at all and that it is better not to get involved. Then follow, however, pages of comments, utopian suggestions for solutions, and dogmatic remarks, all of which contradict the point made at the beginning:

> (67) The war in Israel is really none of our business as Germans. I am also absolutely opposed to our getting involved. [. . .] Maybe the European Jews should put pressure on their country to end this impossible and meaningless war. [ZJD_Gaza2009_238/816_Kla_001]

E-mail (68) has a similar structure:

> (68) I am writing to you although I really don't know much about Jews. [. . .] For me, there are only human beings. I don't recognize any racial differences. .In the meantime I have come to understand those who hate Jews.In my family there are Poles Russians,Indians etc. I wouldn't like to have any Jews in the family. Such shame I wouldn't survive. [ZJD_Gaza2009_349/816_Mah_001]

Although the author of this e-mail claims not to "*know much about Jews*," in the lengthy remarks that follow she encodes one stereotype after the other (see Hate without a Real Object in the present chapter). Despite her admitted lack of knowledge, she is convinced that she "*knows*" "*that Jews are degenerate*" and "*commit mass murder*" in Israel. At the same time she catches herself in a further contradiction: while describing herself, on the one hand, as tolerant and free of prejudices, she reveals, on the other hand, an extreme hostility toward Jews. She is not capable of practicing her "anti-racist tolerance" with Jews, revealing that she shares the traditional conception, communicated especially in the Nazi period, of Jews as THE ENTIRELY OTHER, situated outside the human community of values.

In (69) a striking contradiction occurs when the author, a woman with a PhD in history, does the very thing she previously rejected: she justifies the Palestinian terror attacks:

> (69) I would never go so far as to justify the suicide attacks. [. . .] But the suicide attacks are a desperate reaction, in part motivated by religious fanaticism, to a decades-long Israeli policy of expulsion and permanent humiliation visited on the Palestinians. [ZJD_12.04.2002_Hei_001]

That various statements in one and the same piece of correspondence are incompatible, and that the authors apparently do not notice the contradiction points to their closed minds or to the need they feel to maintain a positive self-image at all costs. The contradictions that occur frequently in letters to the Central Council and the Israeli Embassy turn up likewise in numerous comments on the Internet and in Judeophobic publications, which presumably are not composed as quickly and carelessly as some of the e-mails in the corpus. A telling example from a pamphlet written by Hans Mahler, a right-wing extremist, makes this clear:

> (70) They strive purposefully to break down the soul of the Volk and aim to gain hegemony over the other peoples. For that reason the Protocols of the Elders of Zion are authentic evidence of the Jewish spirit—even if they are a forgery. [Mahler, quoted in BfV 2005, 12]

The terms *forgery* and *authentic* stand in semantic opposition to one another: something that is false cannot be authentic, and a piece of writing recognized as a forgery cannot, according to logical/rational or plausible criteria, be authentic evidence. This text, which according to the principles of normal reason would be recognizable immediately as contradictory, reveals the irrational criteria according to which the author's mind functions. Everything is subsumed under the antisemitic view of the world, even if logical paradoxes and a breakdown of coherence result from the attempt to confirm that view.

Hate without a Real Object: *Jew* as an Abstract Notion

For many people with a recognizable antisemitic attitude, the lexeme *Jew* refers not to anything concrete,[24] but to an abstraction that makes it possible to project everything negative onto this concept without coming into conflict with reality. The dislike these people feel pertains to a mental construct, not an actual object:[25]

(71) I've never had any dealings with Jews, but for some reason I don't like you people. [ZJD_08.08.2007_Bus_001]

(72) You know, Mr. Ambassador, I don't know your story. I've never heard you speak, I don't know who you are and what you think, but simply because you occupy an official position that serves such a misguided policy makes me feel a great dislike for you. But not because you're a Jew, but because you're not a Jew who strives for justice, as your name promises. [IBD_13.07.2006_Hel_001]

(73) I personally don't know a single person from Israel, or of the Jewish faith. [ZJD_Gaza2009_66/816_Her_001]

Statements like (71), (72), and (73) articulate verbatim what has already been mentioned in numerous publications on antisemitism and has been explained by us in detail (see chapter 2, under Conceptual and Verbal Antisemitism, and chapter 3): antisemitic resentment refers not to anything specific in the real world but rather to the concept of the JEW stored in a person's mind. "To the anti-Semite the Jew remains an unknown object; he does not know whereof he speaks" (Glucksmann 2005, 98).

Contrary to all reason, Judeophobic resentment is "an entirely general negative value, a form of rejection that appears without justification and bursts out suddenly, seemingly at random, filled with hate" (Scheler 1912/1955, 36). This outburst can be explained only on the basis of the long-standing, culturally, communicatively, emotionally, and collectively established hostility toward Jews.

The educated author of (74) considers himself self-critical, asserting that he does not presume to judge the Israeli ambassador because he does not know him personally. Nonetheless, he does not hesitate to judge events in Israel, although he has received information about them only through the media. To put it another way, he requires direct personal experience for judging the ambassador, yet he finds secondhand experience perfectly adequate when it comes to evaluating or devaluing Israel:

(74) You yourselves, dear Mr. Ambassador and ladies and gentlemen, I do not know well enough. I will also not make your acquaintance and therefore

> will not presume to reach a judgment about you. I can, however, form an opinion and reach a personal judgment about the things I read in the media, hear, and see, and about which I learn in conversations with friends and acquaintances. And my judgment about your country's government is as definitive as my judgment about a president who conducts illegal wars of aggression that flout international law and threatens the authorities responsible for responding with a military operation if they seriously attempt to negotiate. [IBD_07.03.2007_Mue_001]

Thus even highly educated academics, trained to think systematically and accustomed to working strictly according to rational principles, fail to follow these principles when it comes to Jews and/or Israelis. This contradictory behavior manifests itself when a professor, in the course of an e-mail correspondence extending over several days, is asked whether he has sufficient personal knowledge of a country that he utterly condemns to make such defamatory statements about it, and replies:

> (75) I have never been to Israel/Palestine, but since a lecture by [. . .] in 2002 in [. . .] (where she reported on her support for the boycott-Israel movement), and even more since the Lebanon war, I have studied the problem very closely. [20.12.2009_Has_003]

When asked about the observations and primary sources on which his entirely derealizing and stereotype-filled statements are based, he mentions a speech by Jimmy Carter. This correspondent, who as a scholar conducts research according to the criteria of intersubjective verifiability and so on loses the capability, when it is a question of Israel, to think rationally. Secondary information is accepted without any attempt at verifying it, and beliefs are substituted for facts. People like this do something they would never do in their professional life; they lose their professionalism and the ability to think clearly and logically. They become immune to factual arguments and entertain no doubts about themselves. Chance factors are raised to the status of essential elements, and things they have read or heard but not experienced are declared to be the absolute truth. Speculations that fit their anti-Israel image are privileged over critical thinking. Here we encounter a feature of hostility toward Jews that has remained a constant for centuries: a readiness to believe any and all information that paints Jews as evil, no matter how improbable.[26] This phenomenon shows the immense influence of the emotional and irrational dimension on cognitive perception.

The glaring contradictions just discussed show the power and influence of Judeophobic conceptualizations. The authors succumb to the compulsion to integrate all information and statements into their mental model. They refuse to allow doubts to enter in, and they modify information to make it fit, ignoring the laws of logic, reason, and plausibility.

Conclusion

Emotionally determined attitudes play an extraordinarily important role in the phenomenon of hostility toward Jews. Collective feelings have a major influence on the way in which Jews are conceptualized and evaluated verbally. Research on antisemitism has previously paid too little attention to the emotional dimension and must now confront the challenge of integrating this factor into its analytical explanations.

Many antisemitic utterances reveal through their high degree of textual emotionality that their producers harbor profound hate for and suspicion of Jews and Judaism, which they attempt to rationalize by means of reinterpretation, external attributions, and arguments. Antisemites' worldview is shaped by an irrational selectivity; that is, their perceptions and mental components of knowledge or belief are always chosen and structured in such a way that they can confirm or maintain the subjects' Judeophobic conceptualization and emotional attitude. What results are hermetically sealed reality constructs that resist facts and have a starkly derealizational tendency; that is, they distort reality, irrationally influencing thought structures in defiance of the principles of reason and logic. This derealization is reflected in the texts in the form of false conclusions, rejection of facts, and contradictions.

9 ACTS OF VERBAL VIOLENCE

> You parasites [. . .] you criminal vermin, you should be processed into animal fodder, so you could be useful for a change; we hate you Jewish swine! [IBD_01.08.2006_ano_026]

Language can, as we have already discussed, be deployed as an instrument to harm people mentally, to damage them cognitively and emotionally, to inflict spiritual pain, and to fill them with fear and worry. That words can be used as weapons becomes particularly obvious when statements are formulated deliberately to be semantically pejorative and pragmatically destructive. Destructive means that the action implied by an utterance involves doing something negative to the addressee through completion of the speech act or announces the intention or the wish to do such a thing. The communicative function of the demand expressed as an imperative in (1) shows this destructive dimension and at the same time reveals the author's high potential for aggression:

(1) Croak!!!! [ZJD_10.01.2009_Her_001]

As regards their action value, many Judeophobic utterances are not merely representative and expressive; they convey defamatory assertions of whose veracity the author is convinced, as well as affective attitudes, as in (2) and (3):

(2) I HATE all Israelis that genocidal people [IBD_16.01.2009_Kös_001]
(3) I spit on your feet in disgust! [ZJD_Gaza2009_632/816_Jun_001]

A large percentage of these speech acts actually display a strongly directive character. The feature that characterizes directives (appellatives) as verbal activities is that they are intended to bring about a specific result in the addressee. Usually the recipient is supposed to be induced to commit some action, thereby bringing the extralinguistic world into harmony with the content of the utterance (and in the process carrying out the writer's wish). The reaction a demand intends to achieve is, for instance, to set a particular action in motion on the part of the recipient.

(4) Get out of the land of the Palestinians! [IBD_22.03.2004_Sch_001]

(5) I call on you to intervene to stop the destruction being perpetrated by Israel. [ZJD_Gaza2009_36/816_Fed_001]

As can be seen from (4) and (5), most speech acts cannot be assigned to a single communicative function. With the demand in (4) the author at the same time asserts that Israel is occupying land illegitimately and thus has no right to exist in the Middle East. The directive speech act in (5) contains, in addition to the specific demand for action, the implicit charge that all the destruction is being perpetrated by Israel and additionally the criticism that the Central Council of Jews in Germany does not take a position against violence in the Middle East. That the demand is directed to the Central Council and not the Embassy at the same time demonstrates the speaker's assumption of a factual involvement of German Jews in Israeli matters. Thus the Central Council is indirectly made responsible for Israel's military operations.

Abuse, Insults, Threats, Curses

In our corpus three types of particularly aggressive speech acts predominate: those that entail abuse or insults, threats,[1] and curses directed at Jews. Aggressiveness often manifests itself in the subject lines of e-mails: usually this line, in which the addressee receives essential information at the outset, states the author's concern as a verbal attack, as the following examples, all drawn from the subject lines of e-mails to the Central Council, illustrate:

(6) Re: Jewish Criminal Acts in Hebron: [ZJD_05.12.2008_ano_001]

(7) Re: Hello there you criminals!!! [ZJD_06.01.2009_Hau_001]

(8) Re: You god-damned sons of whores [ZJD_09.01.2009_Hel_001]

(9) Re: Zionist murderers, child-killers, cowardly terrorists, cowardly agresors [ZJD_Gaza2009_92/816_ano_001]

An essential feature of abusive language is the negative evaluation of the addressee, who suffers devaluation as a result of having pejorative words directed at him.[2] In this way the producer gives expression to a strongly affective attitude. Abuse is intended to insult the recipient. The choice of abusive words is decisive: therefore, pejorative terms enjoy a particular status. The chief characteristic of abusive vocabulary is that it predicates something genuinely negative about the addressee. This degrading referentialization can entail dehumanization (e.g., by means of allusions to animals) or delegitimation (e.g., through denial of cognitive ability, as in the term *idiot*). The focus on mental or physical characteristics considered inferior reduces the recipient to negative characteristics.

Pejorative vocabulary, which functions primarily to abuse and insult a person, remains stored in the mental lexicon of the language user, and its use can be classified as customary.[3] Many antisemitic terms of abuse have a very long tradition (see chapter 3), and some have been used for centuries. The following types that can be observed in current usage belong to these categories:[4]

> (a) Animal designations such as *swine*, *rat*, *vultur*e, and *brute*. This category also includes lexemes from the realm of microbiology, such as *parasites* and *bacilli*, as well as *creatures* and *spawn*.
>
> (b) Designations from (pseudo-)religious and fictive discourse referring to beings that personify pure evil, such as *devil*, *Satan*, *anti-Christ*, *fiend*, *demon*, and *monster*.
>
> (c) Abusive terms that refer to inferior substances, pathological growths, and excrement, such as *bones*, *manure*, *filth*, *mess*, *tumor*, *boil*, and *shit*.
>
> (d) Terms for human beings considered physically, intellectually, or morally limited or inferior, such as *idiot*, *freak*, *dummy*, *cripple*, *brain amputee*, *pervert*, *hypocrite*, *liar*, *criminal*, and *murderer*.

These abusive terms often occur in combinations: adjective-plus-noun phrases like *wretched Jewish swine* bring together the pejorative components of dehumanization and moral wickedness, while a composite term such as *Jewish spawn of the devil* brings together the dehumanizing semantics of *spawn* with religious or metaphysical devaluation. In this sense abuse follows the general pattern according to which an image of an enemy is constructed on the basis of dehumanization and demonization (as discussed in chapter 2). Combinations containing the term *swine*, *filth*, or *murderer* turn up particularly often in the messages to the Central Council and the Embassy: *Jewish swine*, *band of murderers*, *child-murderers*, *murderous spawn*, *murderous people*, *people of cripples*, *murderous horde*, *filthy Jews*, *swinish Jews*, *filthy riffraff*. The pejorative elements are intensified by the addition of adjectives such as *stinking*, *miserable*, *revolting*, and *lying*. The state of Israel is often described with composite phrases and metaphorical constructions such as *cancerous growth*, *cripple state*, *thalidomide freak*, *murder machine*, and *nest of terrorists*.

The most common instances of abusive language comprise elliptical exclamations and listings of individual pejorative expressions, addressed directly to the recipient(s):

(10) you Jewish swine [ZJD_08.09.2006_Mon_003]

(11) You child-devourers [ZJD_Gaza2009_9/816_Hai_001]

(12) You terrorists and war criminals!!!!!!!!!!!!! [IBD_11.08.2011_ano_001]

(13) You cowardly piles of shit! [ZJD_Gaza_677/816_Pan_001]

(14) You child-slaughterers. [ZJD_Gaza2009_432/816_Hel_001]

(15) You monsters, You p***sites [ZJD_Gaza2009_92/816_ano_001]

(16) You murderers and criminal gangster regime [. . .] You child-murderers, child-devourers, organ-snatchers [IBD_04.01.2007_Ard_001]

(17) You filthy Jews and GANG OF MURDERERS. [IBD_05.08.2010_ano_001]

(18) You genociders and warmongers. [IBD_06.05.2009_ano_001]

Every one of these abusive epithets amounts to a degradation of the addressees, intended to demonstrate their inferiority vis-à-vis the society's collective value system.

The authors almost always use the German informal mode of address (*du*); this indication of disrespect intensifies the expression of contempt and makes obvious the intention to be insulting. Examples such as (19), in which the German formal mode of address (*sie*) is used, are therefore a rarity:

(19) You scoundrels, sirs, you war-criminals! [IBD_03.04.2009_Kub_001]

In the majority of cases no one is addressed directly; the abusive comments in these elliptical texts take the form of isolated words, phrases, or strings of generic words, often inflated by means of multiple exclamation marks:

(20) Bloodthirstymurderers, criminal fascists, land-grabbers, plunderers human-organ-snatchers [IBD_26.01.2007_Ard_001]

(21) Mass murderers!! [ZJD_09.08.2006_ano_001]

(22) Filthy arrogant Jews!!! [IBD_06.05.2009_ano_002]

(23) Nazi executioners!!!!!!!!!!!!!!!!!!!!!!!!!!! [IBD_11.02.2011_ano_001]

Many of these abusive comments contain adjectives and nouns that have been used for centuries and have become stock phrases, since they activate clichés: *devious*, *cowardly*, *vengeful*, *parasites*, *devils*, and the like are lexemes that were already in habitual use in the Middle Ages for characterizing Jews (see chapter 3, under On the Genesis of Resentment toward Jews). Correspondingly there are many utterances that predicate such negative traits as typical of Jews and thereby, from the producers' point of view, explicitly confirm the old prejudices:

(24) Obviously these [i.e., murdering, disturbing the peace, stealing land] are the basic traits of Jews. [IBD_15.06.2009_ano_001]

(25) JEWS ARE THE WORST LIARS AND GREATEST CRIMINALS IN THE WORLD. JEWS ARE THE SOURCE OF TERRORISM. [IBD_07.07.2006_ano_045]

(26) You Jews just can't leave well enough alone. . . . Your state is an abomination, as you know yourselves. You need to fix your relationship with your neighbors. But of course you see yourselves as the chosen people. [IBD_12.06.2006_ano_001]

While many of the messages are very brief, consisting only of a string of abusive terms, and thus serving primarily to express the emotions of hate and fury, in numerous other e-mails and letters the abuse merely serves to introduce further verbal aggressions consisting of warnings, threats, and curses:

(27) Shame on you..You disgusting filthy pigs. One of these days you'll FINALLY be wiped out.. You arrogant, egotistical, cruel, affected people.. Who misinformed you that you're better than all the rest? [ZJD_Gaza2009_401/816_Jar_001]

(28) You shitty Jews should have your throats slit! [. . .] [ZJD_04.05.2007_Mau_001]

(29) Jewish swine! Too bad that you didn't all croak when Adolf was here. Just to make sure, every single one of you should be poisoned, gassed, and for good measure be shot with 10 bullets. You motherfuckers are like a

plague and for that reason should be wipped out. We're going to stick you filthy pigs in all the places where it hurts. As a people you're pure shit! It's a treat to see on TV, sheer pleasure, after a bombing, a Jewish sow, no matter whether old or young, what matters is that she's laying in the mud blown to bits. There's hardly anyone in the world who likes a Jew, no one has any use for you! It's to be hoped that a whole lot of you super-riffraff end up dead! [IBD_01.01.2006_ano_026]

The lexeme *Jew*, too, is used by some of the writers as a term of abuse at the very beginning in the salutation.

(30) Jew Simon Stein, with what you said [...] [IBD_23.07.2006_Hud_001]

(31) JEW!!!!!!!!!!!!!!!!!!!!!!!!!!!!!!!!!!!!!! [ZJD_23.10.2007_ano_001]

(32) Shalon you Jews [...] [IBD_22.04.2008_Pal_001]

With denigrating adjectives such as *filthy* and *damned*, as well as emotional interjections such as *ick* and *yuck*, the pejorative effect is intensified further:

(33) You filthy Jews!!!!!!!!!!!!!!!!!!!!!!!!!!!!!!!!!! [ZJD_Gaza2009_301/816_ano_001; anonymous frequent correspondent]

(34) Oh, you damned Jews! [IBD_16.04.2009_Kub_001]

(35) how in the world can you be such troublemakers, ugh! [IBD_23.03.2008_ano_001]

(36) Go to hell, you JEWS. [IBD_27.05.2009_ano_001]

The lexeme *Zionism*, which denotes the 'attempt to bring the Jews back to Israel from the diaspora,' turns up in its various grammatical forms exclusively as a term of abuse.[5] The pejorative component can already be recognized as everyday usage; correspondents of all political persuasions use the word with an intent to devaluate, in a wide variety of combinations such as *Zionist swine*, *Zionist foe*, *filthy Zionist crew*, *Zionist whore* (referring to Charlotte Knobloch), *Zionist prisoner-liberation terrorism*, *Zionist state terrorism*, and *Zion's spawn*:

(37) Then Zionist megalomania and war crimes like Sabra and Shatilla will receive their just deserts. [IBD_14.07.2006_Bru_001]

(38) Contempt for human life and callousness on the part of Zionist

criminals are reaching a lonely zenith at present, since before the eyes of the world and according to all the rules of a war machine run amok these gangsters are simply slaughtering a people on the Gaza strip that for decades has been terrorized, robbed, enslaved, bullied, and starved to death. [ZJD_Gaza2009_399/816/Sne_001]

(39) To the national-Zionist gang of murderers [ZJD_Gaza2009_686/816_Fra_001]

The term appears with particular frequency in messages from leftist and left-wing-extremist correspondents. Here *Zionist* is used almost synonymously with *imperialist*, *colonialist*, and *fascist* and turns up particularly often in connection with terms from the semantic field of 'terrorism, violence, and oppression.' War metaphors predominate: Jews and Israelis are characterized without distinction as aggressive, thieving capitalists and imperialists who appropriate land, and the Central Council is correspondingly delegitimized.

(40) In my eyes you have become nothing more than an organization that ought to be banned that has no right at all to exist since you promote warmongering by the state of Israel contrary to the well-being of the peoples and respond to any criticism with discreditation. Shame on you! [ZJD_02.09.2006_Man_001]

(41) Criticism and sanctions for the Zionist war criminals! [ZJD_Gaza2009_194/816_ano_001]

(42) This war is state terrorism pure and simple against an almost defenseless people. [IBD_19.07.2006_Bec_001]

Right-wing-extremist writers, on the other hand, have a particular preference for scatological imagery and like to employ crude animal and filth metaphors (see Hortzitz 1999; Pörksen 2005):

(43) Revolting Israeli horde . . . You rat pack [. . .] [IBD_05.05.2007_Kol_001]

(44) fillthy jeus get out of palestine you stinking parasites [ZJD_22.05.2007_Lan_001]

(45) diseased, sickening and ultra-brutal motherfuckers [IBD_10.06.2006_Bre_001]

(46) Re: stinking, toxic Jewish filth. [IBD_11.01.2009_ano_001]

As in (47), the references apply to all Jews generically. The dehumanizing semantics are further intensified through use of the impersonal pronoun *it*:

(47) The Jew is no human being, it's a decay phenomenon [IBD_01.08.2006_Mar_001]

(48) Monsters! Animals! Filthy pigs! [IBD_18.04.2011_ano_001]

Often terms are borrowed from the lexicon of Nazi ideology, among them *subhuman riffraff, inferior subhumans*, as well as allusions to the Final Solution in the Holocaust (see chapter 5):

(49) Sieg Heil! SUBHUMAN RIFFRAFF ! [IBD_19.01.2004_ano_001]

(50) Farewell, Jew, Zyclon B won't hurt you. The day is nearing when world Jewry will be eliminated at last. We'll exterminate you all but first you're going to have to really suffer, only then will we exterminate you all, without exception. [IBD_11.01.2009_ano_001]

Yet if one surveys the e-mails and letters received in the period from 2002 to 2011, it becomes noticeable that the patterns of language usage increasingly merge. Turns of phrase that previously were employed only by neo-Nazis and right-wing radicals appear more and more in messages from the leftist camp and the mainstream, as the following examples from declared leftists and left-liberal authors, some of them with academic titles, show:

(51) Subject: Revolting Israeli rabble. So have your fascist brothers murdered a couple of Arabs again? [. . .] Only hate and violence for you. And time, you rat pack, is against you. [IBD_05.05.2007_Ler_001]

(52) To hell with the archcriminal Zionistic rabble in Palestine and its comrades in arms in Europe and North America! [ZJD_Gaza2009_521/816_Mel_001]

(53) To me as an anti-fascist it is appalling how the security state of Israel and its elites with blind rage revert time and again to unnecessary inhumanity and degenerate [. . .] to state-terrorist puppets. The monsters Goebbels and Hitler must be laughing themselves sick in hell. [IBD_01.06.2010_Göl_001]

The modes of address do not always clearly include the informal *du/ihr* or the formal *Sie*. Sometimes the authors couch their abuse in impersonal terms, as in (54). Here the writer uses third-person pronouns and thereby presents his negative attributions as generally valid facts:

(54) JEWS ARE THE CANCERUS GROWTH ON OUR WORLD! THE ABSOLUTE FILTH OF MANKIND. ONE DAY THE REAL HOLOCAUST IS COMING. STEIN à THAT'S HOW A GANGSTER LOOKS. NO ONE BELIEVES A WORD HE SAYS ANYWAY: EVERY TIME HE APPEARS IN THE MEDIA IT CREATES ONLY HATE. A PERVERSE LIAR. [IBD_01.08.2006_Mor_001, Postcard]

By means of such generic statements Jews are collectively devalued, and Shimon Stein, the ambassador at the time, is negatively conceptualized as a typical JEW. This argumentation follows the deductive pattern, which moves "from the general to the particular." In (55) the abusive comments are furthermore combined with the threat of violence against the ambassador's children:

(55) Hey you ambassador pig, do you have children by any chance that live in Berlin? Filthy Israeli sow. [IBD_20.10.2003_ano_001]

Most of the abusive comments and insults are collective attributions meant to be read generically—that is, addressed not only to the Central Council or the Embassy but to all Jews or Israelis. But abuse of individuals, addressed to a specific person or persons, also occurs, as in example (56), where the president of the Central Council at the time, Charlotte Knobloch, is accused in pseudo-religious terms of blasphemy and moral degeneracy:

(56) but you [. . .] are a PROVEN BLASPHEMER who has permanently reinterpreted the Jewish God of life into a Zionistic-tribalistic god of destruction and death! [ZJD_Gaza2009_136/816_Kra_001]

While right-wing-radical authors use almost exclusively abusive terms, as in (57) and (58), when they attack individuals, authors from the mainstream prefer to formulate their insults as questions, as in (59):

(57) lying immoral whore Knobloch [. . .] The rancid moral slut Knobloch disgusts me to the bottom of my soul! And she can stick the Holocaust up her you-know-what. [ZJD_19.04.2007_Ber_001]

(58) It's disgustingly cynical that the Jewish Central Council whore still has the gall to comment, when reporting on Gaza is absent, that the press

doesn't represent the Zionistic state enough. [ZJD_Gaza2009_267/816_ano_001]

(59) Dear Frau Knobloch [. . .] The question is: is all your impertinence intentional and backed by conspiracy or are you just plain senile? [ZJD_31.08.2006_Hyp_001]

Paul Spiegel, the previous president, is mocked and held up to ridicule, his communicative and professional activity devalued by means of pejorative terminology:[6]

(60) Dear Herr Spiegel, In your capacity as president of the Central Council of Jews in Germany you've already made a poor choice of words. I can understand that a honky-tonk agent with complicated problems doesn't have an easy time of it. But couldn't you make sure you get better advice in the future? [ZJD_08.04.2005.Hah_001]

In addition to the use of pejorative and abusive terms in the salutation (*Pissing Jew*, *Filthy Jews*), these messages feature overly casual terms of greeting such as *Hey* or *Hello* and distortions of the addressees' names (*Paulie Spiegel* or *Chalotte Knoblauch* [= *Garlic*]). A typical antisemitic strategy is to mock and stigmatize the names of Jews by twisting them or interpreting them negatively (for a more thorough discussion, see Bering 1989a, 1991b):

(61) Re: lotte knoblauch. it's time to muzzle your president. She sticks her nose into internal german matters much too often, which she doesn't have any right to do because jewry is and remains a disliked—but must-be-tolerated—religious minority. lotty should focus her attention more on her matzoh and sabbath slops and keep her impertinent mug out of the german press. [ZJD_23.10.2007_Sch_001]

(62) Dear herr wolffsohn, with this statement you've certainly done your name proud. [13.05.04-m-U1][7]

Right-wing extremists often address members of the Central Council's board of directors by their first names, which communicates a condescending or disrespectful attitude toward them:

(63) Just to make sure you don't get a wrong impression, dear Paul [. . .] [ZJD_27.05.2002_Sor_001]

(64) Hello, there, Charlotte, it's me again, this time from Berlin, my

beloved capital of the Reich, where I was always so close to your predecessor 'Paulie' Spiegel. Too bad about him, because at the end there he was really starting to understand his limits! [ZJD_18.11.2006_Seg_001]

Specific to right-wing-extremist correspondents are also references to the appropriateness of Hitler's "policy toward Jews" ("*Hitler got it right*!") and "speaking names" that hint at revisionist efforts. These extremists usually also mention their pronounced opposition or their political convictions or historical role models, as in (66). In (65) the lexeme *heretic* implies the entire right-wing-extremist position, according to which a taboo against speaking one's mind exists in Germany that supports the so-called *system parties of the FRG* and that one can flout only by being a heretic, or in other words risking death as a martyr. The claim that the Federal Republic is illegitimate, imposed by an allied occupying power that is allegedly still in control, results from the belief on the part of the author of (67) that he is the legitimate successor to the Third Reich:

(65) With a Germanic salute Erik the Heretic [ZJD_08.02.2007_Wol_001]

(66) with best regards, an admirer of Henry Ford [ZJD_22.03.2007_ano_001]

(67) Acting as a volunteer on behalf of the German Reich [IBD_08.11.2006_Pat_001]

Abuse and insults cannot always be clearly distinguished from one another. Both are forms of verbal violence intended to attack or smear the addressees' dignity and integrity. Abusive comments are fundamentally the most primitive form of insult; they are affective expressions of aggression and hate without any argumentative content. Humiliation of the person with whom one is communicating occurs exclusively through strongly pejorative lexemes. Insults, on the other hand, can be based on elaborated argumentation and do not necessarily require the use of invective. An ironic comment as in (68), sarcasm as in (69), a rhetorical question as in (70) and (71), a defamatory observation as in (72), and inappropriate analogies as in (73) and (74) can all be insulting:

(68) The army of the murder-, torture-, and land-grabbing state of Israel has won yet another glorious victory over Palestinian children and youths hurling stones. [IBD_28.03.2004_Wul_001]

(69) Congratulations to your Israeli brothers and sisters! [ZJD_05.01.2009_Nie_001]

(70) ISRAEL—A PEOPLE OF MURDERERS??? [IBD_19.03.2009_Müh_001]

(71) Can you still be called normal? [ZJD_09.01.2009_Cap_001]

(72) Israeli soldiers are murderers! [ZJD_Gaza2009_87/816_May_001]

(73) How well you've learned from the Nazis!!! [IBD_20.03.2008_Voc_001]

(74) You murder Palestinians just as you please, the way the concentration-camp wardens did to you once upon a time. Except that they were punished! [IBD_20.04_2009_ano_001]

Insults can rely on complex stereotypes and pseudo-rational arguments, all of which serve to devalue and degrade the addressee and invariably involve comparisons to the Nazis:

(75) You're campaigning for solidarity with Israel. All I can say is: down with the Jews! You've turned Gaza into a concentration camp. For decades you've kept the natives locked up, have created an apartheid system—no wonder resistance or terrorism springs up. What was it Prime Minister Andreotti said so tellingly: "We would all be terrorists if we had to grow up in a concentration camp like Gaza and live without any prospets." Right. Give up the occupation! Then maybe something will change. What can I do? I strictly boycott everything Jewish—and I spit on you!" [ZJD_Gaza2009_468/816_Kub_001]

(76) The West Bank will be reduced to rubble just like Gaza. The people there will be slaughtered just like in Gaza. Not a trace of peace, because SIrael mows down everything Palestinian without mercy. Especially the beasts of settlers, who are the greatest Israeli scum, are allowed to do whatever they like. Murdering Palestinians, carrying out acts of violence against Palestinians, abusing the children of Palestinians, destroying Palestinian harvests and property, stealing land. And much more. But the Israeli government is no different. It lets the Palestinians starve, die of thirst, refuses medical help, steals the Palestinians' land permanently, destroys the Palestinians' property, slaughters the Palestinians (whether old or young, whether man , woman or child) it has Palestinians abducted and tortured and locked up in concentration camps that rival those of the Nazis. [IBD_18.10.2007_Dro_001]

Equally insulting, however, are statements intended to instruct and chastise those addressed inappropriately, and thereby construct an asymmetric communicative situation in such a way that the addressees are disqualified as intellectually, emotionally, and morally inferior, as in "*Don't you have a spark of compassion?*" or "*Humanists are right to despise you!*" or "*It's time for you to listen to reason!*" These more subtle forms of insult are used primarily by authors from the mainstream and academics who characterize themselves as *left-liberal, not anti-Semitic*, and *concerned* (see Hostility toward Jews as a Missionary Urge in this chapter).[8]

Threats always contain an announcement of actions the producer intends to undertake: these actions invariably have negative implications for the addressee. Specific threats announce a particular form of conduct, whereas nonspecific threats suggest a future action or punishment that is not further described:

> (77) I at least will certainly not hold my tongue and will publicize the crimes of the Israelis, so those of the Jews, everywhere. [IBD_04.07.2007_Dro_001]
>
> (78) [. . .] but you're going to get the bill one of these days. [ZJD_30.05.2002_Kre_001]
>
> (79) YOU'LL LIVE TO REGRET YOUR POLICY , and no state terrorist Bush and his vassal Merkel will be able to help you! [IBD_13.07.2006_Fro_001]
>
> (80) You're going to do penance for these murders, for every little child you've murdered, for what you've done to people...whether here on earth or in the kingdom of eternal justice... But we're not going to wait till Judgment Day. [IBD_12.02.2009_ano_001]

Speech acts like these, in which the author commits to a future action, typically presume that the author is in a position to carry out what he or she has promised. Yet that presumption cannot always be confirmed when it comes to threats against the Central Council or the Embassy. Therefore, realistic and irreal threats must be differentiated. Realistic speech acts primarily take the form of promises to engage in boycotts, protests, and resistance, as well as agitation campaigns:

(81) From now on I will not buy any goods from your country! And I will urge my acquaintances and friends to do the same! [IBD_13.07.2006_Fis_003]

(82) At least on a small scale I will do everything I can not to support your state. I will neither buy any products that I can tell come from Israel nor will I ever give a moment's thought to spending my vacation in the "Holy" Land. I just hope I can be an example for many others. [IBD_05.06.2010_Hüb_001]

(83) I, too, will take part in anti-Israel demonstrations from this moment on. [IBD_16.01.2009_Kel_001]

(84) So long as there is not a government that is really ready for peace, I will not travel to Israel anymore and will do everything to denounce this policy that blocks the important and necessary peace process. As a journalist this opportunity comes up often. [IBD_02.06.2010_Fra_001]

(85) I will do everything to incite my fellow human beings against Israel. [ZJD_Gaza2009_799/816_ano_001]

These threats to engage in boycotts and protests lie within the spectrum of the possible. The same goes for declarations that promise some form of active behavior. In expressing these intentions, most of the writers do not distinguish between Israeli and Jewish matters: the Jews in Germany are made responsible collectively for Israeli military operations and so on, as the following e-mails to the Central Council illustrate:

(86) As already mentioned, I am no friend of force, but I will not allow myself to be deprived of the right to protest peacefully against your actions. [ZJD_Gaza2009_732/816_Kuh_001]

(87) For years I have boycotted everything Jewish—and that will continue. I wish you all the worst! [ZJD_05.12.2008_ano_001]

Irreal threats, on the other hand, relate to scenarios that the author is in no position to realize, as in (88), or that refer to fictive situations, as in (89):

(88) And I belong to the generation that has the good fortune to see Israel crap out.And when Israel dies, when your cities go to rack and ruin and your population craps out—I will go down on my knees,humbly clasp

my hands and thank God for HIS justice. Go to hell—where you belong. For you are the evil in this world.It will be lovely to see you crap out!I thank God for letting me witness this. [IBD_09.05.2010_ano_012]

(89) wherever possible you will be fought until you perish in a "hell." [IBD_26.07.2006_Mor_001]

The threats often appear in tandem with conditional statements that follow the pattern of "If not *X*, then *Y*." Invariably a future circumstance that the producer anticipates is made dependent on the behavior of the addressee, as in (90) and (91):

(90) I am no prophet and do not have insight into the Middle-East problems. It is also not appropriate for me to stick my nose into the '"internal" problems of other countries. But I do believe I understand one thing: freedom is indivisible. If Israel refuses to recognize this, there will be consequences. [IBD_29.03.2004_Sta_001]

(91) but if Israel does not declare an immediate ceasefire, we will demonstrate not only against the NDP but also for peace and thereby [. . .] Israel! [ZJD_30.07.2006_Wel_001]

What is striking about these threats tied to certain conditions is that the Central Council is always charged with lacking moral integrity, as in (92):

(92) Either you behave respectably and are then treated accordingly, or people will never be able to muster understanding for your religion and your people. [ZJD_Gaza2009_732/816_Kuh_001]

The authors, who seem to be filled with missionary zeal, express themselves like stern schoolmasters, articulating rules for proper behavior (see Hostility toward Jews as a Missionary Urge in this chapter). The underlying attitude is that Jews are incapable of recognizing and applying ethical principles. The threats specifically directed at Israel usually reveal a hostility grounded in the conceptualization that ISRAEL DESERVES TO BE DAMNED, INDEPENDENT OF ITS ACTIONS.

(93) If Israel continues to act this way, Israel has no hope of surviving. And that's a good thing. [IBD_16.01.2009_ano_006]

(94) I fear that if Israel doesn't turn itself around, it will bring about its own downfall as a result of its insufficient realism in seeing itself "as the chosen people." [IBD_11.05.2010_Sta_001]

(95) the blockheads in Israel, will bring the jewish state to the brink of destruction if the hitlergovernment in Israel isn't forcib4y removed! [ZJD_Gaza2009_12/816_ano_001]

In making the realization of his threat dependent on certain conditions, the author aims to exert pressure and force the recipient to do or not do something. Correspondents who verbally threaten the Central Council and the Embassy in this manner are convinced of the rightness of their demands and want to impose their will on those to whom they address their comments. Their threats take the approach of the Elf King in Goethe's poem of the same name—"And if you're not willing, then I will use force"—and reveal the traditional conceptualization that JEWS ARE UNREGENERATE AND OBSTINATE and WE HAVE THE DUTY AND THE RESPONSIBILITY TO OPEN THEIR EYES, TO PURIFY THEM, IF NEED BE BY FORCE. This thought process is articulated explicitly in (96). The threat contains not only an announcement of future violence as a moral obligation but also a suggestion for a global solution, made in analogy to the Nazis' Final Solution:

(96) To get the Jews to see reason, it is the duty of every civilized person to beat, hit, stab, or simply release these wretched chosen ones from their delusions. [. . .] In the end there will be another 'Night of Broken Glass' [*Kristallnacht,* 9 November 1938], hopefully a thorough one this time. [ZJD_Gaza2009_676/816_Pan_001]

Many threats do not stand alone but are linked to abuse and expressions of the writer's feelings:

(97) How long do you stinking Jews plan to go on killing innocent civilians with impunity? For every dead Lebanese 1000 of your type should die a miserable death. I can only hope that the chambers will be reopened for you at some point. You just make me sick. At any rate, for every one of you that dies I'm going to have a nice drink. And you can be sure,this isn't just one person's opinion. [ZJD_07.08.2006_ano_001]

Through the reference to the representativeness of his opinion the author intensifies the potential of his threat.

Right-wing extremists couch their threats in announcements of extreme bodily harm. Obscenities and coarse vulgarities predominate. This crude antisemitism is typical of the hatred articulated by neo-Nazis and right-wing extremists on the Internet as well, as (101), a text from the information platform StudiVZ, shows:

> (98) We're going to rip the testicles off you pigs and set your cunts on fire! [ZJD_Gaza2009_677/816_ano-001]
>
> (99) You stinking Jews should have your throats slit, but then instead of blood only stinking shit would come out. [ZJD_04.05.2007_Mau_001]
>
> (100) Fuck Israhell! [ZJD_09.01.2009_Cap_001]
>
> (101) I'm going to give you a grand gassing in Auschwitz! I'm going to rape your women to death. What a pleasure! You wretched rabble will get exactly what you deserve. The German people will emerge from this ethnic cleansing greater than before and purified! You Jewish rabble! Jewry is robbery. Jews are there to be killed [StudiVZ, accessed 2 August 2008, 6:33 PM; subsequently removed from the Internet]

These irreal threats reflect the extreme fantasies of violence and murder harbored by the authors and can be viewed as an expression of their hate-filled wishful thinking. The threats by right-wing radicals, often accompanied by the Hitler salute, always appear in tandem with abusive remarks that contain expressions recognizable from the Nazi period:

> (102) Sieg Heil, SUBHUMAN RIFFRAFF! The way it's looking, our grandfathers didn't do their work thoroughly enough after all! It's getting to be time againe for proper Aryans to turn on the gas! Hey Paul Spiegel can you hear us filthy Jew??? The day of reckoning will come—Sieg Heil and then you all will get your Holcaust which till NOW didn't happen yet.... hahaha...but what hasn't happened yet can still happen! HEIL HITLER!" [ZJD_19.01.2004_ano_001]
>
> (103) I take the liberty of pointing out again that I plan to stick every Jew who crosses my path like a pig. Heil Hitler [...] [IBD_26.04.2009_Kru_001]

The threats made by educated correspondents, like the one in (104), from a man with a PhD, differ only marginally from the right-wing extremists' crude antisemitism:

(104) We'll take you to The Hague, tomorrow, in a year, maybe only much later! You who from Germany fill the tank of the IDF-beasts with gasoline, manipulate the people, and put on such model-citizen airs, you're arsonists, accessories to murder. Gaza is Warsaw, the IDF is the Wehrmacht and the SS, and Livni, Barak, and Olmert are also reincarnations! You're not going to come out of this unscathed, The Hague is waiting! [ZJD_Gaza2009_154/816_Haf_001]

Aggressive announcements relating to the future can be characterized as prophetic threats:

(105) Now I'm going to give you a prophecy, Mr. Ambassador. The state of Israel will begin to fall apart, starting now, it will crack, you'll begin to hate each other for the crimes you've committed. [IBD_13.07.2006_Hel_001]

(106) The time will come when the Israelis will be called to account for their war crimes. [IBD_16.01.2009_Kel_001]

(107) For all that you'll be called to account and you'll die for it. [IBD_03.03.2008_Mie_001]

(108) You're going to be called upon to answer in the court of justice of mankind, of legitimate states that don't approve of your atrocities, and you will be found guilty. [IBD_12.02.2009_ano_001]

(109) But there's one thing you mustn't forget: "Israel will be wiped off the map." [IBD_28.05.2010_Özd_001]

Statements are made about future negative events that affect the addressee. Legal and metaphysical punishments are predicted that are viewed as sure things. The authors of such threatening prophecies feel compelled at the same time to predict a disastrous future for the addressee. The line between announcements of threats and speech acts containing curses is thus fluid[9] (on fantasies of aggression, cf. also Kiener 1983, 220).

(110) Re: You god-damned sons of whores. Don't you ever dare again to shake your finger at us Germans in the 2nd generation since the Nazi

regime because of crimes our grandfathers allegedly committed, you child-slaughterers. I hope to God that Iran really has an atom bomb and puts an end once and for all to your lying carrying-on. If this letter gets me in legal trouble, I will finally have a reason to take action against your lies and murders, committed against a civilian population that's kept locked up. I wish the plague on you and everything bad that can happen. [ZJD_Gaza2009_432/816_Hel_001]

Curses (here synonymous with maledictions)[10] are utterances in which the wish is expressed that the addressee may suffer some misfortune.

(111) Curses on Israel! [IBD_07.08.2006_ano_001]

(112) Thus speaketh the Lord Isreal you have been murdering for 3000 years and stealing others' property. May dogs lick your blood. God will bring misfortune down on you and wipe you out ? your descendants will exterminate what is male down to the last man if God so wills. [IBD_15.07.2006_ano, Postcard]

(113) Stinking riffraff, hey! Go to the devil, you miserable warmongers. [IBD_12.07.2006_ano_postcard]

(114) My wish is: that the Arab peoples may finally ally themselves against you and send you back to hell where you came from. May the "Red Sea" live up to its name. [ZJD_Gaza2009_792/816_ano_001]

(115) May your fields all dry up. [IBD_30.05.2007_ano_001]

(116) These crimes exceed any other in human history! Herr Stein your zynical attitude, your enjoyment of death, famine, murder, torture, imprisoning, and plundering the Palestininian people will hopefully rob you of all peace, health, and happiness. I wish you a long miserable unhappy life. May everything you've done to the Palestininan children happen to you 1000-fold. [IBD_24.01.2007_Ard_001]

(117) Away with you, [. . .] you lying angels, away with you. May the earth open up and swallow you all, that no trace of you may remain and all your walls, tanks, bombers, bulldozers may disappear. Away with you! Long live Palestine in Israel and Isra3el in Palestine [IBD_18.07.2006_Bil_001]

(118) I wish the CC of Jews, the chosen perpetrator people of USrael, the Jewish terrorists,war criminals and their supporters for the New Year all plagues, explosive attacks and evils of this world.May you suffer , after all you're a self-appointed chosen people. [ZJD_Gaza2009_754/816_ano_001]

Educated persons from the mainstream likewise sometimes resort to curses, through which they indulge in the very same atavistic vengefulness that they attribute to the Jews collectively, as the e-mails from a medical doctor (119) and an attorney (120) demonstrate:

(119) [. . .] may Israel find no peace and live in fear of the next suicide bombings. [ZJD_24.06.2002_Mau_001]

(120) God will punish you for that! [IBD_05.02.2009_Kel_001]

Imprecations entail verbal manifestations of hate and aggression that reflect at the same time the extent of impotent rage. A person resorts to imprecations when the real world offers no opportunity to actually inflict harm on the object of hatred.

(121) I wish you everything bad imaginable! [IBD_20.03.2009_ano_001]

(122) I wish you all a long life full of pain, torment, disgrace, and humiliation; may every breath you draw be the utmost torture. [IBD_04.01.2007_Ard_001]

(123) I hope you all die a miserable death! [ZJD_Gaza2009_301/816_ano_001]

(124) I hope to God that Iran really has an atom bomb and puts an end once and for all to your lying carrying-on. [ZJD_Gaza2009_432/816_Hes_001]

(125) It is to be hoped that Israel will have enough dead to mourn as Europe in the 30-years' war, in order to see reason (in the truest sense of the word). [ZJD_Gaza2009_552/816_Mad_001]

In (121)–(125) the authors articulate, through use of the expressive verb *wish* or *hope*, as well as the phrase *it is to be hoped*, their positive attitude toward the horrendous things they wish on the addressee. Sentences like these display a dual proposition: an emotional expression conveys both the producer's emotional attitude and an evaluation. The lexical meaning of such a sentence contains, on the one hand, this specific attitude and, on the other, the situational proposition that refers to the expression of that attitude. In semantic terms we thus have a dual proposition: a proposition within an attitudinal proposition (see Schwarz-Friesel 2007, 174).

In maledictions the writers often refer to higher powers such as heaven or hell: *May hell swallow you up*; *God will punish you*. Idiomatic expressions such as wishing *a pox on* someone and *Go to the devil* often accompany them. Formulaic sayings likewise appear in various guises: *He who sows violence will reap violence*; *He who sows such hate will reap hate*; *May he who plants the seeds of hate reap hate.*

(126) "He who sows hate will reap hate." [IBD_01.08.2006_Ren_001]

(127) Hate sows hate, and todays' Israel has remained stuck in the bloody muck of the Old Testament. [IBD_01.06.2010_Göl_001]

Curses serve as an escape valve for the authors' overflowing feelings (see chapter 8). They are emotion- and affect-laden as well as atavistic forms of communication, atavistic in the sense that they are motivated by a belief in the power of verbal magic. They correspond precisely to Judeophobic resentment: they express profound hate and ill-will toward Jews, but they are also indicators of the authors' rage and their feeling of powerlessness: when the producers of these curses are not in a position to strike a real blow against the "rotten Jewish swine," at least their curses are supposed to have an effect—like voodoo. If it is impossible to actually harm the hated Jews in real life, they deploy the destructive potential of language.

Hostility toward Jews as a Missionary Urge: Moral Appeals and Advice

If extremist antisemitism takes the form of ostentatious aggression, expressed by means of hate-filled curses and fantasies of violence, authors from the mainstream tend to encode their Judeophobic attitude more euphemistically—that is, recode their attitude as one of "concerned criticism," "indignation," and "moral obligation" (see the strategies of legitimation and attenuation in chapter 10, under Strategies of Legitimation and Self-Aggrandizement and Strategies of Avoidance and Self-Defense). If extremists portray Jews on principle as inferior, degenerate beings belonging to an innately criminal people, text producers from the mainstream insinuate that their Jewish fellow citizens and Israelis suffer from intellectual, affective, and moral failings, and they style themselves communicatively as instructors, judges, and/or counselors. These correspondents therefore express their primarily didactic directives in the imperative, challenging the addressees to be ashamed of themselves and/or to mend their ways at long last:

(128) [. . .] you should be ashamed of yourself! (IBD_05.02.2009_Mar_001]

(129) [. . .] and you should be ashamed of yourself! [IBD_03.04.2009_Kub_001]

(130) [. . .] YOU should ALL be ashamed of yourselves!!! [ZJD_Gaza2009_306/816_ano_001]

(131) In conclusion I would like to remind you once more of what I consider Moses' most important commandment: Thou shalt not kill. You should obey that, damn it! [ZJD_Gaza2009_14/816_ano_001]

The producers of these texts obviously see themselves as occupying a superior position to the recipients that allows them to make such demands. The demand that someone be ashamed usually occurs in the context of childrearing when some reason allegedly exists for the child to be ashamed, namely bad behavior. Scolding implies an asymmetric communicative relationship that allows the producer to admonish the recipient out of a sense of superiority. In many messages the authors attempt to prescribe to the Central Council how it should behave. In particular, it is often urged to take a critically distanced stance toward Israel.

(132) But why does the Central Council of Jews in Germany not openly voice criticism and condemn the obvious injustice. [. . .] Why doesn't the vice president of your organization say anything against Israel's aggressive war on Palestine, which is no ordiniary defense against terrorism but is itself terrorizing? [ZJD_09.04.2002_Sto_001]

(133) Why don't you distance yourself from the murderous war of the state of Israel against Palestine's civilian population? [ZJD_Gaza2009_409/816_Pat_001]

(134) Distance yourself decisively from the murderers—enemies of mankind. [ZJD_Gaza2009_325/816_Kis_001]

At the same time these messages often imply that Jews deal with problems in a cognitively inadequate or inappropriate way, make mistakes, have no sympathy for others, and are emotionally deficient:

(135) I hate any kind of violence including violence against Jews. But I wish for a peaceful world for my children's future. Unfortunately you all have no interest in such a thing [. . .] [IBD_20.07.2006_ano_008]

(136) Just think about it! [ZJD_Gaza2009_723/816_Kuh_001]

(137) what didn't you understand when I wrote peace!!! [ZJD_Gaza2009_600/816_ano_001]

(138) This can't go on. You and the state of Israel are behaving with an unparallelled lack of responsibility. [ZJD_27.07.2006_Rau_001]

As the basis for such scolding, the authors verbalize Judeophobic conceptualizations, as in this e-mail from a professor:

(139) The background is most likely the Zionistic notion of being a chosen people. [ZJD_27.07.2006_Rau_001]

The observation or the charge, formulated as a rhetorical question, that Jews have no compassion for others turns up as one of the reproaches most frequently hurled at the Central Council:

(140) I am stunned to observe that you apparently don't care at all about dead children in Gaza and Lebanon. [ZJD_27.07.2006_Rau_001]

(141) You people have no respect for life!!! [ZJD_Gaza2009_210/816_ano_001]

(142) You HAve no human feelings. [IBD_02.06.2010_Bos_002]

(143) Do you people have any such thing as human feelings? [ZJD_22.10.2008_Lie_001]

Another reproach that appears significantly often is that Jews have learned nothing from history or in general are incapable of learning:

(144) Have you and the likes of you learned nothing from history? [ZJD_03.09.2006_Gus_001]

(145) This is all the more regrettable as the Jewish people has learned nothing either from its history of salvation since the days of Abraham or from the dark days of the 3rd Reich ... and now [...] watches the goings-on in the "Holy Land" without a word. [ZJD_15.04.2002_Fal_001]

Many Germans see themselves as preceptors, obligated on the basis of the "lessons of German history" to warn and reprimand the Jews, whom they charge with being perpetrators of or accomplices in "*Israeli crimes*" and "*Zionist state terrorism*":

(146) And those who attempt to justify Israel's deeds thereby make themselves complicit. [ZJD_30.08.2006_Cra_001]

(147) Re: Frau Knobloch—your criticism of us Germans. [. . .] We have learned from our mistakes, but now you're committing the same ones. [ZJD_30.08.2006_Mei_002]

(148) we Germans have learned from history, but it seems to me there's a deficit in that respect in the Central Council of Jews [ZJD_29.08.2006_Bre_001]

(149) We Germans have bitter experience with Chosen Ones, apparently you have yet to learn that. [ZJD_27.07.2006_Rau_001]

Many authors also take it upon themselves to declare that statements by the Central Council and the Embassy are lies, hypocrisy, or fiction, as in (150)–(153):

(150) Evidently you're blind in one eye, because there's no other way to interpret YOUR holier-than-thou attitude. [ZJD_25.10.2006_Sch_001]

(151) Do you believe in all seriousness that the world community accepts your contention that the abduction of Israeli soldiers justifies the battles of the last few weeks? [ZJD_18.08.2006_Kan_001]

(152) In view of the twisting of facts and the dishonesty with which people like Ambassador Stein, Prof.Wolfenssohn, Frau Knobloch, and the Israeli UN ambassador Gillerman legitimate the Israeli war crimes in the Palestinian territories and in Lebanon, no one should be surprised to find justified anti-Zionism in Germany. [ZJD_04.08.2006_War_001]

The demands and admonitions are conveyed primarily by means of the modal verbs *must*, *should*, and *may*. The modal verb *must* serves to express "norms and prescriptions with a high degree of obligation" (*Duden* 2006, 564):

(153) To survive in this world as a Jew, you absolutely must change your behavior [. . .] [ZJD_Gaza2009_20/816_ano_001]

(154) Mustn't one be ashamed, Frau Knobloch .....? [ZJD_05.01.2009_Kil_001]

At the same time many authors refer in this connection to the official culture of memorialization in Germany: they assume the position of "admonishers" vis-à-vis the Jews but firmly reject the Central Council's right to admonish others (see chapter 8, under The Mentality of "Being Fed Up" and Refusal of Empathy).

(155) Herr Spiegel [. . .] When are you finally going to stop harassing and blaming the current generation of Germans? [ZJD_24.06.2002_Pin_001, with the signatures of friends and acquaintances attached]

(156) You absolutey should compare your moral claims against nazi germany, which to this day are plaguing Innocent Descendants, with the morality back home in fascist Israel. Maybe something will jump out at you. In that regard you have a ton of reality to process. And let me make it clear that I personally refuse to accept any paternalism when it comes to morality and claims from the Nazi period! [ZJD_01.09.2006_Len_001]

In content many of these directives employing the modal verb *should* resemble the didactic directives in examples (128)–(130), in which the addressees are ordered to be ashamed of themselves:

(157) You should be ashamed of yourself. [ZJD_Gaza2009_344/816_Bau_001]

(158) You, the representatives of Israel, should be ashamed of yourselves. [IBD_16.01.2009_Bau_001]

(159) You and your country should be thoroughly ashamed of yourselves. [IBD_19.03.2009_Knö_001]

The authors of such messages present themselves as peace-loving humanists who are not antisemitic; they construct an attitudinal and communicative position for themselves that legitimizes moral condemnation of the addressees. They assume a know-it-all attitude toward the Jews. From their point of view, they, as morally upright persons, have a right to instruct the "*stupid Jews*" and/or the "*despicable Israelis*" as to the error of their ways and to rub their noses in their shame. They often articulate this conviction in generalizations that impart moral judgments, such as "*Force is never good,*" "*Oppression of another people is evil,*" or "*Peace and respect for one's fellow man are most important.*" Responsibility for observing ethical principles in conflict situations is always imposed one-sidedly on the Israelis. That another party to the conflict in the

Middle East engages in terrorist and warmongering activities and that other sources of conflict have historically existed in the Middle East is denied or ignored altogether (see chapter 6, under Derealization).

(160) Mr. President, that Israel is fighting for its existence is sheer nonsense. [ZJD_05.04.2002_St_001]

(161) With the greatest indignation I see that your Zionist state to bomb and drive out countless thousands of people who have done nothing other than to live there .... Please recognize that before the arrival of Israel in the Middle East peace reigned there. Since then there has been war. Doesn't that make you think? [ZJD_27.07.2006_Rau_001]

(162) Israel conducted [. . .] a brutal war [. . .] against the helpless civilian population This vicious cycle of violence and counter-violence that has been going on now for abt. 60 years must finally be stopped..... This spiral of violence—injustice—hate must end, otherwise there will never be peace. [ZJD_Gaza2009_63/816_Wil_001]

Sometimes, as in (163) and (164), these generalizations are introduced by phrases that identify them as the author's opinion, such as *in our view* or *as I believe*:

(163) In our eyes every people has a right to exist in dignity and justice. [ZJD_19.04.2002_Lin_001, with several signatures]

(164) But I do believe I understand one thing: freedom is indivisible. If Israel refuses to recognize this, there will be consequences. [IBD_29.03.2004_Sta_001]

The educated author of (165), who comes from Braunschweig, positions herself through the reference to her own mental and emotional normality as opposed to the addressees, who, she implies, lack these characteristics:

(165) I consider myself a person with normal emotions and normal intelligence and with good common sense [. . .] my wish is to have statesmen and stateswomen who are capable of reconciliation, insightful, wise, and smart, and will do the right thing in the right place at the right time. [IBD_12.08.2006_Sch_006]

The wish expressed at the end of this multipage message about the Middle East conflict, which contains all sorts of reproaches and defamatory charges leveled at Israel, implies that such smart people do not exist on the Israeli side.

Hyperbolic demonization as in (166) and referential derealization as in (167) also turn up in messages from members of the educated mainstream, as the following comments by correspondents with PhDs plainly show:

> (166) Israel is far and away the greatest evil in the world [...] [ZJD_25.10.2006_Sch_001]
>
> (167) Israel is the greatest threat to world peace. [IBD_17.05.2009_Lor_002]

While explicit and radical threats appear primarily in messages from right-wing extremists, educated correspondents from the mainstream convey their threats implicitly, usually recasting them as recommendations, as the following e-mail subject lines demonstrate:

> (168) Call to reason from Erwitte [IBD_16.01.2009_Bri_001]
>
> (169) Calm reflection called for [IBD_22.01.2009_Kam_001]

Moral appeals are often couched in the form of rhetorical questions:

> (170) Don't you have a shred of compassion? [ZJD_30.06.2008_Man_001]
>
> (171) Does Israel have no shame? No compassion? [ZJD_Gaza2009_116/816_Sel_001]
>
> (172) Does the community of Jews in Germany really not include any wise, self-critical, and humanely just fellow human beings? [ZJD_Gaza2009_502/816_Cri_001]

In this way the stereotype is collectively coded to imply that Jews lack humanistic qualities. These "polite" insults all serve to discredit Jews' morality, reproaching them for complicity in or even responsibility for Israeli military operations, all of which are classified as illegal, disproportionate, and morally despicable.

> (173) And those who attempt to justify Israel's actions thereby make themselves accomplices. [ZJD_30.08.2006_Cra_001]

(174) drop the victim act, because you've been the perpetrators for a long time already. [ZJD_25.10.2006_Sch_001]

(175) taking the lives of innocent little children, mothers, and fathers in attacks by Israel: I'm ashamed for all Jews! [ZJD_05.01.2009_Kil_001]

(176) You clearly deserve to be brought before an international court for supporting war crimes Frau Knobloch. You and the government rabble in Israel [. . .] [ZJD_Gaza2009_568/816_Cap_001]

In examples (173)–(179) the members of the Central Council are stylized as criminals. The authors of the messages issue general warnings related to the overall political situation. Here hyperbolic assertions play a dominant role:

(177) State-sponsored terrorism of the worst kind. A punishment awaits you, a huge shock, whatever it will be, a natural catastrophe or destruction of some other kind. [IBD_13.07.2006_Hel_001]

(178) the Israeli hitlerstate endangers world peace! [ZJD_Gaza_2009_12/816_Mah_001]

Warnings differ from threats in that they are not linked to announcements of pending sanctions. Threats always include notice of possible negative consequences if that which the producer demands is ignored. Warnings merely predict some danger, although additional consequences and developments can be implied.

(179) Your policy can ignite an inferno! [IBD_07.06.2011_Ört_001]

A warning is predicated on the producer's possessing more knowledge or being better informed than the recipient and on the recipient's not perceiving the danger. Warnings therefore always imply a feeling of superiority toward the Jews and Israelis. This patronizing attitude also finds expression in utterances like (180) and (181):

(180) But it would be a human and ethical miracle if the Central Council of Jews in Germany distanced itself from Israel's manner of waging war. If that were to happen, I would have confidence in you again, and a speck of interest in contact. [ZJD_Gaza2009_11/816_Ges_001]

(181) And because Jews have always lived in Palestine, Jews are supposed to continue to be allowed to live there in perpetuity and have new ones

join them. [...] But I find a "Jewish state" in which other people have fewer rights just as unacceptable as a Germany where Jews, Turks or other people have fewer rights than the German majority. [ZJD_24.07.2009_Has_001]

The authors display an unmistakably exaggerated sense of their own worth when they make the very existence and configuration of the state of Israel, as well as their relationship to the Central Council of Jews, contingent on their personal attitudes. The modal verb *dürfen* carries the meaning of 'to have permission' to do something. The author of (181) considers it appropriate to shape Israel's future according to what he envisions.[11] Utterances of this sort express a goodly measure of condescension and presumption; the authors are convinced of the rightness of their demands and admonitions and believe they have sufficient competence and standing to reprimand the Central Council and the Embassy. This self-assessment, however, clashes with the reality: most of the moralists and "Middle East experts" (who sometimes also disseminate their suggestions through the Internet and send copies of their e-mails to newspapers and politicians) have, by their own admission, never been in the country whose future they are so eager to shape. Correspondingly many of the writers offer "good advice" and behave toward the Central Council and the Embassy like adults toward small children. Typical of this attitude is the use of analogies intended to help Jews or Israelis, allegedly "slow on the uptake," grasp the cognitive and moral implications of their own actions:

(182) Let me perhaps add a tip for the responsible politicians on both sides: when two children in nursery school can't agree on sharing something equally (such as a piece of cake), one of them is allowed to split the object of contention and the other is allowed to pick his piece first—seldom have I experienced a fairer process... [ZJD_28.07.2006_Geh_001]

This communicative asymmetry is often introduced with emotion-laden phrases such as *I'm very sad that . . .* or *I'm disappointed in you*; then come moral appeals and criticisms of the addressees' behavior.

(183) I was very sad to read again (in SPIEGEL Online) that the Central Council has poked its nose into controversy involving Israel again [on the subject of Felicia Langer's receiving the Federal Cross of Merit]. Aren't you supposed to be focusing on the Jews in Germany? [ZJD_21.07.2009_Has_001]

(184) Dear Ladies and Gentlemen, I am very disappointed and indignant [...] [ZJD_Gaza2009_63/816_Wil_001]

(185) Israel is another country altogether, so why are you constantly focusing on it? [...] What if you established a subsidiary, for instance a "German-Israeli Friendship Committee"? It could then publicly express opinions on Israeli matters, and the Central Council could focus on matters that affect German Jews. [ZJD_21.07.2009_Has_001]

In this context, it is striking how often the authors use verbs such as *call on*, *demand*, *appeal*, *forbid*, and *protest*. This usage matches the terms that appear in the public communication space, including the Internet and pamphlets, such as those issued by the Bremen boycott advocates (see Schwarz-Friesel 2012).[12]

(186) hence my demands [...] [IBD_14.07.2006_Mue_001]

(187) I would like to call on you to do likewise, unambiguously. [ZJD_09.04.2002_Sto_001]

(188) I protest against the inhumane policy of the state of Israel and appeal to you and all responsible politicians from your country to end immediately this criminal war against Palestine and Lebanon. [...] It's time the state of Israel recognized the truth and stopped lying to the world and itself. [IBD_19.07.2006_Kno_001]

Implicit demands are formulated as requests, advice, expectations, and admonitions:

(189) Dear Ladies and Gentlemen, dear Fellow Human Beings, A little tolerance, a little less obstinacy would help! Please take these thoughts to heart. [IBD_17.01.2009_Hir_001]

(190) So I would also expect the Central Council of Jews to distance itself from these atrocities in Gaza and also elsewhere and ask the victims for forgiveness in the name of all Jews living here and in the name of Jewry. [ZJD_Gaza2009_64/816_Khu_001]

(191) I exhort your state to behave humanely [...] [IBD_17.01.2009_Sch_002]

(192) Please compare Herr Filbinger with Herr Sharon. Filbinger was certainly no hero who would have been ready to risk his life or livelihood for

> resistance. But your Herr Sharon is considerably worse. In Sabra and Shatila no "superior orders" were in effect. Herr Sharon was the commanding officer there. You should issue some kind of statement on the murders being committed by the Israelis; then perhaps you would be more believable [ZJD_16.04.2007_Rau_001]

These self-appointed humanists seem not to be aware that such "advice" invokes the same ancient defamatory clichés and Judeophobic stereotypes as the abusive comments made by right-wing radicals, merely on a higher stylistic plane and therefore less obvious.

Since many e-mail authors want to be viewed as upstanding, honest people despite their anti-Jewish arguments, they use a variety of strategies to give the radical content of their messages an aura of respectability (see chapter 10). In the "antisemitism of the reputable," as Jean Améry called it in 1969, the masking and trivializing formulations create the impression that the conventions of politeness are being preserved; such formulations should be categorized as pseudo-politeness. These messages differ from the blatantly impolite messages whose authors make no attempt to save face and revel in abuse and insults, but also from e-mails that are genuinely courteous. To imply that the addressee lacks cognitive insight, moral virtues, and the emotional capacity for empathy, or to portray him or her as unable or unwilling to learn, is as much of an insult as calling the addressee a *pig* or *monster*, merely less vulgar. To impute to other human beings a lack of the most important faculties—intelligence and feeling—constitutes dehumanization and denigration. The difference is only a matter of style.

If one surveys the texts received by the Central Council between 2000 and 2009 and those received by the Embassy between 2003 and 2011, it becomes clear that over that span of time the tone becomes more aggressive, the argumentation more radical, and the use of defamatory formulations more frequent and thus more routine. Starting in 2006, the verbal attacks on the Central Council contain more insults and threats. The messages to the Embassy increasingly include abuse and imprecations. Mainstream correspondents become more likely to deny Israel's right to exist. Up to 2006, messages that include aggressive speech acts tend to be sent anonymously, but after that time the authors are more likely to identify themselves by name and address. Although educated antisemites who declare themselves to be anti-antisemites continue to use "verbal velvet gloves," that is, primarily indirect speech acts, their pseudo-rational argumentation reveals an irrational radicalism and emotional aggressiveness that differs little from extremist thinking. Observance of the conventions of politeness dwindles while the verbal forms communicating violence increase. An important factor contributing to this phenomenon is that utterances hostile toward Israel increasingly go unchallenged and unpunished in the public communicative space. Furthermore, starting with the Second Intifada and especially in connection with the Lebanon and Gaza conflicts, reporting on the Middle East was often one-sided, highly emotional, and largely unfavorable to Israel. That numerous authors refer repeatedly to this reporting indicates the role the media play in linking public and individual attitudes and shaping opinion (see Beyer and Leuschner, 2010; Schwarz-Friesel, 2012). The taboo against expressing hostility toward Jews is disappearing and the acceptance of using inflammatory language in public is growing.[13]

Suggestions for Solving the "Jewish Problem": "*Exterminate them for good!*" and "*Dissolve the state of Israel!*"

I hope someday all the Jews will have disappeared from the world. [IBD_07.07.2006_ano_026]

Many of the correspondents are not content with uttering abusive comments, specific threats, and imprecations; they also articulate a variety of comprehensive suggestions for solving the "*Jewish problem*" or, projected onto Israel, for the "*Middle East conflict*," the "*Jewish state*," the "*Holy Land*," or "*Palestine*." Most of these "suggestions" do not distinguish between Jewish existence in general and the existence of the state of Israel. The majority of the educated correspondents from the mainstream, however, do make a clear distinction: seemingly legitimizing themselves by asserting that they are not antisemites and have nothing against Jews in general, they apply their "solutions" only to the state of Israel, which according to them needs to be "*drastically altered*," "*abolished*," "*dissolved*," or "*internationalized*." These suggestions sometimes take the form of appeals, for instance urging Jews to leave Israel, and sometimes convey threats or "promises" or implied threats.

Articulated as expressions of emotion, they resemble prophetic curses and portray wishful images of the future downfall of all Jews and/or the Jewish state of Israel. What they have in common is that they support a final resolution of a situation considered to be problematic and link that resolution to a general approach to the problem of the Jews or Israel.[14]

Many writers, in particular those who write repeatedly to the Central Council or the Embassy over the years, sometimes even several times a month, convey the impression that they see it as their most important task in life to focus on Jewish or Israeli matters. The obsessive nature of antisemitism is unmistakable (see chapter 8). The old, traditional conception that underlies the suggestions is that JEWS ARE THE FUNDAMENTAL EVIL IN THE WORLD. Linguistically this conception manifests itself in statements such as "*Without Jews the world would be better off; Jews are the scum of humanity*" and "*Jews are mischief makers, disturbers of the peace.*" Examples (193)–(195) demonstrate this feature:

> (193) This is my opinion: as long as there are Jews there will be no peace in the world.[15] [ZJD_08.01.2008_Hei_001]
>
> (194) You yourselves create the basis for antisemitism in the world [. . .]!!! [ZJD_Gaza2009_70/816_ano_001]
>
> (195) I view you as the scum of humanity. [IBD_15.07.2006_Dei_001]

The ultimate goal of anti-Jewish resentment is to see to it that the evil embodied by Jews in the world is eliminated, for the well-being of humankind. This salvational antisemitism formed the ideological basis of the Nazis' Final Solution (see chapter 3, under Survival and Resistance of Judeophobic Stereotypes in Modern Times).

Three types of proposed solutions can be distinguished, occurring regularly in the messages from correspondents of different backgrounds, educational levels, and political orientations: radical calls for killing not only Israelis but also Jews all over the world; utopian programs for resettlement intended to end the Middle East conflict; and recommendations for dissolving the state of Israel. In the radical-extremist extermination plans, the things wished on Jews include "*the plague*," "*downfall*," "*extermination*," "*nuclear annihilation*," and "*the second Final Solution, but the right one this time.*" These suggestions do not differentiate between Jews and Israelis. Accordingly, Jewish and Israeli concerns become indistinguishable:

(196) Hello, you blood-dripping Jewish swine! I contest Israel's right to exist and the Jewish pestilence's right to live. [IBD_26.04.2009_Kru_001]

(197) Get out of germany, out of Gaza, out of the world, out of the universe! [ZJD_Gaza2009_102/816_ano_001]

(198) One of these days you will be FINALLY exterminated. The world is praying for that. [ZJD_Gaza2009_401/816_Jar_001]

(199) I hope you all bite the dust soon [. . .] From this moment on, I'm an ANTISEMITE. [ZJD_Gaza2009_178/816_ano_001]

(200) you should be processed into animal fodder so you can be useful for a change. [IBD_01.08.2006_ano_026]

(201) get out of our peaceful life for good and fight your wars on the planet Moon for all I care but leave us here on earth in peace. [IBD_12.08.2006_ano_001]

(202) All of you need to be WIPED OUT!!! [IBD_01.05.2010_ano_024]

Many of these radical suggestions, which have the character of irreal imprecations, are pure murder fantasies, but there are also repeated references to the Final Solution that was put into actual effect during the Nazi period, "for the good of mankind." The completion of the Nazis' Final Solution by means of their practices is often proposed, and in the same language used by the Nazis (see chapter 5).

(203) It's getting to be time again for proper Aryans to turn on the gas! [ZJD_19.01.2004_ano_001]

(204) In the end there will be another "Night of Broken Glass," hopefully a thorough one this time. [ZJD_Gaza2009_676/816_Pan_001]

(205) It's my burning wish to get the gas chambers back [. . .] [IBD_05.08.2008_Dro_001]

(206) Get back in the oven you came from! [ZJD_30.07.2006_Ger_001]

(207) and off to the gas chambers! [ZJD_Gaza2009_677/816_Per_003]

Similar solutions are proposed for the state of Israel, which symbolizes Jewish life in the world: the country is supposed to be "*destroyed*," "*smashed*," "*radically changed*," "*dissolved*," or "*modified*."

(208) I hope Iran has the BOMB. [IBD_01.06.2010_Thi_001]

(209) The Israelis are the rats of the world and should one and all be poisoned with cyclon gas, the way you do with rats. [IBD_11.04.2007_Dro_001]

In example (210) the proposals for a solution are cloaked in pseudo-rational justifications and affective expressions that contain several characteristic components of extreme verbal antisemitism, this time in the anti-Israeli variant (see chapter 6):

(210) Hey, you disgusting Israeli gang of criminals, by now I've come to be really happy about every Israeli asshole that is offed somewhere—the only good Israelis are dead Israelis....hopefully your filthy fascist state will be wiped off the map real soon. I'd be glad to help that along... I think it's really time to treat your "representatives" here in this country now and then the way you rats have just shown us. [IBD_28.05.2010_ano_018]

The closed nature of the author's mental image of the world, in which the Israelis figure as the current representatives of the "inhumane, abysmally evil Jew," becomes evident here.

Less drastically formulated but no less irreal suggestions by certain authors call for the resettlement of the Jews living in Israel; a frequent correspondent from Bochum expresses this idea as follows:

(211) My suggestion is that Israel be moved to Texas. Then the murdering would stop. The Americans like the hardworking Jews, but your people won't go for that, of course, the solution would be too easy, they prefer the endless killing. [IBD_12.06.2006_Sch_001]

(212) I hope my suggestion to move Israel to Texas/USA might still be acted on after all so this terror finally stops. [IBD_13.07.2006_Sch_004]

(213) My suggestion is that the Israeli government find a sufficiently large piece of land in Texas/USA and transfer its people there. [ZJD_27.07.2006_Sch_002]

(214) You'd have an opportunity to stop the murdering if you'd relocate Israel to the USA. [IBD_11/06.2008_Sch_001]

These utopian suggestions undergo some elaboration; that is, they are presented with many explanations and justifications, as in (215), sent by an author from Erkrath who offers a detailed argument:

(215) Doesn't the Israeli government have an opportunity to acquire land in Egypt, for example by purchase, rental, or lease? (Sinai Peninsula or something like that.) Egypt is only about 10% populated, the rest is desert

or steppe. Since it's fairly poor, Egypt would gain additional revenue. The millions that Israel receives from the US could be put to use in part for land purchases. Also the EU would certainly be willing to contribute. But Syria or Jordan could perhaps also provide additional living space. Then Israel wouldn't have to build new houses in West Jordanland or in East Jerusalem. Instead it would rent land for example for 100 years in Egypt. [IBD_16.09.2009_Dap_001]

Resettlement plans and the dissolution of the state of Israel are sometimes presented together, as in the following from a twenty-five-page e-mail to the Central Committee:

(216) I have thought about how this potential breeding ground for a third world war can be eliminated, and in my considered opinion there is just one lasting solution to this conflict: [. . .] Only the dissolution of the Israeli state can blockthe Jews from banding together and thus also their highly aggressive tendencies as a united people that gives free rein to its inherited aggression and inherited frustration. The Jews who have moved away from Israel will then have a chance to settle somewhere else. [ZJD_30.11.2006_Gel_001]

In the utopian suggestions, too, usually no distinction is made between Jews and Israelis:

(217) The Jewish question must be solved. One suggestion would be to prepare refugee camps in Iran for the religious Jews. [IBD_18.01.2009_ano_001]

The suggestions made by educated authors from the mainstream of society are billed as "peaceable, humanistic" solutions to the Middle East conflict and world peace. These solutions usually entail dissolving the state of Israel:

(218) The best thing for world peace and also for the Jews would be to have Israel dissolve itself without a fight, and for the Jews from all over the world to make restitution for the crimes against the Palestinians by means of generous donations and the rebuilding of Palestine for the Palestinians. [IBD_30.06.2006_Bec_001]

The proponents always vehemently deny that these suggestions entail a projection of anti-Jewish resentment based on the conceptualization of ISRAEL AS A COLLECTIVE JEW. In direct analogy to the Judeophobic conceptualization of Jews as evil per se and disturbers of the peace in the world, Israel is demonized and ostentatiously devalued (see the detailed discussion in chapter 6):

(219) But it's a fact that the state of Israel is disturber-of-the-peace No. 1 in the Middle East. [IBD_24.07.2006_Ehr_001]

(220) Israel is the disturber of the peace in the Middle East. [IBD_02.08.2006_Ser_002]

(221) Next to the usa israel is the worst UNJUST STATE. ...now we're convinced of that once and for all: you and your people are Sick, in spirit and body! [IBD_15.08.2006_Deu_001, with five signatures]

(222) You are the EVIL in this world, may sickness and misery befall you and your offspring. [IBD_31.05.2010_Sch_014]

Right-wing extremists prefer to degrade Israel with terms such as *cancerous growth*, *cripple state*, *thalidomide monster*, *murder machine*, *freak*, *monster state*, and *nest of terrorists*. Educated and left-wing liberal correspondents delegitimize Israel by means of lexemes such as *unjust state*, *apartheid regime/state*, *Zionist anachronism*, and *colonialist throwback*. The writers who express such judgments or condemnations (usually without conflating anti-Israeli defamation with Judeophobic collective attributions or assuming that the groups are synonymous) make a point of emphasizing that all this has nothing to do with antisemitism:

(223) Have you grasped where the evil lies? The world is beginning to get sick and tired of the professional nurturing of terrorists by the state of Israel. [. . .] Why are the Jews persecuted again and again? That you must ask yourselves. [. . .] Don't call me an antisemite, because that's not accurate. [IBD_04.07.2006_Str_001]

(224) I'm of the opinion, by the way, that criticizing the behavior of the Israeli government or army has nothing to do with antisemitism or right-wing radicalism. [ZJD_31.07.2006_Baa_001]

Most of the authors who characterize themselves as "open-minded" and as imbued with the "spirit of the Enlightenment" display, when it comes to Jewry and the state of Israel, a marked intolerance, usually articulated as condemnation or negation of a Jewish national state.

(225) Dear Ladies and Gentlement of the Jewish Faith, I am sorry to say this, but Israel is just as little Jewish as Germany is Christian. Why do you always equate Judaism with Israel [. . .] ? [ZJD_Gaza2009_28/816_Pah_001]

A business consultant from Bavaria offers—in a subordinate clause—a suggestion that he characterizes as "*just*" and "*humane*":[16]

(226) I don't care about the Zionist state, which should be peacefully dissolved. [ZJD_Gaza2009_72/816_Som_001]

A gentleman from Wesseling sends "cordial greetings" and points out:

(227) A plenary session of the UN really should be called as quickly as possible to discuss the dissolution, the dissolution of the state of Israel. [IBD_03.03.2008_Moe_001]

And a gentleman from Offenbach with a PhD has a similar approach:

(228) Dear Mr. Ambassador Stein, The best solution for a lasting peace in the Middle East is the dissolution of the state of Israel and the destruction of all weapons. [IBD_23.03.2007_Hof_001]

A professor tries to make clear to the Central Council in several e-mails that the Jewish character of the state of Israel must be altered to make way for a multinational state without religious preferences. The history of Israel's founding is portrayed as illegitimate and morally despicable; the author uses a crude analogy to colonial racist policies:

(229) The creation of Israel in this form would have been completely impossible after 1960. In 1947 the UN was still dominated by the colonial powers, which found it perfectly normal that the whites ruled over broad swaths of the non-white world. [ZJD_24.07.2009_Has_002]

When the secretary general of the Central Council, who responded several times to the professor, pointed out that Israel also represented a guarantee for Jewish persons and gave many Jews a sense of security after the Holocaust, the professor reiterated his delegitimation of Israel, which included equating it with the former apartheid regime in South Africa. He also made the patronizing remark that "*the Zionist dream of a national state ruled by Jews must be relinquished.*"

(230) The notion of finding safety in the Holy Land may have made sense during the colonial period, but since decolonization in the '60s it is clear that the Europeans can't simply seize possession of others' land in Africa or Asia. Israel is an anomaly that will not survive. Sooner or later a solution will have to be found. [ZJD_27.07.2009_Has_003]

In order to block any possibility of a radical reading hostile toward Israel or Jews by the addressees but also by themselves, such authors always invoke generally recognized precedents and declare their solutions to be the result of their humanistic thinking and feeling.

(231) For Palestine the best solution is the one-state solution already advocated by Albert Einstein and Hanna Arendt: a secular state in which all people, regardless of their religion and ethnicity, have the same rights and no one tries to rule over anyone else. [ZJD_24.07.2009_Has_002]

(232) that we, too, in Germany commit ourselves primarily to justice, and not primarily for the descendants of the Holocaust victims (since the latter are a small minority in Israel). [ZJD_20.12.2009_Has_005]

Formulating proposals for solving the "Jewish problem" has been a feature of Judeophobia for centuries. The "oldest hatred in the world" has a destructive dimension that turns up in demands for assimilation or aggregation, depending on the period and worldview or ideology (see the examples in chapter 3; see also Schwarz-Friesel and Friesel 2012). In the religious realm this solution meant abandoning the Jewish faith and accepting (compulsory) conversion; in the social and political realm it meant ghettoization, discrimination, expulsion, murder, or assimilation. The wishful thinking about Jews on the part of non-Jews is reflected to this day in utterances such as those in examples (233)–(236):

(233) Willingness to accept real integration would be something to wish for and would represent a step in the right direction [...] [ZJD_30.05.2007_Gir_001]

(234) Adapt, for heavens sake! [ZJD_01.05.2008_Kro_001]

(235) Get out of Palestine! [IBD_24.03.2009_Pet_001]

(236) Make yourselves scarce so mankind can live in peace again. [ZJD_Gaza2009_577/816_ano_001]

The "solution" from a non-Jewish point of view means only one thing for the Jews: extermination or abandonment of their birthright as Jews.[17] Although two hundred years have passed since the fanatical hater of Jews Hundt-Radowsky suggested in his book *The Jewish Mirror* two basic solutions to the problem of Jewish "vermin," the modern variants have not changed, despite the experience of the Holocaust:

(237) The best would be, however, to purge the country entirely of this vermin, and for this purpose there are likewise two means. Either to exterminate them altogether or, as Pharoah and the people of Meiningen, of Würzburg, and of Frankfurt have done, to chase them from the land. [Hundt-Radowsky 1819, 146]

That Israel styles itself the Jewish state, and thereby boldly declares Jewish existence to be legitimate and asserts its right to realize that existence, constitutes an immense provocation to antisemites. They inevitably demand the annulment or "dejewification" of this state as a necessity. In Christian anti-Judaism the call was issued for the Jewish "unbelievers" to convert, and in racist-eliminatory antisemitism, Jews were classified as subhuman and targeted for the Final Solution. Today, "in the name of justice," and "in the interest of world peace," the dissolution of Israel is demanded. The modern antisemites take their place with their proposals in the unbroken line of those vowing to "solve the Jewish question."[18] They thereby preserve to this day the continuity of hostility toward Jews.

Conclusion

The aggressiveness that becomes evident in modern texts manifests itself in linguistic acts of violence that abuse Jews for being Jews and insult, mock, disparage, and threaten them. The violent and discriminatory potential of language also expresses itself in speech acts through which Jews are lectured and reprimanded. They are treated—particularly by academic writers—as if they were immature persons who depended on advice from non-Jews. They are denied the ability to judge critically or intelligently and to experience human emotions. Questions and observations that call into question, or declare to be nonexistent, the moral integrity and rational competence of Jewish fellow citizens correlate to these charges. Even future "solutions to the Jewish question," often projected onto Israel as "suggestions for solving the Middle East conflict," which call for either the complete assimilation of Jews or dissolution of the state of Israel, are proposed without critical reflection, either with regard to the parallels to the Nazi plan or with regard to the actual consequences such a measure could have in the future. The language in which these proposals are couched echoes that of nineteenth-century nationalist racism and Nazi antisemitism.

10 TEXTUAL STRATEGIES AND PATTERNS OF ARGUMENTATION

Communicative Strategies and Argumentative Elaboration

In contrast to right-wing-radical or fundamentalist correspondents, who express their Judeophobic opinions primarily through invective and obvious forms of discrimination, the educated correspondents go to considerable lengths to defend and justify their antisemitic positions by employing a range of argumentative strategies. Simple invective, such as use of the term *Jewish sow* or a threat like *You're all going to croak!*, does not constitute an argument. The messages from educated correspondents, most of whom have university degrees and some of whom have academic titles, tend to be lengthy.[1] They offer numerous patterns of argumentation and often display considerable stylistic sophistication. But as we showed in chapter 4, these messages often draw on the same traditional stereotypes as those from extremists. Typical of these correspondents is that they almost always vehemently deny having the very antisemitic attitudes that emerge unmistakably from their words. The denial itself can be viewed as a strategy that enables the authors to legitimize themselves and justify the resentment-laden views they express (see Strategies of Legitimation and Self-Aggrandizement and Strategies of Justification in the present chapter).

To clarify the connection between mental orientation, communicative function, and verbal realization in this type of verbal antisemitism, we must first offer a brief explanation of several linguistic terms: *function*, *strategy*, and *means*. The communicative function of an utterance corresponds to its action value. A statement such as *Jews have too much influence in the financial sector* expresses a general observation by means of which the writer intends to realize a certain function (e.g., criticism or devaluation). A statement's communicative function extends beyond the statement's meaning and constitutes the action that the producer carries out (cf. Schwarz and Chur 2007, 28–32). One must also distinguish between the function intended by the author of the text and the potential functions the text can also have for the recipients.

Thus Nazi comparisons (e.g., *Sharon is the Hitler of the Middle East; Israel is a Nazi state*) have the function of expressing particularly drastic criticism of a person or thing, or ascribing particular meaning to the realm referred to (e.g., *pogrom atmosphere in Palestine*; *Palestinians today experience the same harassment the Jews once did*). Every Nazi comparison, however, automatically not only relativizes the Nazi period but also mocks its victims. Intentionally or unintentionally, the comparison robs the Nazi period of its status as a unique and unprecedented occurrence.

Realization of communicative functions takes place by way of certain verbal strategies.[2] Verbal strategies are communicative patterns for action. A strategy, *S*, such as the reversal of perpetrator and victim, is employed in order to realize the function, *F*, for instance criticism of the state of Israel and, furthermore, its delegitimation, and bring about a reaction, *R*, for instance emotional indignation or acceptance of a boycott of Israeli goods. Acting strategically means choosing particular arguments and words suited to realizing a particular communicative function. Thus the function of criticism, depending on a strategic calculation, can be realized directly, in the form of invective or, indirectly, in the form of irony or a rhetorical question, in order to insult, attack, or convince the recipient. Thus strategies represent relationships between ends and means and can be designated according to generalized functions (criticizing, disqualifying, fending off blame, denying, etc.) and objectives (insulting, discriminating against). While right-wing-radical correspondents intend to insult and denigrate, and verbalize these ends by means of direct speech acts (invective, mockery, threats; see chapter 9, under Abuse, Insults, Threats, Curses), the mainstream antisemites first want to save face and second want to convince the recipients that the criticism leveled at them is justified.

The strategy of reversing perpetrator and victim, for instance, currently rests on the conceptualization that nowadays Jews' shameless and exploitative behavior makes them the perpetrators and the Germans their victims or that the Israelis, despite their Jewish origins and their parents' past persecution, and so on, have now become perpetrators vis-à-vis the Palestinians, the new victims. The function of this reversal strategy resides, on the one hand, in the criticism or defamation of Jews and/or Israelis and, on the other hand, in the relativization of German guilt—even if this relativization is not always intended.

As for their content, strategies are thus based on mental representations. In the case of the reversal strategy, these representations consist of beliefs such as 'Israelis use excessive force. They have learned nothing from the past. They have not achieved any moral stature' and/or 'Jews are not really citizens of the German state. They identify with and support Israel. They exploit the German state.'

Such informational structures also occur individually in antisemitic discourse, verbalized as arguments.[3] Arguments are usually verbally encoded "marshaling of evidence," for the most part realized through several statements. The statements often represent pseudo-causal linkages, for example 'Jews by nature are evil and greedy. The Israelis are Jews, therefore evil and greedy, and they have stolen the Palestinians' land. Germany shares responsibility for the Palestinians' suffering because it has supported the state of Israel. As a German one has a particular responsibility and must therefore stand up for the Palestinians.'

From the perspective of the language producer, arguments are thus true and well-founded assertions or observations; that is, they take as a premise that they can be justified. Three types of argument can be distinguished:[4] factual arguments can be verified (through historical knowledge, documents, resolutions, etc.) and tested for truthfulness (e.g., *X resolutions against Israel were proposed in the UN*); conceptual arguments (plausibility arguments), on the other hand, rest solely on beliefs or on assumptions generally assumed to be valid (e.g., *Common sense dictates that . . .*, or *No one will want to support this/an immoral state . . .*). Pseudo-arguments are used for strategic purposes (against one's better judgment) (e.g., opinions are presented as facts, as in *Everyone agrees that Israel is an apartheid state*, or the speaker presents him- or herself as an authority, as in *I've been to Israel five times, so you can believe me . . .*).

The strategy of quoting authorities (*X, too, calls it a war of extermination*) can be employed as in (1) and (2) to legitimate the speaker's own position. Bolstering one's position is the communicative function of the strategy based on the factual argument that 'prominent figures/experts see it my way.'

(1) Mosche Zimmermann spoke in Tübingen on 14 May (Lucas Prize) of the "Nazi-like potential of a certain segment of society in Israel." [ZJD_05.06.2002_Rud_001]

(2) The political scientist and professor at Bar Ilan University in Tel Aviv, Menachem Klein, recently stated publicly in an interview [. . .] [ZJD_22.04.2002_Gie_001]

Those who employ verbal antisemitic strategies usually provide several arguments to reinforce their effectiveness. For instance, the strategy of delegitimizing Israel is often supported by the factual argument about 'UN resolutions,' a conceptual argument about 'weapons of mass destruction,' and pseudo-arguments about 'theft of land,' 'state-sponsored terrorism,' 'apartheid,' or the like.

Every strategy can be realized with a variety of linguistic means (lexemes, syntax). Thus strategies should not be seen as identical with the linguistic means employed. The perpetrator–victim reversal strategy can be expressed crudely and with simplified syntax, as in "*Now you're the fucking criminals!*" (IBD_14.08.2006_Auf_001) or elaborated and elevated stylistically, as in "*Your status as victims can no longer be maintained. Through your brutal use of force . . . you make yourselves guilty of crimes against humanity*" (ZJD_18.06.2002_Oeh_001).

Accordingly, the strategies of verbal antisemitism[5] can be characterized as communicative patterns of action with specific functions that make use of specific arguments and can be realized in different ways, depending on the producer and/or the context.

Our textual analyses of the corpus show that messages from mainstream correspondents that reveal an antisemitic orientation often display similar strategies, argumentative patterns,[6] and linguistic characteristics. On the basis of the striking similarities in the structure of the texts, one might gain the impression that the authors, despite their differences in age, sex, background, and so on, have conspired to use the same templates. This merely proves the extent to which the cognitive stereotypes and emotional resentments against Jews are deeply anchored and consistent as a result of their long cultural tradition.

When it comes to their communicative function, the verbal utterances in the corpus can be assigned to various strategies.[7] We must differentiate among strategies of legitimation, avoidance, justification, relativization, as well as inclusion and exclusion. In addition, characteristic forms of realization and patterns of argumentation can be described. A clear one-to-one assignment of an argumentative pattern to a strategy is not always possible, however, for, depending on the context, concrete verbal manifestations can have differing communicative functions. Thus in example (3) the author mentions his age in order to document his personal lack of responsibility for German crimes during the Nazi period and thereby also to reject any suggestion of contemporary German responsibility:

> (3) As someone born in 1966 I do not feel responsible for the crimes of the 2nd world War [...] [ZJD_01.03.2002_Lue_001]

Here the primary aim is to relativize the question of guilt. But an indication of the author's age can also be used to suggest wisdom gained from experience and responsible action, as in (4). Here the information legitimates the author:

> (4) I am 65. My life has always been guided by humanistic principles. [ZJD_21.04.2005_Lan_001]

Since the strategies chosen have a close relationship to the topic and in part condition and supplement one another, a variety of connections and overlaps can result. Denying one's own antisemitism, for instance, can result in both legitimation and avoidance. Nonetheless, within the structure of a text the strategies can be identified separately, and through analysis the specific argumentative structure of Judeophobic texts can be made visible.

The following sections explicate the individual strategies by means of examples from the corpus.

Strategies of Legitimation and Self-Aggrandizement: "*I am a humanist through and through!*"

The global textual structure of many messages in the corpus reveals strategies of legitimation in the beginning that serve to justify the act of writing and/or proactively deflect a possible charge of antisemitism.[8]

Legitimation strategies are characterized by arguments that serve to construct a positive image of the author (positive self-representation)[9] and demonstrate his respectability. The authors of the texts portray themselves as democratic, politically correct persons of human and moral integrity, and attribute to themselves such characteristics and competences as experiential and technical knowledge, rationality, and objectivity. These characteristics authorize them, in their estimation, to turn to the Israeli Embassy in Berlin and/or the Central Council of Jews in Germany to present their concerns, to express their thoughts and opinions, and to be considered serious correspondents and interlocutors.

Positive self-representation can take the following verbal forms:

(a) Attributions of positive qualities are statements authors make about themselves in the first person singular, such as *I am/I do X* (cf. also Wodak et al. 1990, 353). If the authors express their support for a principle valued in democratic societies, such as 'all men are created equal,' they intend to thrust their tolerance and freedom from prejudice into the foreground:

> (5) I am one of those citizens for whom a person is and remains a person. No matter what religion or worldview he subscribes to. [ZJD_08.04.2002_Lud_001]

The word *humanist* is the term most frequently used by the correspondents to characterize themselves. That is significant insofar as this self-referential assessment can imply that Jews and/or Israelis are not humanistically oriented (see chapter 4, under Current Stereotypes and their Verbal Manifestations, and chapter 9). The portrayal of moral and/or political integrity further takes the form of the author's positioning him- or herself in the Social Democratic camp and/or alluding to a "higher" nexus of values such as international understanding, as in (6), and world peace, as in (7):

> (6) Dear Ladies and Gentlemen, I am speaking here in the spirit of Social Democratic values and out of a wish for peaceful international understanding. [IBD_25.06.2006_Rei_001]
>
> (7) I beg you in the name of peace on earth to put an end to this senseless war. [ZJD_01.04.2002_Ask_001]

(b) Biographical information, such as age, career, educational level, or professional attainment, as well as expertise on the subject of "Jews" and/or "Israel,"[10] serves as a positive self-representation, which is accomplished by means of references to knowledge gained through personal experience, as well as general knowledge, and to interest in social policy, as well as specialized topical knowledge.

Information about the correspondent's age can thus indicate a personal democratic orientation, as in example (8), in which the author makes his political orientation explicit, even though he speaks of himself in the third person singular:[11]

> (8) The analysis by a 27-year-old german interested in politics and an Upstanding democrat who fights for peaceful coexistence [. . .] [IBD_18.02.2006_Bri_001]

Indications of age can also be used to express life experience, in which case the authors are invoking a notion of wisdom conferred by age, as in (9):

> (9) I don't want to claim that Herr Friedmann knowingly evokes the impression I have described, it's well known that no one can jump over his own shadow, something I as a retired secondary-school teacher know well, since in this respect I have had a wealth of professional experience (born in 1934). [ZJD_06.06.2002_Hau_001]

When writers of the older generation explicitly mention their age, they often accompany that information with emphatic disavowals of Nazism:

> (10) I am 74 years old and by God no Nazi. [ZJD_24.10.2006_Bon_001]
>
> (11) I am now 62. By the mid-1950s at the latest—when I was gradually coming to grasp German history—I was ashamed as a German of our past. [IBD_22.07.2006_ano-003]

Some of the correspondents offer specific educational and professional information in order to document that they are qualified to form an opinion and take a position, and to refute any suggestion that they may be prejudiced:

> (12) I am well aware of the historical developments since the founding of Israel, and through my studies of political science I have repeatedly examined the issue thoroughly. [IBD_10.06.2006_Sch_002]

In the following example, antisemitism is portrayed as a predisposition that correlates with a low level of education and is thus minimized as a problem:

(13) as an educated person [. . .] and therefore not prone to antisemitic 'prejudging,' I would like to comment as follows on the attempts at justification of the sort mentioned that you have published [. . .] [ZJD_08.04.2002_Ram_001]

For the producer of this text, a quasi-syllogistic conclusion results from the major premise that 'educated people are no antisemites.'[12] The minor premise reads, 'I am an educated person'; hence the deduction will be, 'Because I am an educated person, and educated people are not antisemites, I am no antisemite.' While the major and minor premises can be discerned implicitly, the author makes a point of explicitly marking the process of reaching a conclusion by inserting the causal expression *therefore.*

Writers' references to their own knowledge, garnered from encounters with Jews, as well as to a long-standing preoccupation with Jewish and Israeli themes, can likewise serve as evidence that they have formed their opinions free of prejudice and in tune with reality; that is the case with the following e-mail from a man from Emden with a PhD:

(14) for a good while I—born in 1930, raised in a one-family house next door to a Jewish family, with whose only son, who escaped the Holocaust by going into exile, I met up three years ago—have delved into the problems of Jewry and Israel, but also into the problems caused by Jewry and Israel. [IBD_21.01.2008_Seg_001]

(c) A positive self-representation can also be constructed by means of a congruence of norms—that is, the generally valid affirmation of positive social and political norms. In distinction to (a) and (b), correspondents do not use the first person singular when speaking of themselves but identify themselves with a group about which they make positive comments, with the implication that its positive features apply to them as well. In the following example, the desire for peaceful coexistence of religions is posited as a general goal of German society and, through use of the pronoun *we*, imputed to the author:[13]

(15) But in Germany we want a good and harmonious to-gatherness with the Jews living here and also Muslims. [ZJD_07.05.2007_Zie_001]

(d) The quasi-prejudice-free argumentation, in which the rejection of all prejudices is stressed (cf. also Wodak et al. 1990, 353), likewise forms part of the positive self-image. In (16) the text producer distances himself and his group explicitly from right-wing and Nazi thinking and condemns the Nazis' crimes against the Jews. In contrast to admirers of the Nazis, to right-wing ideas, and thus implicitly to the antisemitism associated with these groups, the text producer locates himself in the democratic mainstream of society:

> (16) I expressly emphasize that we are no "brownshirted old boys' club" but perfectly normal Germans with a strong sense of justice and good democracy. We are also no admirers of the Nazis. We condemn and regret the evil deeds committed by the Nazi regime—especially against the Jewish people—most deeply. [ZJD_07.05.2007_Zie_001]

This exercise, in contrast, functions to enhance the value of the author's argumentation. A striking feature is an emphatic use of language with respect to the modality of the utterance. Thus the word "*expressly*" serves in this representative speech act to establish the author's position vis-à-vis the contents of the utterance. Furthermore, the text producer underlines, through phrases like "*perfectly normal Germans*" and "*with a strong sense of justice and good democracy*," that he vigorously accepts the fundamental concepts on which the modern German state rests and that therefore no opinions tainted by prejudice need be feared from him. In the expressive speech act of condemning and regretting, the adverbial phrase *most deeply* serves to intensify his rejection of the Nazis' crimes. By offering these details the author legitimates himself as "quasi-prejudice-free" (for the antisemitic sentiments that usually follow).

(e) Positive self-representation is further characterized by references to the author's own rationality[14] and objectivity, often marked linguistically by a sober style free of emotional expressions and by presentation of factual knowledge, as in (17):

> (17) Dear Herr Spiegel, I am enclosing an outline of historical facts and would ask that you give these facts your careful attention. [ZJD_08.04.2002_Lud_001]

(f) Placative philosemitism, with Jewish culture emphasized as something special, admired and recognized, or ostentatious philo-Israelism, in which an admiring and appreciative attitude is expressed toward Israel, can likewise figure in an author's positive self-representation. Linguistic characteristics of such utterances are positive evaluative terms or often lexemes that describe emotions, joined with philosemitic stereotypes, as in (18), or exclusively positive attributions expressed in emphatic language:

> (18) I love Kishon and your music from the bottom of my heart. Having access to 'The Seventh Cross' and to a great, great deal of other information, I always had heartfelt compassion for your tormented people! [IBD_10.06.2006_Reb_001]
>
> (19) From after 1947 to today I have felt a profound admiration for the Israeli people, the way they have built up the land of ISrael through hard work and high intelligence. [ZJD_09.04.2002_Hor_001]

Such overtly positive evaluations always appear in the introductory part of the messages when antisemitic stereotypes follow immediately or particularly harsh criticism of Israel is verbalized. The authors intend to secure their position and justify themselves at the same time by going on the offensive.

Strategies of Avoidance and Self-Defense: "*I am no antisemite!*"

Argumentation patterns with whose help the possible inflammatory effect of an argument is mitigated can be categorized as strategies of avoidance. The authors want to avoid the risk of being situated by others outside the bounds of political correctness and/or the social and moral values and attitudes characteristic of the mainstream. Avoidance strategies generally serve to preserve the authors' positive self-image and/or specifically to fend off direct or indirect charges of antisemitism and the resulting societal sanctions. At the very least they indicate that the author of the text is aware that the reader might interpret his or her comments as prejudiced.

Within the argumentative patterns used to maintain a positive self-image and deflect suspicion of antisemitism (see examples [26], [30], and [31]), individual arguments turn up that can likewise be found among the legitimation strategies (cf. examples [8], [9], and [10]). The difference lies, however, in their function: in the case of the legitimation strategies, the arguments serve to support a positive self-representation, legitimating the fact of writing per se, whereas in the avoidance strategies they serve to protect concrete contents and expressions of opinion from the charge of antisemitism. Legitimation strategies function offensively, while avoidance strategies function defensively.

The statement *I am no antisemite* (in several variants) is by far the most frequently verbalized form of avoidance strategy in the texts sent to the Central Council and the Embassy. More than half of the mainstream authors use it. In its various manifestations it occurs either at the beginning or at the end of the messages and is sometimes also repeated several times, especially in longer texts. The authors take great pains to prevent the addressee from suspecting that the motivation for writing the message might be dubious and disreputable; on the contrary, they want to sound reasonable and politically correct.

> (20) Herr Kramer [. . .] I am NOT anti-Semitic. [ZJD_18.05.2005_Ben_001]
>
> (21) I am most definitely no anti-Semite and will not tolerate any such imputations—my criticism is directed solely at Israel's policies. [IBD_20.07.2006_Fle_001]
>
> (22) I vote for the SPD, always have. [. . .] As I said, as an average German I am simply expressing my thoughts to you. I'm not a Nazi. Not a right-wing voter and no hater of Jews. [ZJD_Gaza2009_14/816_ano_001]

In theory the strategy of denying their own antisemitism also functions to legitimate the correspondents. By claiming not to be hostile toward Jews, they can imply that their fierce criticism must have a different, legitimate basis.

> (23) I am not a right-wing radical and have no desire to become one. It's just that the behavior of This Violent State is detestable. The state of Israel always trots out what happened in the Second World War. That wasn't right either, what happened back then. [ZJD_30.07.2006_Bus_001]
>
> (24) I'm no Nazi! But your greedy club with its constant demands for money makes me madd. [ZJD_30_07.2006_Kei_001]

In (23) and (24) the authors anticipate the reproach that could be leveled at them. By forestalling and negating that reproach, they try to show that it has no justification. Messages that begin with such denials reveal that their authors are well aware of the potential inflammatory nature of their comments. At the same time, however, they defend their criticism as important, correct, and necessary. Their compulsion to express criticism, rage, and indignation ultimately overrides their fear of being taken for resentment-driven antisemites.

For educated correspondents, to be viewed as antisemitic, whether by themselves or others, would pose no small problem. To be an antisemite contradicts their self-image, shaped by the concepts of a modern, enlightened, and tolerant society that has learned from the experiences of the two world wars and especially from the atrocities of the Holocaust. For those born after 1945, an important element of their socialization was to accept "never again" as an unshakable ethical commandment. Educated citizens who know about the Holocaust, and therefore have a cognitive grasp of the dangers stemming from mentalities shaped by resentment and prejudice, cannot present themselves against this background as confirmed antisemites—not if they want to be taken seriously by the members of their modern society and accepted (also by themselves) as decent human beings.

Accordingly, citizens who wish to preserve an image of themselves as responsible and free of prejudice must deny their own antisemitism. The researcher must ask to what extent the authors of these texts actually believe their own protestations when their messages articulate one antisemitic stereotype after the other. Can they really be unaware of the contradiction? The motivation for their behavior stems first from the taboo imposed since 1945 against publicly expressing antisemitism; they insist on denying any hostility toward Jews out of fear of social disapproval. Second, they wish to maintain a positive self-image. From the psychological perspective, one can, of course, surmise that in some of the correspondents massive repression has occurred. It would be too painful for them to admit the extent to which they are motivated by resentment.

> (25) As a German who is no antisemite, I ask [...] [IBD_17.07.2006_Wei_001]; I am a German citizen and no antisemite, but [...] [IBD_20.02.2009_Wei_001]; I am no fascist and no antisemite, on the contrary, I have Jewish friends myself [...] [IBD_06.05.2009_Fil_001]

At the linguistic level we find correspondents resisting the charge of antisemitism both explicitly and implicitly. One verbal form in which the resistance manifests itself explicitly is negative self-characterization along the lines of *I am no X*, with *X* being *antisemite*, *fascist*, *right-winger*, or the like. Positive self-characterizations that adhere to the pattern *I am X* can use the terms *a leftist*, *a democrat*, and so on. All of these characterizations are connected with the notion of 'not being antisemitic' or with the rejection of antisemitism. Representative speech acts of this sort often precede speech acts containing negative evaluations that express a critical position. In (26) and (27) the writers even mark this break in coherence explicitly by inserting the conjunction *but* (see also example [45]):

> (26) I am no fascist and see myself as positioned halfway on the left. But Israel has been making me absolutely SICK TO MY STOMACH recently [. . .] [IBD_05.02.2006_ano_001]
>
> (27) P.S. I'm not hostile to Jews , but this kind of thing really makes me angry ! [IBD_09.10.2007_Gro_001]

Indirect resistance to charges of antisemitism can take the form of an analogy, for instance when the relationship between Germany and Israel is conceptualized as friendly and egalitarian, such that Jews and Germans can be viewed as belonging to the same group. In example (28) this function is realized through the use of the modal verb *may* along with the insertion of the analogy claiming that Germans and Jews behave the same:

> (28) It's all right to say such things among freinds; you do the same to us, up to now someone's not done it often. [IBD_18.02.2006_Bri_001]

Biographical information such as an explicit reference to when the correspondent was born (e.g., "*the blessing of being born late*") and mention of Jewish friends, acquaintances, or family members (see [30]) likewise serve to fend off charges of antisemitism, as well as blame, implicitly (as in [29]) or explicitly (as in [30]):

> (29) As a German citizen born only in 1968 [IBD_20.07.2011_Vul_001]
>
> (30) Prhaps you think I'm antisemitic, but I'm not, also I have Jewish relatives and think what happened earlier in Germany sucked. [ZJD_23.04.2002_Doe_001]

Indirect resistance to the charge of antisemitism can take the form of the author's accepting German guilt and moral responsibility on the basis of the Nazi past but at the same time using this admission to justify criticism of Israeli policy, as in (31). In (31) the author's high educational level and choice of profession are cited as additional guarantees for her having learned from history that one must take a stand against discrimination and persecution:

(31) As a PhD candidate in history and future secondary-school teacher, I consider it a particular obligation for Germany to turn against discrimination and persecution—precisely also in the case of the Palestinian people. [ZJD_09.04.2002_Sto_001]

The major premise in this argumentative pattern goes as follows: 'Germany's past obligates the Germans to criticize injustice and genocide.' The minor premise would be 'The Palestinian people are suffering from discrimination and persecution,' which leads to the conclusion, 'The Germans are obligated to criticize the discrimination and persecution to which the Palestinians are subjected.' It is assumed that Israel's policies are responsible for the discrimination and persecution, which leads to the expanded conclusion 'The Germans are obligated to criticize the Israeli policy toward the Palestinians.'

On a linguistic level, defense against charges of antisemitism and against possible sanctions can take the form of the author's rejecting, excluding, or negating in advance a possible reading of his views as antisemitic:

(32) [. . .] to forestall any misunderstanding. The following lines are not intended to justify yesterday's suicide attack in Tel Aviv. [IBD_18.04.2006_Bor_001]

The possibility that his comment might be understood as antisemitic leads this correspondent to negate explicitly any such motivation:

(33) I hope you will not take this letter as criticism but as an indication of sympathy and esteem. [ZJD_25.09.2006_Hip_001]

In (33), a message from a professor of law, the author prescribes the preferred interpretation of his message. Defense against the charge of antisemitism can also be expressed through mention of social discreditation or criminal prosecution as possible results of what is said. In example (34) the author engages in an explicit defense against sanctions but without revoking his defamatory statement:

(34) if it wouldn't get me in legal trouble, I would ask you who pumped shit into what's left of the brains of the Israeli politicians responsible for

setting the current war crimes in motion. But since I prefer to spare myself criminal proceedings, I'm not asking you this question but am asking myself. [IBD_02.09.2005_Lur_001]

In this example, the author expresses his fantasy in the conditional so as not to have it pinned on him explicitly.

All of these defensive statements are metacommunicative; that is, the authors comment on their own statements and postulate ways in which they might be read or interpreted. As a result of their obvious need to avoid being misunderstood, they reveal their awareness of a possible problem. They seem to be aware that the attitude they are communicating may be politically or socially inacceptable.

Strategies of avoidance, which function to reduce the inflammatory content of what is being said, at least formally, and at the same time to preserve the author's positive self-image, can take the following linguistic forms:

(a) Attenuation: with the help of expressive speech acts such as apologies, often in association with modal words such as *unfortunately*, the inflammatory potential of the proposition is supposed to be mitigated or reduced, without, however, calling the proposition itself into question:[15]

(35) Excuse me, I have a few questions[16] that are very important to me! [IBD_13.06.2007_Fis_001]

(36) unfortunately I must say , that slowly but surely one understands , also as a German , what people turn up again and again who manage to get the masses behind them to move against the Jews . Unfortunately I must also say , you are the only people in all of Biblical history that is constantly and again and again hated by the whole world. [ZJD_27.07.2006_Zaj_001]

The attenuating function is achieved through the semantics of the words and phrases that express emotion, since they verbalize regret and at the same time signal a desire to preserve the conventions of politeness.

In example (37), a message from a sociologist to the Embassy, the Nazi comparison—of whose political inflammatory force the author is well aware—and the moral discreditation of the Israeli population are formally deradicalized by various linguistic means, such as the modal particle *please*, the adjective expressing emotion *concerned*, and the quasi-apologetic *please forgive me*:

(37) That is a crime and—please forgive this comparison—these types of attack remind me unfortunately more and more of the behavior of the German Nazis toward the Jewish population in the ghettos! [...] I very much hope that the Israeli decision-makers and the population will grow with respect to moral maturity [...] With appalled and deeply concerned greetings Shalom [IBD_12.06.2006_Goe_001]

The author immediately follows up the speech act of defamatory criticism with a verbal reinterpretation that presents the criticism as an expression of concern. Thus the author assumes the guise, on the formal plane of communication, of a morally intact personality. The marked tendency toward self-righteousness that manifests itself in this e-mail is typical of writers from the mainstream (see chapter 9, under Hostility toward Jews as a Missionary Urge).

(b) Rhetorical questions, as in (38), and conditional constructions, as in (39), are deployed to avoid explicit expression of a viewpoint that could be tied to the author:

(38) So is Israel untouchable vis-à-vis Germany as a result of the German past? [ZJD_08.04.2002_Nie_001]

(39) If Jews should feel discriminated against by the criticism that is also expressed internationally, in my view complaints should be addressed to Israel, not to those who supply the reports. [ZJD_11.08.2006_Bla_001]

Here, too, it is merely the form of the comment that is chosen carefully; the communicative meaning emerges unmistakably from the reproaches.

(c) Discrimination can be downplayed by means of quantifiers, as in (40), and/or a contrastive division into "bad" versus "good" Jews and/or Israelis, as in (41). When it comes to Israel in particular, the authors often distinguish between the *corrupt, criminal government* and the *good, suffering civilian population*, as in (42):[17]

(40) [...] and I' m firmly convinced that there are also many people in Israel who don't agree with what Herr Sharon is up to. After all, not all Israelis voted for that man, and some who did vote for him are surely already regretting doing so. [ZJD_10.04.2002_Kem_002]

(41) It's always just a minority that pours gas on the conflict and

Israel's policies also contribute to escalating the conflict time and again. [IBD_18.02.2006_Bri_001]

(42) I pity the Israeli population for their government, which does everything inits power to make sure that this state has fewer and fewer friends in the world. [ZJD_10.04.2002_Rot_001]

It also happens that the author attempts to contrast the groups of "(good) Holocaust victims" and "(bad) Israeli perpetrators," as in (43):

(43) I view linking the crimes of the contemporary Israeli govt. with the murder of millions of Jews by the fascists as an unspeakable smear on your fellow Jews who fell victim to Hitler's terror. Sharon is a murderer and a racist warmonger. He is a willing executioner of the USA's policy. The terrorists are not the Palestinians but the Israeli military and the settlers who occupy stolen land. [ZJD_14.04.2002_ano_004]

The various concessions are meant to demonstrate that the author does not condemn all Israelis and all Jews, but only the "bad" ones. It is a strategy intended to counter the charge of being generally hostile toward Jews.

(d) *Yes–but* constructions constitute a particular form of avoidance strategy. They serve primarily to present thematic information in the text and often contribute to the author's construction of a positive self-image. *Yes–but* constructions that link the positive self-description to a prejudiced statement or ones that might be interpreted as such are deployed in order to preserve the positive self-image as well as to fend off accusations of antisemitism and the accompanying disapproval. At the linguistic level, a *yes–but* construction can mark the transition explicitly from a positive self-description to a statement expressing prejudice.[18]

In the examples in which the writers describe themselves as democratic, responsible, and moral, these qualities that society prizes are instrumentalized as pretexts for writing to express criticism. The general pattern at work takes the following form: *Precisely because I am X, I must say this*, with *X* being one of the positive self-attributions just discussed.

The correspondent may explicitly mark this transition linguistically by employing adversative conjunctions or causal adverbs that signal a concessive relationship, as in (44), and thus create an apparent break in coherence, as in (45):

(44) These incomprehensible events [in the concentration camps] must not be forgotten or viewed as past and gone. But I can't stand it anymore that Herr Spiegel and Herr Friedmann constantly wag their finger at the Germans and put on airs as apostles of morality. [ZJD_08.06.2002_Her_001]

(45) I'm no antisemite, and yet I'm of the opinion that the Central Council should stay out of politics as much as possible. [ZJD_20.09.2006_Glo_001]

The switch from a positive self-characterization to a prejudice-laden statement, or one that lends itself to interpretation as such, can also, as in (46) and (47), occur by way of the construction of an (apparent) causal relationship that employs consecutive conjunctions or causal adverbs to avoid an explicit break in coherence:

(46) All the more I disapprove of and condemn the current actions [...] [ZJD_11.08.2009_Man_001]

(47) I'm basically a relatively nonpolitical person, aside from the fact that I am a dyed-in-the-wool "anti-Nazi" and also make this known in many forms. Precisely because of this fact I'd like to voice serious criticism of your behavior by getting some critical statements about the state of Israel off my chest. [ZJD_14.09.2006_Man_001]

The strategy of avoidance theoretically includes all implicit forms of verbal antisemitism (cf. [b] above; on this subject see chapter 2). The strategy entails the use of verbal utterances with a particular form–function combination (e.g., statement–observation) with a divergent function. These statements follow the pattern: The speaker says *X* but actually means *Y*.

Example (48), from a message sent by a prominent physician to the Central Council, seems at first sight to be a pure assertion—that is, a speech act with which the speaker says something about the world or vouches for the truth value of something, in other words verbalizes very generally a claim that can be verified:

(48) Violence will always breed new violence if there is no pause for reflection. [ZJD_07.04.2002_Bin_001]

Though (48) is an assertion, its meaning is unclear. This information is not news to the Central Council. Why would the doctor want to inform the Central Council of this truism? The communicative intention does not consist of enlightening the recipient but rather of calling for a pause in or cessation of something. Example (48) can thus be described as a speech act with directive import, although the words themselves merely express an observation. At the same time, the statement conceptually equates German-Jewish and Israeli issues, and the author stigmatizes the Central Council as an accomplice or coresponsible agent in the violence taking place in Israel (see chapter 4, under Current Stereotypes and Their Verbal Manifestations, and chapter 6, under Derealization).

Many statements employ the performative verb *say*, *emphasize*, or *observe* and contain attenuation devices such as the modal particles *please* and *unfortunately*.

(49) Unfortunately I must tell you now that I have nothing but scorn for this primitive type of "policy." [ZJD_10.08.2006_Koe_001]

In fact these are verbal attacks that subject the addressee to discrimination and defamation. The authors' communicative intention of insulting or threatening is defused, with defamation and abuse presented as "justified criticism" or even, as in (50), as "sympathy":

(50) take this message as a sign of sympathy for your people. [IBD_23.07.2006_Vol_001]

Speech acts such as saying and observing normally function to establish the truth value of the content expressed. In the messages to the Central Council and the Embassy, on the other hand, these speech acts convey insults, defamation, and/or subjective assessments (see chapter 9).

Argumentation that engages in discrimination and is fraught with resentment is usually defended as "*legitimate criticism of Israel*"; the charge of antisemitism is anticipated and repelled (on the distinction between anti-Israelism and criticism of Israel, cf. chapter 6, under Criticism of Israel versus Anti-Israelism).

(51) Please don't haul out the old clichés to argue that anyone who criticizes Israel, that anyone who attests that Israel has a murderous government, is an antisemite. [ZJD_06.04.2002_5]

For the correspondent the communicative strategy of attacking Israel has the advantage of projecting the blame and making the addressee the perpetrator without exposing the author to the suspicion of being an antisemite (as with the perpetrator–victim reversal). Although Israel is named, the accusation is in fact directed, by way of a verbal detour, against Jews and Judaism.

A similar situation obtains with the directives (demands for action), but there we must note a difference between the number of demands addressed to the Central Council and those addressed to the Embassy. The latter receives far fewer demands. Regardless of the recipient, most of the demands are expressed in the imperative, which makes them classic formulations of calls for action.

(52) Stop your brothers in Israel and make peace at last! [ZJD_30.07.2006_Mra_001]

(53) bring justice to bear so that these crimes may be atoned for and peace may finally return—a peace that you, we, and the entire region around Israel needs. Peace and not always fanning the flames of hate. [ZJD_03.12.2008_Oet_001]

Such directives always convey implicitly negative evaluations, such as *You occupy illegally land that belongs to others* or *Up to now the Central Council has not advocated for peace*. The expressives that occur in the corpus, or in other words speech acts that express an author's emotional attitude,[19] are often formulated with performative verbs, primarily *protest*, *condemn*, and *thank*, or realized by means of conventionalized stock phrases, such as *it's a shame, it's unacceptable, that X*... Thus messages often begin as follows:

(54) I protest vigorously and firmly against the continued and intentional violation of human rights. [...] It's a disgrace that nothing can justify. Israel thereby places itself, in my opinion, in the ranks of the rogue states. [IBD_29.03.2004_Sta_001]

If commissives are verbalized—that is, are speech acts with which the speaker pledges to carry out some action in the future—they are usually to be understood as threats. This type of speech act turns up explicitly, for instance, in the form of promises to join a boycott, as in example (55):

> (55) From now on I will not buy any goods from your country! And I will urge my acquaintances and friends to do the same! [IBD_13.07.2006_Fis_003]

Ostensibly all that is being said in (56) is that Ariel Sharon is a monster, but at the same time a second type of speech act, an expressive, plays a role, since the statement conveys the author's attitude, as well as delivering an insult:

> (56) A monster is what he is, not a head of government. [ZJD_10.04.2002_Alt_001]

To sum up, two different types of implicit verbal antisemitism can play a part in an avoidance strategy: what is said can be expressed, reinterpreted, and revalued by means of reclassifying verbal forms that seemingly negate what is actually meant; alternatively, what in fact is meant is conveyed by way of additional conclusions (implicatures) that can be drawn. The first type may be paraphrased thus: 'What is meant is something other than what is said.' The second type adheres to the pattern 'What is meant is something more than what is said.'

The advantage for correspondents of indirectly verbalizing what is meant or renaming it is that they need not pin themselves down; they can always point to what was said and deny what was meant, which was conveyed only by implication. The indirect speech acts entail an encoding of prejudices against Jews that allows the authors to convey a radical semantics in a deradicalized form.

Strategies of Justification: "*You provoke that!*"

The strategies of justification include patterns of substantiation with which the author's argumentation can be defended as rational and well-founded or proved. Such substantiations come into play when a personal or societal (moral) guilt or responsibility that Germans have vis-à-vis Jews or Israel must be deflected or delegitimized.[20]

The core of the strategies of justification can be found in patterns of argumentation intended to show that the argumentation presented, the linking of individual arguments, is correct in its content, accepted by society, or widespread. The motivations mentioned are characterized as "based on facts." The allegedly factual arguments cited are actually subjective. These "facts" include the "*silence*" and "*moral failure*" of the Central Council, Israel's "*unjust policies*" and the "*state-sponsored terrorism*" that supposedly compel the authors to sit down and write.

(57) I must write to you because I am extremely worried about world peace and about our children's future. [ZJD_28.07.2007_Gab_001]

(58) And I say: those who don't speak out against these crimes, against this horror, make themselves guilty by their silence. [ZJD_30.08.2006_Cra_001]

(59) By now I am so disappointed by your years of one-sided portrayal of the Palestinians and your many provocations, your lack of compassion, your provocative settlement policy, your clash with Turkey, etc. [IBD_01.11.2011_Ber_001]

Beyond the strategies of legitimation and avoidance, which foreground justification of the act of writing to the Central Council or Embassy, and the individual statements or arguments presented, the strategy of justification helps to preserve the authors' positive self-image, and in particular to fend off charges of antisemitism and exonerate the Germans of historical guilt. But in addition to stressing a global concern (*worry about world peace, awareness of responsibility, normality for Germans*, etc.), this strategy prioritizes discrediting the addressees and conveys an impression of facticity and objectivity. At the same time, the authors' attempts at justification often reveal an effort to fend off guilt and responsibility. This effort involves patterns of argumentation that construct a rationale or causal explanation for the authors' position or portray that position as socially accepted and held by the majority. Because the following examples are particularly complex in their patterns of substantiation and the underlying conceptualizations, several will be discussed at greater length.

(a) Example (60) uses an analogy to portray Jewish and non-Jewish Germans as equal victims of and sufferers from the effects of Nazism. On the basis of this calculation and comparison of suffering, the extent of the Nazis' crimes against the Jewish community and the personal guilt incurred by non-Jewish Germans alive at the time are negated. Accordingly, contemporary German responsibility vis-à-vis the Jewish community can be contested (cf. also the strategies of relativization).

> (60) My grandfather also died in the war, and my father had to care for his mother and three younger siblings. If my grandfather had refused to serve, they would have shot him. So exactly what are you asking for? [ZJD_01.08.2006_Mue_001]

On the linguistic level the analogy is accomplished by the addition of the particle *also*, as well as through the use of an *if–then* construction, which signals causality. The rhetorical question at the end draws a conclusion from the analogy: 'Jews have no reason to complain.' The comparison rests on the argument that 'Germans suffered just as much as Jews during the Nazi period.' To illustrate German suffering, the correspondent draws on a specific family experience as the basis for a generalization that makes his experience representative of the suffering of all Germans. At the same time, the analogy remains vague, for the Jewish victims are never explicitly designated as such, nor is the nature of their suffering described. The use of the personal pronoun *you* makes the Central Council a stand-in for the Jewish community.

(b) In example (61) deductive reasoning is employed, along with an indirect comparison to the Nazis, to demonstrate the rationality of the attitude being presented:

> (61) The Jews rightfully reproach the Germans for having looked the other way during the Nazi regime. Now, however, you are demanding that we look the other way again. But that is something I am not willing to do. [ZJD_01.08.2006_Fle_001]

In the first assertive speech act, the Germans are characterized as *cowardly*, a negative attribute. This trait is evaluated as the source of the guilt German society shares for the crimes of the Nazis. Thus the writer first explicitly acknowledges a moral failing on the part of the Germans. In the assertion that follows, the Central Council is accused of demanding that Germans look the other way again, which would be tantamount to committing the same moral failure. With the verb *demand* and the adverb *again*, the statement implies first that the act of looking the other way was not voluntary, second that the current situation in Israel is comparable to the Nazi period, and third that, according to the Central Council, Israel's policies may not be criticized. The author of the text then rejects the behavior of looking the other way as immoral, on the grounds that in the past it has incurred legitimate reproach. The author's critical attitude toward the Central Council is thus deductively justified as rational and moral in light of the historical precedent.

(c) Citing others can likewise be seen as a strategy of justification, although this strategy is also strongly linked to the function of avoidance, since the technique allows authors to avoid acknowledging as their own the opinion they cite. In (62) an antisemitic statement is explicitly characterized as the opinion of another person or group:

> (62) Here one has the impression that Jews feel better the more enemies they have around them. And I am not speaking of myself, but that is the reaction among my circle of acquaintances. These people, usually moderate voters on the right or left, actually develop extremist thoughts when this topic comes up. [ZJD_24.03.2005_Dei_001]

On the one hand, the author of this text denies responsibility for the antisemitic content (which employs the stereotype of the QUARRELSOME AND VENGEFUL JEW), assigning it to others, but at the same time does not reject the statement and thus implicitly accepts it. On the other hand, he justifies and legitimizes the sentiment by pointing out that an entire group of upstanding citizens thinks this way. The author of (63) uses the same method, along with the attenuation strategy, expressed by "*unfortunately*," by means of which he distances himself, presenting an antipathy to the Central Council of Jews that is allegedly shared by the majority:

> (63) My work takes me to the states of Hessia, Rhineland-Palatinate, and Saarland, and every day I am privy to the opinions of many citizens of our fatherland, of both sexes. [. . .] Unfortunately (!) I can and must point out that the overwhelming sympathy when it comes to the increasingly harsh exchange of blows between Friedmann and Möllemann is—unambiguously!—on Möllemann's side. [ZJD_11.06.2002_Win_001]

Along with the technique designed to exclude the author from a generalization, as in (62) and (63), there is a technique that includes the author, as in (64). This technique has the purpose of giving the author backing by maintaining that his view is in no way exceptional but rather a normal view held by many Germans:

> (64) In my circle of friends, the thinking about Israel has changed so much for the worse over the past 5 years that we ourselves are surprised. No, we are not antisemites. Most of us are middle-aged Germans with above-average education, leftist leanings, and humanistic attitudes. [IBD_08.07.2011_Wac_001]

(d) Speaking in the name of the majority thus becomes a way for an author to express the general acceptance and prevalence of the attitude he or she presents, as in (65):[21]

> (65) A citizen of the Federal Republic [IBD_24.03.2004_ano_002][22]
>
> (66) Greetings from a member of the 'indecent majority' that sees Israel's nefarious doings as a violation of international law. [IBD_23.07.2004_Sch_001]
>
> (67) With greetings from one of the 65% of Germans who see in the state of Israel a threat to world peace [. . .] [IBD_25.03.2004_War_001]

Particularly noticeable at the level of language is the way the authors refer to themselves in the third person singular, as well as the underspecification. The authors often describe themselves in the closing as part of a collective, as in (65), which is characterized as a majority, as in (66), and as morally upstanding, as in (67). In this connection lexemes such as *world peace* and *international law* often appear, as do concepts and phrases derived from them, as in (66).[23]

Speaking in the name of the majority can also entail an explicit reference to an unspecified collective, as in (68):

> (68) The Israeli leadership has created doubt as to Isreal's right to exist, and not only for me. [IBD_date illegible, Letter]

This strategy also sometimes involves multiple signatures, as in (69), or appended lists of signatures or petitions:

> (69) W.L., Berlin, R.S., Berlin, H.D., Fürth, A.H., Berlin [etc.] [ZJD_19.04.2002_Lin_001]

If this kind of generalizing argument shows up in the text's closing, in addition to implementing a particular strategy of justification it also serves to justify the entire text.

When the authors invoke what they characterize as a widely shared opinion in order to portray antisemitic thinking as socially acceptable and declare it to be anti-antisemitic, they legitimize their radicalism to the addressees and to themselves as well.

(e) Explicit invocation of socially recognized authorities or institutions likewise serves to protect authors,[24] who thereby relinquish responsibility, while at the same time suggesting general support for any inflammatory contents in the text. These producers thus situate their views as societally accepted and legitimate themselves.

> (70) "It's an atrocity what is being perpetrated as punishment on the people in Gaza. [. . .] It's a crime. [. . .] I think it is an abomination that this continues to go on," said the former American president Jimmy Carter on Friday. [IBD_21.04.2008Gel_001]
>
> (71) "Israel is pursuing an apartheid policy" (J. Carter). [IBD_17.01.2009_Boc_001]

When it comes to argumentative substantiations, but also strategies of justification and legitimation, references to authorities play a prominent role. In order to support their own opinion, correspondents cite statements by politicians, Middle East experts, or historians. In this connection the comments of various well-known personalities and dignitaries are often cited as well.[25] A person whose status and integrity enjoy general respect qualifies as an authority. Anyone who can invoke such an authority profits from this integrity; his or her opinion becomes easier for others to accept or assent to. Such "proofs by authority" turn up primarily in messages hostile toward or critical of Israel sent by mainstream authors and by leftists or left-wing extremists.

The strategy of referring to institutional authorities in statements directed against Israel often invokes UN resolutions:

> (72) You accuse Lebanon of failing to comply with UN Resolution 1559. Is there even one of the innumerable resolutions with which Israel has ever complied ? This is pure hypocrisy and dumbing-down. [ZJD_21.07.2006_Gie_001]

The "proofs" cited by the writers for the "degeneracy" of Israelis and/or Jews always omit important information, for instance that certain UN resolutions were revoked and that the resolutions condemning Israel always originated with Arab member states.

The authorities cited are by no means always prominent. Some writers canonize as an authority anyone who is somewhat familiar from the mass media or has attracted attention by taking an excessively critical position toward Israel.

> (73) The courageous and convincing argumentation of Dr. Norbert Blüm, Ulrich Kienzle, and Udo Steinbach surprised me greatly and made a deep impression. [IBD_22.01.2009_Wei_001]
>
> (74) You should follow the example, Frau Knobloch, of Frau Evelyn Hecht-Galinski, the daughter of your predecessor Galinski; as an activist with "Jews for a Just Peace" she doesn't close her eyes, but honorably calls this injustice by name instead of joining the herd of sheep trotting along behind Herr Olmert. [ZJD_31.08.3.2006_Goe_001]

(f) All the correspondents, no matter what their political orientation, often cite Jewish authorities, obviously considering it a particularly powerful and effective justification strategy. Here we have the classic persuasive strategy of proving something through appeal to authority, especially an authority representing the group being criticized, whose voice is thought to carry particular weight.

Altogether three different forms can be differentiated by means of which the authors strategically invoke Jewish "authorities" in order to buttress their own opinion or interpretation of happenings in the Middle East:

1. a reference to a specific Jew or Israeli;
2. a vague reference to Jewish or Israeli friends or acquaintances;
3. a contrast between "good" and "bad" Jews without reference to specific persons (i.e., generalization by means of dichotomization).

The most common variant is the explicit reference to individual Jewish or Israeli authorities; these are invoked as *good* or *positive representatives of the Jews*, in contrast to the *bad Jews*, deserving of criticism. The primary representatives of the *bad Jews* are the Central Council and the Embassy, whom the correspondents intend to criticize by citing authorities. A close second are German-Jewish or Israeli figures Charlotte Knobloch, Dieter Graumann, Salomon Korn, Ehud Olmert, and Schimon Stein. If no individuals are mentioned, various vaguely defined Jewish and Israeli groups are named as collective representatives of the bad Jews/Israelis, as in (75):

> (75) in our Western Hemisphere there are serious-minded and devious people. One can probably also classify the Jews as "hawks" and "doves.: The "doves"include community-minded, intelligent, educated, likeable, sensitive, and artistic people. The "hawks" include aggressive, greedy, power-mad people—Paul Wolfowitz—Jewish media moguls of the German press—Israeli politicians, etc., at least that's how I see it. [ZJD_16.04.2007_War_001]

Example (75) offers a striking example of the explicit contrast set up between the two groups. The author assigns antisemitic stereotypes to the group of *bad Jews*. This kind of stark distinction characterizes primarily the messages of right-wing radicals and left-wing extremists, but also occurs now and then in messages from mainstream authors.

A contrast between "good" and "bad" Jews without direct reference to individuals occurs primarily when Israel becomes the subject of sweeping condemnation. Generic criticism of all Israelis suggests the formation of new stereotypes applied specifically to Israel, for the blame is leveled not at an individual politician or soldier but at the state of Israel or the community of Israelis as a whole (see chapter 6). Juxtaposed to these generalized bad Jews are the exceptional admirable Jews or Israelis who take a critical position toward Israel. The authors of the texts conscientiously invoke their statements and texts, some of which are anti-Israeli, to discredit all the other "unenlightened" Jews and Israelis. For the most part well-known left-wing critics of Israel are quoted, Uri Avnery above all, but also Tony Judt, Benny Morris, Michael Lerner, and Reuven Moskovitz. The most frequently quoted German Jews are Felicia Langer, Rolf Verleger, and Evelyn Hecht-Galinsky (cf. example [76]). As Israeli moral authorities David Grossman, Abraham B. Yehoshua, and Amos Oz also figure in the messages. Groups like Jews for a Just Peace or Defenders of Civil Rights in Israel (cf. example [77]) count as *good Jews*:

> (76) Dear Frau Knobloch, dear Herr Dr. Graumann, I am happy that there are people like Frau Hecht-Galinski, Frau Wieczorek-Zeul, and Dr. Verleger

who speak out openly about the events in Lebanon. [. . .] But above all it is cynical when you attack the minister in this way. And you know, Herr Dr. Graumann, what is also cynical? This quote: "The Israeli armed forces do their utmost to spare civilians and avoid collateral damage. Nonetheless, their mission is to put the rocket launch-sites out of commission so as to spare their own population further attacks." With barrel bombs? [. . .] So we must wait for the findings from this inquiry, but above all my thanks to the people I mentioned at the beginning of this e-mail and their express disapproval of your behavior, Frau Knobloch and Herr Dr. Graumann. [ZJD_02.09.2006_Fis_001]

(77) Obviously some of the Israelis are blessed with a more humane attitude than this Central Council! The army can obviously do whatever it pleases and all you do is cheer it on. Let the defenders of civil rights in Israel be an example to you. What's supposed to happen after this holocaust? You're quite something when it comes to humane behavior! [ZJD_22.11.2006]

The explicit reference to Jewish authorities often follows the same pattern. The reference usually comes at the beginning of the message. The writer emphasizes the authority's distinguished position, for instance by using academic titles or noting that the persons named are "*renowned*" or "*well-known*." In the following example, the explicit reference to the professor's origins, as well as the typographic emphasis, are typical:

(78) ". . . Israel is willfully blind to the danger that its indulgent excesses might ultimately push its imperial mentor beyond the point of irritation. . . . Such a radical realignment of strategy would entail a difficult reappraisal of every illusion under which the country and its political elite have nestled." Tony Judt, (Jewish!) prof. at New York University [IBD_20.07.2006_Hau_001]

The authors' use of modal particles such as *even* or *also*, as in (79), signal the implication that Jewish criticism of Israel is somehow remarkable or worthy of particular attention:

(79) One can understand the partisan attitude of Frau Knobloch as a Jew, but not accept it. She really should stay somewhat within bounds. From the beginning the Israeli army has fought brutal offensive wars. Even the Israeli historian Benny Morris confirmed that. [ZJD_25.07.2006_Wie_001]

Example (79) ignores the fact that in Jewish communities inside and outside of Israel constant debates on Israeli policies take place and controversial points of view are aired, which means that Jewish criticism of Israel is by no means exceptional. The use of the modal particles implies the rhetorical gambit 'Even those who are criticized say . . .' In order to introduce this argument implicitly, the authors often refer explicitly to the fact that the authorities they cite are Jewish.

(80) Maybe you should take the time to read what Uri Avneri says about the Middle East conflict and Frau Patricia Langer, who received death threats after her comments, and who rightly says, "The only lesson from Auschwitz is justice." Both Jews. [ZJD_30.03.2002_Kos_001]

Jewish authorities are assumed to have greater relevance or persuasive clout or also closeness to the topic or personal involvement than non-Jewish authorities, for when "those affected" share the correspondents' views, those views cannot be wrong. According to the principle *Jews say so themselves . . . so it must be right*, the authors conclude implicitly that critics of Israel like Avnery are the positive exception that confirms the rule.

The authors also like to refer to Jewish friends and acquaintances who take the same position as they do, entirely objectively and believably, for they are Jews after all. Being Jewish in itself heightens authority as far as the authors are concerned and confers inside knowledge of the situation or the right to comment on it. At the same time, these references allow the authors to exonerate themselves and implicitly deflect any suspicion of antisemitism. If they have Jewish friends, so the reasoning goes, they cannot be antisemitic. In distinction to the defense against guilt or responsibility accomplished by mentioning when they were born, the reference to Jewish friends tends to come at the end of the message, as in (81), a message from man with a PhD:

(81) If you find this statement presumptuous, may I also inform you that for decades I have been able to count several Jewish families among my friends, including abroad. [ZJD_30.6.2002_Pol_001]

In addition to Jewish authorities, the authors appeal to a goodly number of non-Jewish authorities, whose statements they take out of context and work into their arguments at random.

(82) I can understand how hard it is for Jews and Israelis to hear criticism from Germans, but the following comes from the pen of one of our greatest writers, Theodor Fontane, who was of Huguenot origin and whom one cannot accuse of being an antisemite. Fontane wrote this toward the end of the nineteenth century—out of genuine concern, I think: "From earliest childhood I have been a friend of Jews and have personally experienced only good things with Jews. Nevertheless I have such a keen sense of their guilt, of their boundless presumptuousness, that I do not merely not begrudge them a serious rout but actually wish it for them. And this much is certain to me: if they do not suffer it now and do not change, in times that we both"—the letter is addressed to the abbess Mathilde von Rohr—"will ourselves not live to see, a terrible fate will be visited upon them."[26] [ZJD_Gaza2009_17/816_Mie_001]

These authorities usually enjoy a greater degree of name recognition and can be described as "general moral" authorities. Among these universally respected figures one finds Mahatma Gandhi, Dietrich Bonhoeffer, Goethe, and Machiavelli. It is certainly no coincidence that all these figures are no longer alive.

(83) We quoted to him [an "old Israeli friend and Holocaust survivor"] a "new wise saying," that of the German pastor Dietrich Bonhoeffer, an adversary of the Nazis and a Nazi victim: "There is no peace along the path of safety. Peace must be risked." [IBD_25.05.2006_Ste_001]

Biblical quotations occupy a special place, as in (84), referring to a nonpersonal moral or religious authority:

(84) In the Bible it says, "He who sows hate shall reap hate." [IBD_23.04.2006_Ren_001]

The author of (85) combines various subforms of appeals to authority to buttress his criticism of the Central Council, whose behavior he classifies as "*scandalous*," "*horrifying*," "*perfidious*," and "*indecent*." He also presents himself as philosemitic by using "*Shalom*" as his closing:

(85) Perfidious above all because you know perfectly well that (along with hundreds of resolutions blocked by the U.S.) 9 resolutions exist that call on Israel **unambiguously** to, for exemple, withdraw to the borders of the 6day

war (to name just one of the resolutions). I recommend to you in-stead the pages www.Jews for a just peace.com and jewish voices. Shalom PS: eye for an eye, tooth for a tooth in your Thora is ultimately a commandment for proportionality. After all, it doesn't say 10 eyes for one eye, as the current victim ratio looks!" [ZJD_24.07.2006_Sch_001]

Generally recognized authorities can be distinguished from those specific to certain groups. Thus Uri Avnery is usually known in leftist circles and among people who pay attention to the Middle East conflict and criticism of Israel. To the vast majority, however, he would be relatively unknown and therefore no real authority.

The authors furthermore refer to political, scholarly, or cultural authorities such as politicians, professors, or writers who express views critical of Israel:

(86) The wife of the British prime minister, Blair, and the British foreign minister, Straw, have recently expressed ideas similar to Mr. Annan's. I wonder whether in the judgment of the Central Council of Jews Mr. Anan, Mrs. Blair, and Mr. Straw must now also be viewed as antisemites? [ZJD_23.06.2002_Gra_001]

(87) 2 noted professors at the Harvard+ Chicago universities, Walt and Mearsheimer describe under the title: The Israel-Lobby and US Foreign Policy how current policy in the "Middle East" is dictated by Israel that the US has to follow [...] [IBD_10.05.2006_Hue_001]

Such "up-to-date" references to critics of Israel very often constitute the actual impetus for writing; that is, not until they encounter the statements of (Jewish) authorities, who more or less offer them the argument on a silver platter, do the writers feel sufficiently motivated to write to the Central Council or the Embassy. Some of the frequent correspondents even send a letter or an e-mail whenever they come upon a new text or interview with Uri Avnery or others. The moment the text appears, it is sent off as an attachment, with the writer's explicit or implicit assent and a message urging the Central Council or the Embassy to take these positions to heart at long last and act accordingly, as in (88):

(88) I can understand of course that the sympathies of the Central Council of Jews in Germany lie with Israel. But wouldn't some critical

> distance to Israel's violent excesses be appropriate? You surely know who Reuven Moskowitz is. Would that Israel would embrace the wisdom he has made his guiding principle in life: A hero is one who turns his enemy into a friend. [ZJD_15.08.2006_Heu_001]

Often the "proofs" obtained from authorities came at "just the right moment" or were "available," but were not specifically sought out or subjected to any thorough and thoughtful analysis. The opportunistic nature of the resort to authorities becomes evident when the authors who cite them get their names wrong—for example, Patricia Langer instead of Felicia Langer—or quote textual passages incorrectly or in abbreviated form. A further question one might ask is whether the persons cited actually qualify as authorities. Not infrequently they fall more into the category of pseudo-authorities because they possess no superior knowledge of the issue under discussion or particular moral integrity; in example (86), Cherie Blair's authority or political clout is probably limited to her being married to Tony Blair.

In most cases the references are explicitly verbalized, introduced through the use of verbs such as *say, describe, express the opinion, that.* Implicit invocations of authorities occur very seldom, and when they do, it is at the textual macro-level, as when quoted passages appear at the beginning or end of a message or entire articles are attached but the message itself does not comment on the quotation or attachment; biblical passages or aphorisms make up the bulk of such citations. In any case, the only plausible function of the citation is to lend support to the author's opinion.

It is striking that the authors of the messages almost never explicate the connection between their own opinions and those of the authorities they invoke. A formulation such as *I see this the same way* or *I share this opinion* or *Thus my opinion coincides . . .* is extremely rare. Since citing authorities is one of the most commonly used rhetorical devices, the authors likely assume that invocation of an authority's opinion speaks for itself.

When it comes to citing authorities, those who are Jewish and criticize or boycott Israel and its policies are regarded as morally superior and praised accordingly. Jews who express solidarity with Israel, defending the state or refuting criticism, become subject to attack and lecturing. Thus the purportedly upstanding correspondents make the relationship to Israel and its policies a test of conscience to which every Jew must submit.

Relativizing Strategies: "*After all, it's 2007!*"

Relativizing strategies are based on patterns of argumentation that seek to minimize German guilt and/or responsibility on the level of society as a whole. At issue here is less the correspondents' desire to safeguard their own opinions and attitudes than a wholesale reconceptualization of the German past. Obviously, however, a global defense against guilt and responsibility entails personal absolution as well. Relativizing strategies, of which the perpetrator–victim reversal is the most common, can thus always be read both individually and collectively (cf. also Wodak et al. 1990, 352; Bergmann and Erb 1991; Holz 2001, 2005).

The perpetrator–victim reversal strategy is based on the concept that THE JEWS ARE NOT VICTIMS BUT PERPETRATORS.

Max Horkheimer offers a telling description of the psychological features inherent to the perpetrator–victim reversal: "Injured pride constitutes a wound inflicted on the collective no less than on the individual. The Jews, who were the victims, are associated with the catastrophe, with the violence perpetrated by Germans, as well as on Germans. In the unconscious, the roles are reversed. 'Not the murderer, the victim is guilty.' To overcome narcissistic hurt is exceedingly difficult, and even the generation that was not involved suffers from the wound with which it has no personal acquaintance" (1961/1997, 314).

A further aspect that must be mentioned is that the phenomenon Horkheimer describes is not always unconscious. Those who engage in perpetrator–victim reversal as a communicative strategy do so purposefully and consciously. Several forms of this strategy appear in the corpus. Right-wing-radical and neo-Nazi correspondents employ it with reference to the past, mentioning the *danger to Germany emanating in those days from the Jews* and the *necessity of mounting a defense against the Jewish enemy.*

(89) HITLER WAS CRAZY BUT HE RECOGNIZED THAT YOU PEOPLE ARE A PACK OF MURDERERS. FILTHY JEWS, YOU'RE PURE SHIT [. . .] [IBD_07.05.2010_ano_040]

(90) HITLER was RIGHT, you're a sick race. [IBD_01.06.2010_ano_017]

(91) HitlerWARNDED US ABOUT YOU PACK OF FILTH. [IBD_01.06.2010_ano_024]

(92) So why were they persecuted all over the world? [. . .] Maybe Herr Hitler had good reason after all? [ZJD_25.07.2006_ano_007]

Writers from the mainstream construct similar justifications (see also chapter 5, example [23]):

(93) In the past few weeks I've come to understand Hitler why he wanted to exterminate the Jews! [ZJD_01.09.2006_Sch_002]

(94) If all Jews are like you, we now know why the past in Germany happened the way it did. [IBD_19.04.2008_Bec_001]

After making such references the authors usually mention the current danger posed to the world by *Jewish conspiracies* and by Israel:

(95) Why do you insist with all your might on ruling the whole world? [ZJD_28.09.2007_Sch_001]

(96) Israel controls America and tomorrow certainly the entire world. [ZJD_Gaza2009_522/816_ano_001]

(97) The atom bomb you Jews built in seecret have disturbed the balance. And you and the Neo-Cons are most likely to also deploy this weapon. [IBD_31.10.2006_ano_001]

In combination with deflecting charges of guilt and responsibility, this strategy also occurs in exclusive reference to the present, as in (98), an e-mail from a thirty-seven-year-old woman who works as an editor and journalist:

(98) The German people has had to do enough penance for generations—in the form of crushing taxes for the Jews. So what is there to complain about? Things are just peachy for you—at the state's expense, at my husband's and my expense, for instance as taxpayers! Is that still not enough? [ZJD_04.05.2005_Kar_001]

Here the reversal of perpetrator and victim serves the purpose of exoneration and meets the felt need for normality. The Jews living in Germany are portrayed as blackmailing exploiters of the Holocaust who impose financial and moral debts on the Germans. In this variant, awareness of the Jews' status as victims in the Nazi period remains a factor, but often a correspondent will expressly deny any obligation it might impose:

> (99) This "oh, the poor Jews" has played out by now! [IBD_30.06.2006_Wor_001]
>
> (100) It's high time you stopped playing the role of eternal victims and faced up to your own crimes. [ZJD_31.07.2006_Wol_001]

Crude jumbles of references and time periods, as in (101), reveal the conceptual conflation of Jews with Israelis:

> (101) Israel likes to portray itself as a victim. They kept this role after the 2nd World War, although in the meantime they've become perpetrators. [ZJD_13.04.2002_ano_002]

Educated correspondents from the mainstream who engage in perpetrator–victim reversal project their anti-Jewish resentments less onto the past than onto the current situation in Israel. Here the conceptualization of ISRAEL AS A COLLECTIVE JEW plays a decisive role:

> (102) the victims' descendants themselves become indescribable perpetrators. [ZJD_01.08.2006_Bah_001]

The Jews living in Germany and the Central Council are accused of complicity in the "Israelis' criminal activities." Many authors do not want to accept the social pressure or moral burden that goes with taking responsibility for the historical treatment of the Jews in Germany. They minimize their "German mark of shame" by constructing perpetrator profiles on the Jewish side and applying a double standard and unidirectional focus (see chapter 6, under Targeting, Unique Standard, and Delegitimation). They portray the crimes ascribed to modern Jews as particularly base (since the Jews should have been cleansed of their sins by their past).

> (103) The Jews of all people, who have endured such suffering, are now brutal war criminals. [ZJD_28.05.2007_Blu_001]
>
> (104) After your own terrible experiences actually inconceivable. [IBD_30.11.2007_Rat_001]

The argument contained in such statements, that 'Jews are doing to the Palestinians today what the Germans did to the Jews in the past,' both deprives the Holocaust of its uniqueness and minimizes its status as caesura in civilization, as well as the dimensions of its inhumanity. Mainstream correspondents always try to conceal these semantics by using strategies of avoidance and attenuation.

> (105) I am appalled to observe that more and more people in my own circle of acquaintances, people whom one would really not classify as right-wing radicals, are directing massive criticism at Israel. At present they still do so in a whisper. But I fear that the taboo against open criticism of Israel could easily be broken. An entire generation's sympathy for Israel and for the Jewish people is in the process of dissolving in horror and disappointment. It is becoming increasingly hard to understand how a people that itself endured a long history of suffering can inflict so much suffering on another people. [ZJD_01.05.2002_Sch_001]

Such messages encode the inappropriate conceptual transference that ISRAELI ACTIONS ARE JEWISH ACTIONS and thereby minimize past German crimes while constructing an image of moral degeneracy on the part of the Jews and justifying the authors' own dislike for Jews, which, however, they attribute to others, portraying Jews as evildoers.

Connected to the perpetrator–victim reversal, several patterns of argumentation turn up, embedded in strategies of relativization: argumentatively the revision of German guilt in the messages always takes the form of historical revisionism; see (a) below. On the other hand, when German guilt or responsibility is being relativized—see (b) below—as well as when German responsibility is being relativized in the context of acknowledgment of German guilt—see (c) below—the historical facts of Nazi history are not denied; rather, their current historical relevance is called into question. Relativization and rejection of German responsibility further results from denial of the antisemitism manifesting itself in Germany today or from its minimization as a fringe phenomenon—see (d) below.

(a) The revision of German guilt shows up explicitly in (106) at the level of wording when the Nazis' crimes are denied by means of the term *Auschwitz lie*. As one of the worst sites of Nazi crimes against Jews, Auschwitz has become synonymous with the entirety of the Nazis' atrocities against the Jewish population (cf. Eitz and Stötzel 2007, 25). Such overt denial of the Holocaust and reconceptualization of the German past can be found primarily in communications from right-wing radicals, most of whom remain anonymous.

(106) Auschwitz lie [IBD_2004_ano, Postcard]

(107) Ah, yes, I almost forgot: the Jews were gassed, and we must all believe this 'fact'; the FRG courts make sure of that. [IBD_16.01.2009_ano_008]

In addition to such global relativization, more specific forms and rejections of facts turn up, as in (108):

(108) "From the skin of murdered prisoners they cynically made useful objects, such as lampshades for SS members [. . .]" This story is a pure fabrication! [. . .] the fairy tale about making lampshades. [ZJD_25.04.2007_Sch_001]

Calling the fairy tale a fabrication is striking, for here two semantically related concepts—they both have a fictional component—are linked. In distinction to a fairy tale, in which the fictional element is expected and accepted and therefore evaluated positively, the concept of the FABRICATION carries a negative valuation and invites punishment for the untruth that has been expressed.

(b) Relativization of German guilt can occur at the sentence level, as in example (109), which weighs the author's own suffering against that of the Holocaust victims:

(109) I am no antisemite, and our family also suffered under the 3rd Reich. [ZJD_06.04.2002_Ses_001]

This statement uses the following logic: 'Because my family also suffered, I can't be an antisemite,' and that implies a further premise: 'When one belongs to a victimized group oneself, one cannot be a perpetrator.'

In example (110) German responsibility and guilt are relativized at the textual level through the use of rhetorical questions and the construction of an analogy, as well as comparisons to the Nazis.[27] At the level of language, the statement is also characterized by exaggeration and trivialization:

> (110) Why do you all weep crocodile's tears when someone happens to throw an object at a Jewish synagogue, yet you remain silent when our Church of the Nativity in Bethlehem is destroyed by the Jewish military hordes? What do the Jewish Nazi hordes have to do to get German "dignitaries" to take a stand? [ZJD_08.04.2002_Sch_001]

The author is using the expression *crocodile's tears* to characterize as hypocritical German public reaction to the series of anti-Jewish attacks in France and Belgium that took place during the Easter holidays in 2002.[28] This formulation trivializes the extent of the attacks by means of the verb *happens to*, calling the perpetrators *someone*, and mentioning only *an object*. The statement also falsifies the situation by referring to only one synagogue and one object, minimizing the antisemitic events. By contrast the Israeli military operation, which was undertaken to liberate the Church of the Nativity from occupation by armed Palestinians, is described as *destruction*, and the Israeli soldiers are abused as a *Nazi horde*. The entire account misrepresents the reality, refocusing attention from European antisemites onto the Israelis to make them the perpetrators. The expression *our Church of the Nativity* establishes Christians as the in-group and excludes Israelis as the out-group on the basis of the concept that ISRAELIS = JEWS.

One-sided portrayals such as this one, which oversimplify complex situations and add inflammatory and emotional details, express a closed view of the world (cf. Schwarz-Friesel 2007, 226).

(c) Relativization of German responsibility can also take place in the context of acknowledgment of German guilt, as in (111) and (112), when a specific demand for drawing a line under the past is articulated:

> (111) After all, it's 2007, not 1945 anymore. The latter date goes back almost two generations. What happened in those days should not by any means be relativized. But enough is enough! [ZJD_16.04.2007_Sch_001]

The author justifies the demand for an end to admonitions and reminders simply by calling attention to the long time that has passed since the Nazi crimes took place.

In (112) the demand for drawing a line under the past is justified by means of the vague term *enough*, with emphasis added by the modal verb *must* and the expression *at long last*:

> (112) Germany has done enough for Israel and the Jews, and it's time to let bygones be bygones. [ZJD_13.05.2007_Lud_001]

(d) Whereas in (a)–(c) relativization of the German past occupies the foreground, for the purpose of avoiding charges of responsibility a different pattern of argumentation aims to deny that antisemitism exists in the present or to relativize it. Example (113) uses the former approach, example (114) the latter. Such utterances focus less on the individual writer's attitude than on the alleged absence of prejudice in the society as a whole. The author of the text, however, sees himself as part of that society and thus protected from any charge of antisemitism. These statements minimize the extent of antisemitism and deny the societal relevance of any examination of it (see example [182] in chapter 4).

> (113) Antisemitism is unknown here. [IBD_23.07.2006_Her_002]

Thus in (113) the existence of antisemitism is explicitly denied, while in (114) it is minimized as a right-wing-extremist phenomenon or in (115) portrayed as harmless by comparison with Israel's misdeeds. Frequently the writers consider a right-wing-extremist attitude innocuous, and they point in this context to what they see as Israeli racism.

> (114) These activities in Israel strike me currently as considerably more dangerous to world peace than neo-Nazi goings-on in Germany. [ZJD_24.10.2006_Bud_001]
>
> (115) So what if there are right-wing-radical harbingers of a new Hitler; CRAP. These people are far more dangerous. [ZJD_24.10_2007_ano_003]

These attempts to exonerate antisemitism reveal three different conceptualizations, all of which place blame on the Jews (see also chapter 4): (a) IN GENERAL JEWS PROMOTE ANTISEMITISM THROUGH THEIR BEHAVIOR (cf. [116]); (b) JEWS IN GERMANY PROMOTE ANTISEMITISM THROUGH THE POSITION THEY TAKE ON ISRAEL (cf. [117]); and (c) ISRAEL AND ITS POLICIES ARE TO BLAME FOR ANTISEMITISM IN

GERMANY (cf. [118]). Thus a civil servant who has worked for the Bundeswehr for thirty years comments:

> (116) somehow a new hatred of jews is springing up in the frg—also thanks to your contributions. [ZJD_02.05.2007_Moh_001]

A citizen from Hildesheim combines his complaint with a reproach that asserts a direct causal connection:

> (117) It is simply reprehensible of you to equate every word of criticism of Israeli policies with antisemitism. Do you realize that your statements are calling forth the very thing you complain of? [ZJD_02.09.2006_Pap_001]

A man from Bedburg states in no uncertain terms that antisemitic activities result solely from the intolerable behavior of all Israelis:

> (118) And you complain about the growing anti-Jewish actions in Europe? Well, you're to blame. [. . .] See, the Israelis engage in racisism, xenophobia, and intolerance. [IBD_04.07.2007_Dro_001]

At the same time, these writers deny or relativize genuinely antisemitic tendencies on the part of Germans, thereby rejecting responsibility or projecting it onto others:

> (119) You know, Herr Kramer, that the antisemitism mentioned so often has no foothold at all in the population? If the Central Council of Jews claims that antisemitism is increasing in Germany, citing 200 ridiculous e-mails from various online junkies, I consider that pretty irresponsible. [ZJD_27.07.2006_Gro_001]
>
> (120) But maybe you need that to confirm your view of the world, that Germans have an "antisemitic" attitude. [ZJD_30.07.2006_Cla_001]

Trivializing the existing antisemitism always occurs in the context of a claim that there is no hostility toward Jews among the majority of Germans, or none that need be taken seriously.

Strategies of Differentiation: "*You are one team*"

The separation and exclusion of Jews as an out-group constitutes a consistent semantic feature of antisemitic discourse that takes the form of emphasizing contrasts (cf. chapter 4). In part the differentiation entails the textual strategies already discussed, but there are also specific techniques of differentiation at play. On the linguistic level, the patterns of argumentation involve setting up an opposition between Germans and Jews or Israelis. One striking characteristic is the concept that JEWS = ISRAELIS, expressed through the use of the lexemes *Jew(s)* and *Israeli(s)* as if they were synonymous. A corollary of this usage is often the one-sided perception of Israel as an aggressor.

Since strategies of differentiation are based on establishing contrasts or juxtapositions, they may be realized linguistically in a number of ways and can appear throughout a text. In what follows the most common variants will be presented.

At the level of word choice, juxtaposition occurs through the use of second-person pronouns, singular or plural, in combination with denigrating descriptions, as in (121)–(123):

> (121) [. . .] your outfit [. . .] You, Herr Spiegel and your organization [ZJD_12.06.2002_Sta_001]
>
> (122) Your money-grubbing crew. [ZJD_04.05.2006_Kel_001]
>
> (123) To your revolting horde of lobbyists. [ZJD_17.03.2002_Lue_001]

Often this contrast also makes use of first-person pronouns, singular or plural, for the in-group of which the text producer considers him- or herself a member, while Jews are assigned to the out-group (on the inclusive versus exclusive use of *we*, cf. Mautner 1998).

> (124) [. . .] I wonder what business of yours this eulogy is. [ZJD_16.04.2007_Moh_001]

The writer of (124), a civil servant, expresses in his message his inability to understand why the Central Council would comment critically on a speech delivered by the prime minister of Baden-Württemberg upon the death of Hans Filbinger, a former Nazi navy judge. The rhetorical question, and the use of the pronoun *I* in contrast to *you*, imply that the eulogy is strictly the business of the (German) in-group and outside the (Jewish) Council's area of competence. The underlying concept is that JEWS ARE NOT GERMANS.

The exclusion of Jews as non-Germans and of Israelis as monsters often takes the form of strongly pejorative adjectives and nouns (see chapter 9, under Abuse, Insults, Threats, Curses):

(125) revolting Israeli mob [. . .] you rat pack [IBD_08.05.2007_Kol_001]

(126) diseased, disgusting, and ultra-brutal motherfuckers [IBD_10.06.2006_Bre_001]

(127) Heartless creatures, that's what you are. [ZJD_01.08.2006_Mon_001]

Dehumanization, sometimes through descriptions of Jews or Israelis as animals, and moral devaluation play a prominent role here.

On the sentence level, differentiation and exclusion also find expression through directive speech acts such as demands:

(128) keep your criticism of german activities abroad to yourself. this is interference in the internal affairs of the German state that is not appropriate for you as a non-european sect. [ZJD_29.05.2007_Sch_002]

In (129), just the pileup of rhetorical questions and the use of the modal particle *actually* points to the conclusion, even without contrasting pronouns, that the text producer does not conceptualize Jews living in Germany as Germans. The sentence that follows shows that this analysis is correct:

(129) What are the members of the CENTRAL COUNCIL actually: Jewish citizens in Germany ? German Jews ? Israeli Jews in Germany ? This last interpretation makes sense, because don't Frau Knobloch and Herr Korn—like Herr Bubicz and Herr Spiegel before them—behave like a 5th column from a foreign country with regard to German politicians and citizens? [ZJD_02.11.2006_Buh_001]

Although strategies of differentiation and exclusion based on traditional Judeophobic stereotypes appear especially often in messages from right-wing extremists, educated correspondents also resort to this pattern of making contrasts, as in (130), in which a man from Lauf with a PhD sees the German Jews as Israelis:

(130) Instead of whining about antisemitism, Herr Friedmann should show some backbone and ask himself whether there isn't a morsel of truth in Möllemann's criticism. Dignified restraint, particularly with your country

in such difficult straits, would serve good German–Jewish relations well. [ZJD_07.06.2002_Ban_001]

A recurring pattern of argumentation that serves to differentiate Jews is the 'moral discreditation' expressed directly by right-wing-radical correspondents, while those from the mainstream accomplish the same thing through references to Israel.

In his e-mail to the Central Council a correspondent from Kornwestheim isolates Israel as a barbarous country by focusing on its degeneracy and thereby legitimizing his hope that it may endure violence and suffering:

> (131) Israel is undertaking the holocaust against the inhabitants of Palestine. [. . .] It is becoming apparent that Israel simply does not belong to the circle of humanistic peoples, but culturally, spiritually, and morally has remained in a barbaric condition. It is to be hoped that Israel will have enough dead to mourn as Europe in the 30-years' war, in order (in the truthest sense of the word) to come to see reason. [ZJD_2009Gaza_552/816_Mad_001]

The Middle East conflict is often seen, primarily by left-wing-extremist and leftist writers, as purely the result of Israel's policies, and this oversimplified interpretation is presented in declarative sentences as fact:

> (132) Hezbollah in particular was founded precisely in response to the continued state-sponsored terrorism of the Israeli government and military against its neighboring states. After all, it is thanks to Hezbollah that in the most recent past the pro-fascist Israeli soldateska was unable to advance into defenseless Beirut and with tanks cut a swath of death and destruction through the refugee camps of Sabra and Shatila as was done a few years ago under General Sharon. [ZJD_07.10.2006_Zim_001]

Characteristic of the slanted account in (132) are the one-sided informational structure on the textual level and the negative references to Israel on the word level. Lexemes like *state-sponsored terrorism*, *pro-fascist*, *swath of death*, and *destruction* criminalize and demonize Israel. By contrast, the terrorist organization Hezbollah is not associated with the concepts of TERROR, DEATH, INJUSTICE, or GUILT, but rather conceptualized as PROTECTOR. Thus a striking derealization takes place.

When Jews and Israelis are portrayed as morally reprehensible or as situated beyond the pale of general ethical values and norms, a wide variety of antisemitic arguments and demands can be voiced. Thus German guilt and responsibility for the Holocaust and its consequences can always be relativized and denied on this basis, and the Israeli state can be delegitimized, while a Judeophobic attitude is justified. The immorality attributed to the Jews serves as a premise that can be employed in a variety of ways for any antisemitic or anti-Israeli position and argument.

The most common form of moral discreditation takes the form of comparisons to the Nazis. Thus in (133), a relativization of guilt and/or denial of responsibility is accomplished by means of the implicit Nazi comparison and with the help of the perpetrator–victim reversal:

> (133) How come after more than 60 years since the end of Nazism there is still so much useless blabber about this period that was put to rest long ago? Clean up your own country first. What's going on there anyway with the Palestinians? [ZJD_13.04.2007_ano_001]

In such texts sent to the Central Council the conceptual identification of ISRAELIS with JEWS always plays a part. German Jews are differentiated as non-Germans from the majority society. Moral discreditation usually occurs, often in conjunction with the application of a double standard to Jews, as in the following e-mail from an engineer from Upper Bavaria:

> (134) Despite your painful past you seem to lack any compassion for the suffering of other peoples. [ZJD_12.12.2006_Oeh_001]

This double standard is based on a conceptualization that can be summarized thus: 'People on whom suffering was imposed must be morally cleansed and sensitized to the suffering of others. But the Jews are particularly depraved and coarse, for they have not learned any lessons from the past.' Israeli policies are blamed on all Jews and seen as a violation of the norms of the in-group—Western democratic societies. Those policies are accordingly cited as justification for the exclusion of Jews (cf. also Holz 2005, 23–53).

Strategies of differentiation rest conceptually and emotionally for the most part on traditional Judeophobic stereotypes. Therefore, Jews are portrayed as the Other, as the epitome of evil and depravity. Strategies of differentiation enable the authors to present and articulate their own antisemitism as legitimate.

Here an argument entailing Judeophobic thinking and communicative acts comes full circle with respect to the strategies we have outlined: the exclusion of Jews must—according to antisemitic thinking—take place, for the language producers see it as (pseudo-)causally justified. At the same time they must avoid any impression that they are racists or antisemites. Offensive self-aggrandizement and defensiveness interact as they attempt to preserve a closed view of the world and to transmit it convincingly to others.

The Right versus the Middle

The various linguistic strategies are not spread evenly through the messages we have examined. Rather, striking differences exist between extreme and more moderate messages. Strategies of legitimation and avoidance occur especially frequently in those from correspondents who locate themselves in the mainstream of society or the middle of the political spectrum. The analyses of our examples show that authors who articulate eliminatory or crudely rightist antisemitism for the most part dispense with these strategies. Right-wing-extremist authors find it unnecessary to conceal their antisemitic views or to provide arguments to support them. At the same time, the few correspondents who express only legitimate criticism of Israel hardly ever use strategies of legitimation or avoidance. This suggests that the writers who represent anti-Israeli and antisemitic positions must recognize that their opinions are inflammatory and dubious, or at least subject to discussion and challenge. Without this awareness there would be no motivation for them to employ the various strategies. Therefore, the absence or presence of these strategies is an important indicator of verbal antisemitism when combined with unambiguous or strongly implied statements, and in particular when the strategies serve the communicative function of fending off charges of antisemitism or sanctions.

Conclusion

Analysis of the messages sent by authors from the mainstream of society reveals, despite all the individual differences among them, a remarkable degree of homogeneity with respect to textual structure, the use of specific strategies, and patterns of argumentation. The e-mails and letters read for the most part like copies of a common original, with minor deviations. The contents and the linguistic forms are often almost interchangeable. It becomes clear how powerfully the Judeophobic stereotypes are mentally present and influential, transcending individual differences, but also how the use of antisemitic language in the twenty-first century is shaped by awareness of the catastrophe that was the Holocaust. The educated authors of Judeophobic texts certainly know that the ideas they express are inflammatory and/or morally dubious, or could be perceived as such. Yet the desire, the compulsion to articulate their rage and indignation to the "Jewish disturber of the peace," the "adversary and enemy," embodied in these cases by the Central Council and the Embassy, proves stronger than the reservations they sense as they do so. Thus even educated antisemites from the mainstream reveal the obsessive component that characterizes the entire phenomenon of antisemitism.

By denying their antisemitism to others and themselves, they manage to preserve their image of themselves as responsible citizens free of prejudices. This constellation is typical of German discourse, informed by Germany's particular history. The authors of antisemitic messages who can be classified as mainstream often encode their Judeophobic prejudices by means of implicit or reclassified linguistic forms. They use a variety of legitimation and justification strategies to justify their semantically radical arguments, on the one hand, and to reinterpret them conceptually, on the other, by means of verbal coding. The writers present themselves as anti-antisemites whose conscience, moral integrity, and sense of responsibility demand that they take a position against what they view as the morally despicable Jews and/or Israelis. This "antisemitism without antisemites" presents itself as antiracist and honorable, but draws on most of the common Judeophobic stereotypes and prejudices, uses demonizing Nazi comparisons, and expresses itself through extreme anti-Israelism. These features also characterize the authors of extremist e-mails.

Here we find clear commonalities between the verbal antisemitism produced by right-wing and left-wing extremists, as well as correspondents from the mainstream. Extremists for the most part, however, use vulgar, abusive lexis, as well as the syntax of threat, and engage in a rather primitive rhetoric of defamation. But if one looks at the underlying patterns of thought and resentment, the same semantic and conceptual contents come to light in all the messages. They show the pervasive influence of basic stereotypes and paradigms for interpreting the world.

Despite all ideological differences, the ways in which most of the authors use language are remarkably similar and reveal fundamental patterns that inform the details of their arguments. Not only the conceptual foundations of Judeophobic language but also the communicative strategies of its implementation are largely homogeneous, transcending political and social differences.

APPENDIX

The Basic Corpus—Letters to the Central Council of Jews in Germany and the Israeli Embassy in Berlin, 2002–2012

The Relevance of Corpus Analysis and the Necessity of Enlarging the Methodological Tool Kit for Research on Antisemitism

This study focuses on the verbal manifestations of hostility toward Jews in present-day Germany and the thought structures and feelings those manifestations reveal. In order to be in a position to make empirically grounded statements on a particular linguistic or communicative phenomenon, researchers in linguistics, communication, and cognitive science increasingly make use of corpus analysis.[1] Corpora are large quantities of texts on a certain topic that have been compiled over a specific period for the purpose of acquiring data that lend themselves to comparative analysis, both quantitative and qualitative (Scherer 2006, 36f.; Bubenhofer 2009). The size of a corpus can vary according to the field, the occasion, or the subject matter. Several hundred texts may be sufficient for discerning basic patterns and frequencies, but usually several thousand or even tens of thousands of examples are involved. Compilation of a corpus can occur over several days, months, or, in the case of longitudinal studies, years. Thus our collection of data in reference to the public debate waged on the Internet over Günter Grass's anti-Israel poem took place over only a few days, whereas reporting on the Middle East in print and online media extended over several years and included reports and commentaries in the mainstream media on specific crises. The focus can be directed toward one particular medium and a specific topic within a particular area—for example, online comments by readers of the mainstream media during the period when the Gaza flotilla action was in the news or readers' comments in the print media on the Lebanon conflict.

The fourteen thousand e-mails, letters, postcards, and faxes in our corpus, sent between 2002 and 2012 to the Central Council of Jews in Germany (Zentralrat der Juden in Deutschland, referred to as the Central Council) and the Israeli Embassy in Berlin (henceforth the Embassy), all address the topic of Jews or Judaism in Germany and/or Israel.[2] Their authors come from German-speaking areas, and they were sent entirely spontaneously to the two institutions. We also had access to a control corpus of well over a thousand e-mails and letters sent to German Jewish professor Michael Wolffsohn in 2004 (Schwarz-Friesel 2007, 354) and a collection of communications sent between 2010 and 2011 to the Israeli embassies in Vienna, Berne, The Hague, Madrid, Brussels, London, Dublin, and Stockholm. Additionally we considered twenty-nine letters or e-mails sent to Esther Schapira, a journalist with Hessian Radio and Television, in response to the film *Three Bullets and a Dead Child*, broadcast on 18 March 2002 in the ARD series *The Red Square*. The Forum against Antisemitism in Vienna also provided us with a summary of anti-Jewish incidents, including a selection of typical defamatory letters sent between 2000 and 2012 to Jewish organizations in Austria.

We did not undertake any specific selection; all the communications, including those expressing positive sentiments and solidarity, were considered. The data from these sources were augmented by specific data collected from the public communication space, primarily the print media and the Internet, that addressed the same topics and thus proved useful for purposes of comparison and for amplification of our results. Examination of these types of texts reveals that similar patterns recur, with the majority of the authors who engage in (semi-)public discourse expressing themselves in the same fashion as the authors of the personal e-mails and letters in the corpus. Furthermore, comparative analysis of texts sent in 2010 and 2011 to the Israeli embassies in Austria, Switzerland, Belgium, England, Ireland, the Netherlands, Sweden, and Spain affords us insight into anti-Israeli sentiment elsewhere in Europe.

Although by now many disciplines have adopted the method of corpus analysis, most research on antisemitism still depends primarily on single examples (e.g., Benz 2004; Rensmann 2004; Wistrich 2010). Corpus-based analysis proves superior to an approach based on unsystematically selected quotations, for the validity of the data yields more convincing empirical evidence. The validity stems from the large number of texts available, for the most part electronically, in the corpora (cf. Bubenhofer 2008, 407ff.,

2009; Stefanowitsch and Gries 2006). Over the past ten years corpus-based linguistics research has demonstrated how electronic searches and statistical analyses can be deployed to gather reliable data of a sort not available through unsystematic searches and assessment.[3] It must be emphasized, however, that when it comes to analyzing language usage and the characteristics of discourse, quantitative analysis is no substitute for qualitative analysis. Many relevant phenomena, such as implication, evaluation, and stereotyping, can be captured only by analyzing details in a way that takes into consideration the context and specific character of a given text, and to discern such features one must have a human researcher. Only by methodically combining qualitative cognition-based linguistic textual analysis with quantitative statistical analysis of the corpus can the researcher evaluate adequately the results of detailed analysis. When engaging in microstructural analysis of the texts, one must first determine the specific verbal forms that antisemitic stereotypes take and the patterns of argumentation. Quantitative analysis can reveal the frequency with which certain antisemitic verbalizations occur, both in general and within a particular chronological span.

Quantitatively oriented surveys on Jews and things Jewish, as well as on Israel and the conflict in the Middle East, that are administered on a fairly regular basis by sociologists and psychologists do not capture the subjects' thinking and emotional patterns, or do so only in a very limited sense, because they always make use of a few preformulated general statements that tend to influence the responses. These statements take the form of semantically circumscribed value assertions such as "Jews have too much influence in our society" or "Israel is an aggressor." The subjects' patterns of verbal expression are not captured at all, since they merely check off a response or answer "Yes," "No," or "I don't know."

Such preformulated utterances can create so-called priming effects. Sometimes it would not occur to the subject to give a certain response without exposure to the researcher's formulation. Factors such as the social desirability bias can likewise come into play (cf. Brosius and Koschel 2001, 113f.). This tendency makes it impossible to determine whether the attitudes indicated by the responses to such a survey were already present in the subjects as established mental orientations or whether they were activated or actualized by the wording of the survey or a specific context and situation (Scherer 2006, 2).

Along with such quality criteria as the validity and reliability of the survey instrument, quantitative studies of antisemitic attitudes in Germany (e.g., Bergmann and Erb 1991; Heitmeyer 2002–2012; Bergmann and Heitmeyer 2005b) rely on a structurally identical sampling from the entire population. Samples are drawn from randomly selected subjects assumed to be representative of the entire population. The scope and structure of the sample constitute the key criteria for the quality of the surveys, although logically the range of characteristics can never be portrayed comprehensively in all their variety, and the concept of a "representative sample or cross section" must thus be understood as a kind of metaphor (Diekmann 2008, 430).[4]

Given this background, the following must be acknowledged with respect to the representative value of the corpus on which this study rests:

We cannot, nor do we presume to, make any statistical claims for the entirety of the German population. As a rule, the correspondents give only their names and addresses, often augmented by their age and profession, but no other demographic information is available. Yet on the basis of the identifying facts provided and the form and content of the texts, one can see that the corpus is clearly not limited to fringe groups of the right-wing-extremist or other persuasions, or to individuals clearly identifiable as antisemitic (in contrast to those described by Decker et al. 2006; Scherr and Schäuble 2007; and Salzborn 2008). Right-wing extremists represent 11 percent of the corpus and are assigned to the categories "right-wing" and "right-leaning," but they do not constitute the majority, which is made up of political and socioeconomic centrists. Thus along with high-school students and white-collar workers one finds many self-employed persons, civil servants, university students, and academics. Many of the writers make a point of mentioning their political preferences and generally locate themselves in the middle of the political spectrum or even mention their membership in one of the major political parties. The corpus also includes a wide range of ages and geographical locations.[5]

Not all Germans are equally motivated to give expression to their views on Jews and Israel, quite apart from whether those views are positive, negative, or even antisemitic. Thus, among the writers in our corpus, the level of emotional intensity or the pertinence to their core convictions and conceptions is very high. This state of affairs offers the advantage that the criterion of centrality is indubitably fulfilled for the corpus and that we do not have to take expressions of "no opinion" into consideration (cf. Atteslander 2008, 61f.).[6] Thus one must assume that the material we have analyzed affords us insight into typical patterns of antisemitic conceptions and stereotypes held by Germans with antisemitic attitudes.[7] The criterion of "representativeness" applies in conjunction with corpus analysis to current linguistic expressions of antisemitism. The data in the corpus are representative with respect to the patterns of linguistic usage in antisemitic discourse; that is, they reveal the methods and strategies typical of anti-Jewish usage in Germany. That does not mean, however, that they are also representative of all communication about Jews in Germany or of the views of all Germans.

When compared with quantitative surveys, a comprehensive corpus analysis offers the following advantages: the texts that make up the corpus represent spontaneous verbal expressions of independently held ideas and emotions, not responses to questions formulated by researchers that focus on particular subjects or individual aspects. Thus our approach extends beyond capturing spontaneous reactions and allows us to consider the information gleaned from the corpus as evidence of deep-seated thoughts and emotions pertaining to Jews, Judaism, and Israel. Any influence by the researchers over the ideas expressed is out of the question; and the spillover effect, whereby one question affects the response to the next, cannot occur, as it does in questionnaires like Heitmeyer's because of the number and proximity of tendentious questions (cf. Brosius and Koschel 2001, 122; Kirchhoff et al. 2003; Porst 2008). The corpus methodology also eliminates undesirable effects such as those that can occur as a result of reactive responses to polls, for instance the "looking-good effect" or unintentional predetermination of responses by the researcher (cf. Brosius and Koschel 2001, 146ff.; Diekmann 2008, 446ff).

The kind of discrepancy that can occur between the attitudes elicited by a survey or interview and the subject's actual behavior (cf. Atteslander 2008, 161) does not occur in the corpus we have chosen to analyze. The linguistic utterances in question manifest persisting attitudes, because linguistic utterances in the form of a written communication constitute acts and at the same time express an emotional and cognitive position.

Most surveys do not do justice to the complexity inherent in the phenomenon of antisemitism.[8] A differentiated survey that would address both critical views of Israel and antisemitism, as well as their multiplicity of forms, is not likely to be undertaken.

While empirical surveys do offer important ways to establish tendencies in society as a whole, they do not support more probing analyses or even explanations. They fail to reveal mental connections made among stereotypes, they elicit no information as to the ways in which verbal formulations and strategies convey cognitive and emotional patterns of hostility toward Jews, nor do they offer insight into attitudinal patterns and worldviews.

Thus sociological studies must be augmented by application of the methods of cognitive analysis to the expressions representative of individual attitudes that appear in the spontaneous patterns of verbalization in our corpus. Only in this way can we determine actual mental images of Jews and Israel and postulate a possible continuity or change in stereotypes and clichés. Contemporary research on antisemitism must open itself up methodologically and include, in addition to traditional "conservative" sociological methods such as opinion surveys and historical description of individual events, interdisciplinary corpus analysis and detailed textual and cognitive analysis, if it wishes to do justice to the challenge of capturing hostility toward Jews in its many facets and manifestations and with appropriate attention to its content. As Rensmann and Schoeps put it, this undertaking "calls for a broad set of discourse-analytic and discourse-historical approaches" (2008, 31).

Specific Characteristics of the Corpus

Dimensions of the Corpus, Subcorpora, and Sample Analyses

Of the more than 14,003 communications in our corpus that we cataloged, those received by the Central Council of Jews in Germany arrived between 31 March 2002 and 24 July 2009, while those received by the Israeli Embassy in Berlin arrived between 17 October 2003 and 10 April 2012. Most of the letters are addressed to Charlotte Knobloch, then president of the Central Council, or her predecessor, Paul Spiegel, and to the Israeli ambassador, Yoram Ben-Zeev, and his predecessor, Shimon Stein, but some were sent to the two institutions without an addressee.

Thematic Emphases or Connection to Relevant Discursive Events The number of messages fluctuates depending on political events. For the year 2006 about two-thirds of the material came from the Israeli Embassy, which between 2006 and 2009 received more mail than the Central Council. In 2006 the

Figure 1. **Number of Messages by Month in 2006**

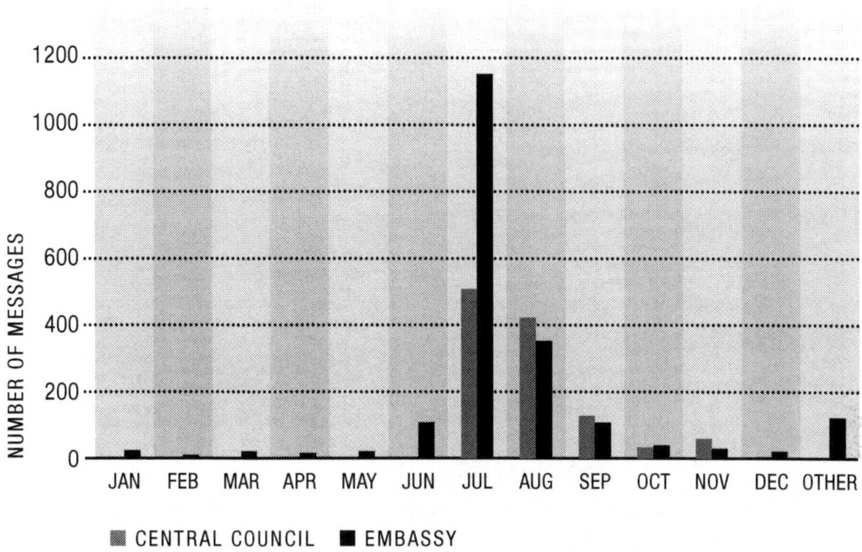

war in Lebanon occasioned 1,170 messages to the Central Council, while the Embassy received 2,100. In 2009 Operation Cast Lead again occasioned twice as much mail to the Embassy. In 2002 the Central Council received the lion's share of the correspondence in connection with the Möllemann–Friedman debate, which placed the Council at the forefront of attention.[9]

As a rule, thematic pretexts stem from announcements by the Central Council or reports in the media on political developments in Israel or in the Israeli–Palestinian conflict. In 2006 it was the war in Lebanon, in 2007 the escalation in the Gaza Strip. The summer months of 2006 alone saw about 2,000 letters reach the Embassy, and more than 1,000 were sent to the Central Council, with both institutions receiving the largest number in July (1,155 for the Embassy; see figure 1).

As the graph in figure 1 indicates, between July and September 2006 the Central Council received a large number of written communications (n = 1,067) urging it to intervene in the Lebanon situation. The authors see a need for action on the part of the Council when Israel's foreign policy or military operations are at issue. This expectation may have something to do with the Council's calls for solidarity with Israel,[10] but it strongly suggests that the writers hold Jews in Germany responsible for the Israeli state's policies.

These communications furthermore provide evidence of the conflation of the concepts JEW(S) and ISRAELI(S), which are discussed further in chapters 4 and 6. In the conflict between Hezbollah and Israel that took place in 2006 in Lebanon, statements by Germany's minister for economic development, Heidemarie Wieczorek-Zeul, remained at the center of attention for weeks. The minister's criticism of Israel's use of cluster bombs turns up in most of the letters from this period. The Central Council is reproached for a partisan attitude toward the Middle East conflict, and its calls for solidarity with Israel are castigated. In 2007 the volume of letters to the Embassy remains fairly consistent, arriving at a rate of about 100 per month, while the Central Council receives between 10 and 20 per month, with April the only exception.

The Gaza conflict of 2008–2009 occasions a new increase, with the Embassy receiving 4,028 letters and the Central Council 867. The increase largely mirrors the attention paid by the media to each escalation of the conflict; the more thorough and controversial the coverage of events in the Middle East and the debates in the German and international media, the more communications the Embassy and the Central Council receive (see figure 1). The authors usually write immediately after an announcement by the Central Council or a broadcast. The authors display a sort of stimulus-response, reacting either immediately after hearing a statement or the very next day. Since 2006, reports in the media have constituted the primary incentive for writing. Reports or announcements in the press often appear as attachments or links, or the letters contain direct references to them (see chapter 6). Between 2002 and 2012 the number of attached photographs and PDFs shows a sharp increase, as does the number of round-robin e-mails, petitions, and lists of signatures.

In May 2008 the sixtieth anniversary of the founding of the state of Israel provided the occasion for most of the letters. For the first time in the entire corpus, a large number of the letters received expressed solidarity and, above all, congratulations. A similar trend appeared in connection with the prisoner exchange between Israel and Hezbollah that resulted in the return of the bodies of Eldad Regev and Ehud Goldwasser to Israel. Here we find many expressions of solidarity with the victims' families, but also with the state of Israel. In an increasing number of letters that express positive attitudes toward Israel, the authors write to the Embassy, mentioning Israel's need for security and the dangers to which the country is exposed, and sometimes criticizing the media for anti-Israeli or one-sided reporting.

On the other hand, the letters critical of Israel or antisemitic in tone include an unmistakable increase in explicit and very aggressive hate mail. Starting early in 2009, contemporaneous with the Gaza conflict, more and more of the writers use brutal speech patterns, insults, invective, direct threats, and curses (see chapter 9).[11] With noticeable frequency, explicit references to Nazism occur. The language used by mainstream correspondents also displays noticeable radicalization. Reports on the Israeli Defense Force's halting of the Turkish Gaza flotilla at the end of May 2010 occasion a flood of 830 messages to the Embassy, the majority of which contain drastic verbal aggression.

Cataloging, Sample Size, and Subcorpora We were unable to undertake a detailed classification and individual analysis of each and every communication received according to all the relevant categories of form and content (see the set of variables), especially not after the exorbitant increase in messages that set in with 2009. In addition to the sheer number involved, the length of the communications comes into play; a quantitative analysis would have necessitated reading all the multipage letters in their entirety. To make the collection of quantitative data possible, however, a representative sample was selected. During the period extending from 1 January 2002 to 31 December 2007, the Central Council and the Embassy received 4,912 communications addressing events relevant to this study. The chosen time span includes a considerable number of thematic pretexts and is large enough to allow changes occurring over time to become evident. It should also be noted that with the large increase in communications starting in 2009, many of the letters were identical or nearly identical copies, sent almost entirely by e-mail. The incentive for writing is always Israeli policies or military interventions. The material received from 2008 on was therefore sampled randomly to identify noticeable features or changes. If specific verbalizations, argumentative patterns, or particular new features could be discerned, their quantitative relevance was estimated by means of corresponding keyword searches or skimming. The analyses were carried out by coders with backgrounds in linguistics who had been informed of the criteria involved; that is, no blind coding was involved. The coders received specific training to enable them to analyze and categorize prototypical cases. During the pilot phase, practice coding was carried out. During the coding process some duplicate coding was undertaken independently, with the results later calibrated by the research group.[12]

Figure 2. **Distribution of Messages along the Political Spectrum**

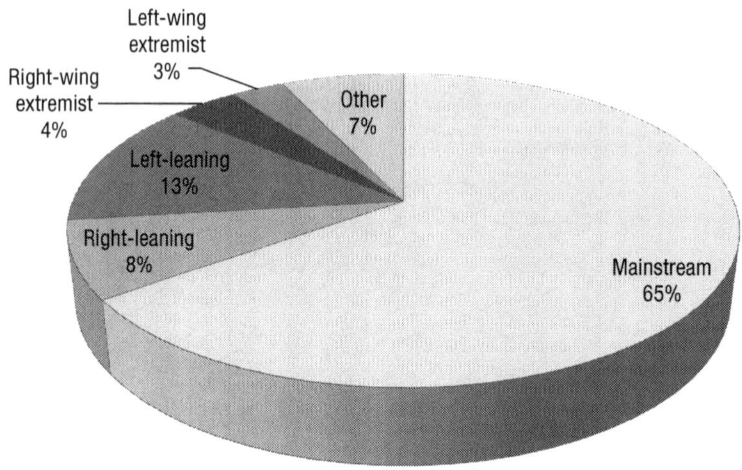

In the qualitative individual analyses, textual examples from 2009 to 2012 were included to show that the changes indicated here affected only a few specific aspects, with most of the verbalized stereotypes and textual strategies remaining constant, changing little since 2006–2007. The results that refer to the quantitatively classified sample can thus be generalized for the entire corpus.[13] The content analyses of the 4,912 communications in the sample allow the following political attitudes to be identified among the authors: Mainstream: 65 percent; Left-leaning: 13 percent; Right-leaning: 8 percent; Right-wing-extremist: 4 percent; Left-wing-extremist: 3 percent; Other: 7 percent.

The clear majority of the correspondents can be assigned to the political mainstream (n = 3,204, or 65 percent);[14] this finding confirms the relevance of the topic "Antisemitism: A Mainstream Phenomenon" (Schwarz-Friesel et al. 2010).

The concept of the mainstream shapes our image of political normality and stability (cf. Heitmeyer 2007, 27). As a rule, a mainstream position is understood to be one that eschews extremist and antisemitic attitudes or can be distinguished from these fringe phenomena (cf. Backes 1989; Backes and Jesse 1989). The analyses undertaken in this project reveal, however, that opinions that veer off into extreme positions also exist in broad segments of society, including the mainstream or majority.

University-bound high-school graduates, students, lawyers, journalists, physicians, pastors, self-employed persons, and local politicians, but also professors, make use of numerous stereotypes in their correspondence (see chapter 4). Nine percent of those writing to the Embassy and 7 percent of those writing to the Central Council use academic titles, an indication that they have at least completed college or university studies. It is thus clear that the correspondents expressing antisemitic sentiments include members of educated societal elites.

The texts expressing extreme right-wing or left-wing political views are about equally divided. With each position constituting less than 4 percent of the total, one may say that these views are surprisingly rare. Texts that can be classified as "left-leaning" occur almost twice as frequently as those from "right-leaning or conservative" correspondents (left-leaning: 12.7 percent; right-leaning/conservative: 7.6 percent). The number of right-leaning/right-wing-extremist correspondences addressed to the Central Council is twice that of the correspondences received by the Embassy, presumably a function of the themes that occur more frequently in the Central Council's corpus; right-wing extremists more frequently adduce classic stereotypes and attitudes than new prejudices relating to Israel, hence their tendency to write to the Council. The Embassy receives a larger number of messages from left-wing extremists than the Central Council; they communicate hostile or critical attitudes toward Israel, some of them differentiating between Judaism and Israel, others defining themselves as anti-Zionist and antisemitic.

Clearly the messages from extreme groups on the fringes of German society do not constitute the bulk of the corpus. Rather, it is primarily persons from the social mainstream who are motivated to communicate their views to the Central Council or the Embassy. The occurrence of letters to the Central Council from extremists at either end of the political spectrum seems to be roughly equivalent to the numerical presence of such persons in German society, as noted in the annual reports issued by the Federal Office for Protection of the Constitution.[15] The numbers match the self-declared political orientations recorded by Zick and Küpper (2006b, 118); in 2005, of those surveyed, 7 percent considered themselves leftists, while 22 percent characterized themselves as left-leaning; 13 percent thought of themselves as right-leaning, and barely 4 percent as right-wing. Meanwhile 54 percent placed themselves squarely in the middle (see also Hradil and Schmidt 2007, 174).

Table 1. **Number of Communications According to Political Sympathies**

	CENTRAL COUNCIL		EMBASSY		TOTAL	
	n	%	*n*	%	*n*	%
Mainstream	1,418	65.3	1,786	65.2	3,204	65.2
Left-leaning	244	11.2	379	13.8	623	12.7
Left-wing extremist	37	1.7	125	4.6	162	3.3
Right-leaning	247	11.4	126	4.6	373	7.6
Right-wing extremist	106	4.9	76	2.8	182	3.7
Islamist	23	1.1	106	3.9	129	2.6
Psychol. aberrant	14	0.6	71	2.6	85	1.7
Other	82	3.8	72	2.6	154	3.1
TOTAL	**2,171**		**2,741**		**4,912**	

The remaining portion of the corpus that may be described as ambiguous or not clearly classifiable, Islamist, or psychopathological consists of 368 letters, or 7.5 percent of the total.[16] More authors express Islamist tendencies in messages to the Embassy than in messages to the Central Council; these communications tend to include references to the writer's own ethnic or religious identity, to solidarity with the "Palestinian brothers," or to a kind of "religious solidarity," but the number of these communications makes them negligible for our purposes. Among the Muslim correspondents a limited command of the German language may account for the small number of messages received.

Few differences can be discerned that relate to the writers' social class or geographical location. The messages come about equally from East and West Germany and from cities, towns, and rural areas.

Within the complete corpus, specific subcorpora were analyzed separately in order to allow clearer contrasts to be established among groups. Thus differences in the linguistic usage of extremists and mainstream correspondents could be established, as could differences between messages addressed to the Central Council and the Embassy, and differences among messages occasioned by the Möllemann–Friedman debate and those pertaining to other events. An interesting partial corpus consists of messages responding to the eulogy the prime minister of Baden-Württemberg, Günter Oettinger, delivered for

Hans Filbinger, or to the Central Council's critical comment on this speech, since this discussion directly adumbrates the Nazi past. Looking at the corpus in chronological terms also proves illuminating: it reveals changes in usage, for instance in the use of comparisons to Nazism or the decline of indirect speech acts in favor of direct speech acts, as well as in the articulation of classic anti-Jewish stereotypes.

In order to identify collocations—that is, significantly frequent occurrences of specific terms in conjunction with other terms—co-occurrence or collocation analyses were conducted on subcorpora (cf. Perkuhn and Belica 2004). In addition, samples of approximately one thousand texts were studied for the occurrence of prominent words or semantic fields (cf. Schwarz and Chur 2007, 60f.).

Message Types and Anonymity The types of messages received by the Central Council and the Embassy between 2002 and 2007 fall into a consistent pattern: in both cases, the vast majority consist of e-mails (65 percent), followed by letters and postcards (28 percent), and more rarely faxes (both less than 10 percent). But a change can be seen over the years: while in 2002 regular letters predominate, by 2006–2007 most correspondents choose e-mail. This rapid and inexpensive method of communication, which since 2008 has come to constitute about 90 percent of all information transmitted, offers the possibility of conveying one's views quickly and easily, as well as anonymously in some cases.

Nonetheless, most of the messages include the senders' names and addresses, with only about 13 percent remaining anonymous. About 41 percent of the messages received by the Central Council and 37 percent of those

Table 2. **Type of Message**

MESSAGE TYPE	CENTRAL COUNCIL		EMBASSY		TOTAL	
	n	%	*n*	%	*n*	%
Letter/postcard	599	27.6	755	27.5	1,354	27.6
Fax	171	7.9	159	5.8	330	6.7
E-mail	1,401	64.5	1,827	66.7	3,228	65.7
TOTAL	**2,171**		**2,741**		**4,912**	

received by the Embassy include the sender's complete mailing address, sometimes accompanied by a telephone number or a home page. The majority of the e-mails, however, provide only the sender's name, place of residence, and of course the e-mail address. Most of the anonymous communications come by e-mail. Between 2002 and 2007 the percentage of anonymous e-mails per year varies between 9 and 15 percent, with no clear trend noticeable. On the other hand, it is unmistakable that more writers to both the Central Council and the Embassy identify themselves by name and address, yet nonetheless articulate antisemitic attitudes, including some extreme forms of those attitudes.

The distribution of the anonymous messages along the political spectrum is revealing. Messages that can be categorized as coming from the mainstream are rarely sent anonymously. The senders of these messages seldom perceive a need to conceal their names and addresses. They clearly consider their sentiments perfectly acceptable and defensible, and would presumably not hesitate to voice them in public. This finding corresponds to the senders' frequent references to their own integrity and denials of antisemitism. These individuals view their opinions as neither antisemitic nor problematic; rather, they consider their standpoints necessary and justified, and show their willingness to accept responsibility for them by signing their names.

The extremists among the senders, whether on the right or left, as well as those who lean right or left, differ sharply from those in the mainstream in that the percentage of anonymous messages from them is in the double digits.[17] These writers clearly recognize their messages as problematic and conceal their names, either out of fear of possible sanctions or out of the paranoid delusion that the Israeli secret police will hunt them down. The right-wing extremists account for the highest percentage—43 percent—of the anonymous messages, with this group constituting fully half of all the anonymous messages received by the Embassy. This phenomenon reveals that the senders do not consider their views generally acceptable or consensual. Here the individuals' perceptions coincide with the ideology of the right-wing-extremist parties and associations, which see their classic positions of xenophobia, rejection of the European Union, and so on as subject to persecution in Germany and portray themselves as victims of censorship. In order to express their views, right-wing extremists thus often resort to writing under cover of anonymity. In addition to the previously mentioned criteria, anonymity can therefore be taken as an indication that the writer holds extremist views.

The messages offer multiple forms of direct and indirect evidence of their authors' socioeconomic status. For one thing, they often provide explicit information on the senders' educational level, profession, or family and life circumstances. Many letters begin with formulations such as "*As a __year-old retiree from __*," or "*As a __year-old student, I have the following questions . . .*" Further sources of information can be found in the extensive descriptions of their family history, interests, or reasons for writing that some correspondents offer, such as "*As a teacher, I have long studied the history of the Jews . . .*" or "*I would like to be able to explain to my children why . . .*" or "*. . . committed to tolerance and honest expression, I . . .*" These formulations usually reveal a desire on the part of the writers to present themselves in a positive light (see chapter 10, under Strategies of Legitimation and Self-Aggrandizement). Certain pieces of factual information, such as indications of the writers' professions—especially pastor, teacher, civil servant, businessperson—or academic titles, but also letterheads and links to websites, make it possible to situate the authors in the middle class. Furthermore, the writers often make a point of mentioning their political orientation, sometimes stressing that they are not adherents of any extremist ideology, particularly of the right-wing persuasion, but rather identify with the "normal" political center. Here it becomes evident that those who write to the Central Council and the Embassy use entirely different criteria to characterize themselves as mainstream.

In view of this degree of explicitness, it is striking that extreme and crude expressions of antisemitism, especially of the right-wing- and left-wing-extremist variety, tend to be sent as e-mails, and short ones at that, while writers who express themselves cautiously, arguing primarily by indirection and implication, write longer messages and often prefer more formal conventional letters. Many of their e-mails are lengthy, extending over several pages. Mainstream senders often forward copies of their messages to newspapers and politicians.

During the time period we studied, the number of explicitly antisemitic and aggressive messages increased noticeably. Explicit expressions of hatred and threats of the sort found from 2006 on occur seldom if at all in the period 2002–2005.[18]

Criteria for Classification (Set of Variables) Employed in the Qualitative Analyses of Individual Texts

The individual messages were analyzed for their textual characteristics and content on the basis of a set of variables using specific linguistic and discourse-analytical criteria of classification. The set of variables (see table 3) consists of formal variables that include identifying factors ("Message Number and Storage Location") but also information about the sender ("Last name, First name, Title, Address, Geographical Location, E-mail Address/Telephone Number") and indications of length, as well as evaluative or valence variables.[19]

The majority of the variables are scaled nominally; only in a few cases were multiple designations possible, for instance in the dominant class of stereotypes that we characterized as "Traditional/New." Because of its wide distribution, the variable "Conspicuous/Particular Verbal Features" was coded openly, meaning that the coders could indicate, without assigning the features to a particular category, what verbal or conceptual patterns stood out or predominated in a given message. The evaluative variables include a series of dichotomous criteria with which the occurrence of certain strategies or manifestations can be identified, with their presence or absence indicated by "Positive" or "Negative."

The variable "Nazi Comparison" indicates whether a message contains at least one comparison to the Nazis. The variable "Emotion" is used to code the occurrence in the message of reference to or expression of emotions through lexemes or such paraverbal signals as the use of colors, emoticons, or extensive punctuation. Furthermore, the coding notes whether the writer alludes in general terms to the media ("Media Reference"), using phrases such as "*I read . . .*" or "*I recently learned . . . ,*" or whether there are specific references to the media ("Concrete Media Reference") such as "*Yesterday I read the article by* __ *in the* Frankfurter Allgemeine Zeitung." Under "Stereotype yes/no" the verbalization of antisemitic stereotypes is captured, a crucial indicator for whether a text is verbally antisemitic or not. The variable "Type of Stereotype" allows for differentiation by means of appropriate abbreviations among the specific dominant stereotypes that can occur.[20] The subtypes include those that are classic antisemitic stereotypes (CIA, such as <u>JEWS = MURDERERS OF GOD</u>, <u>JEWS = USURERS</u>, <u>WORLD CONSPIRACY</u>), post-Holocaust antisemitic (PHA, such as <u>JEWS EXPLOIT THE HOLOCAUST</u>;

TABOO AGAINST CRITICISM), or anti-Israeli (Anti-I, such as ISRAEL'S SPECIAL STATUS; DISTURBER OF THE PEACE).[21] The variables make it possible to use multiple characterizations, for instance KIA/PHA or KIA/Anti-I, and a cluster of stereotypes is coded with "Conspicuous/Particular Verbal Features." The most important evaluative variable is "Verbal Antisemitic Status."[22] Depending on the occurrence of stereotype variables and of the Nazi-comparison variable, and after consideration of the strategies verbalized in the text (such as legitimation strategies, denial of antisemitism) and of denials of responsibility for the Holocaust or relativizations of guilt, as well as a perspective and conceptualization hostile to Israel, the coder makes a judgment as to whether the message as a whole should be classified as antisemitic, critical of Israel, or hostile toward Israel. Texts are also coded as verbally antisemitic if they deploy anti-Judaic sayings and formulations, such as "*An eye for an eye, a tooth for a tooth*," to argue against Jews or Israelis, or whether antisemitic conceptualizations are used unintentionally, for instance when Jews are referred to as *guests* or *foreigners* but otherwise wholly positive or supportive attitudes toward Jews are expressed. The coding "Supportive" is used for messages that contain no antisemitic sentiments or criticisms of Israel, instead expressing solidarity. Messages are coded as philosemitic if they contain positive stereotypes of Jews.

The linguistic and argumentative character of the messages or the eloquence of the verbal formulations is categorized as "Normal" (or "Unremarkable"), "Uneducated," "Vulgar," or "Elaborated." Thus under some circumstances connections can be established between the level of education and the verbalization of antisemitic stereotypes or comparisons to the Nazis.

A further evaluative variable is the "political bias" of the authors. In addition to indicators in the messages' contents, formal contextual factors must be considered that suggest where the sender's political attitude fits on the classic spectrum extending from right to middle to left. Usually the letterhead, the e-mail header, or the running text provides explicit or implicit information. The attenuated or moderated form of these indicators points to the categories "left-leaning" or "right-leaning." The absence of such indicators is also relevant, as is the presence of class markers characteristic of the socioeconomic center, for instance title, profession, educational level, or membership in or affinity to one of the established parties. Additional indicators can be found in the senders' explicit assignment of themselves to the societal majority or

Table 3. **Overview of Variables and Specific Values**

I. Formal Variables

Code	*ZJW_TT_MM_JJJJ_No.*	*Signature*
Type	E	E-mail
	B	Letter
	Bh	Letter (handwritten)
	F	Fax
	Fh	Fax (handwritten)
	P	Postcard
	Ph	Postcard (handwritten)
Name	[. . .]	
First name	[. . .]	
Title	Prof./Dr./degree/etc.	Academic title
Address	Yes	Street and town given
	No	Street and town not given
Place	[. . .]	Place name
E-mail/telephone	T	Telephone number given
	E	E-mail address given
	E/T	E-mail and telephone given
Length	Short	Text just a few lines
	Medium	Text less than one page
	Long	Text more than one page
How filed	Binder	Text filed in paper form
	PC	Text filed electronically
	PC and binder	Text filed in paper form and electronically

center or, alternatively, in their strict rejection of antisemitism and right-wing extremism.

While the results of the analyses are captured digitally, the analysis itself was not conducted by means of a software package; among other things, the available software cannot assess the significance of the data in any meaningful way. The analysis focuses on the significance of a given opinion within a specific context, which allows us to counteract the tendency of numerical coding to eliminate semantic and contextual elements (cf. Brosius and Koschel 2001, 202).

II. Evaluative Categories/Valence Variables

Category	Code	Description
Political orientation	r.ex.	Right-wing extremist
	Mr.	Right-leaning/conservative
	Mitte	Social mainstream
	Ml	Left-leaning
	l.ex.	Left-wing extremist
	islam	Islamist
	psych	Psychopathological
Verbal level	norm	Normal/not noticeable
	elab	Elaborate/high linguistic level
	bild	Uneducated/low linguistic level
	vul	Vulgar/crude
Antisemitic status	neutr	Neutral (descriptive; not antisemitic)
	sol	Expressing solidarity
	phil	Philosemitic
	ik	Critical of Israel (but not antisemitic)
	eas	Explicitly verbally antisemitic
	ias	Implicitly verbally antisemitic
Type of antisemitism	KIA	Classic antisemitism
	PHA	Post-Holocaust antisemitism
	IA	Israel-related antisemitism
Stereotypes yes/no	Yes	Judeophobic stereotypes present
	No	No stereotypes present
Type of stereotypes	KIA	Classic antisemitic stereotypes
	PHA	Post-Holocaust antisemitic stereotypes
	IA	New (Israel-related) stereotypes
Nazi comparison(s)	Yes	Comparisons to Nazis present
	No	No comparisons to Nazis present
Reference to media	—	No references to media
	ind. MB	Indirect references to media
	konk. MB	Concrete reference to media (to single medium/text)
Emotion	Yes	Emotions are expressed/named
	No	No emotions are expressed/named
Noticeable features	[. . .]	Most noticeable verbal/conceptual characteristics
Other/notes	[. . .]	Comments for team (e.g., "parts of text missing")

Verbal Antisemitism: Quantitative Findings

Although our analysis of the corpus is primarily qualitative, we also conducted quantitative analyses in order to identify such things as meaningful patterns of distribution.

When one examines the evaluative valence of the messages, it becomes apparent that the majority of opinions expressed about Jews and Judaism are negative: 72.6 percent of all the messages can be categorized as antisemitic. If one looks only at the messages from extremists at either end of the spectrum, it can be seen that almost all of them are antisemitic. But more than a third of the correspondents from the middle of the spectrum articulate traditional antisemitic notions, confirming sociological findings that indicate a rate of antisemitism among Germans that exceeds 20 percent.[23] It is striking that the percentage of those expressing such notions is higher among those writing to the Central Council than among those corresponding with the Embassy.

The other communications include only 9 percent expressing neutral attitudes or legitimate criticisms and 14 percent that can be categorized as positive or supportive. Only 0.4 percent can be classified as philosemitic. The majority of messages expressing solidarity stem from a postcard campaign initiated by the Embassy that brought in 230 declarations of sympathy. Others were written to acknowledge the anniversary of the founding of the state of Israel. Other messages indicating solidarity or positive views occur only sporadically, but beginning in 2007 they have a constant presence in the corpus. In addition to expressing solidarity, these messages often characterize German media coverage of Israel as one-sided or hostile.

The messages declaring solidarity (from mainstream correspondents) are all addressed to the Embassy: unqualified expressions of solidarity relate only to the state of Israel, whereas messages to the Central Council calling or advocating for commemoration of the Holocaust are few and far between.

About 4 percent of the messages could not be assigned to any category because they were completely incoherent and semantically confused. More than half of the messages received by the Central Council were classified as explicitly antisemitic (n = 1,209, or 55.7 percent); these texts contain unmistakable indicators for verbal antisemitism, and the authors cite traditional stereotypes expressive of hostility toward Jews (Jews as USURERS, LIARS; denial of guilt or antisemitism, historical revisionism, etc.). For the subcor-

Figure 3. **Frequency of Nazi comparisons by political orientation**

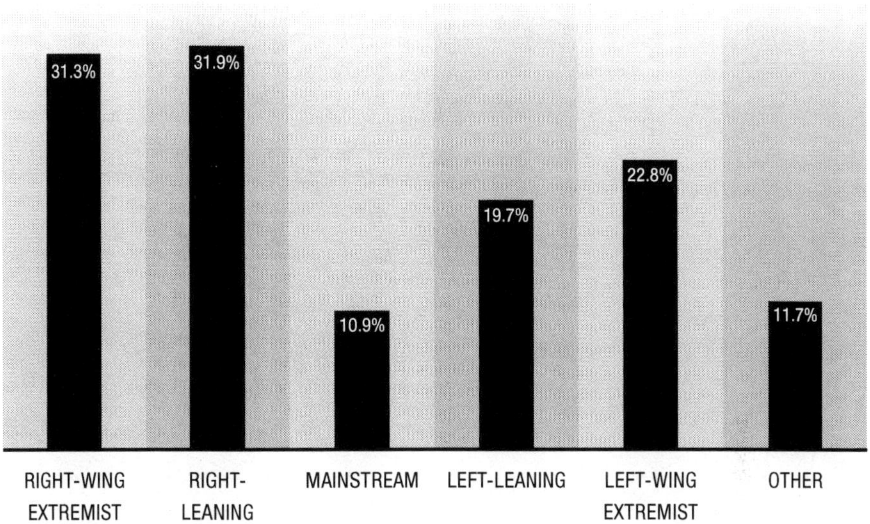

pus of messages received by the Embassy, this value is lower by 25.8 percent, with anti-Israel messages making up 33.9 percent of the total. These messages, however, often lend themselves to coding for implicit stereotypes and often use Nazi comparisons. These communications display frequent conceptual slippage and expansions of traditional stereotypes to include current negative clichés (see chapter 6).

The distribution of comparisons to the Nazis can be detected in the random sample of messages received between 2002 and 2007, as shown in figure 3. The samples drawn from the material received from 2008 on reveal a steadily increasing frequency of comparisons to the Nazis, starting with the escalation of conflict in the Gaza Strip. Representative samples drawn from this new material through the end of 2011 reach more than 30 percent; that is, no difference can be detected between messages from mainstream and extremist correspondents with respect to such patterns of linguistic usage.

■

For an additional appendix of selected complete texts included in the corpus, visit http://bir.brandeis.edu/handle/10192/26034.

NOTES

Preface to the English Edition (2016)

1. For instance, one of the authors of this book has been asked to write an expert report for a lawsuit appeal concerned with the question of whether a German journalist might be deemed an antisemite (see *Ditfurth v. Elsässer*).

1. Introduction

1. Researchers on antisemitism have noticed for quite some time that "the zone of acceptance of antisemitic prejudices has changed or expanded in recent years" (Rensmann and Schoeps 2008, 19). See also Schwarz-Friesel et al. (2010) and Schwarz-Friesel (2010a); cf. BMI (2011, 68).

2. The most recent detailed linguistic studies of postwar verbal antisemitism based on empirical data go back twenty years; see Wodak (1990) and Wodak et al. (1990), both of which analyze usage in Austria. The German Bundestag's commission of experts (BMI 2011) noted, "While comparable phenomena of antisemitic stereotyping and the entrenchment of antisemitic codes have been relatively well researched for earlier eras, a considerable research deficit exists for everyday usage in the present, precisely from the point of view of 'modernized antisemitism'" (72).

3. Cf. BMI (2011): "The relatively widespread presence of antisemitic attitudes in the population and the existence of hostility toward Jews in everyday life raise the question, up to now unanswered, as to how antisemitic stereotypes, prejudices, and attitudes are transmitted in our society. This question must be answered if effective counterstrategies are to be developed" (179).

4. In light of the recurring debates that usually ignore existing scholarship (as witness the intense debate over Günter Grass's anti-Israel poem "What must be said"), as well as numerous libel suits and other legal proceedings, the ability of scholarship to provide clear information as to whether an utterance can be classified as antisemitic becomes highly significant. Currently, when someone is accused of "hate speech," it is standard procedure for the perpetrators to resort to an excuse or a redefinition, styling themselves as victims of an alleged "antisemitism bludgeon" with which they are being beaten over the head. In such situations a societally accepted classification of verbal antisemitism, based on scholarly research, could prove very useful.

5. Corpus analyses have become the most important method in linguistics and cognitive science for establishing the systematic and representative characteristics of linguistic

and cognitive phenomena. A qualitative corpus analysis concentrates on the identification, classification, and interpretation of linguistic phenomena. A quantitative analysis, however, focuses on determining the frequency of certain phenomena (see on this point Scherer 2006, 36f.; Bubenhofer 2009). Only qualitative corpus analyses can capture the actual content of current hostility toward Jews.

6. The majority of the communications can be classified as hostile toward Jews, even though a number of them are either philosemitic or simply expressive of solidarity or support (see the summary in chapter 2, under The Power of Language as Violence through Language).

7. The criterion of representativeness applies here to the thematically relevant corpus and therefore to antisemitic language. The data that make up the corpus represent this specific discourse. They reveal which modalities and strategies are typical in Germany of linguistic expression of hostility toward Jews. This does not, of course, mean that they should be considered representative of *all* communication about Jews in Germany or of *all* Germans' attitudes.

2. Hostility toward Jews and Language

1. As a knowledge system, language includes certain subsystems (lexicology, morphophonology, syntax, semantics), all with their own specific rules. The decisive element is that forms are always associated with content. Forms by themselves have no meaning, and intellectual content cannot be communicated without resort to forms.

2. Obviously not all Jews are Israelis; they can be German, French, American, etc. Additionally, not all Israelis are Jews; there are also Arab Israeli citizens (both Christian and Muslim).

3. Utterances evoke not only single concepts but also complex schemata, i.e., conceptual combinations that as model constructions reflect mental reality structures (see Schwarz 2008, 115ff.).

4. In the nineteenth century Jews constituted about 1 percent of the German population and faced massive hostility and social impediments. It was thus patently absurd to suggest that Jews could exert any significant influence that would harm the German people (see Friesel 1990). The statement was equally at odds with reality during the Nazi period.

5. Even if we do not assume the existence of an objective reality but rather accept the constructivist argument that reality always arises in the mind of the observer, we cannot dispense with undertaking assessments of reality in the form of comparisons, since otherwise we would find our society becoming completely subjective. In our lives we always posit the existence of a reality that can be used as the basis for distinguishing between true and false. The real world has the character of a binding system of relations not normally called into question; it provides the basis for our judgments, our assertions of truth, and our legal verdicts. We orient ourselves by this reality, and it is characteristic of our cognitive abilities that we can normally tell the difference between the real world and fictional worlds.

6. *The Protocols of the Elders of Zion* have been printed and disseminated in some Muslim countries as often as Hitler's *Mein Kampf*. On right-wing radical home pages the *Protocols* are cited as sources of the validity of antisemitic ideology. In the *Hamas Charter*, article 32 includes a reference to the correctness of the *Protocols*. For a more thorough discussion of this topic, see Wistrich (2011).

7. Cf. Marcuse (1984): "Language does not merely define and damn the enemy; it also creates him; and this creation does not represent the enemy as he really is but rather as he has to be in order to fulfill his function" (303).

8. Indirect speech acts do not express overtly what is meant. They are forms of communication by indirection: the speaker says *X* but means *Y*. The function performed by the grammatical surface is not identical with the intended function. Thus an assertion can be clothed in a question when in fact the speaker is convinced of the truth of the implied answer. In the case of indirect speech acts, a second meaning can be recognized by any communicatively competent speaker or listener from the same language community (see, e.g., Liedtke 1995; Wagner 2001).

9. That language can carry out action has been recognized at least since the development of speech-act theory and forms an uncontested basic starting point for any theory of language and communication (cf. the classic statements by Austin 1962 and Searle 1969; see also Habermas 1981).

10. The topic of nonverbal violence has been explored in recent years by philosophers, political scientists, linguists, and social scientists, especially in connection with so-called hate speech (cf., e.g., Butler 1998; Corbineau-Hoffmann and Niklas 2000; Erzgräber and Hirsch 2001; Haubl and Caysa 2007; Krämer and Koch 2010). Previous scholarship has been limited largely to theoretical reflections relating to the philosophy of language and discussion of legal consequences (cf. Zimmer 2001; Delgado and Stefancic 2004; Herrmann et al. 2007). The point is made that "violence in language" must be distinguished from physical violence as a purely mental phenomenon with different possible effects (see Krämer and Koch 2010). Insufficient analysis has been devoted to the emotional component as the underlying phenomenon, as well as to the verbal component (but cf. Kiener 1983; van Dijk 1984; Jäger 2001; Reisigl and Wodak 2001; Graumann and Wintermantel 2007; Havryliv 2009; Meibauer 2012). There is a particular lack of empirically grounded studies that could provide decisive insight into current forms of verbal violence in their various facets (cf. other critical comments along these lines by Haubl and Caysa 2007; Schwarz-Friesel 2012).

11. The legal concept of violence deals essentially with physical violence. Cf. *Strafgesetzbuch* [the German Criminal Code], §240ff. Nonverbal forms of violence are treated in §130 and elsewhere as instigation.

12. That nonverbal violence in the sense of assertion of control stigmatizes and discriminates against its victims and at the same time manipulates their consciousness can be seen especially in the case of state control over speech, as was true of Nazi propaganda.

13. Power in a positive as well as a negative sense: the power of words reveals itself in a poem that moves us to tears, a novel that shakes us to the core and fills us with delight,

a love letter that makes us happy, a speech that fills us with apprehension, a text that enrages us.

14. Exposure to certain words has the ability not only to intensify emotions but also to cause pain (cf. Richter et al. 2010).

15. Most mental processes in human cognition occur unconsciously and automatically, unaffected by intentions and intellection and outside the control of our conscious will (see, e.g., Schwarz 2008, 162ff.; Kahneman 2011). Accordingly, the semantics of verbal utterances can awaken or intensify resentments without a person's becoming aware of this effect or preventing it.

16. In the Nazi period *Jew* was a term of abuse, with real consequences for the civil rights of those so designated; it became a matter of life and death. Bering (1991b, 2010) has written extensively about the use of Jewish names as stigmata. In the past few years we have conducted surveys among students at German universities to examine the denotative and connotative significance of various religious descriptors. More than 90 percent of the subjects considered *Jew* (as opposed to *Protestant* or *Catholic*) not to be a neutral noun, associating it with characteristics such as 'inflammatory' or 'highly emotional.' These attributions, which can be explained by reference to the German past, contrast with the normalization of membership in other religions. If the processes described above are added to the mix, the word *Jew* can have further features attached to it.

17. The "forms of expression . . . are the product of a long historical past" (Bering 2004, 378).

18. Cognitive linguistics is an interdisciplinary theory of language and cognition that has developed and established itself over the past twenty years as the most influential form of modern linguistics. It rests on the assumptions that language is a mental system of knowledge that interacts with other components of knowledge and that notions expressed through language provide insight into mental structures and processes (see, e.g., Schwarz 2008).

19. Of course, it is also possible to lie through language, i.e., consciously say something false; one can also consciously conceal one's notions and attitudes and express oneself in such an indirect and/or vague manner that it is difficult, if not impossible, to pin down or determine and reconstruct one's actual intentions (on lies as linguistic acts see, e.g., Meibauer 2007). Yet in principle one may assume that a person's linguistic utterances about a particular extralinguistic phenomenon reveal much of the person's opinion and his or her emotional attitude and state.

20. Conceptualizations are cognitive representations in the sense of model mental images formed and stored in reference to a certain realm, e.g., images of a person or group (see Schwarz-Friesel 2007, 81f., 329f.; Schwarz 2008). Following the conventions of cognitive science, conceptual entities and structures are indicated in small capitals; e.g., the conceptualization attached to the word *Jew* is represented as JEW.

21. This mechanism revealed itself recently with particular clarity in the emotional discussion of the poem "What must be said" by Günter Grass, who explained he had written it in order to criticize Israel and express concern about world peace. Many people

were incapable of recognizing anything antisemitic in this text, although it made use of nearly all the traditional Judeophobic clichés. But because the word *Jew* was not used and the informational component of Israel's atomic policy was placed in the foreground, many interpreted the text as "merely critical," as "freedom of speech," and as "fact." What was overlooked was that the poem contained distortions of reality and demonizing charges that bore all the characteristics of a modern antisemitic text in the guise of criticism of Israel (see chapter 6). Modern forms of antisemitism can often be recognized and understood only if one knows the long tradition of hostility and its cultural and communicative grounding in verbal expression that employs particular strategies.

22. It could be a matter of a latent conceptual antisemitism, i.e., one of which the speaker is unconscious. The memory of the speaker is stocked with stereotypical anti-Jewish conceptualizations that influence the process of verbalization; yet the speaker may be entirely unaware of the antisemitic potential (e.g., because knowledge of anti-Jewish stereotypes and their established place in Western structures of thought and argumentation is not present or because the speaker represses all awareness of being an antisemite because it does not fit his or her self-image). We must distinguish between this phenomenon and performances based on a strategy of denying antisemitism; the producers of such denials characterize themselves as anti-antisemitic but clearly employ anti-Jewish stereotypes and feelings (see chapter 10).

23. Collective or cultural memory includes knowledge familiar to many members of a society and conveyed from generation to generation. Such memory includes not only fact-based information but also myths, legends, beliefs, and set phrases. Each person's individual memory is significantly shaped by elements of cultural memory, and collective knowledge functions in many respects to form cultural identification. Cultural memory also contains patterns of linguistic usage that are stored in the communicative memory. In the twentieth and twenty-first centuries many elements of collective and individual memory show marked effects of emotional and media influence. On collective memory see, e.g., J. Assmann (1988) and A. Assmann (2006), and on communicative memory Welzer (2002).

24. Equivalent phrases with additive designations that indicate a differentiation between other groups, such as *Germans and Catholics* or *Germans and Protestants*, do not occur in normal usage.

25. A fourth analytical step has to do with the previously discussed category "intentional/nonintentional," which, however, often is not amenable to textual analysis. An example of verbal antisemitism that lends itself to unambiguous categorization would be a statement like *I'm an anti-Semite and I hate all Jews!* Yet such explicit and self-defining utterances occur after 1945 almost exclusively in right-wing-extremist and neo-Nazi circles. To be sure, for some years now such bald expressions of antisemitism have been turning up on the Internet, and not only in extremist forums, but increasingly in chat rooms, on Facebook, in information portals, etc. that cater to the social and political mainstream (Schwarz-Friesel 2012). At the same time one can observe that in right-leaning publications like the *National-Zeitung* and *Junge Freiheit* the verbal antisemitisms used

are almost all implicit, which allows them to reach in a persuasive guise a wider public that might be frightened off by explicit, radical forms of hostility toward Jews.

26. "Manifest" and "latent" are thus used in accordance with the theory of communicative latency and refer to a concept of systemic latency. In this usage, all forms of antisemitism are considered manifest if they can be observed in the majority, i.e., in society, whereas latent antisemitism does not occur in public communication and appears only in more minor, private discourses. This contrast is expressed more clearly through the concepts "public" versus "private."

27. Thus Pollak and Eger (2002) and Stern (2002), among others, characterize implicit verbal antisemitism or the communication of Judeophobic thinking by means of indirect speech acts as a "latent form of antisemitism." See also Rensmann and Schoeps (2008, 16) and the contributions in Pelinka and Wodak (2002). Bergmann and Erb (1986) characterize these phenomena, on the other hand, as "communication by indirection" (cf. also Rensmann 2004, 78f). Adorno (1962/1971, 109) used the term "crypto-antisemitism." But the terms "explicit" and "implicit," drawn from linguistics and communication studies, are best suited to express the variations in realization. They have proved their durability over decades of theoretical and empirical analysis devoted to language and discourse.

28. On this topic see also Graumann and Wintermantel (2007), who point to the processes of separation, accentuation or fixation, and devaluation as typical of verbal discrimination. Cf. also Haubl and Caysa (2007, 22f.), for whom the essential markers of hatred are devaluation of the object of hatred and isolation of the person or thing hated.

3. Hostile Stereotypes of Jews and Their Historical Roots

1. We are dispensing with extensive descriptions and explanations, as well as a complete chronology. For our purposes it is important to show that the stereotypes that can be observed in current communication have a long tradition and should be viewed as part of the cultural knowledge transmitted through speech, sometimes consciously, sometimes unconsciously and without reflection. We concentrate, therefore, on a few texts chosen from the past five centuries and cite in particular texts from the nineteenth century that show how widespread and habitual negative conceptualizations of Jews had become in all social circles. Extensive discussions of most of the stereotypes that will be touched on here can be found in Schoeps and Schlör (1999). For fundamental treatments see also Katz (1980), Almog (1988), Wistrich (1991), Klamper (1995), and Laqueur (2006).

2. According to surveys and studies undertaken in 2011, fully 20 percent of Germans harbor antisemitic resentments and believe the corresponding clichés (see BMI 2011; see also Schwarz-Friesel et al. 2010).

3. Hostility toward Jews arose after 500 BCE as a result of various Jewish emigrations after the destruction of the first Temple. As a minority distinctly set apart from other groups in eating habits, clothing, living customs, and observance of the Sabbath, Jews resisted assimilation into the countries where they were guests and thereby attracted much attention, which sometimes took the form of admiration and conversions to Judaism but

also resulted in much rejection. Practice of Judaism was already seen in ancient Rome as a provocation. In this very early period, fear and suspicion attached to Jews, giving rise to the idea that they were out to undermine the existing society. This anxiety in turn bred the notion that Jews aimed to take over the world (see Heinemann, 1931; oral communication from Moshe David Herr).

4. Two central characteristics of the Jewish community were already seen in antiquity as negative distinctions separating Jews from Greeks, Romans, and Egyptians. One was the monotheistic belief in an invisible god, the other the notion of being the chosen people. Both were viewed by the Jews' neighboring peoples as strange and abnormal. The stubborn refusal to recognize the gods of the other faith communities struck those communities as inflexible and arrogant (cf. Heinemann 1931). In antiquity xenophobic attitudes toward other minorities manifested themselves as well. The profound hatred toward Jews that affected all dimensions of life did not arise until after Christianity split off from Judaism.

5. Marcion in the second century CE voiced the demand for strict separation between Christianity and Judaism. In his theology, the "good Lord" proclaimed by Jesus is distinguished from the "wrathful God" of the Jews. He portrays Judaism as an obsolete religion that no longer deserves to exist (cf. Parkes 1981; Rokeah 1988). Justin declares that the Christians, not the Jews, are the "true Israel." The writings of Augustine in the fifth century (see *De civitate Dei*) were particularly influential, shaping the relationship of the Christian Church with the Jews for many centuries. He distinguishes between "Israel in the spirit" (the Christians) and "Israel in the flesh" (the Jews). According to him, the Jews are sinners because they deny the true faith, but as witnesses to the true story of Jesus (until they accept the true faith) they must be tolerated (though despised). This toleration includes the prohibition on killing Jews (see Simon 1996). That the "sinful, despicable unbelievers" could not, according to Augustinian doctrine, simply be done away with was a further reason for the anger and impotent rage of non-Jews and thus the basis of resentment.

6. The contention that the Jews had murdered God (cited as the Jews' collective guilt for the death of Jesus) began to be disseminated from the second century CE on. Not until the Second Vatican Council in 1965 did the Catholic Church officially part company with this legend. Fanatical Christian groups to this day do not accept this resolution (e.g., the Society of St. Pius X). See also Grözinger (1999).

7. According to Max Scheler's classic definition, still recognized as salient today, resentment is "the recapitulation and reliving of a specific emotional response to another person" (Scheler 1912/1955, 36). The grudge leads to rejection, to hatred. While individual feelings are directed toward some specific aspect of the other (appearance, actions, etc.), resentment is directed toward the very existence of the other. It is "an entirely general negative value judgment, a hate-filled rejection that suddenly appears without reason and seemingly erupts at random" (Scheler 1912/1955, 61).

8. Until the third century CE, when the so-called Milan Tolerance Edict was issued, Christianity faced massive hostility and demonization, which it in turn projected onto the

Jews. The projection took the form of asserting that Christianity was not a child of Judaism but that Judaism was a perversion of Christianity. The Barnabas epistle (fourth century) provides insight into the theological disputes between the early Christian Church and Judaism (see Rokeah 1988). There Jewish doctrine is described as "obsolete," Jews are called "unworthy" and influenced "by an evil angel." Jewish Israel is portrayed as "in decline." This early text manifests the same spirit as the subsequent *adversus-judaeos* texts of the church fathers, which represent a categorical rejection and absolute devaluation of Judaism. Jewish figures are Christianized, i.e., interpreted as forerunners of Christianity. Just as the Jew Jesus of Nazareth was torn out of his Jewish context, Abraham is stylized in the Barnabas epistle and subsequent texts as the first Christian (see also Parkes 1981, 84).

9. Among fundamentalist Christians this intolerance persists to this day, e.g., among the brothers of the Society of St. Pius X and the adherents of kreuz.net. It is significant that these religiously motivated haters of Jews also deny or minimalize the Holocaust. The Good Friday prayer for the Jews calls upon God to open the Jews' hearts so that they can recognize Jesus Christ as the Savior and to receive Israel into his church so that Israel may be saved.

10. In the Middle Ages conceptualizations of Jews as devils, allies of the devil, ritual murderers, desecrators of the host, heretics, and witches were dominant and widespread (cf. Trachtenberg 1943, 32ff.).

11. His treatise "On the Jews and Their Lies" should not be seen as an anti-Jewish tract per se. Nonetheless, it contains all the typical verbal demonizations and the view that one should take active steps against Jews. Bering (1989b), who has studied Luther's vocabulary extensively and critically, identifies *lie, to lie, devil, harmful, evil*, and *blaspheme* as the negative terms that appear most frequently in Luther's writings (148). Bering also points out that Luther did not create this anti-Jewish vocabulary himself but rather drew on existing patterns of pejorative usage (155). This fact does not, of course, diminish the influence Luther had on the transmission of hostility toward Jews through language. Bering (1990) considers Luther's angry attacks on Jews to originate in his affinity to other theological positions. This phenomenon coincides with the formation of resentment discussed earlier.

12. Correspondingly Luther's verbal aggression was often instrumentalized, e.g., by Julius Streicher, who at the Nuremberg Trials in 1946 declared that Luther should be seated next to him in the dock (see Bering 1989b, 140).

13. This concept continues to be reactivated to this day. Thus placards carried at anti-Israeli demonstrations often say such things as *Israel kills children* and *Let the blood of children flow*. Muslim antisemitism often adopts these conceptualizations as well (see Wistrich 2011, 64f.).

14. This form of derealization constitutes to this day a significant component of antisemitism, especially of the anti-Israeli variety, which demonizes Israel (see chapter 6, under Derealization).

15. Between 325 and 1139 the Church at various councils had forbidden Christians to lend money for interest. Yet the medieval economy depended on financial transactions of this sort. Even monasteries sometimes needed to borrow money. Thus clerics often

sharply criticized the Jews' alleged avarice and condemned moneylending for interest as immoral while themselves taking advantage of its availability for practical reasons. Bernhard de Clairvaux (eleventh to twelfth century), for instance, considered Jews and usurers identical, but at the same time condemned Christian moneylenders as worse than the Jews. Christians who engaged in usury thus became "*christened Jews*." This is the first known example in which the lexeme *Jew* appears in writing as invective. We thank Joseph Shatzmiller for this reference.

16. Shatzmiller (2007) was able to show, however, that in witness statements made at the trial of a Jewish merchant in the fourteenth century, his non-Jewish contemporaries and business partners described him as generous, helpful, and especially trustworthy. The generally accepted image according to which Jewish merchants and moneylenders were met with rejection and scorn must thus be revised (see also Shatzmiller 2007, 9).

17. Goethe's writings do not provide any evidence of an anti-Jewish attitude (see Low 1979; Homann 2002). Nonetheless, the passage quoted in the text is often invoked by individuals on the right and by right-wing extremists to document the famous writer's alleged skepticism and antipathy toward Jews (see Schwarz-Friesel 2012).

18. Cf. also Voltaire (1785): "The Jewish people has the audacity to display an irreconcilable hatred toward all peoples. It rebels against all its masters, always superstitious, always greedy for the goods of others, always barbarous, groveling in misfortune and impudent in good fortune" (186).

19. On the stereotype of RITUAL MURDER, see Erb (1999).

20. Similarly one wonders today why Hitler, with his crude conspiracy theories and the hate-filled fantasies he articulated from the very beginning of his political career, was not recognized as mentally ill or at least disturbed, but instead was made Reich chancellor. Demands for elimination (Jews must be driven out or eliminated) as the "solution" to the "Jewish problem" constitute a central aspect of anti-Jewish argumentation to this day (see chapter 9, under Suggestions for Solving the "Jewish Problem"). Of course, by no means all Germans actually wanted to banish or kill Jews, but as Low (1979) remarks, "The number of Germans who hoped for the disappearance and 'death' of Judaism was quite large: they included adherents of the most diverse political and ideological currents" (7).

21. A satirical poem by Wilhelm Busch incorporates such features, as do numerous postcards that caricature Jews (see Bajohr 2003): "Short the trousers / long the coat / crook'd the nose and walking stick / eyes pitch-black and soul all gray / hat pushed back, expression sly / That's Shmul Bowleg, believe you me / (We're far prettier, don't you see?)" (Busch 1882, ch. 5).

22. Bering (2002) characterizes this conceptualization as follows: "To the anti-Semite Jews appear as naturally bad and incorrigible in their negative traits. Because of these necessarily present characteristics, Jews must always be viewed as a collective that remains congenitally alien to the societies in which it lives and exerts a hidden destructive influence on the 'host people.' This negative influence and the factual foreignness must be unmasked in order to reveal the true, unchanging being of the Jews" (174).

23. Secular and racist hostility toward Jews does not differ radically from religious

anti-Judaism. The hostility is merely exacerbated by the addition of new elements of devaluation to the traditional stereotypes and resentments. These new elements are dressed up as scientific. Hostility toward Jews has "several historical layers, with the older layers of prejudice not being 'forgotten' in the next phase but merely overlaid with new ones" (Bergmann 2001, 38).

24. Stoecker was a cofounder of the "Berlin Movement," which in 1880–1881 launched the "Antisemite Petition," with the objective of placing limits on the legal equality enjoyed by Jews in Germany. The petition received a quarter of a million signatures.

25. In the nineteenth century a "linguistically established system of prejudice thus became codified as standard practice" (Bering 1991a, 342), based on notions going back almost two thousand years. Fuchs (1921) tellingly describes anti-Jewish resentment expressed by means of caricature: "Caricatures almost always assume the role of accuser when it comes to Jews. Therefore most anti-Jewish caricatures reveal, according to circumstances, a greater or lesser degree of hatred and at the same time a contempt that encompasses all gradations and not seldom goes to the ultimate extreme. . . . Some caricatures of Jews express unmistakably a helpless rage against the alleged mortal enemy of Christian society, who is hated, despised, and feared, yet whom one cannot go after as one would secretly wish to" (104).

26. Until 1945 the Grimms' *Fairy Tales* included a story called "The Jew amid the Thorns," which contains a grisly anti-Jewish scene that justifies physical violence against Jews and draws on the cliché of the avaricious Jew. The Jew unmasked as a traitor is executed at the end of the story.

27. Cf. also statements by Theodor Fontane such as "It was very lovely here, except for the Jews" (see Benz, 2001, 9, 58f.).

28. According to Nipperdey and Rürup (1994), the "first known use [of the term *antisemitism*] occurs in the *Allgemeine Zeitung des Judentums* [General Jewish news] on 2 September 1879" (138). Under the heading "Jewish Polemical Pamphlets" one finds the following: "We have received an anonymous communication from Hamburg, for whose contents we cannot therefore vouch in any way. It asserts that Marr's pamphlet has gone into its tenth printing—that would be of little moment were it not for the size of the printings; he wants to issue it as a little treatise in 150,000 copies—we must wait and see whether he can manage that—and claims to have found friends through whom this 'antisemitic weekly' will come into existence" (*Allgemeine Zeitung des Judentums*, 2 September 1879, 564). Etymologically and semantically this concept makes no sense, since there is no *anti* against Semites involved. It is a question only of Jews, not of Semitic peoples (see also Berger Waldenegg 2000; Bauer 2011).

29. The belief in having right on one's side when one rejects Jews and Judaism and the contention that one was merely pointing to facts remains to this day a typical marker of antisemitic thinking and expression. Modern antisemites are blind and deaf to anything that does not correspond to their conceptually sealed image of the world and the enemy, and declare the demands they make on Jews to be humanely motivated (cf. chapter 9 and chapter 10, under Strategies of Legitimation and Self-Aggrandizement).

30. The public debate caused deep emotions to come to the surface among readers. For instance, a young man, a student of Treitschke's, wrote from Greifswald, "I do not hate the Jews, but I hate Judaism. The Jews' way of being repels me, and this makes me feel like an ancient German tribesman. Never will the German find the French way of being as repellent, as hateful, as that of the Jews. Therefore the term 'antisemite' is much more accurate than 'anti-Jew'" (Boksch 1880, quoted in Benz 2001, 64f.).

31. The complete sentence reads as follows: "All the way into the highest circles of education, from men who would reject with utter disgust any thought of churchly intolerance or national arrogance, one hears as if with one voice: the Jews are our misfortune!" (Treitschke 1879, 575). Treitschke's comments gave rise to a fierce political debate that continued for two years (see Boehlich 1965; Meyer 1966; Krieger 2002).

32. For that reason any comparison with other forms of prejudice (e.g., against Muslims) is misleading and obscures the unique aspects of hostility toward Jews. This hostility is not merely one system of prejudice among many but an ideology for interpreting the world that has persisted for two thousand years. Accordingly, antisemitism research cannot supply a paradigm for general explanations of prejudice. See Schwarz-Friesel and Friesel (2012).

33. Cf. the "scientific" definition offered by so-called "Race"-Günther (Rasse-Günther), a professor during the Nazi era at the University of Jena. According to him, a race is "a group of people who differ from every other by virtue of their shared physical features and spiritual characteristics and time and again produce offspring only of the same kind." He asserts that mental characteristics and inclinations, character or creativity are linked to certain physical properties (Günther 1936, 65, in Stuckart and Globke 1936, quoted in Priester 2003, 239). Under Chancellor Adenauer, Globke later became secretary of state. On continuities and discontinuities in racist antisemitism, see Volkov (1990); cf. also von Braun and Gerlach (2000).

34. The racist antisemitic conceptualization is based on a strictly binary code: the homogeneous, generally positively valued *we*-group, which embodies the positive principle and must defend it existentially against the generally negatively evaluated *they*-group of the Jews, who embody the evil principle (cf. Wistrich 1999; Rensmann 2004). This conceptualization usually goes hand in hand with a veritable demonization of the Other (cf. Befu 1999).

35. Within the framework of this ideologically motivated extermination policy, certain factors came into play, such as social envy of the economic success of individual Jewish citizens. But only the conceptualization of Jews as an entity harmful to the German people can explain the dimensions of the Shoah (see also Bauer 2001, 2011). Attempts at explanation, such as the most recent one by Aly (2011), that concentrate on economically motivated antisemitism (see Pulzer 1966, 32ff.; Adam 2003, 85ff.) fail to capture the relevance of ideological and emotional factors underlying hatred for Jews; they reduce the phenomenon to components and by-products that may have been important, especially when the Nazis first took power, but were not central. Such explanations oversimplify and distort the motives for the implementation of the Final Solution. See also Bauer's

(2011) critical commentary. The fact that in spite of resource shortages Eichmann always received enough rail cars for the Final Solution shows that the ideological hatred and his extermination program took precedence over economic and military interests (see Friedländer 2006, 647).

36. This resentment rests on the belief that those motivated by it are acting correctly and truthfully and must defend themselves against evil, ills, the influence of the Other, in the form of inferior beings or those who would do harm.

37. Not until the end of the 1960s, twenty years after the collapse of the Nazi regime, did the Auschwitz trials and the student protest movement bring about lengthy discussions and analyses involving the entire society (cf. Frei 2005). Yet even into the late 1980s historical accounts of the Nazi period tended to minimize the mass murder perpetrated against the Jews (Herbert 1998, 15). And not until Friedländer (2006), did a historian make the perspective of the victims the focus of research.

38. References to Western Christian culture consistently belonged to the repertory of public discourse in the postwar period, yet no critical reckoning with the dark sides of that culture took place. No awareness of a watershed situation manifested itself in language or discourse (see Kämper 2005).

39. In their influential analysis the Mitscherlichs showed the extent to which processes of repression were responsible not only for the Germans' "inability to mourn" but also for their inability to empathize with the victims (Mitscherlich and Mitscherlich 1967; see also chapter 8, under Cruelty and Emotional Coldness).

40. To this day the notion survives in some circles that virulent antisemitism and its implementation were confined to just a few obsessed Nazis. The historians' debate of the 1980s revealed the intensity of the need within Germany's academic elite to relativize the Nazis' atrocities (see Augstein 1987; Evans 1991). Goldhagen, who broke with this tendency in his book *Hitler's Willing Executioners* (1996) and showed that hatred for Jews was widespread among Germans, encountered vehement resistance. The debate over his thesis displays a high degree of emotionality, and the partially justified criticism of his methodology often gets buried under irrational polemics.

41. This orientation constitutes the basis of the current strategy of resistance (see chapter 8, under The Mentality of "Being Fed Up" and Refusal of Empathy). The Holocaust is minimized by reference to one's own suffering; as in the Borchert passage just quoted (1947/2009, 53), the argument is put forward that while the Second World War caused the Germans similar or identical suffering, their suffering was not seen as worthy of the same exaggerated commemoration.

42. In a survey conducted in 2011 by the Institute for Research on Youth Culture, sixteen- to nineteen-year-olds living in Vienna were asked to respond to the statement "Hitler also did a lot of good things for people." Of those asked, 11.2 percent responded affirmatively. More than 18 percent agreed with the statement "The Jews still have too much influence on the world economy, as they did in the past." Similar views exist in Germany. At a press conference on 6 September 2007, e.g., the former anchor woman Eva Herrmann responded positively to the concept of motherhood current during the

Nazi period, and on 10 October of that year, when she was asked on the Kerner talk show about her use of the Nazi term *Gleichschaltung* (forcible alignment), she responded that the autobahns built in the Nazi period were also still in use.

43. In (German-language) antisemitism research, the term *secondary* is applied to post-1945 antisemitism (see Benz 2004, 19ff.; Bergmann 2006). The term goes back to Peter Schönbach, a collaborator of Adorno's (see Adorno 1962/1971, 107f.) We do not, however, accept this usage, which distinguishes between *primary* antisemitism (also described as "classic" by Heyder et al. 2005, 147) and *secondary* antisemitism. The latter concept is misleading, because it suggests that the postwar phenomenon constitutes a derivative, possibly less virulent hatred of Jews. But that notion is not accurate. We therefore specifically argue for rejecting these inadequate categories.

44. Bergmann and Erb describe (first in 1986) this move from the public to the private realm as "communication latency," using the term *latency* not in the cognitive-linguistic sense to refer to unconscious conceptualizations but rather to designate the change in the level of openness and later also the form of expression. The concept of communication latency, nowadays used by many authors inconsistently, implies in its original application that the expression of Judeophobic slogans shifted from the public to the private plane of discourse (cf. Benz 2004, 19f.; Bergmann 2006, 117f.).

45. The German Basic Law includes an article on inciting persecution of an ethnic group; its purpose was to prevent discriminatory use of language that, on the one hand, damages a person's dignity and is insulting and injurious and, on the other hand, can represent and create the basis for prejudice, hatred, and violence.

46. Up to now no political scientists or sociologists have undertaken a comprehensive study of these new variants of expression. Our analysis therefore offers an important and innovative contribution.

47. The term *new antisemitism* was used by Marrus as early as 1986 to designate a newly motivated hostility directed against Israel. Taguieff (2002, 196) notes a wave of antisemitism between 1998 and 2002 and speaks of a *nouvelle Judéophobie*, expressed primarily by Muslim immigrants. He maintains that this phenomenon consists of a demonization of Israel that simultaneously applies to everything seen as Jewish. Taguieff sees left-wing anti-Zionism as providing the ideological foundation for this trend. Cf. also Gessler (2004).

48. The Stephen Roth Institute (2010) reports a worldwide increase in acts of antisemitic violence since 2001, reaching a climax in 2009; see also BMI (2011). Anti-Israel demonstrations featuring hate slogans on posters as well as worldwide demands for boycotts and antisemitic Internet activities strengthen the impression of increasingly virulent hostility. With respect to the attitudes elicited by opinion polls, however, Bergmann (2008, 476) does not see a longer-term negative trend and interprets the increase in hostile statements between 1998 and 2003 as the result of a "normal" periodic fluctuation (cf. Whine 2006; see also EUMC 2004, 319; FRA 2009, 23). But we explained in chapter 2 why opinion surveys as an empirical method have limited usefulness when it comes to capturing Judeophobic attitudes together with their mental and emotional components.

49. We will show, however, that current arguments justifying hostility toward Jews consist largely of rejection of culpability for the past combined with assignment of blame in the present by means of a strategy that reverses perpetrators and victims.

50. Benz and Wetzel (2007, 12) also believe that radical Islamists are functioning as agents of current antisemitism, having appropriated the old antisemitic concepts and with them worldwide anti-Jewish attitudes, prejudices, and images of the enemy. On the one hand, the Middle East Media Research Institute (MEMRI) determined on the basis of analyses of Arab media that the main marker of Muslim antisemitism is the presence of anti-Jewish opinions derived from traditional Islamic sources, and antisemitic stereotypes, images, and accusations motivated by Christian and racist thinking imported from Europe. On the other hand, denial of the Holocaust, identification of Zionism with National Socialism, and denial of Israel's right to exist are characteristics of Muslim antisemitism (see Milson 2008). The main representatives of anti-Israel views are considered to be young migrants inclined to violence because their Arab and/or Muslim backgrounds cause them to feel uncritical solidarity with the Palestinians and make them vulnerable to the influence of Islamist propaganda (see Amadeu Antonio Stiftung 2009; FRA 2009, 23; cf. also Küntzel 2007).

51. This circuitous communication led Bergmann and Heitmeyer (2005a, b) to determine that the scope of what is permissible to say along antisemitic lines can expand, especially in the social mainstream (something that today must be seen as having already taken place).

52. This position does not take into consideration that traditional stereotypes need not simply be reactivated in response to a current trigger but can also undergo conceptual shifts and elaborations.

53. The term *democratic antisemitism* is misleading because use of the positive adjective *democratic* can imply that this antisemitism represents a democratic majority view based on human rights, which would be a harmless phenomenon.

54. We will show that this is by no means the case (cf. chapter 6). Antisemitism directed at Israel shows all the characteristics of traditional Judeophobia.

55. Even if any monocausal explanatory systems must be rejected in the case of antisemitism, today no doubt can exist as to the connection between the increase in antisemitism in its anti-Israel variant and the altered media reporting on the Middle East conflict since 2000. This reporting has become one-sided: unfavorable to Israel, extremely negative, and in part highly emotional (cf. Behrens 2003; Jäger and Jäger 2003; Wistrich 2003; Schwarz-Friesel 2007, 2012c; Schapira and Hafner 2010; Beyer 2012; cf. also Langenbucher and Yasin 2009 and chapter 6, under "*As I just read in my paper . . .*").

56. According to the U.S. expert Andrew Baker, the crucial factor has been that this new antisemitism turns the state of Israel into a particular target for nontraditional racist groups; i.e., it is embraced not only by the "usual" right-wing extremists but above all by Arab or Muslim migrants (cf. Baker 2006, 157).

57. Shortly after publication of the German edition of this book, David Nirenberg (2013) published a study illustrating that Judeophobic thought is anchored in Western culture.

4. Present-Day Verbalization of Stereotypes

1. Cf. the 2011 report of the Bundestag's expert commission: "The terms *stereotype, cliché, prejudice*, and *resentment*, which are used largely interchangeably in this report . . ." (BMI 2011, 7). In other scholarly treatments likewise no precise definitions are offered. See, e.g., Benz (1995): "Present-day antisemitism derives from traditional stereotypes, aversions, and constructs (such as that of the worldwide conspiracy . . .), as well as from Nazi resentments (exploiters of reparations . . .)" (367). Here and elsewhere concepts are conflated without being sufficiently and adequately explained. What Benz describes as resentment actually constitutes a stereotype (which obviously did not exist as such in National Socialism); aversions are resentments and therefore emotional states; and constructs such as the worldwide conspiracy are complex combinations of stereotypes. On this problem, cf., e.g., Ehlich (1998), Banaji (2001), Kilian (2005), and Hart (2007).

2. ". . . we define first and then see" (Lippmann 1922, 81).

3. The function of stereotypes need not be defined negatively: we cannot manage without mental representations that provide categories for the efficient storage of general knowledge and for organizing our own observations. Stereotypes become the basis for discrimination and hostility only when they employ crude simplification and distortions of reality to portray situations and groups and when they are tied to negative emotions. There also exist concepts that categorize objects and situations (in the broadest sense) by type. But in cognitive science these are labeled prototypes and schemas (see Schwarz 2008, 115ff.). Often, however, conceptual representations are inextricably connected to human beings, things, and processes. For instance, the stereotype of the RAPACIOUS JEW is linked to prototypic information about the money economy and the use of capital, while the stereotype of the JEWISH CHILD-MURDERER is associated with information about violence and the cult of blood (see Barkai 1999; von Braun 1999; Erb 1999; Raphael 1999).

4. In the case of anti-Jewish stereotypes, we are dealing exclusively with constructs that lack any empirical basis, i.e., with pure products of the imagination (see, e.g., stereotypes of the BLOOD CULT or PLANS FOR WORLD DOMINATION).

5. See Allport (1954, 23), who recognized early on that prejudices are based on "a faulty and inflexible generalization." Cf. also Operario and Fiske (2001).

6. Here a further difference between cliché and prejudice becomes apparent: prejudices always have a negative connotation, whereas clichés can imply strongly positive assessments, for instance in the case of eternal or romantic love.

7. Stereotypes can be expressed not only in words but also in images. The infamous caricatures in the *Stürmer* during the Nazi period offer examples of historical antisemitism. But today visual manifestations of stereotypes exist as well, for instance in the anti-Israeli caricatures on Cologne's "Wailing Wall," which show the Israelis as barbarians devouring children, or on the posters used to incite boycotts, such as those in Bremen that depict bleeding oranges, thereby evoking the stereotype of the BLOOD CULT.

8. "A stereotype is the verbal expression of a belief about social groups or individuals as members of those groups. It takes the logical form of a judgment that, in an unjustifiably

oversimplifying and generalizing manner, with an emotionally subjective tendency, ascribes or denies certain traits or behaviors to a class of persons. Linguistically it can be described as a statement" (Quasthoff 1973, 28). But this is precisely *not* what stereotypes are!

9. In the scholarly literature one quite often encounters expressions such as "stereotypes with negative connotations" (see also BMI 2011, 31). But connotations are (affective) attributes of meanings that assign value, are homogeneous within a society, and form part of the verbal knowledge of the person using the language. As mental elements, stereotypes cannot have connotations. Only words have connotations, i.e., combinations of expressions and significations (see Schwarz-Friesel 2007, 162ff.).

10. Cf. statements such as *The best eating is in France* or *The British are always courteous* or *Germans are always punctual and hardworking*. These sentences verbalize stereotypes, but they express positive judgments.

11. As a result, stereotypes prove to be largely resistant to empirical facts. Antisemitic stereotypes in particular rest not on primary but on secondary experiences (i.e., antisemites rarely have any actual experience with Jews). Rather, antisemites derive their "information" from cliché-laden discourses or texts, but have an unshakable belief in their truthfulness (see chapter 8, under Hate without a Real Object).

12. Statements of belief that represent generalizations have the status of generally valid assertions; i.e., those who use them assume that the language portrays the world accurately. The producers of such statements are convinced of the truthfulness of their semantic content. Accordingly, their thinking and feeling are decisively shaped by these formulations. They never entertain the possibility that these statements constitute mental constructs that mirror a very specific view. On the contrary: every attempt to challenge belief in these supposed truths meets with embittered opposition on the part of antisemites (see chapter 8).

13. "The foreignness of the Jews seems to be the most handy formula for dealing with alienation in society. Blaming the Jews for all existing evils may brighten the darkness of reality like a floodlight that provides speedy and comprehensive orientation" (Adorno 1950/1973, 124).

14. An exception can be seen in the phenomenon of so-called self-hatred. Jewish self-hatred or Jewish Judeophobia (see Friesel 2010, 164ff.) consists in Jews subjecting Judaism to extreme criticism or (in the current variant) Jews and/or Jewish Israelis taking a critical attitude toward Israel and in part adopting antisemitic strategies.

15. This e-mail to the president of the Central Council, Charlotte Knobloch, also demands an end to behaviors that the writer views as inappropriate (designated as extremely negative by means of the phrase "*insolent instigation*"). The term *instigation* was used particularly often during the Nazi period in connection with negative judgments of Jews. The stereotype coding of Jews as non-Germans usually occurs in combination with additional negative attributions, as in an e-mail from a fifty-seven-year-old man from Hamburg who describes himself as "*born in Germany*": "*Paul Spiegel, you are a person suffering from megalomania, and Michel Friedmann is an arrogant wannabe journalist. Focus on your own country, Israel*" (ZJD_20.06.2002_ano_001).

16. A mental schema contains slots that depending on the situation and context can be occupied by specific (typical) contents; in the nineteenth century the slot JEWS AS FOREIGNERS was occupied by the value NON-GERMANS/NON-CHRISTIANS, in the Nazi period by JEWS AS NON-ARYANS.

17. As regards Muslims, such statements do occur from time to time, but mostly in right-wing-extremist circles.

18. Cf., e.g., "*the Jew-Zionist-riffraff in IsraHELL*" (ZJD_Gaza2009_549/816_Grä_001) and "*Jewish zionistic Israelis*" (IBD_27.05.2010_Ekk_001).

19. The entire e-mail can be found as text 1 in the online appendix as an exemplary illustration of verbal antisemitism from the educated mainstream.

20. An explicit version (the speaker says *X* and also means *X*) would go like this: *Jews are foreigners* or *Jews are not Germans*. Indirect speech acts (the speaker says *X* and means *Y*) require the addressee to make an inference; e.g., for (21), the inference would be 'Since Jews and foreigners are named together as a group, Jews are like foreigners, not Germans.' The stress on a "*purely German concern*" in (22) implies that Jews have nothing to do with it and are thus not Germans.

21. The metacognitive monitor that normally steers the process of language production (see Levelt 1989) and, in the case of Freudian slips, for instance, but also that of affective missteps such as curses and spontaneous outbursts involving expletives like *shit!*, takes control and usually causes the speaker to correct him- or herself or apologize, is more or less put out of commission by Judeophobic conceptualizations and the powerful emotional impulse that accompanies them (see chapter 9).

22. See also Salzborn's study (2005). This stereotype manifests itself among fundamentalist Christian groups, e.g., on the Internet site kreuz.net.

23. What is striking about this letter is that the author believes more strongly in traditional thought patterns than in any information from external sources that convey a different message. Facts and contrary versions could neither alter nor shake his view of the world.

24. Along with the CHRIST-MURDERER stereotype, this e-mail encodes a specific variant of the perpetrator–victim reversal: Jews who for centuries were the victims of Christian Church doctrine are here stylized as perpetrators who hate Christians. On the perpetrator–victim reversal, see chapter 11.

25. Excessive use of punctuation, especially exclamation points, often occurs in these texts as an expression of emphasis and strong feeling (see also chapter 9).

26. The stereotype of CHILD-MURDERER goes back to the story of child-murder under the rule of Herod. Thus the violent deed of a single ruler is overgeneralized and interpreted as typical of the entire Jewish people. The concept of Jews as child-murderers gained currency as a cliché in the Middle Ages (see Trachtenberg 1943, 124ff.). Many medieval texts contain stock phrases that express this notion together with the blood-cult legend, according to which Jews practiced rituals involving the blood of Christian children, e.g., baking matzos for Passover with children's blood (see chapter 4, examples [4] and [6]; cf. also Erb 1999).

27. Reactivation of this stereotype shows up in 2012 in numerous messages and commentaries (especially on the Internet) in connection with the debate over circumcision in Germany: Jews are described as *primitive*, *atavistic*, *brutal*, and *perverse* because they have boys circumcised. Cf. a statement like this: "*You backward barbarians! What kind of a bloody mutilation ritual are you engaging in?*" and "*It's a damn shame that you and your religion are still living in the Middle Ages*" (see http://www.youtube.com/watch?v=BXeERg6JrEg, 2012).

28. In the corpus some texts could be identified, on the basis of information the authors themselves provided, as the work of Islamists. In recent years various Muslim film productions have graphically portrayed the motif of the blood cult (cf. BMI 2011, 44).

29. Lists of traditional religious stereotypes and modern patterns of defamation occur (often together with relativizations or denials of the Holocaust) on the Internet, particularly elaborated in texts that appear on the Catholic fundamentalist forum kreuz.net.

30. Intertextuality refers to specific, intentional, and marked allusions to other texts and textual patterns. Biblical passages tend to be particularly favored for citing strategically as authorities.

31. In John 8 Jesus tells several Pharisees that they must be descended from the devil because they are planning to murder him. The author of (51) quotes this passage to verbalize his own hostility toward Jews, although what Jesus, himself a Jew, says is not addressed to Jews at all.

32. Relevant in this context are stereotypes of Jewish appearance that persist in caricatures, because there external features function as identifiers: intentional use of the cliché of the UGLY JEW occurs particularly in Muslim countries, especially in antisemitic newspapers (cf., e.g., Stav 1999; Wistrich 2011, 151ff.).

33. If one looks at the various commentaries on the Internet, thousands of which appear in forums and chat rooms, and in social networks like Facebook, it is clear that this conceptualization turns up constantly and is communicated with particular frequency (cf. also Blum 2010). In cultural memory, this mental image possesses a particular place value among the stereotypes handed down over the centuries. This cliché has been not only passed down through oral communication in the form of numerous stock phrases, but also disseminated since the nineteenth century by way of caricatures, postcards, and many literary texts.

34. In many of these texts the lexeme *eternally* appears in this connection. This hyperbolic reference is intended to focus semantically on the disproportionality of reminders and at the same time emphasize the Jewish attitude of holding a grudge and being unable to forgive.

35. Such positive self-characterizations implicitly convey the message that a person with such qualities cannot be an antisemite or racist. A rich emotional life, education, and love of culture are not, however, incompatible with Judeophobic resentments. The commandant of Auschwitz, Rudolf Höss, was a loving father and wrote after the war, "Today I bitterly regret that I did not spend more time with my family" (Höss 1958, 138). Many active Nazis loved their children, were kind to animals, listened to Beethoven, and

read poetry (see Goldhagen 1996). This did not prevent them from first harassing Jews, then gassing and burning them. Their love for children did not extend to Jewish children, whom they killed without a moment's hesitation. But to this day the mistaken notion persists that culturally sensitive and educated people, kindhearted in their everyday lives, are immune to antisemitism.

36. On the concept of ISRAEL AS A COLLECTIVE JEW, see chapter 7.

37. This example comes from a corpus of letters and e-mails that Michael Wolffsohn kindly placed at our disposal (see the analyses in Schwarz-Friesel 2007, 353ff.).

38. In the process, partially mistaken attributions either go unrecognized or are made intentionally. The rule "an eye for an eye, a tooth for a tooth" (from Deuteronomy 19:21) was supposed in Mosaic Law to guarantee equity, but in the context of this e-mail it is quoted as an example of excessive vengeance, thereby reinforcing the cliché of JEWISH VENGEFULNESS.

39. Indirect speech acts allow the person producing them to avoid being pinned down to the implicit message, which he or she can always deny, i.e., informationally cancel, for instance by saying, 'The fact that I quoted the Bible to refer to actions in the past or to Jews' attitudes does not mean that I want to imply that Jews alive today are the same.' Indirect speech acts of this sort function as a communicative protective measure.

40. *Collocation* is the technical term for words that appear frequently in close proximity to each other.

41. A generic reference refers to all members of a category or group: in this case all Jews are meant.

42. On the stereotype of the CORROSIVE INFLUENCE, see Faber (1999).

43. Intentional distortion of names and their specific semantic meanings are examples of typical manifestations of this stigmatization (see Schwarz-Friesel 2007, 358). A person's name stands for his or her personality; this polemical device therefore aims to discredit totally the person thus insulted and defamed (see Bering 2010, 217).

44. These e-mails are taken from a corpus placed at our disposal by Esther Schapira, a producer at Hessian Broadcasting. The e-mails were sent in response to a feature that reported and commented critically on the one-sided and distorting anti-Israeli media reporting on the Middle East, taking the case of Mohammed al Durah as an example.

45. Cf., e.g., the essay "Does Israel No Longer Believe in Peace?" by Chen Tzoref-Ashkenazi in the *Tagesspiegel* of 11 April 2010 or Ulrich Kienzle on the ARD talk show broadcast on 21 January 2009, "Tough but Fair: Bloody Ruins in Gaza—How Far Does Our Solidarity with Israel Extend?" in which he said, "I have the feeling the Israelis are no longer interested in peace, and that is what I find most disappointing." This and other such statements disseminated by the mass media are used by many authors intertextually to legitimate the content of their communications (e.g., *As I heard yesterday on television* . . .; see chapter 6, under "*As I just read in my paper* . . .").

46. In the meantime this cliché has turned up increasingly in public settings such as the Internet and in letters to the editor appearing in the mainstream press. The following letter from a reader of the *Hannoverische Zeitung* offers a good example: "The hatred of

Germans . . . is being kept alive forever. . . . The Jews will still be reminding us of our guilt 100 years from now; no further memorial plaques will be needed." The perpetrator–victim reversal combines here with the stereotype of the GRUDGE-BEARING NAG. That texts of this sort do not go straight to the editors' wastebaskets but are published without any kind of critical commentary shows the extent to which the taboo threshold has been lowered in the communication space (see Braune 2010). That such a letter manifests antisemitic thinking is either not recognized or accepted as free speech.

47. Cf., e.g., a segment in the series *Horizons* on the Hessian Broadcasting Network that carries the title "How Much Is One Allowed to Criticize Israel? Of Human Rights, Antisemitism, and Christian–Jewish Dialogue." Questions formulated this way imply that it is problematic or even impossible to criticize Israel, an idea that is utterly misleading and counter to reality, given the excessive criticism that actually takes place.

48. In the meantime this cliché has made its appearance in public and mass-media communications. Cf., as a prime example of such discourse, the ARD talk show "Tough but Fair: Bloody Ruins in Gaza," broadcast on 21 January 2009 (see also chapter 6, under "*As I just read in my paper . . .*").

49. Cf. "[. . .] Why do we keep on paying reparations for something that happened over 50 years ago??? That debt's been paid!!!!!" (ZJD_26.08.2007_Kar_001). By itself, the lexeme *reparations payment* is an indicator of an insensitive attitude toward the crimes of the Holocaust (cf. Schwarz-Friesel 2007, 325). The very meaning of the term implies the possibility of making amends financially for the mass murder committed in the Holocaust. In view of the 6 million murdered, this is a problematic form of referentialization.

50. In the scholarly literature this conceptualization is therefore seen as the most prominent marker of so-called secondary antisemitism. As already explained, we reject the term *secondary* since it is semantically misleading. We also point to the unbroken continuity of the stereotypes, whose fundamental conceptual character persists, while their concrete instantiation assumes a contemporary form. The *traitor and usurer* has become the *land-grabber*.

51. Cf. "The Germans will never forgive us for Auschwitz!" (Zvi Rex, quoted in Heinsohn 1988, 115).

52. In this connection Trachtenberg's observation on hatred of Jews in the Middle Ages remains apt: "Why? There can be but one answer: people believe such things because they want to believe them" (1943, 2). Even the Holocaust could not put an end once and for all to the universal suspicion to which Jews have been subjected for centuries, the ancient "rumor about the Jews" (Adorno 1951/1980, 123).

53. HOLOCAUST EXPLOITATION and CRITICISM TABOO are the stereotypes most often verbalized in the messages from writers belonging to the educated and comfortably situated mainstream. Among right-wing-extremist writers these stereotypes correlate to Holocaust denial and/or Holocaust relativization (see chapter 5). Cf. "Worse than the Holocaust, if in fact that even happened" (ZJD_Gaza2009_153/816_Rie_001).

54. Günter Grass also used this term (*Gleichschaltung*) when he was criticized for his anti-Israel comments.

55. This often occurs in the form of dual propositions of the EP(P) variety, with the author's emotional attitude expressed first (*It makes me sick . . .*), followed by the embedded proposition (*that . . .*) representing a state of affairs as factual (cf. Schwarz-Friesel 2007, 173ff.).

56. That the authors remain anonymous is actually rare within the corpus, occurring primarily in the case of extremists. The very fact that most of the correspondents give their names and addresses and often send copies of their messages to the press and to political figures refutes the very taboo about which they complain so bitterly.

57. Using samples, we have analyzed mass-media linguistic usage in the reportage on political crises (comparing Middle East reports with those on North Korea's nuclear policy, the India–Pakistan conflict, or human-rights violations all over the world) and have been able to demonstrate that, first, no conflict in the world preoccupies and upsets the Germans emotionally as much as the Middle East conflict and, second, that no country on earth is as massively and intensely criticized and (pre)judged as the Jewish state of Israel. That this is connected with Germany's past is obvious (see chapter 6).

58. This cliché also occurs widely in the realm of public communication. In Internet forums and chat rooms it is the stereotype most often verbalized, next to the alleged instrumentalization of the Holocaust. Nowadays even some recipients of the Nobel Prize do not hesitate to articulate it. Since these are people who serve as role models and authorities, there is a danger they will be believed.

5. Echo of the Past

1. Thus we cannot confirm the thesis sometimes put forward in antisemitism research (cf., e.g., Rabinovici et al. 2004, 8) that the process of coming to terms with the past elicits less and less reaction from contemporary antisemites and that anti-Zionist and anti-Israeli tendencies now predominate. We believe instead that current antisemitic texts offer an amalgam of arguments referring to the past and the present. Our contrastive analysis of texts from other European countries will show that this mixture is particularly characteristic of Germany. In other European countries, forms of anti-Israeli sentiment and combinations of classic Judeophobic and current anti-Zionist clichés do in fact predominate, while the theme of guilt plays either no role or only a marginal one (see chapter 7).

2. Eitz and Stötzel (2007, 2009) have employed keyword analysis, looking at approximately fifty "Nazi terms" to establish the extent to which lexemes from the Nazi period are employed in current public discourse, in part intentionally, for purposes of persuasion, in part inadvertently. According to this analysis, since the beginning of the twenty-first century, the use of Nazi comparisons has virtually exploded. In particular, the terms *Auschwitz*, *Holocaust*, and *Final Solution* turn up with great frequency (Eitz and Stötzel 2007, 175), a finding that reflects precisely what we discovered in our corpus. In the mass media, comparisons with the Nazis are deployed primarily to sharpen an insult or reinforce a polemical position (Eitz and Stötzel 2007, 304f.). Most comparisons with the Nazis by no means represent verbal slips or inadvertencies; rather, they form part of

intentionally chosen patterns of communication (see Schwarz-Friesel 2007, 197). Comparisons to the Nazis in anti-Jewish statements are intended to stigmatize and defame.

3. The phrase *language of National Socialism* designates a specific vocabulary and particular rhetorical strategies that were employed frequently during the Nazi period. Typical lexical characteristics include the use of nationalist catchwords (*Volk*, *Vaterland*), metaphors based on biological or pathological concepts (*pest*), and lexemes drawn from radical racism (*Aryan*, *degenerate*, *alien influence*, etc.; see Cobet 1973, 238; Schmitz-Berning 1998; von Polenz 1999, 541ff.). From a strictly scientific point of view, this is not a distinct language, for which reason Braun (2007), e.g., speaks of the "Nazi style."

4. Braun (2007) examines, in addition to rhetorical and stylistic features of Nazi usage, the role the media played in disseminating the ideological semantics and stock phrases. Along with Hitler, prominent Nazis like Goebbels and Rosenberg provided models for a group-specific linguistic style. Racist thinking became a standard feature of official juridical discourse in April 1933, when terms such as *Aryan*, *documentation of Aryan descent*, and *Aryan clause* were incorporated into legislation (see also von Polenz 1999). According to Römer (1985), the development of racism revealed that radical nationalistic and especially extreme racist tendencies had been articulated and established since the mid-nineteenth century, even in educated circles, especially prominently in (Indo-)Germanic philology.

5. Collocations are typical combinations of words, i.e., linguistic units that occur with some frequency in different contexts. By means of so-called co-occurrence or collocation analysis, linguists study whether and to what extent the words in such collocations have a close semantic relationship to one another and in what sort of contexts they tend to be used (see the appendix).

6. Carinhall was the name given by Göring in honor of his wife, Carin, to a large estate he acquired in Brandenburg.

7. To be sure, the term *race* still occurs nowadays (often without any indication of a critical perspective) in scholarly papers. In comments on students' essays and theses on verbal antisemitism and racism, the instructor must regularly point out that the concept of race is obsolete, now that biology has refuted the notion and replaced it with the concept of "ethnicity."

8. A striking lexical difference can be observed here: whereas right-wing authors use the term *National Socialist* when comparing Jews or Israelis to the Nazis, left-wingers almost without exception use the term *fascist*; instead of *Holocaust* they characterize Israel's military operations as *ethnic cleansing*. Right-wing extremists encode conspiracy theories as *Jewish*, while to left-wing extremists they are *Zionist*. Cf. on this subject the anti-Israeli texts in the *Red Flag*, in which, for instance, the death of Barschel and the scandal over Dominique Strauss-Kahn are portrayed as events instigated by Zionists.

9. Between 2002 and 2007 only 10.9 percent of the mainstream authors make explicit comparisons to the Nazis, equating or comparing Jews and/or Israelis to persons and actions from the Nazi period. Starting in 2008 the number of such comparisons grows markedly: representative samples from the newer material, up to the end of 2011, yield

more than 30 percent. Since 2008–2009 such comparisons also appear more often on the Internet in defamatory references to Israel.

10. On the semantics and pragmatic significance of Nazi comparisons in public discourse, see Schwarz-Friesel (2007, 195ff.) and Eitz and Stötzel (2007, 312f.).

11. The corpus contains a series of e-mails from members of the party known as "Die Linke" (The Left). These use explicit Nazi comparisons with significantly greater frequency than other left-leaning authors.

12. Those who sign and support calls for boycotts always energetically reject the charge that their activities are perpetuating an antisemitic tradition from the Nazi era.

13. Cf., e.g., "*Germans, be on guard, don't buy from Jews!*" (Berlin, 1933; cf. Königseder 2011, 61). In many texts the phrase "*the forcibly aligned press*" is used to point out the alleged imposition of political correctness. Cf. Günter Grass's response to the criticism of his anti-Israel poem, in which he spoke of a "seemingly almost forcibly aligned press" (cf. chapter 6).

14. This tendency can be observed in other contexts as well: the inflationary use of comparisons to the Nazis (cf. expressions such as *the Holocaust on your plate*; *Baby-Caust*; *Holocaust against the Palestinians*) in the public communicative space can decontextualize and alter awareness of the historical connection and uniqueness of this crime, with the result that the meaning of 'the Holocaust' changes as well. The term's referential potential is enlarged to constitute something along the lines of 'Holocaust = crime.' In the process, the crime against the Jews in the Nazi period becomes relativized (cf. also Soric 2005).

15. Thirty-eight messages in which these lexemes appeared in collocations were subjected to closer qualitative analysis in order to determine whether this usage was embedded in antisemitic argumentation. The textual analysis revealed that the character trait 'insolent' is seen as typically Jewish and thus represents a common cliché. Persistent effects of Nazi propaganda may be at work here.

16. In current German usage the adjective *insolent* carries pejorative connotations, e.g. in the negative sense of *cocky*, when someone fails to show deference to and respect for others and is characterized as 'shameless' or 'antisocial.' Possible synonyms are *cocky*, *snotty*, *snooty*, *snarky*, *rude*, *ill-bred*, *unabashed*, *shameless*, *obstreperous*, *smart-alecky* (cf. *Duden*, 2002). In an explanation that goes beyond that of the *Duden*, *Wikipedia*, which serves as an information portal for and by the general public and thus also demonstrates the sense in which the lexemes function in everyday language, offers the gloss that the term *insolent* conveys moral devaluation or negative evaluation. Furthermore, *Wikipedia* offers a cross-reference to the lexeme *chutzpah*, from the Yiddish. This entry shows that in current usage an association exists between *insolent/insolence* and *Jews/Jewish* (cf. http://de.wikipedia.org/wiki/Frechheit, accessed 2 September 2012).

17. In light of decades of attention to and analysis of Nazi ideology in German educational institutions and the mass media, such an effect is not surprising. Speeches and writings by prominent Nazis that have been discussed and analyzed with particular frequency can be viewed as part of collective knowledge and can thus be 'rapidly activated' in long-term memory. That lexical units display different capacities for activation is a

phenomenon that has been intensively researched in psycholinguistics and cognitive linguistics (see, e.g., Aitchison 2012; Schwarz 2008, 228).

18. At present this conceptualization of Jews finds explicit expression in right-wing-extremist propaganda; e.g., the lyrics to a song by the group White Aryan Resistance resort to this old antisemitic verbalization: "*Should cocky Jews our masters be? Where can Germany's worst foes be found? Among the Jews—just look around!*" (DÖW, Dokumentationsarchiv des österreichischen Widerstandes, available at http://de.doew.braintrust.at/b163.html, accessed 2 September 2012).

19. Of the thirty-eight messages containing the phrase *insolent Jews* or *Jewish insolence* that we analyzed separately and in detail, only two can be described as right-wing-extremist, with all the others attributable to authors from the social mainstream. One would expect such correspondents to have a heightened sensitivity to the Nazi style and rhetoric vis-à-vis 'the enemy,' but that is by no means the case.

20. The German terms are *hetzen* and *Hetze*, originally used in hunting to describe the process of chasing down or siccing hounds on prey. In contemporary German the words can also refer to moving with great haste, equivalent to the English *rushing* or *racing*. The expanded meaning of the terms suggests hatemongering, whipping up hostile feelings against someone or something, instigating, or agitating. The Nazis created a number of composite terms incorporating *hetz-*, such as *Hetzblatt*, *Hetzartikel*, *Hetzschrift*, and *Hetzrede*, referring to agitational journals, writings, or speeches (Paul 2002, 471) by Jews and others considered political enemies.

21. In the Central Council corpus, two-thirds of the messages describe Jews and/or Israelis as agitators. In the Embassy corpus approximately one-third of the messages make such accusations. These messages also contain antisemitic conceptualizations. About four-fifths of the authors of such texts belong to the mainstream.

22. Thus Hitler wrote, "In fact it was primarily Jews and Marxists who attempted here with all the means at their disposal to ignite and fan the flames of war between the two countries" (1934, 162) and "So today the Jew is the great instigator of the total destruction of Germany" (1934, 702).

6. Anti-Israelism as a Modern Variant of Verbal Antisemitism

1. Many members of the party Die Linke (The Left) have a particular problem with this form of verbal transgression toward Israel (on antisemitism on the left, see Salzborn and Voigt 2011; cf. also Kloke 1994, 2010; Haury 2001, 2007).

2. In April 2012, e.g., on the occasion of the publication in several mainstream newspapers of the anti-Israel poem "What must be said" by Günter Grass—notably, a Nobel Prize winner—which unleashed a passionate debate.

3. Since overt antisemitism has been frowned upon and subject to sanctions since 1945, circumlocution has become established as a variant of implicit verbalization (see chapter 3, under Hostility toward Jews after 1945). Speakers can always hide behind the

claim that they are not in the slightest antisemitic but are simply expressing criticism of Israel. In part, however, at issue is not a "communicative detour" but a form of communication that employs dual reference, in the sense that Jews and the state of Israel are attacked simultaneously (see the examples in the present chapter, under Characteristics of Antisemitic Anti-Israelism).

4. Cf., e.g., such headlines as "*Is Criticism of Israel Allowed?*" or "*How Much Criticism of Israel Is Allowed in Germany?*" as well as a variety of similar formulations that appear regularly in the print media and in radio and television broadcasts. On the basis of the semantic information they transmit, such questions imply the existence of political correctness and a taboo against freedom of expression. A similar situation obtains with respect to the metaphor of the *antisemitism bludgeon*, which suggests that critics of Israel are always accused of antisemitism, even though this charge is leveled only when an actual antisemitic statement has been made. Questions and assertions of this kind by no means stem from naive stupidity or ignorance; rather they serve the media as populist attention getters. Antisemites purposefully style their criticism of Israel as breaking a taboo in order to immunize themselves against the charge of antisemitism. Criticism thus serves as a distraction from their Judeophobic attitude and at the same time delegitimizes criticism aimed at them.

5. Some of those criticizing Israel's settler and military policies most harshly are Israelis.

6. E.g., Günter Grass distorted reality in his portrayal of the atomic conflict between Iran and Israel when he implied that Israel was planning to attack the Iranian people, whereas the actual threats of extermination being voiced by the Iranian president, Ahmadinejad, who was described as a "braggart," were minimized. The implied taboo against criticism of Israel contained in the title of Grass's poem "What must be said" likewise represented a drastic, stereotype-based derealization. Nonetheless, people like the president of the German Academy of the Arts defended Grass as follows: "*One should be allowed to speak out without being denounced as an enemy of Israel.*" He argued that Grass had "*the right to free expression on his side*" and was only "*expressing his concern*" (Klaus Staeck on 5 April 2012 in the *Mitteldeutsche Zeitung*, published in Halle). The writer Rolf Hochhuth resigned from the Academy to protest against the support given to the position expressed by Günter Grass.

7. Contrastive studies of media reporting on crises and conflicts show that Middle East reporting in Germany occupies appreciably more space than other reporting, e.g. on the India–Pakistan conflict or on North Korea, even though these conflicts actually pose far greater risks. The distribution of comment on the Internet matches this finding. Furthermore, the emotional quotient is markedly larger in texts critical of Israel (see Schwarz-Friesel 2007, 228). Altogether, more attributions of guilt and more monocausal explanations occur in conjunction with Israel, as well as totalizing identifications of victims and perpetrators.

8. Anti-Zionism is a third variant. But because anti-Israelism and anti-Zionism are often inextricably linked and because usually no linguistic distinction is made, we subsume

this variant under anti-Israelism. Cf. detailed and more differentiated examinations of this topic by, e.g., Kloke (1994, 2010), Claussen (1995), Mertens (1995), Orland (1999), and Haury (2001).

9. The symbol # is used in the analysis of linguistic examples to indicate the presence of a semantic and conceptual implausibility or incompatibility.

10. Hedges are words and phrases that are used when speakers or writers recognize that they are expressing something difficult and should choose their words with care (cf., e.g., Schwitalla 2006, 155). In critical discourse such expressions indicate politeness toward and consideration for the addressee, showing respect and a genuine interest in achieving an understanding.

11. Most of the other e-mail authors, many of whom are highly educated, lack this self-critical dimension and fail to reflect on the ways in which their opinions on the Middle East situation are shaped by the reporting on the region. Media reports critical of Israel are either accepted uncritically or taken as a pretext for excessive blaming and insults.

12. Cf. chapter 3 on the definition of verbal antisemitism. Verbal antisemitism by no means always results from hypocritically claimed ignorance and conceptual hatred of Jews. A lack of background knowledge and inadequate awareness of the inflammatory potential of certain patterns of verbal usage can equally well be the source. But whether the utterances in question are articulated in full awareness that they are hostile toward Jews and with the intention of discriminating against Jews has no real importance. Unintentional verbal antisemitisms can also play a major role in communicating anti-Jewish stereotypes.

13. Verbal courtesy indicates that the author socially recognizes and values the addressee as a communicative partner.

14. Pfahl-Traughber (2007a, 50, 53) sees the reconstruction and designation of the "actual motifs contained" in an utterance or the "concrete motivation" as salient for the distinction between criticism of Israel and antisemitism. In practice, however, a writer's actual motivation cannot be detected, or only very seldom, and it is not necessary for the classification of utterances as antisemitisms. Relevant here are solely the forms of verbal coding that can be described precisely and determined on the basis of their semantic characteristics as hostile toward Jews.

15. On the discussions of this topic, which tend to be general and polemical, see in particular Rabinovici et al. (2004), Rauscher (2004), Kreis (2005), and Zuckermann (2005).

16. Only Heyder et al. (2005, 146f.) assert that criticism of Israel is antisemitic if only one of the following criteria is fulfilled: the denial of Israel's right to exist and to defend itself; the comparison of Israel's policy toward the Palestinians to persecution of Jews in the Third Reich; application of a double standard to Israel's policies; the transfer of antisemitic stereotypes to the Israeli state. Cf. also Pulzer (2003, 96ff.).

17. Cf. also "Your history is full of blood. You are perpetrators, not victims" (IBD_20.07.2006_ano_008).

18. With reference to this example, the contextual information that the author is an extremely antisemitic habitual correspondent (writing to both the Embassy and the Central Council) should also be taken into consideration.

19. Anti-Israelism can be understood, on the one hand, as a mental attitude and, on the other, as tangible behavior based on an attitude hostile toward Israel. We see both phenomena as inseparable. Since in what follows we will be looking at forms of anti-Israelism manifested verbally, we stress here the action-oriented and tangible dimension of this complex phenomenon.

20. On the phenomenon of bias see, e.g., Assmann (2009) and Stangor (2009).

21. A speech act that does not offer the addressee any options is not criticism but a command, intended to impose something in an authoritarian and power-conscious manner, and it patronizes the addressee from an asymmetrical position. If no command is issued, the speech act articulates intolerance. A speech act that attacks and degrades without proposing alternatives is an insult and a threat.

22. Derealization or depersonalization is described in psychopathology as a syndrome that can cause those so afflicted to experience themselves and/or their surroundings as strange and abnormal (cf., e.g., Wolfradt 2001). We, on the other hand, see derealization as a phenomenon that results when a mental interpretive schema applied to a specific extralinguistic situation or, in the case of anti-Israelism, to a country results in a distorted, narrowed, or completely false perception and assessment of the state of affairs. The criterion of falsity or distortion emerges from the incongruence between the subjective perspective of the observer and the objective or intersubjective situation. We have already pointed out in chapter 3 the problem involved in verifiability of (absolute) truth. What derealization and derealizing have in common is that they both entail disturbances in the perception of reality. Mitscherlich and Mitscherlich (1967, 76) have discussed the phenomenon in the context of the avoidance of mourning after the Holocaust. Cf. also Hegener (2006, 18f.), for whom antisemitism represents a disturbance of the thought process as well as a disturbance of the sense of reality.

23. In representative (assertive) speech acts the speaker swears to the truthfulness of his or her statement about the world. A prerequisite is that the speaker be convinced of the truth of what he or she says and that sufficient reasons exist to support this conviction. As a result, under some circumstances such utterances have a powerful effect on others.

24. Some of the arguments in this piece actually occur, in polemically pointed form, in current discussions of the role played by Germany in the European Union and its economy.

25. In the past four years derealized texts about Germany, France, Australia, and Israel like (15) have been presented as reading experiments in university seminars taking place in Jena and Berlin. While more than 95 percent of the test subjects immediately and without hesitation identified the texts about the first three countries as "false," "grotesque," "crazy," or "insane," more than 60 percent saw nothing striking in the anti-Israel texts (see Schwarz-Friesel 2011b).

26. The majority of Israelis, according to polls conducted in the country, would like to have peace with the Palestinians and are willing to accept a variety of compromises and concessions to achieve it. Yet only rarely does the correspondence mention this fact, and usually only in e-mails that express legitimate criticism. In the anti-Israel messages

Israel's population is lumped together as if it consisted only of fanatical settlers and/or members of the National Religious Party, right-wing politicians, and troops engaged in military operations.

27. This book does not have Israel or the Middle East conflict as its subject, but to clarify the discrepancy between the real world and the derealizing utterances in the corpus, and to reveal the manipulative and antisemitic potential of anti-Israel utterances, we must comment briefly on extralinguistic matters.

28. This defamatory analogy does not turn up only in German discourse, as Wistrich (2010) points out: "The big lie that Israel is an apartheid state has become firmly entrenched in recent years in many Western countries" (35f.).

29. Thought experiments and mental analogies can illustrate how out of proportion such judgments are (see double standard). One should try to picture what the German government would do to protect its citizens if terrorists in neighboring regions fired rockets toward German cities or suicide bombers came to Germany to blow up school buses, and how German citizens would react to such attacks.

30. Cases of harassment that do occur become the pretext for accusing all of Israel, as in the following e-mail: "What are Israel's soldiers doing at the checkpoints? They humiliate people from the Palestinian areas! ISRAEL, YOU SHOULD BE ASHAMED!!!" (IBD_29.09.2008_Eng_001). That unlawful acts of brutality on the part of individual soldiers are punished by the Israeli military leadership goes unmentioned.

31. Emotion-laden terms such as *shame* and *ashamed*, often combined with the word *disgrace*, occur with significant frequency to express the author's moral superiority to Israel. Here the reversal of perpetrator and victim is used to apply to Israel the emotional dimension of shame and disgrace that should or must be felt collectively in regard to the Nazi past (see chapter 8, under The Mentality of "Being Fed Up" and Refusal of Empathy).

32. Very recently forms of populist anti-Israelism have manifested themselves. That a prominent politician with a nonextremist ideology would use derealizing formulations to defame the state of Israel did not often occur in the past. The example presented by Sigmar Gabriel shows, however, how quickly anti-Israel stock phrases that appear habitually in right-wing-extremist and fundamentalist discourse can find their way into everyday language. On Monday, 14 March 2012, Gabriel posted the following text on his Facebook page: "I just came back from Hebron. That is an area where Palestinians have no rights. That is an apartheid regime for which there is no justification whatsoever." Even if this statement was not intended to discredit Israel, such distortions of reality through words convey anti-Israel thinking to the mainstream, and their articulation must therefore be condemned as particularly irresponsible.

33. A collocation and word-field analysis (see appendix) of a partial 450,088-word corpus (1,266 pages), consisting of messages sent to the Central Council and the Embassy in 2006 and available in digital form, showed that the lexeme *disproportionate* is a key term in communications critical of Israel. Analysis of the sample by means of the software package antconc 3.2.1.0 turned up 60 instances in which *disproportionate* was used as an attributive or predicate adjective and 5 instances in which its negated antonym, *not*

proportionate, occurred. The noun *disproportionality* came up 12 times. Furthermore, 280 instances were found of quasi-synonyms like *excessive* and *incommensurate*.

34. Usually the authors of these messages do not answer the question as to what they would consider a "normal/appropriate" military response to terrorist attacks and rocket firings.

35. Here we find expressed overtly something characteristic of an antisemitic attitude: obsessive fixation on Jews and unalterable resistance to facts. The author admits what most haters of Jews deny: having in his mind a certain fixed conceptualization as a belief system with absolute truth value that under no circumstances should be altered.

36. Among serious-minded critics one does not find these verbal forms.

37. All categorizations and arguments constructed on traditional stereotypes show that in the case of anti-Israelism the old patterns of hostility toward Jews have been updated. It is by no means the Middle East conflict, as Klug (2004, 237) and others assume, that plays a decisive role here. The reporting on this conflict merely provides a specific pretext for the processes of projection.

38. Often the equation or identification appears already in the salutation: "Dear Israeli Diplomats, dear Jews" (IBD_22.12.2006_Mar_001).

39. This is a further variant on antisemites' derealizing worldview that rests on the concept of the WORLDWIDE JEWISH ALLIANCE AND SOLIDARITY.

40. Cf. Kreis (2005): "It must be said clearly again and again, not to the impervious hardened antisemite but to the greater public . . . in the decent mainstream that no action on the part of Israel, however worthy of criticism, can be made responsible for antisemitism and its spread. Nothing in the world (neither targeted killing of Hamas leaders, nor predatory taking of land, nor destruction of family and community bonds by the 'protective wall,' nor any form of arrogance of power), no circumstantial conditions are responsible for the manifestation or growth of antisemitism. Responsible is solely the person who develops and strengthens such an 'ism'" (29).

41. A statement like (91) involves a double implicature of the perpetrator–victim reversal. For one thing, Israelis are stigmatized as perpetrators, and for another the Germans, not the Jews, are made the focus as victims of the "*terrible memories*."

42. This term, however, is ambiguous and its semantics do not indicate that a unique evaluation is involved. We prefer, therefore, "unique standard of evaluation."

43. Up to now no commentaries such as "Syria has lost its right to exist as a state" or "The Serbian people are drunk on blood" or "North Korea is a disgrace to humankind" or "Nazi methods in China" have been heard. Such verbal excesses occur almost daily in comments on Israel.

44. Following the same pseudo-logic, one would have to assume that on the basis of their brutal past the Germans are particularly experienced in and destined for the use of force. Such an assumption would legitimize the concept of the perpetrator people, a concept that has been rightfully rejected.

45. Most recently this communicative pattern of defensiveness and legitimation has manifested itself openly in the media. The Social Democratic mayor of Jena felt com-

pelled to heed the prompting of his "broken heart," becoming one of the first to sign a call initiated by Pax Christi to boycott fruit and vegetables from Israeli settlements. The right-wing National Democratic Party promptly hailed his action.

46. Günter Grass used almost exactly the same stock phrases in defending himself against massive criticism of his poem. In speaking with the journalist Tom Buhrow, he said on 5 April 2012, "*It's time this was finally discussed. But what I have experienced is not all that different from a forcibly aligned press. No dissenting voices are raised.*"

47. The author of this message emphasizes several times in his e-mail that he is a "sensitive citizen": "I am particularly sensitive and dedicated to [resisting] antisemitism in particular and exclusion of and generalizations about all religious, ethnic, and individual people in general!" (ZJD_01.09.2006_Tef_001).

48. Reactions to a television feature by the TV station Hessischer Rundschau make this apparent: because the piece reported critically on, among other things, anti-Israeli propaganda and falsification of the facts of an alleged child-killing, the producer received a series of intemperate letters, accusing her of spreading untruths and of manipulation. We thank Esther Schapira for making these messages available to us.

49. "Intertextuality" designates the specific, intentional, and marked technique of referencing in one text to other texts or discourses and textual patterns. In the corpus, intertextual references generally serve the purpose of legitimating the position taken by the writer (see chapter 10, under Strategies of Legitimation and Self-Aggrandizement).

50. Hove (2008, 159) has shown how omissions and falsification in Norwegian television's reporting on the beginning of the Second Intifada had the effect of portraying Israel one-sidedly as the aggressor. Despite repeated queries and presentations of the facts, the producers refused to comment on this charge.

51. On this phenomenon, see also Braune (2010), who, on the basis of a corpus analysis focused on readers' letters to the mainstream press, was able to show that antisemitic comments are increasingly published uncensored and without any critical intervention by the editors.

52. These analyses are based on a corpus of more than five hundred texts on the Middle East conflict from the mainstream press that were published in conjunction with the Lebanon and Gaza conflicts in 2006.

53. In a few cases this one-sided reporting unfavorable to Israel also receives critical mention in the e-mails. Since 2010 an increase in correspondence can be noted in which the authors express displeasure at the anti-Israel bias in the media. Cf. a comment such as, "Dear Ladies and Gentlemen, Yet again a fearmongering news item has been disseminated: with a grim expression the anchorwoman announced (essentially) that Israel had struck again and launched an attack on Gaza. The related news item about rockets from Gaza sounded like an afterthought. The type of news item, the image created, the body language, the barely contained outrage intuitively reinforce an anti-Israeli atmosphere. For weeks beforehand we heard as good as nothing officially about the attacks by terrorists from the other side. Now the victim is once more the perpetrator, being held up for blame. 'It's your own fault. Why do you defend yourselves . . . !' Since Israel is a democracy, in

which secret misdeeds immediately come to light, as in our country, and are discussed out in the open, the following documentation cannot be unbelievable. I would like to share it with you. There are so many reports on 'medical malpractice'—how would it be to have research on 'media or journalistic malpractice' for a change? Half-truths are always also half-lies [. . .]" (IBD_12.03.20012_Kau_001).

54. Behrens (2003) has already pointed out that the *Spiegel* strikingly often uses inflammatory language when it is a matter of characterizing Israel and Israelis. Our analyses confirm this impression: *Spiegel* articles on Israel repeatedly employ hyperbole and metaphors, and references to Israel display sensationalist and melodramatic tendencies.

55. Since Israel is the best-known symbol of Jewish life and is conceptualized as a Jewish state, every anti-Israel text automatically creates a mental connection between the concepts JUDAISM and ISRAEL. From the point of view of cognitive linguistics, the association "Israeli–Jewish" can be viewed as part of a customary and automatic mechanism.

56. This danger is shown by the survey results reported at the beginning of this chapter as well as by the flood of thousands of anti-Semitic comments and slogans that appeared on the Internet in conjunction with the debate over Günter Grass's anti-Israel poem. Within a matter of days the Israeli Embassy received a large number of messages on this subject. Time did not allow us to analyze these within the scope of this book.

7. A Comparison with Other Countries in Europe

1. Our current project analyzing antisemitism on the World Wide Web and in American discourse reveals patterns of conceptual devaluation and verbal demonization of Jews that are similar to those evident in the context of German and European communication. Current research on antisemitism has up to now established indications of a broad distribution of anti-Israeli antisemitism (see, e.g., Faber et al. 2006; Rensmann and Schoeps 2008). Empirical surveys document this tendency (cf. EUMC 2004; Zick and Küpper 2006a, b; Zick 2010). On anti-Israel antisemitism in the United States, see Reinharz 2010).

2. The subcorpus consists of a random sample of communications. According to the staff of the Israeli Embassy in Paris, whom we also asked about possible material, since 2010 the Embassy has received very few e-mails or letters. Instead those who wish to comment post their (numerous) critical messages on the Embassy's Facebook page.

3. This similarity becomes evident also in the numerous abusive letters sent between 2000 and 2011 to the Israelite Cultural Community in Vienna and to a variety of Jewish organizations in Austria (we had access to a selection of these letters).

4. The Norwegian writer Jostein Gaarder published in *Aftenposten* on 5 August 2005 an anti-Israeli piece,"Guds utvalgte folk" [God's chosen people], in which he projected onto Israel almost all the traditional anti-Jewish stereotypes ("*We call child-murderers 'child-murderers'. . .*," "*not the spiral of vengeance involving blood revenge of 'an eye for an eye, a tooth for a tooth'. . .*") and employed all the familiar strategies of demonization and delegitimation to defame the Jewish state. Nonetheless, he protested vehemently that he had not produced an antisemitic text.

5. One reason might be the strong Catholic orientation of Spanish society, but without further empirical studies this explanation remains speculative.

6. But a noticeable feature of the Spanish subcorpus is that in addition to the numerous hate-filled messages there are equally many positive e-mails, in which the authors express dismay at the virulent antisemitism and anti-Israelism of their fellow Spaniards and express solidarity with Israel. A similar phenomenon exists in the messages from Belgium in connection with the Gaza flotilla operation in 2010: the Embassy in Brussels received more positive messages than negative ones at that time. Many Belgians sent e-mails in which they stress that they are not Jews but condemn the "pro-Palestinian hysteria" in the Belgian public. Cf. "I believe I am fortunately not the only Belgian who condemns the pro-Palestinian hysteria" (IB_Brüssel_07.06.2010_Sim_001).

7. On various current manifestations of antisemitism in the Scandinavian countries see Gerstenfeld (2008).

8. This correlates to survey results within the European Union, where antisemitic crimes have been on the rise since the turn of the millennium (see Rensmann and Schoeps 2008, 10, and, e.g., the results of the ADL 2007).

9. Thus the qualitative text analyses match only partially the results from surveys. Zick and Küpper (2006b, 118) detect as a significant trend in Europeans' opinion profile "a shift from traditional antisemitic opinions to subtle, surreptitious, and secondary antisemitic prejudices that are marked as transformed antisemitism." We, however, see the traditional opinions manifesting themselves also in implicit forms of verbalization. Traditional Judeophobic stereotypes are projected onto Israel (see chapter 7). Thus, in explicit references to Israel, circumlocutions are used to mobilize all the available means of denigrating Jews.

8. The Emotional Basis of Modern Hostility toward Jews

1. Sartre (1948, 47) describes antisemitism as the fear of being human. He emphasizes that the antisemitic worldview is mentally constructed and irrational: "If there were no Jew, the antisemite would invent him" (10).

2. The separation of cognition and emotion, of thinking and feeling, has a long cultural tradition: the modern image of the human being in the Western world is permeated by a fundamental dualism between mind and feeling. For that reason emotions long had the status in both everyday and scientific conceptualizations of incidental phenomena and marginal by-products. On the inclusion of emotions as pertinent to historiography, see Jensen and Morat (2008) and Frevert (2009).

3. In the case of antisemitism, the destructive emotions predominate, disrupting, destroying, and deranging cognitive operations. They can derail reason and intellect and defy the rules of logic (see the present chapter, under Contrary to Reason). Yet emotion and cognition need not stand in polar opposition to one another. And emotional evaluations are not always irrational or even destructive. Positive and productive emotions that are

consistent with rational cognitive processes also exist. Emotional states can optimize and accelerate such cognitive processes as processing, learning, retaining, and remembering (see Schwarz-Friesel 2007, 115f.).

4. This cognitivistic approach to emotion views evaluation as the constitutive and central element of emotions (cf. Scherer 2004; Schwarz-Friesel, 2007, 72ff.). See Solomon (2001): "What are feelings? As fundamental judgments or complexes of judgments, they form existential initiatives that . . . determine us and our position in the world, create values, ideals, structures, and mythologies by which we are guided and within whose framework we live. In that sense feelings depend greatly on opinions and convictions. . . . We can be angry only if we assume that someone has wronged or harmed us. . . . Feelings are evaluative (or 'normative') judgments: about my situation as well as about myself and/or all others" (172f.).

5. The emotional potential of a given verbal utterance stems, as a characteristic internal to the text, from all linguistic forms of named emotions and of the (explicit as well as implicit) expression of emotion (see Schwarz-Friesel 2007, 210f.).

6. Quantitative analysis of a subcorpus of approximately 4,695 messages from the years 2002–2006 revealed that 68.9 percent of the e-mails to the Israeli Embassy contained emotional passages, that is to say, lexemes expressive or descriptive of emotions. In the messages to the Central Council, the figure is 60.1 percent. Starting in 2007, more than 70 percent of the messages to the Central Council contain emotional formulations.

7. Lexemes descriptive of emotion, such as *fear*, *hate*, and *furious*, refer explicitly to certain feelings; lexemes expressive of emotion convey emotional states and processes by way of the expressions' (evaluative) semantics (e.g., by means of affective adjectives such as *disgusting* or modal particles such as *unfortunately*; interjections such as *ick!* also function to express emotion).

8. Feelings are experienced emotions, i.e., evaluations of emotional states that can be experienced subjectively. Conscious representation of emotion requires that it first be conceptualized. Thus feelings are cognitively influenced states (see Scherer 2004; Schwarz-Friesel 2007, 77ff.). In the psychology of emotions a distinction is made between "hot emotion" and "cold emotion," i.e., between different states or processes of an emotion (see, e.g., Teasdale 1999). Cf. also Haubl and Caysa (2007): "True hate need not be either primitive or precivilized, uncontrolled or irrational; rather it can appear as sublime, controlled, noble, civilized, calculating, clever, and rational" (82).

9. When human behavior is being judged, a causal attribution always takes place (see, e.g., Weiner 1986). This attribution reflects convictions about the causes of events and situations. External attributions see the causes in external factors (the environment, the need to defend oneself, danger, etc.), whereas internal attributions ascribe behavior to human character (see chapter 7).

10. In this sense the reversal of perpetrator and victim can also be observed on the emotional level: the hate-filled antisemites are forced by the "Jews' misdeeds" to develop negative feelings. They thus see themselves emotionally as victims. Cf. also Haubl and

Caysa (2007, 96): "The scapegoat is to blame for being hated. The victim is . . . always responsible for everything, and is also responsible for the charges thrown at him, regardless of whether they correspond to the facts or not. Hate produces its own enemy."

11. In the conceptual belief system of the "antisemitic ethos" there is a "just-world thinking, which is the tendency to believe that people who suffer, especially those already devalued, must deserve their suffering as a result of their deeds or their character; and scapegoating, or blaming others for one's problems" (Staub 1995, 17). Cf. also Haubl and Caysa (2007): "Fighting and exterminating them takes place without any sense of guilt" (33ff.).

12. Such statements are by no means limited to the e-mail corpus. In numerous Internet communications sentiments turn up that refuse, sometimes explicitly, sometimes implicitly, to entertain feelings such as compassion for Jews or Israelis. In the online audience-comments sections on ARD and ZDF, for instance, in March 2011 dozens of entries like the following appeared: "He who sows violence harvests violence. That's something the Bible-versed Jews must know" (12.03.2011_17:23_Raimon) or "These settlements were, are, and will remain ILLEGAL. Why is not a word said about that in this article??! [. . .] The Israeli settlers seem to lack all common sense, putting their children into such a dangerous situation [. . .]" (12.03.2011_20:35_Maysoon). The occasion was an article on a particularly brutal murder of an Israeli family in Itamar; the parents and three small children, the youngest of whom was a three-month-old girl, were all stabbed, and the youngest had her throat slit.

13. "Empathy can be refused to the object of hatred all the more easily when that object is portrayed with all linguistic and graphic tools as an Other whose feelings are impossible to share" (Haubl and Caysa 2007, 46). We proceed from the premise that verbal dehumanization results from a mental evaluation that denies the object human qualities.

14. Correspondingly, the results of antisemitism research that show the persistence of anti-Jewish thinking in mainstream German society are vehemently denied and minimized. Observance of the never-again resolution with regard to the Holocaust is limited for many Germans to a few days of remembrance each year. Watchwords such as *Remember the victims* and *We acknowledge our responsibility* have become empty stock phrases. Thus a more critical engagement with problematic phenomena in the present fails to materialize.

15. On this subject see, e.g., the Forsa survey undertaken for *Stern* magazine in conjunction with Holocaust Remembrance Day in 2012. Twenty-one percent of the eighteen- to twenty-nine-year-olds asked did not know what the term *Auschwitz* stood for; 31 percent of those surveyed did not know in what country Auschwitz is located. Forty percent, however, wanted to draw a line under the past, and 65 percent felt that Germans did not have any special responsibility toward other peoples on the basis of their past. In the 2009 ADL poll 44 percent of the Germans surveyed checked off "Jews refer to the Holocaust too often."

16. Argumentation means a language producer's attempt to justify a claim by invoking the assumed validity of another claim (see, e.g., Kopperschmidt 1989). Arguments thus

aim to get the recipient to accede to the author's point of view, specifically through cognitive processes (cf. Sornig 1986, 251). These processes rest on ordinary logical conclusions, and thus on an explicit or implicit logical relationship (see Toulmin 1958).

17. Adorno (1946/2002) long ago pointed out some peculiarities of this pseudo-argumentation as manifested in fascist propaganda: "It follows no discursive logic but rather can be recognized—especially in rhetorical manifestations—as a sort of organized sequence of ideas. The relationship between premises and conclusions is replaced by a linkage of thoughts based on mere similarity, with one and the same characteristic word often figuring in two assertions not connected in any way but linked associatively through this word. This procedure not only eludes the control mechanisms of rational scrutiny but also makes it easier for the listener to 'follow'" (153).

18. Cf. Löhner (1996) and van Eemeren (2001). In (historical) rhetoric a distinction is made between a false conclusion, i.e., a formally incorrect conclusion reached on purpose to deceive others, and an erroneous conclusion (paralogism), i.e., a conclusion in which the language producer inadvertently reaches a wrong conclusion. The erroneous conclusions that occur often in the corpus texts were presumably not reached intentionally. The authors are convinced of the correctness of their statements and judgments, for they represent the basis for their anti-Jewish attitude. Ultimately, however, the question as to whether the authors are aware of the falsity of the theses they present cannot be answered with certainty simply from an analysis of the corpus. The speech acts could theoretically also be outright lies.

19. Self-fulfilling prophecies bear that name because those who believe in the predictions they articulate often behave in such a way as to create a reality that brings about the predicted result. Smith and Mackie (2000) offer the following definition: "the process by which one person's expectations about another become reality by eliciting behaviors that confirm the expectation" (94).

20. On this point see also Sartre (1948): "It is not experience that creates the concept of the Jew; rather prejudice falsifies experience" (10).

21. On the unique evaluation (double standard) of Israel, see chapter 6, under Targeting, Unique Standard, and Delegitimation. Here the unique evaluation consists in Israel's being denied the right to fight terrorism—a right denied to no other country in the world.

22. Hacker (1990) characterizes this phenomenon tellingly as a "use of irrational concepts that presents itself as rational" (33).

23. Many correspondents apparently do not consider it necessary to check, correct, or revise their messages before sending them off to representatives of official institutions such as the Embassy, to the president of the Central Council, or (as a copy) to cabinet ministers and the like. The many spelling and grammatical errors reflect a lack of the thoughtful control that might be expected of writers who attest to their own level of education and knowledge or to the self-censorship they claim to have imposed on them.

24. Concrete concepts are characterized by their potential to refer to a reality that can be experienced and perceived. Members of a given group are subsumed under an overarching, concrete category and can display many individual characteristics. In the case of abstract

concepts, no direct, empirically perceptible connection to reality exists. These concepts are hypostases of the human mind. Abstractions cannot be perceived by the senses (see Schwarz 2008, 123f.). *Jew* as a lexeme is a concrete concept, but for many antisemites it functions as an abstraction, since it refers not to actual Jews but to a category in their minds.

25. On this subject see also Hacker (1990, 46) and Hegener (2006, 19).

26. Correspondingly the anti-Israel reports in the mass media, some of which convey only one perspective, are believed immediately and cited as authoritative sources (see chapter 6, under "*As I just read in my paper . . .*"), although most (academic) authors certainly view reports in the mass media on other topics with at least as much skepticism as Luhmann (1996): "What we know about our society, indeed about the world in which we live, we know through the mass media. . . . On the other hand, we know enough about the mass media to know that we cannot trust these sources" (9).

9. Acts of Verbal Violence

1. According to the categories in speech-act theory, threatening belongs to the class of so-called commissives. In speech acts of this type the producer of the utterance commits to do or refrain from doing something in the future that has negative implications for the recipient. In the case of threats, however, a directive dimension of action is also present, since the recipient is supposed to be either mentally intimidated or induced to act. Abuse is primarily expressive; i.e., the producer articulates his or her feelings with regard to the recipient, but wants to achieve the effect of offending, destabilizing, or intimidating the addressee. Since abuse and threats belong to aggressive speech acts, we subsume these types here accordingly.

2. Abuse (*Beschimpfen*) differs from ranting (*Schimpfen*) in that it is directed at a person, whereas ranting can apply also to an object or a situation.

3. Certain terms acquire a pejorative character only in a specific context. *Jew* is the term for a member of a specific religious community. But if this word appears in a context that can be recognized contextually as degrading, it becomes a term of abuse (see examples [30]–[36]).

4. Here we will concentrate on the frequent terms of abuse found in language hostile toward Jews. A treatment of general aspects of abusive terms can be found, e.g., in Havryliv (2003); see also Kiener (1983).

5. This communicative practice has a background in reality: on 10 November 1975 the United Nations General Assembly passed Resolution 3379, condemning Zionism on the grounds "that Zionism is a form of racism and of racist discrimination." This official and institutional devaluation of Zionism was not revoked until December 1991, under pressure from the United States and with the assent of Russia. To this day antisemites invoke this resolution. That the lexeme *Zionist* or *Zionism* has undergone a shift in meaning can be clearly seen: in the entire corpus we found not one textual example with a neutral or positive reading. In the communication space of the Internet, too, the terms appear primarily in a pejorative context (see Schwarz-Friesel 2012).

6. The speech act of mockery is understood here as a particular form of insult: a specific characteristic of a mocking insult is that the addressee is made fun of by means of irony, sarcasm, or puns.

7. These texts come from a collection of approximately 1,000 e-mails and letters sent to Michael Wolffsohn, a German Jewish professor of history at the University of the Bundeswehr in Munich, in the spring of 2004. Professor Wolffsohn had given an interview to Sandra Maischberger of N-TV on new methods of combatting international terrorism, in which he supported the use of torture (see Schwarz-Friesel 2007, 353).

8. Some authors, however, show genuine concern and write to the Central Council and the Embassy in real perplexity either to request information or to ask questions. These writers eschew reproving moral appeals that imply that Jews and Israelis have cognitive and emotional deficits. Cf. the examples in chapter 6, under Derealization.

9. In the case of threats (including irreal ones), the speaker makes a commitment to see to it that the announced punitive measures are carried out; he or she portrays their future realization as a certainty. In the case of curses, however, the person expressing them relies on "higher powers" to bring misfortune to the recipient. Threats are announcements, while curses are expressions of wishes on the part of the producer.

10. Curses/maledictions relate to the addressee. Curses, like abusive comments, can be purely dependent on a situation or object and relate to vexing situations (*Damn! To hell with . . . ! That's jinxed! Damnation!*).

11. The author, a prominent scholar, who, according to the information he himself provides, has never been to Israel but defames the country as an apartheid and colonial state, derives his information exclusively from the media (cf. chapter 8, under Contradictions and Paradoxes).

12. The call for the boycott can be found at http://steinbergrecherche.com/20110500schinaglanchristlichjuedisch.pdf. Accessed 9 February 2012.

13. In the past few years hardly any guest on a talk show dealing the with Middle East has been reprimanded or challenged for using inaccurate, demonizing, and derealizing vocabulary such as *apartheid state* and *state-sponsored terrorism*, as well as Nazi comparisons. Even the moderators often conflate Israelis and Jews, as occurred in "Tough but Fair: Bloody Ruins in Gaza," broadcast on 21January 2009 (discussed in chapter 6, under "*As I just read in my paper . . .*").

14. This factor sets these suggestions apart from the threats and curses discussed in this chapter, under Abuse, Insults, Threats, Curses, which had a particular focus. The suggestions address an alleged global problem and are embedded in general considerations or fantasies of salvation. To be sure, many of the emotionally motivated curses likewise display this feature.

15. The statement that peace will not reign until there are no more Jews implicitly conveys the suggestion that one must take steps to see to it that in the future there are no more Jews.

16. Many of the authors are not content to write only to the Central Council and the Embassy but also send their messages, as well as various commentaries, to the press,

politicians, and the federal government. They also post their "suggested solutions" to the Middle East conflict on the Internet and send out chain letters calling, e.g., for a boycott of Israeli products.

17. The idea that Jews should not exist as Jews often turns up on the Internet, and in various contexts—forums, chatrooms, social networks, etc. A prime example appeared in a customer review, on the Amazon site, of Albert S. Lindemann's *Esau's Tears: Modern Anti-Semitism and the Rise of the Jews* (2000). The reader explicitly presents the thesis that Jews are hated because they are Jews and that they should therefore give up their Jewishness in their own interest and that of non-Jewish society: "I am firmly convinced that the separation demanded by Jewish religion is the primary cause of anti-semitism, simply because of the implied insult to the majority culture. If Jews could stop being separate, they would gradually stop being hated, but they would no longer be Jews, either. It's an uncomfortable situation for Jews, dealt with mostly by denying that there is any inherent insult in the traditional refusal to socialize, eat together, and intermarry" (http://www.amazon.ca/product-reviews/0521593697, accessed 2 September 2012). The "implied insult" refers to the concept of God's chosen people as well as the preservation of Jewish customs and laws. That Jewish existence as such is felt to be an insult and a challenge forms the core of Judeophobic resentment.

18. Cf. also the campaign video for Dietmar Moews, the candidate for the Pirates' Party (http://www.youtube.com/watch?v=04jo8Z5RVfs, posted 4 April 2012). After Moews articulates the usual conspiracy theories, e.g., the one about "world Jewry," at the end of his speech he makes the recommendation that every minority join the majority.

10. Textual Strategies and Patterns of Argumentation

1. To avoid a possible misunderstanding: the only texts analyzed in this chapter are those that have been classified as clearly antisemitic; they contain Judeophobic stereotypes and arguments. From these one must differentiate messages that express genuine concern and legitimate criticism without verbalizing anti-Jewish notions. These two categories of texts sometimes resemble each other in their verbal formulations. Only a cognitive and textual linguistic analysis can pinpoint the difference between verbal antisemitism and, e.g., justified criticism of Israel (see chapter 7).

2. Cf. also Brinker (1986, 180), Hoffmann (1998, 63), Ortak (2004, 135), and Schwarz-Friesel (2007, 198). The concepts of function and strategy relate not merely to a single utterance but also to larger portions of text or an entire text. Thus local and global strategies can be differentiated from one another, depending on whether they are realized through a single speech act or a number of speech acts (cf. Jucker 1986, 186). Likewise a distinction can be made between the communicative function (illocution) of a single utterance and the communicative function of a text (global illocution).

3. In rhetoric, argumentation is defined as identifying suitable arguments and connecting them to form a persuasive series of statements (cf. Ottmers 2007, 66). The starting point for an argument consists of a contested state of affairs, or one perceived as contested,

that is supposed to be rendered uncontested in its claim to validity. Arguments regarded as uncontested, such as information and assertions, are mustered either to support or to refute the definition of the state of affairs (cf. Ottmers 2007, 68–70, 72). In linguistics, we can define argumentation with Herbig (1992) as a speech act "with whose help a speaker can undertake, on the basis of his assessment of a situation, the attempt that will be recognizable to one addressee or several to move the addressee(s) by means of one or more supporting statements to accept claims to validity or truth that are actually contested or contested only according to his assessment of the situation" (62).

4. On analyzing arguments, cf. also Toulmin (1958), Kopperschmidt (1989), Herbig (1992), and Bayer (2007).

5. This is an abbreviated formulation: *strategies of verbal antisemitism* is shorthand for the specific strategies employed to express antisemitism through certain linguistic (formal) means. On the other hand, the formulation *antisemitism as a verbal strategy* refers to the general tendency in mainstream society to use language, rather than cartoons or the defacement of graves, to express antisemitic resentments. Antisemitism as a verbal strategy aims to deradicalize and legitimate antisemitism by replacing nonverbal actions with verbal manifestations.

6. Recurring arguments and series of arguments can be referred to as patterns or argumentative patterns.

7. Cf. also the descriptive categories of Wodak (1990), Wodak et al. (1990), and Reisig and Wodak (2001), as well as Van Dijk (2002).

8. Textual analyses of the complete messages reveal what seems to be a distributional pattern for the respective textual strategies within the global structure of the text: first comes self-legitimation, followed by strategies of demarcation, avoidance, and relativization; toward the end, justification strategies emerge. A text that displays this pattern very clearly can be found in the appendix (ZJD_01.09.2006_Tef_001).

9. Wodak et al. (1990) classify positive self-representation as a strategy of argumentation with which the speaker "emphasizes his innocence, integrity, philosemitic attitude, etc." (353).

10. Biographical information does not appear exclusively in the introductory part of the message (legitimation strategy); see this chapter, under Strategies of Avoidance and Self-Defense, and the appendix.

11. At the same time, members of the younger generation refer to their age as a way of absolving themselves of historical German guilt.

12. Such patterns of justification also turn up in public discourse: a well-known example is Norbert Blüm's statement on various talk shows that as a Christian he cannot possibly be an antisemite (see the discussion in chapter 4, which shows how absurd such a contention is).

13. In the context of the message, a statement like this can imply that those who are not included in the we-group (i.e., the Jews) are not interested in harmonious coexistence and thus, in contrast to the we-group, do not feel obligated to honor generally accepted norms and values.

14. Wodak et al. (1990, 353) use the term "pseudo-rational judgment," calling the rationality of the arguments into question.

15. Reisigl and Wodak (2001, 44f.) describe attenuation, which they call mitigation, as a general strategy within antisemitic usage, that results, they argue, in attenuation of the speaker's own utterance. But the utterance is not really attenuated. The authors merely feign being considerate toward the addressee.

16. Here a double proposition is constructed. A statement appears embedded in a description of the speaker's attitude (see Schwarz-Friesel 2007, 174f.).

17. In this way situations such as the rocket strikes on southern Israel that do not fit the author's view of the world can be relativized. The reasoning might be that although these attacks must of course be condemned, one should not forget the far more serious crimes committed by the Israeli army of occupation.

18. The patterns of argumentation pointed out by Van Dijk (2002) also adhere to the pattern of ostensible general agreement, which is then, however, divided, limited, or even revoked. Statements along the lines of *I have/am/think . . . but . . .* usually follow and can be used to articulate antisemitism and anti-Israelism: apparent denial: *We have nothing against Jews, but in general . . .* ; apparent concession: *Some of them are nice, but in general . . .* ; apparent empathy: *Of course the Israelis have problems, but . . .* ; apparent cluelessness: *I have no idea, but . . .* ; apparent apology: *Excuse me, but . . .* ; reversal of charges: *Not you but we are the true victims*; transference: *It doesn't bother me, but my friends and acquaintances. . . .*

19. Classic speech-act classification sees almost only the expressives as providing an opportunity to express feelings linguistically or activating utterances with emotional content. But ultimately we can address and activate emotional conditions and processes with all types of speech acts. Every verbal utterance can convey emotional contents (see Schwarz-Friesel 2007, 27).

20. At the same time, this kind of defense entails taking a position contrary to the official mainstream societal consensus that acknowledges the singularity of the Holocaust, German guilt, and Germans' responsibility to Israel. Such a defense therefore involves a conflict with the accepted norms, and the authors resolve this conflict by portraying themselves as courageous defenders of the freedom to form their own opinions in the face of the political correctness allegedly imposed by Jews.

21. Consider also in this connection the in-group and out-group constructions.

22. Examples like (65) can also represent a technique by which the author makes him- or herself anonymous, sometimes not giving a name on the envelope, on the letterhead, or in the letter itself. Those with a university education, however, who identify themselves as such, always share their names and addresses.

23. Statements of this sort also signal faithful adherence to norms and a positive self-evaluation, such that several strategies coincide.

24. Citing authorities is an argumentative and persuasive strategy that goes back to classical rhetoric (cf., e.g., Klein 1994).

25. Here we concentrate first on personal authorities; medial authority in the form of

opinion-molding media and mainstream reporting will be discussed in connection with the phenomenon of intertextuality.

26. It has been documented that Fontane held the Judeophobic prejudices that were widespread in the nineteenth century and articulated them in, e.g., letters (see chapter 4, under Current Stereotypes and Their Verbal Manifestations). The Fontane quotation in this example displays the classic argumentative pattern *I have nothing against Jews, but they are so depraved.* The author of (82) brings this pattern into the present without being aware of its inflammatory potential. In the process he upgrades Fontane into a truly concerned person.

27. On the specifics of the Nazi comparison, see chapter 6, under Tools of Demonization.

28. In many places synagogues and Jewish stores were set on fire. Cemeteries were vandalized, and stones were thrown at synagogues and human beings (cf. *Neue Zürcher Zeitung*, 2 April 2002, and *Tagesspiegel*, 4 April 2002).

Appendix

1. Proceeding on the assumption that verbal utterances contain traces of the cognitive and emotional activity of those who generate them, one can infer from them the authors' attitudes (see chapter 2).

2. See Busse and Teubert (1994), who view as discourse a virtual textual corpus whose "composition is determined in the broadest sense by criteria of content or semantics" (14). The texts belonging to a particular corpus are those that relate thematically to a specific discursive phenomenon and may therefore be considered representative of this particular discourse. Cf. also Bubenhofer (2009).

3. Critical discourse analysis has likewise emphasized for years the relevance of discourse-oriented analyses that combine methods of textual analysis with historical and cultural studies (Wodak 1997; Reisigl and Wodak 2001; Jäger 2001).

4. Diekmann (2008) notes: "'Representative' cross sections, especially random cross sections, are important in sociological research for certain purposes: for estimating distributions, such as, for instance, percentages or means in the population. For other purposes, such as testing general hypotheses, representative samples can usually be dispensed with. If one also considers that 'representative cross sections' do not literally exist, one can with some justification call this concept a myth" (432). On the subject of opinion-survey errors, see Diekmann (2008, 446f.). See also Brosius and Koschel (2001, 122), Kirchhoff et al. (2003), and Porst (2008).

5. The representative value of the results can also be increased by the fact that individual quota samples can be drawn from the entire corpus or, in accordance with considerations pertaining to the logic of the matter at hand, a conscious selection can be made (cf. Brosius and Koschel 2001, 91). Furthermore, all the messages that unambiguously emanate from right- or left-leaning sources have been filtered out and assigned to a separate category, from which a discrete sample has been taken and analyzed. The results from these partial

corpora can then be considered representative of the respective groups within the population, whether left-wing-extremist, right-wing-extremist, mainstream, etc. Establishing such quotas makes it legitimate to undertake comparisons between these groups. Since, however, consciously assigning the data to the various categories is a prerequisite for such comparisons, testing the results according to probability theory is no longer possible. It is thus the researchers' experience and knowledge that guarantee the reliability of the results (cf. Atteslander 2008, 259).

6. Centrality refers to the level of concern among the subjects of a survey, or to the relevance to central convictions and conceptions (cf. Atteslander 2008, 61f.).

7. Particular significance attaches in the analysis to the periods during which the number of communications received by the Central Council and the Embassy remained relatively constant (2002, 2006, 2008–2009), because with the mounting number of communications the influence of confounding factors declines or such factors constitute a normal distribution. At peak times for attention to and awareness of Jews and Israelis, persons feel empowered to chime in who otherwise experience little motivation to do so and are more inclined to take moderate positions.

8. They probably cannot do so because the short time available for a survey would make it impossible to confront the large number of persons one would need for a valid sample with detailed questions on Judaism or their understanding of history and Israel, or to standardize the questions. In addition, participants in surveys tend to view the survey questions more and more critically as they work their way though the instrument, and they increasingly formulate their answers more cautiously. This effect constrains the validity and reliability of surveys in general.

9. Only the letters to the Central Council commenting on the 2002 Möllemann–Friedman debate have been considered here. Whether the Embassy also received letters on this topic, and in what numbers, could not be established.

10. In 2006 the Central Council called several times for solidarity with Israel, e.g., on 19 July (http://www.zentralratdjuden.de/de/article/1060.html, accessed 2 September 2012).

11. The European Union's Agency for Basic Rights (FRA) notes an increase in antisemitism in connection with the Gaza conflict (see FRA 2009). In April 2009 the Federal Interior Ministry published statistics on antisemitic criminal acts that our findings confirm to the extent that increasingly radical forms of verbal expression occur. The Federal Interior Ministry noted a record number of politically motivated crimes, starting with the beginning of the Second Intifada in 2001; 31,000 offenses were recorded. Right-wing-extremist acts rose by 16 percent to 20,422. In 2008 this phenomenon included a large number of "propaganda misdemeanors" glorifying the Nazis, carried out largely by unknown perpetrators. Such propaganda actions eventually amounted to 69.9 percent of all right-wing offenses.

12. The coding was always carried out conservatively. Thus an unclear tendency or a gradation appearing in a given communication would always be assigned to the less prominent variable.

13. For purposes of comparison, it is worth noting that trends within the entire popu-

lation of Germany, currently at 82 million, are identified by the Forsa organization on the basis of between 2,000 and 4,000 persons polled. The Heitmeyer study *Germany Today* draws on 2,000 subjects for its primary poll and a total of 23,000 over a span of many years.

14. Political and social moderates are often not identical (cf. Heitmeyer 2007, 28); the definition according to socioeconomic characteristics therefore makes more sense for our analysis. Typically those situated in the mainstream are not politically radical. They are economically secure, educated citizens (cf. Hradil and Schmidt 2007, 169f.; Nolte and Hilpert 2007, 31ff.). On the phenomenon and concept of the mainstream, see also Rensmann (2004, 104) and Zick and Küpper (2006b): "The middle is multilayered and multidimensional. When one is analyzing social prejudices it appears primarily as a political position" (115).

15. On right-wing-extremist membership in political parties and free associations, see http://www.verfassungsschutz.de/de/arbeitsfelder/af_linksextremismus, accessed 2 September 2012.

16. So few messages were received from Islamists or exiled Palestinians that separate treatment is not indicated.

17. Coding indicators of right-wing extremist messages include salutations such as *Germanic greetings*; language patterns from the Nazi period, such as *the Jew Sharon*; isolated lexemes such as *the capital of the Reich*; ironic formulations such as *the so-called Federal Republic of Germany*; red-flag and high-value expressions, such as *Volk* and *Reich*; extensive use of the adjective *deutsch* (*German*); conceptualizations and verbalizations that are markedly racist or hostile toward immigrants; conspicuous e-mail handles or pseudonyms, such as *wotan . . . @web.de* or *a true German*; and references to party membership in or sympathy for the NPD (Nationalist Party of Germany) or the German Republican Party. Indicators of left-wing-extremist messages include references to recognized left-wing-extremist media, such as *The Red Flag*, but also to the Israeli peace movement, as well as to Amnesty International and its sharply critical opinions of globalization and capitalism; interface with extreme anti-Americanism (directed toward George W. Bush); and references to party membership in or sympathy with the German Leftist Party.

18. Here we have an indication that the opportunity structures of antisemitism have changed, as Rensmann (2004) and others have established, and that the realm of what can be expressed has expanded.

19. No distinction is made between the unit of analysis or selection, or rather these two designations always coincide because the entire set of pertinent variables refers to the entire message.

20. These codes, of course, appear only when the variable "Stereotype yes/no" is coded in the affirmative.

21. We reject the distinction between *primary* and *secondary* because these terms do not yield semantically appropriate readings and have the potential to activate inadequate inferences (see chapter 3, endnote 43).

22. Here the coding is determined primarily by the classification of Judeophobic stereotypes. Additional factors—with respect to antisemitism involving Israel—are comparisons

to the Nazis, rejection of Israel's right to exist, and references to a double standard, moral as well as political (cf., e.g., EUMC 2004, 229; Gessler 2004, 10, 15; Heyder et al. 2005, 146f.; Pfahl-Traughber 2007a).

23. For example, the Pew Research Center (2008) finds 25 percent of Germans to be antisemitic. The higher value of 32 percent in our study might be explained by noting that surveys tend to activate social desirability and reactivity effects that influence the results in the direction of lower percentages.

BIBLIOGRAPHY

Primary Sources

Arndt, Ernst Moritz (1814). *Blick aus der Zeit auf die Zeit.* Frankfurt: Eichenberg.

Augustine, Aurelius (413–426/1479). *De civitate Dei.* Basel: Wenssler.

Bacon, Francis (1620/1974). *Neues Organ der Wissenschaften.* Darmstadt: Wissenschaftliche Buchgesellschaft.

Boksch, Rudolf (1880). Treitschke Papers, Box 5, No. 68. 19 November 1880.

Borchert, Wolfgang (1947/2009). "Kartoffelpuffer, Gott und Stacheldraht: KZ-Literatur." In Wolfgang Borchert (2009). *Das Gesamtwerk.* Reinbek: Rowohlt.

Busch, Wilhelm (1882). *Sämtliche Bildergeschichten.* Munich: Bassermann.

Calic, Edouard (1968). *Ohne Maske: Hitler-Breiting Geheimgespräche 1931.* Frankfurt: Societätsverlag.

Chamberlain, Houston Stewart (1899/[30]1944). *Die Grundlagen des neunzehnten Jahrhunderts.* Munich: Bruckmann.

de Lagarde, Paul (1884). *Programm für die konservative Partei Preussens.* Göttingen: Dieterich.

de Lagarde, Paul (1887). *Juden und Indogermanen.* Göttingen: Dieterich.

Dühring, Eugen (1881). *Die Judenfrage als Racen-, Sitten- und Culturfrage: Mit einer weltgeschichtlichen Antwort.* Karlsruhe: Reuther.

Feder, Gottfried (1927). *Das Programm der N.S.D.A.P. und seine weltanschaulichen Grundgedanken.* Munich: Eher.

Fichte, Johann Gottlieb (1793/1845). *Sämmtliche Werke.* Vol. 6, Sec. 3: *Populärphilosophische Schriften.* Vol. 1: *Zur Politik und Moral.* Berlin: Veit & Comp.

Finkelstein, Norman ([5]2001). *Die Holocaust-Industrie: Wie das Leiden der Juden ausgebeutet wird.* Munich: Piper.

Freytag, Gustav (1855). *Soll und Haben.* Leipzig: Hirzel.

Fries, Jakob Friedrich (1816). *Ueber die Gefaehrdung des Wohlstandes und Charakters der Deutschen durch die Juden.* Heidelberg: Mohr & Winter.

Friesel, Evyatar (ed.) (2006). *Quellen zum Antisemitismus in Deutschland, 1850–1935.* Brochure.

Glagau, Otto (1878). *Der Bankrott des Nationalliberalismus und die "Reaction."* Berlin: Luckhardt.

Gobineau, Joseph Arthur de (1853). *Essai sur l'inégalité des races humaines.* Paris: Firmin-Didot.

Goebbels, Joseph (1943). *Das eherne Herz: Reden und Aufsätze aus den Jahren, 1941–1942*. Munich: Eher.

Goethe, Johann Wolfgang von (1773/[2]1973). *Poetische Werke: Dramatische Dichtungen*. Vol. 1. Berlin: Aufbau.

Grattenauer, Karl Wilhelm Friedrich ([3]1803). *Wider die Juden: Ein Wort der Warnung an unsere christlichen Mitbuerger*. Berlin: Schmidt.

Hegel, Georg Wilhelm Friedrich (1907). *Hegels theologische Jugendschriften nach den Handschriften der Kgl. Bibliothek in Berlin*. Ed. Hermann Nohl. Tübingen: Mohr.

Himmler, Heinrich (1943). Speech delivered in Posen, 4 October 1941. http://www.nationalsozialismus.de/dokumente/text/heinrich-himmler-posener-rede-vom-04-10-1943-volltext.html. Accessed 9 February 2016.

Hitler, Adolf (1934). *Mein Kampf*. Munich: Eher.

Hitler, Adolf (1945). Political Testament.

http://www.ibiblio.org/pha/policy/1945/450429a.html. Accessed 9 February 2016.

Holst, Ludolf (1821). *Judenthum in allen dessen Theilen aus einem Staatswissenschaftlichen Standpuncte betrachtet*. Mainz: Kupferberg.

Höss, Rudolf (1958). *Kommandant in Auschwitz: Autobiographische Aufzeichnungen*. Stuttgart: DVA.

Hundt-Radowsky, Hartwig von (1819). *Judenspiegel: Ein Schand- und Sittengemälde alter und neuer Zeit*. Würzburg: Schlagehart.

Kant, Immanuel (1798/1839). *Schriften zur Anthropologie und Pädagogik: Nebst einer Sammlung von Briefen und öffentlichen Erklärungen und einem chronologischen Verzeichnisse sämmtlicher Schriften Kant's*. Vol. 10. Leipzig: Modes and Baumann.

Luther, Martin (1543/1577). *Von den Juden und ihren Lügen*. Leipzig: Berwald.

Marr, Wilhelm ([3]1879). *Der Sieg des Judenthums über das Germanenthum: Vom nicht konfessionellen Standpunkt aus betrachtet*. Berne: Costenoble.

Mommsen, Theodor (1880). *Auch ein Wort über unser Judenthum*. Berlin: Weidmann.

Naudh, H. [Nordmann, Heinrich] 1861. *Die Juden und der deutsche Staat*. Berlin: Nicolai.

Nigrinus, Georg (1570). *Juden Feind: Von den Edlen Früchten der Thalmudischen Jüden, so jetziger Zeit in Teutschlande wonen, ein ernste, wolgegründe Schrift*. Oberursel: Henricus.

Phelps, Reginald H. (1968). "Hitlers 'grundlegende' Rede über den Anti-Semitismus." *Vierteljahresheft für Zeitgeschichte* 16, 4.

Raabe, Wilhelm (1864). *Der Hungerpastor*. Berlin: Janke.

Sachs, Nelly (1961). *Fahrt ins Staublose: Gedichte*. Frankfurt: Suhrkamp.

Salomon, Felix ([3]1924). *Die deutschen Parteiprogramme: Vom Erwachen des politischen Lebens in Deutschland bis zur Gegenwart*. No. 2: *Im deutschen Kaiserreich, 1871–1918*. Leipzig: Teubner.

Saltzmann, Balthasar Friedrich (1661). "Jüdische Brüderschaft: Predigt anlässlich der Taufe eines Juden." N.p.

Sauerwein, Wilhelm (1831). *Beleuchtung der Judenemancipation: Ein Wort ans deutsche Volk*. Offenbach: Hauch.

Scharff-Scharffenstein, Hermann von (1871). *Das entlarvte Judenthum der Neuzeit.* Vol. 11: *Die Juden in Bayern.* Zurich: Verlagsmagazin.

Smith, Bradley and Agnes Peterson (eds.) (1974). *Heinrich Himmler: Geheimreden 1933 bis 1945 und andere Ansprachen.* Frankfurt: Propyläen.

Steiner, Rudolf (1888). "Robert Hamerlin: 'Homunkulus': Modernes Epos in 10 Gesängen." *Deutsche Wochenschrift* 16–17 (= GA 32).

Steiner, Rudolf (1919). "Vergangenheits- und Zukunftsimpulse im sozialen Geschehen." Seventh lecture, 5 April 1919, Dornach (= GA 190). http://www.anthroposophie.byu.edu/vortraege/190.pdf. Accessed 2 September 2012.

Stuckart, Wilhelm and Hans Globke (1936.) *Kommentare zur deutschen Rassengesetzgebung.* Munich: Beck.

Treitschke, Heinrich von (1879). "Unsere Aussichten." *Preussische Jahrbücher* 44.

Voltaire (1785). "Essai sur les Moeurs et l'Esprit des Nations, et sur les principaux faits d'histoire depuis Charlemagne jusqu'à Louis XIII." Vol. 1. *Oeuvres complètes de Voltaire.* Vol. 16. Gotha: Ettinger.

Wagner, Richard (1850). "Das Judenthum in der Musik." In Richard Wagner ([2]1888). *Gesammelte Schriften und Dichtungen von Richard Wagner.* Vol. 5. Leipzig: Fritzsch.

Secondary Sources

Adam, Uwe Dietrich (2003). *Judenpolitik im Dritten Reich.* Düsseldorf: Droste.

ADL (Anti-Defamation League) (2007). *Attitudes toward Jews and the Middle East in Five European Countries.* New York: ADL. http://www.adl.org/anti_semitism/european_attitudes_survey_may_2007.pdf.

ADL (Anti-Defamation League) (2009). *Attitudes toward Jews in Seven European Countries.* New York: ADL. http://archive.adl.org/public%20adl%20anti-semitism%20presentation%20february%202009%20_3_.pdf.

Adorno, Theodor (1946/2002). "Antisemitismus und faschistische Propaganda." In Ernst Simmel (ed.) (1946/2002a).

Adorno, Theodor (1950/1973). *Studien zum autoritären Charakter.* Frankfurt: Suhrkamp.

Adorno, Theodor (1951/1980). *Minima Moralia: Reflexionen aus dem beschädigten Leben.* Frankfurt: Suhrkamp.

Adorno, Theodor (1962/1971). "Zur Bekämpfung des Antisemitismus heute." In Theodor Adorno (1971). *Kritik: Kleine Schriften zur Gesellschaft.* Frankfurt: Suhrkamp.

Aitchison, Jean ([4]2012). *Words in the Mind: An Introduction to the Mental Lexicon.* Chichester: Wiley-Blackwell.

Allport, Gordon (1954). *The Nature of Prejudice.* Cambridge, MA: Addison-Wesley.

Allport, Gordon (1971). *Die Natur des Voruteils.* Cologne: Kiepeneheur & Witsch.

Almog, Shmuel (ed.) (1988). *Antisemitism through the Ages.* Oxford: Pergamon.

Aly, Götz (2011). *Warum die Deutschen? Warum die Juden? Gleichheit, Neid und Rassenhass.* Frankfurt: Fischer.

Amadeu Antonio Stiftung (ed.) (2009). *"Die Juden sind schuld": Antisemitismus in der Einwanderungsgesellschaft am Beispiel muslimisch sozialisierter Milieus: Beispiele, Erfahrungen und Handlungsoptionen aus der pädagogischen und kommunalen Arbeit.* Berlin: Amadeu Antonio Stiftung. http://amadeu-antonio-stiftung.de. Accessed 2 September 2012.

Améry, Jean (1966/[6]2008). *Jenseits von Schuld und Sühne: Bewältigungsversuche eines Überwältigten.* Stuttgart: Klett-Cotta.

Améry, Jean (1969). "Der ehrbare Antisemitismus." *Die Zeit,* 25 July 1969. Also in Jean Améry (1971). *Widersprüche.* Stuttgart: Klett-Cotta.

Arendt, Hannah (1955). *Elemente und Ursprünge totaler Herrschaft.* Frankfurt: Europäische Verlagsanstalt.

Assmann, Aleida (2006). *Der lange Schatten der Vergangenheit: Erinnerungskultur und Geschichtspolitik.* Munich: Beck.

Assmann, Aleida (2009). "Introduction." In Anton Pelinka, Karin Bischof, and Karin Stögner (eds.) (2009). *Handbook of Prejudice.* Amherst, NY: Cambria.

Assmann, Jan (1988). "Kollektives Gedächtnis und kulturelle Identität." In Jan Assmann and Tonio Hölscher (eds.) (1988). *Kultur und Gedächtnis.* Frankfurt: Suhrkamp.

Atteslander, Peter ([12]2008). *Methoden der empirischen Sozialforschung.* Berlin: Schmidt.

Augstein, Rudolf (ed.) ([6]1987). *"Historikerstreit": Die Dokumentation über die Kontroverse um die Einzigartigkeit der nationalsozialistischen Judenvernichtung.* Munich: Piper.

Austin, John L. (1962). *How to Do Things with Words.* Cambridge, MA: Harvard University Press.

Backes, Uwe (1989). *Politischer Extremismus in demokratischen Verfassungsstaaten: Elemente einer normativen Rahmentheorie.* Wiesbaden: Westdeutscher Verlag.

Backes, Uwe and Eckhard Jesse (1989). *Politischer Extremismus in der Bundesrepublik Deutschland.* Bonn: Bundeszentrale für politische Bildung.

Bajohr, Frank (2003). *"Unser Hotel ist judenfrei": Bäder-Antisemitismus im 19. und 20. Jahrhundert.* Frankfurt: Fischer.

Baker, Rabbi Andrew (2006). "Sachverständigenaussage zum Antisemitismus in Europa. Aussage vor dem Ausschuss für Auslandsbeziehungen des Senats der Vereinigten Staaten, Unterausschuss für europäische Angelegenheiten. 8 April 2004." In Klaus Faber, Julius H. Schoeps, and Sacha Stawski (eds.) (2006).

Banaji, Mahzarin R. (2001). "Social Psychology of Stereotypes." In Neil Smelser and Paul B. Baltes (eds.). *International Encyclopedia of the Social & Behavioral Sciences.* Vol. 22. Amsterdam: Elsevier.

Barkai, Avraham (1999). "Einundzwanzigstes Bild: 'Der Kapitalist.'" In Julius H. Schoeps and Joachim Schlör (eds.) (1999).

Bauer, Yehuda (1982). *Antisemitism Today: Myth and Reality.* Jerusalem: Hebrew University, Vidal Sassoon International Center for the Study of Antisemitism.

Bauer, Yehuda (1992). "Vom christlichen Judenhass zum modernen Antisemitismus: Ein Erklärungsversuch." In Wolfgang Benz (ed.) (1992). *Jahrbuch für Antisemitismusforschung,* Vol. 1. Frankfurt: Campus.

Bauer, Yehuda (2001). *Rethinking the Holocaust*. New Haven, CT: Yale University Press.

Bauer, Yehuda (2011). "Current Anti-Semitism Problems." Manuscript of speech. Berlin.

Bauer, Yehuda, with Nili Keren (1985). *A History of the Holocaust*. New York: Watts.

Bayer, Klaus ([2]2007). *Argument und Argumentation: Logische Grundlagen der Argumentationsanalyse*. Göttingen: Vandenhoeck & Ruprecht.

Beck, Ulrich (2003). "Der neue europäische Antisemitismus: Globalisierte Emotionen." *Süddeutsche Zeitung*, 17 November 2003. http://www.info3.de/ycms_alt/printarticle_1213.shtml. Accessed 2 September 2012.

Befu, Harumi (1999). "Demonizing the 'Other.'" In Robert S. Wistrich (ed.) (1999).

Behrens, Rolf (2003). *"Raketen gegen Steinewerfer": Das Bild Israels im* Spiegel. Münster: Lit.

Benz, Wolfgang (1995). "Antisemitische Stereotype in Deutschland." In Elisabeth Klamper (ed.) (1995).

Benz, Wolfgang (2001). *Bilder vom Juden: Studien zum alltäglichen Antisemitismus*. Munich: Beck.

Benz, Wolfgang (2004). *Was ist Antisemitismus?* Munich: Beck.

Benz, Wolfgang and Juliane Wetzel (2007). *Antisemitismus und radikaler Islamismus*. Essen: Klartext.

Berger Waldenegg, Georg Christoph (2000). "Antisemitismus: Eine gefährliche Vokabel? Zur Diagnose eines Begriffs." In Wolfgang Benz (ed.) (2000). *Jahrbuch für Antisemitismusforschung*, Vol. 9. Frankfurt: Campus.

Bergmann, Werner (1997). *Antisemitismus in öffentlichen Konflikten: Kollektives Lernen in der politischen Kultur der Bundesrepublik, 1949–1989*. Frankfurt: Campus.

Bergmann, Werner (2001). "Antisemitismus." In BpB (Bundeszentrale für politische Bildung) (ed.) (2001).

Bergmann, Werner ([3]2006). *Geschichte des Antisemitismus*. Munich: Beck.

Bergmann, Werner (2008). "Vergleichende Meinungsforschung zum Antisemitismus in Europa und die Frage nach einem 'neuen europäischen Antisemitismus.'" In Lars Rensmann and Julius H. Schoeps (eds.) (2008).

Bergmann, Werner and Rainer Erb (1986). "Kommunikationslatenz, Moral und öffentliche Meinung: Theoretische Überlegungen zum Antisemitismus in der Bundesrepublik Deutschland." *Kölner Zeitschrift für Soziologie und Sozialpsychologie* 38.

Bergmann, Werner and Rainer Erb (1991). *Antisemitismus in der Bundesrepublik Deutschland: Ergebnisse einer empirischen Forschung von 1946 bis 1989*. Opladen: Leske & Budrich.

Bergmann, Werner and Wilhelm Heitmeyer (2005a). "Communicating Anti-Semitism: Are the 'Boundaries of the Speakable' Shifting?" In Moshe Zuckermann (ed.) (2005).

Bergmann, Werner and Wilhelm Heitmeyer (2005b). "Antisemitismus: Verliert die Vorurteilsrepression ihre Wirkung?" In Wilhelm Heitmeyer (ed.) (2005a).

Bering, Dietz (1989a). "Gewalt gegen Namen: Ein sprachwissenschaftlicher Beitrag zur Geschichte und Wirkung des Alltagsantisemitismus." *Muttersprache* 99.

Bering, Dietz (1989b). "Gibt es bei Luther einen antisemitischen Wortschaft? Zur Widerlegung einer politischen Legende." *Zeitschrift für Germanistische Linguistik* 17.

Bering, Dietz (1990). "Eine Tragödie der Nähe? Luther und die Juden." In Ulrich Ernst and Bernhard Sowinski (eds.) (1990). *Architectura Poetica: Festschrift für Johannes Rathofer zum 65. Geburtstag*. Cologne: Böhlau.

Bering, Dietz (1991a). "Sprache und Antisemitismus im 19. Jahrhundert." In Rainer Wimmer (ed.) (1991). *Das 19. Jahrhundert: Sprachgeschichtliche Wurzeln des heutigen Deutsch*. Berlin: de Gruyter.

Bering, Dietz ([3]1991b). *Der Name als Stigma: Antisemitismus im deutschen Alltag, 1812–1933*. Stuttgart: Klett-Cotta.

Bering, Dietz (2002). "Gutachten über den antisemitischen Charakter einer namenpolemischen Passage aus der Rede Jörg Haiders, 28 Feb. 2001." In Anton Pelinka and Ruth Wodak (eds.) (2002).

Bering, Dietz (2004). "Vom kleinen Teil zum grossen Ganzen: Etappen der Antisemitismusforschung in der Sprachwissenschaft." In Werner Bergmann and Mona Körte (eds.). *Antisemitismusforschung in den Wissenschaften*. Berlin: Metropol.

Bering, Dietz (2010). "Namen-Polemik." In Wolfgang Benz (ed.) (2010). *Handbuch des Antisemitismus: Judenfeindschaft in Geschichte und Gegenwart*. Vol. 3. Berlin: de Gruyter.

Berliner, Bernhard (1946/2002). "Einige religiöse Motive des Antisemitismus." In Ernst Simmel (ed.) (1946/2002a).

Bertelsmann (2009). "Deutsche und Juden: Verbindende Vergangenheit, trennende Gegenwart? Eine Studie der Bertelsmann-Stiftung zum Deutschland-Bild unter Juden in Israel und den USA und zum Israel-Bild in Deutschland." PDF available at http://www.bertelsmann-stiftung.de. Accessed 2 September 2012.

Beyer, Robert (2013). "'Olmert ertrinkt in Blut': Mediale Israelfeindschaft als aktuelle Formvariante von Antisemitismus? Textlinguistische Analysen antisemitischer und israelfeindlicher Medienbeiträge." In Michael Nagel and Moshe Zimmermann (eds.) (2013).

Beyer, Robert (2015). "Israelkritische, einseitig perspektivierende und evaluierende Nahostberichterstattung in der deutschen Qualitätspresse: Eine Inhaltsanalyse mit linguistischem Schwerpunkt." Dissertation. Berlin: Technische Universität.

Beyer, Robert and Eva Leuschner (2010). "Aktion und/oder Reaktion: Funktionale Konvergenz von medialen Diskursen und antisemitischen Äusserungsformen." In Monika Schwarz-Friesel, Evyatar Friesel, and Jehuda Reinharz (eds.) (2010).

BfV (Bundesamt für Verfassungsschutz) (ed.) (2005). "Argumentationsmuster im rechtsextremistischen Antisemitismus: Aktuelle Entwicklungen." http://www.verfassungsschutz.de/de/publikationen/pb_rechtsextremismus/.
broschuere_2_0511_argumentationsmuster_im_rechtsextremistischen_antisemitismus. Accessed 2 September 2012.

Blum, Johanna (2010). "Explizite und implizite Verbalisierungen antisemitischer Stereotype in Onlinekommentaren: Zur Konstruktion eines feindlichen Judenbildes im aktuellen Diskurs der gesellschaftlichen 'Mitte.'" Thesis. University of Jena.

BMI (Bundesministerium des Inneren) (ed.) (2011). *Antisemitismus in Deutschland: Erscheinungsformen, Bedingungen, Präventionsansätze: Bericht des unabhängigen Expertenkreises Antisemitismus*. Rostock: Publikationsversand der Bundesregierung.

Boehlich, Walter (ed.) (1965). *Der Berliner Antisemitismusstreit*. Frankfurt: Insel.

Botsch, Gideon, Christoph Kopke, Lars Rensmann, and Julius H. Schoeps (eds.) (2010). *Politik des Hasses: Antisemitismus und radikale Rechte in Europa*. Hildesheim: Olms.

BpB (Bundeszentrale für politische Bildung) (ed.) (2001). *Informationen zu politischen Bildung 271: Vorurteile; Stereotype; Feindbilder*.

Braun, Christian A. (2007). *Nationalsozialistischer Sprachstil: Theoretischer Zugang und praktische Analysen auf der Grundlage einer pragmatisch-textlinguistisch orientierten Stilistik*. Heidelberg: Winter.

Braune, Holger (2010). "Expliziter und impliziter Verbal-Antisemitismus in aktuellen Leserbriefen." In Monika Schwarz-Friesel, Evyatar Friesel, and Jehuda Reinharz (eds.) (2010).

Brinker, Klaus (1986). "Strategische Aspekte von Argumentationen am Beispiel eines Mediengesprächs." In Franz Hundsnurscher and Edda Weigand (eds.) (1986).

Broder, Henryk M. (1986). *Der ewige Antisemit: Über Sinn und Funktion eines beständigen Gefühls*. Frankfurt: Lembeck.

Brosius, Hans-Bernd and Friederike Koschel (2001). *Methoden der empirischen Kommunikationsforschung: Eine Einführung*. Wiesbaden: Westdeutscher Verlag.

Browning, Christopher (2003). *Die Entfesselung der Endlösung: Nationalsozialistische Judenpolitik, 1939–1942*. Munich: Propyläen.

Bubenhofer, Noah (2008). "Diskurse berechnen? Wege zu einer korpuslinguistischen Diskursanalyse." In Ingo H. Warnke and Jürgen Spitzmüller (eds.) (2008). *Methoden der Diskursanalyse: Sprachwissenschaftliche Zugänge zur transtextuellen Ebene*. Berlin: de Gruyter.

Bubenhofer, Noah (2009). *Sprachgebrauchsmuster: Korpuslinguistik als Methode der Diskurs- und Kulturanalyse*. Berlin: de Gruyter.

Bublitz, Wolfram ([2]2009). *Englische Pragmatik: Eine Einführung*. Berlin: Schmidt.

Bunzl, John (2005). "Spiegelbilder: Wahrnehmung und Interesse im Israel/Palästina–Konflikt." In Moshe Zuckermann (ed.) (2005).

Burger, Harald ([3]2007). *Phraseologie: Eine Einführung am Beispiel des Deutschen*. Berlin: Schmidt.

Busse, Dietrich and Wolfgang Teubert (1994). "Ist Diskurs ein sprachwissenschaftliches Objekt? Überlegungen zu einer linguistischen Diskurssemantik." In Dietrich Busse, Fritz Herrmans, and Wolfgang Teubert (eds.) (1994). *Zeichengeschichte, Begriffsgeschichte, Diskursgeschichte*. Opladen: Westdeutscher Verlag.

Bussmann, Hadumod (ed.) ([4]2008). *Lexikon der Sprachwissenschaft*. Stuttgart: Kröner.

Butler, Judith (1998). *Hass spricht: Zur Politik des Performativen*. Berlin: Berlin Verlag.

Chesler, Phyllis (2004). *Der neue Antisemitismus: Die globale Krise seit dem 11. September*. Hamburg: Schwartzkopff.

Claussen, Detlev (1995). "Versuch über den Antizionismus: Ein Rückblick." In Gudrun

Hentges and Reinhard Kühnl (eds.) (1995). *Geschichte, Interessenstruktur, Aktualität.* Heilbronn: Distel.

Cobet, Christoph (1973). *Der Wortschatz des Antisemitismus in der Bismarckzeit.* Munich: Fink.

Cohen, Haim (1977). *The Trial and Death of Jesus.* New York: Ktav.

Corbineau-Hoffmann, Angelika and Pascal Nicklas (eds.) (2000). *Gewalt der Sprache—Sprache der Gewalt: Beispiele aus philologischer Sicht.* Hildesheim: Olms.

Damasio, Antonio (2000). *Ich fühle, also bin ich: Die Entschlüsselung des Bewusstseins.* Berlin: List.

Decker, Oliver, Elmar Brähler, and Norman Geissler (2006). *Vom Rand zur Mitte: Rechtsextreme Einstellungen und ihre Einflussfaktoren in Deutschland.* Berlin: Friedrich-Ebert-Stiftung & Forum Berlin. http://library.fes.de/pdf-files/do/04088a.pdf. Accessed 2 September 2012.

Decker, Oliver, Marliese Weissmann, Johannes Kiess, and Elmar Brähler (2010). *Die Mitte in der Krise: Rechtsextreme Einstellungen in Deutschland 2010.* Berlin: Friedrich-Ebert-Stiftung.

Delgado, Richard and Jean Stefancic (2004). *Understanding Words That Wound.* Boulder, CO: Westview.

Dichanz, Horst and Barbara Breidenbach (2001). "Antisemitismus in den Medien: Beispiele und Analysen." In Christina Tuor-Kurth (ed.) (2001). *Neuer Antisemitismus—alte Vorurteile?* Stuttgart: Kohlhammer.

Diekmann, Andreas ([19]2008). *Empirische Sozialforschung: Grundlagen, Methoden, Anwendungen.* Reinbek: Rowohlt.

Duden ([3]2002). *Deutsches Universalwörterbuch.* Mannheim: Dudenverlag.

Duden ([7]2006). *Die Grammatik.* Mannheim: Bibliographisches Institut, Brockhaus.

EC (European Commission) (2003). *Eurobarometer: Iraq and Peace in the World.* Pdf. http://ec.europa.eu/public_opinion/flash/fl151_iraq_full_report.pdf. Accessed 2 September 2012.

Edelman, Murray J. (1976). *Politik als Ritual: Die symbolische Funktion staatlicher Institutionen und politischen Handelns* Frankfurt: Campus.

Ehlich, Konrad (ed.) (1989). *Sprache im Faschismus.* Frankfurt: Suhrkamp.

Ehlich, Konrad (1998). "Vorurteile, Vor-Urteile, Wissenstypen, mentale und diskursive Strukturen." In Margot Heinemann (ed.) (1998). *Sprachliche und soziale Stereotype.* Frankfurt: Lang.

Eitz, Thorsten and Georg Stötzel (2007). *Wörterbuch der "Vergangenheitsbewältigung": Die NS-Vergangenheit im öffentlichen Sprachgebrauch.* Vol. 1. Hildesheim: Olms.

Eitz, Thorsten and Georg Stötzel (2009). *Wörterbuch der "Vergangenheitsbewältigung": Die NS-Vergangenheit im öffentlichen Sprachgebrauch.* Vol. 2. Hildesheim: Olms.

Erb, Rainer (1999). "Drittes Bild: Der 'Ritualmord.'" In Julius H. Schoeps and Joachim Schlör (eds.) (1999).

Erler, Katja (2004). *Deutschlandbilder in der französischen Literatur nach dem Fall der Berliner Mauer.* Berlin: Schmidt.

Erzgräber, Ursula and Alfred Hirsch (eds.) (2001). *Sprache und Gewalt*. Berlin: Spitz.

EUMC (European Monitoring Centre on Racism and Xenophobia) (ed.) (2003). *Manifestations of Antisemitism in the EU, 2002–2003. First Semester 2002. Synthesis Report*. http://www.spiegel.de/media/0,4906,3553,00.pdf. Accessed 2 September 2012.

EUMC (European Monitoring Centre on Racism and Xenophobia) (ed.) (2004). *Manifestations of Antisemitism in the EU, 2002–2003. Based on Information by the National Focal Points of the RAXEN Information Network*. http://fra.europa.eu/sites/default/files/fra_uploads/184-AS-Main-report.pdf. Accessed 9 February 2016.

Evans, Richard (1991). *Im Schatten Hitlers? Historikerstreit und Vergangenheitsbewältigung in der Bundesrepublik Deutschland*. Frankfurt: Suhrkamp.

Ewen, Elizabeth and Stuart Ewen (2009). *Typen und Stereotypen: Die Geschichte des Vorurteils*. Berlin: Parthas.

Faber, Klaus (2002). *Nach Möllemann: Antisemitismus und Antizionismus in Deutschland: Eine gefährliche Verbindung in Medien und Politik*. In Tobias Kaufmann and Manja Orlowski (eds.) (2002).

Faber, Klaus, Julius H. Schoeps, and Sacha Strawski (eds.) (2006). *Neu-alter Judenhass: Antisemitismus, arabisch-israelischer Konflikt und europäische Politik*. Berlin: Verlag für Berlin-Brandenburg.

Faber, Richard (1999). "Zwanzigstes Bild: 'Der Zersetzer.'" In Julius H. Schoeps and Joachim Schlör (eds.) (1999).

Fleischer, Michael (1995). *Fontane auf Norderney*. Norderney: Soltau.

Fodor, Jerry (1983). *The Modularity of Mind*. Cambridge, MA: MIT Press.

FRA (European Union Agency for Fundamental Rights) (2009). *Anti-Semitism: Summary Overview of the Situation in the European Union, 2001–2008*. Vienna. http://fra.europa.eu/sites/default/files/fra_uploads/347-Antisemitism_Update_2009.pdf. Accessed 2 September 2012.

Frei, Norbert (1997). *Vergangenheitspolitik: Die Anfänge der Bundesrepublik und die NS- Vergangenheit*. Munich: Beck.

Frei, Norbert (2005). *1945 und wir: Das Dritte Reich im Bewusstsein der Deutschen*. Munich: Beck.

Freud, Sigmund (1926). *Die Frage der Laienanalyse: Unterredungen mit einem Unparteiischen*. Leipzig: Internationaler Psychoanalytischer Verlag.

Frevert, Ute (2009). "Was haben Gefühle in der Geschichte zu suchen?" *Geschichte und Gesellschaft* 35.

Friedländer, Saul (2006). *Die Jahre der Vernichtung: Das Dritte Reich und die Juden, 1939– 1945*. Munich: Beck.

Frindte, Wolfgang (1999). "Antisemitismus." In Wolfgang Frindte (ed.) (1999). *Fremde, Freunde, Feindlichkeiten: Sozialpsychologische Untersuchungen*. Opladen: Westdeutscher Verlag.

Friesel, Evyatar (1990). *Atlas of Modern Jewish History*. New York: Oxford University Press.

Friesel, Evyatar (2010). "Aktuelle jüdische Judeophobie: Juden gegen Israel." In Monika Schwarz-Friesel, Evyatar Friesel, and Jehuda Reinharz (eds.) (2010).

Fuchs, Eduard (1921). *Die Juden in der Karikatur: Ein Beitrag zur Kulturgeschichte.* Munich: Langen.

Gerstenfeld, Manfred (ed.) (2008). *Behind the Humanitarian Mask: The Nordic Countries, Israel, and the Jews.* Jerusalem: JCPA.

Gessler, Philipp (2004). *Der neue Antisemitismus: Hinter den Kulissen der Normalität.* Freiburg: Herder.

Glucksmann, André (2005). *Hass: Die Rückkehr einer elementaren Gewalt.* Darmstadt: Wissenschaftliche Buchgesellschaft.

Goldammer, Peter (1993). "Nietzsche-Kult—Antisemitismus—und eine späte Rezension des Romans *Vor dem Sturm*: Zu Fontanes Briefen an Friedrich Paulsen." *Fontane-Blätter* 56.

Goldhagen, Daniel J. (1996). *Hitlers willige Vollstrecker: Ganz gewöhnliche Deutsche under der Holocaust.* Berlin: Siedler.

Goldhagen, Daniel J. (2004). "Die Globalisierung des Antisemitismus." In Doron Rabinovici, Ulrich Speck, and Natan Sznaider (eds.) (2004).

Grammel, Eva (2002). "Antijudaismus, Antisemitismus, Antizionismus: Versuch einer Definition." In Tobias Kaufmann and Manja Orlowski (eds.) (2002).

Graumann, Carl Friedrich and Margaret Wintermantel (2007). "Diskriminierende Sprechakte: Ein Funktionaler Ansatz." In Steffen K. Herrmann, Sybille Krämer, and Hannes Kuch (eds.) (2007).

Grice, Herbert P. (1975). "Logic and Conversation." In Peter Cole and Jerry Morgan (eds.) (1975). *Syntax and Semantics.* Vol. 3: *Speech Acts.* New York: Academic Press.

Grigat, Stephan (2009). "Israel als Jude unter den Staaten." http://www.hagalil.com/01/de/israel.php?itemid=3188. Accessed 2 September 2012.

Grözinger, Elvira and Karl E. Grözinger (1998). "'Judenmauschel': Der antisemitische Sprachgebrauch und die jüdische Identität." In Karl E. Grözinger (ed.) (1998). *Sprache und Identität im Judentum.* Wiesbaden: Harrassowitz.

Grözinger, Karl E. (1999). "Erstes Bild: Die 'Gottesmörder.'" In Julius H. Schoeps and Joachim Schlör (eds.) (1999).

Grunberger, Béla (1962). "Der Antisemit und der Ödipuskomplex." *Psyche* 5.

Grunberger, Béla and Pierre Dessuant (2000). *Narzissmus, Christentum, Antisemitismus: Eine psychoanalytische Untersuchung.* Stuttgart: Klett-Cotta.

Habermas, Jürgen (1981). *Theorie des kommunikativen Handelns.* Vol. 1: *Handlungsrationalität und gesellschaftliche Rationalisierung.* Frankfurt: Suhrkamp.

Hacker, Friedrich (1990). *Das Faschismus-Syndrom: Psychoanalyse eines aktuellen Phänomens.* Düsseldorf: Econ.

Hart, Christopher (2007). "Critical Discourse Analysis and Conceptualisation: Mental Spaces, Blended Spaces and Discourse Spaces in the British National Party." In Christopher Hart and Domink Lukeš (eds). *Cognitive Linguistics in Critical Discourse Analysis: Application and Theory.* Newcastle: Cambridge Scholars.

Haubl, Rolf (2007). "Gattungsschicksal Hass." In Rolf Haubl and Volker Caysa (eds.) (2007).

Haubl, Rolf and Volker Caysa (eds.) (2007). *Hass und Gewaltbereitschaft*. Göttingen: Vandenhoeck und Ruprecht.

Haury, Thomas (2001). "Der Antizionismus der Neuen Linken in der BRD: Sekundärer Antisemitismus nach Auschwitz." In Arbeitskreis des deutschen Antisemitismus (ed.) (2001). *Antisemitismus—die deutsche Normalität: Geschichte und Wirkungsweisen des Vernichtungswahns*. Freiburg: ça ira.

Haury, Thomas (2007). "'Das ist Völkermord!' Das 'antifaschistische Deutschland' im Kampf gegen den 'imperialistischen Brückenkopf' und gegen die deutsche Vergangenheit." In Matthias Brosch, Michael Elm, Norman Geissler, Brigitta Elisa Simbürger, and Oliver von Wrochem (eds.) (2007). *Exklusive Solidarität: Linker Antisemitismus in Deutschland*. Berlin: Metropol.

Havryliv, Oksana (2003). *Pejorative Lexik: Untersuchungen zu ihrem semantischen und kommunikativ-pragmatischen Aspekt am Beispiel moderner deutschsprachiger, besonders österreichischer Literatur*. Frankfurt: Lang.

Havryliv, Oksana (2009). *Verbale Aggression: Formen und Funktionen am Beispiel des Wienerischen*. Frankfurt: Lang.

Hegener, Wolfgang (2006). "Antisemitismus—Judentum—Psychoanalyse: Einleitung." In Wolfgang Hegener (ed.) (2006). *Das unmögliche Erbe: Antisemitismus—Judentum—Psychoanalyse*. Giessen: Psychosozial.

Heil, Johannes (2001). "Fremde, Fremdsein: Von der Normalität eines scheinbaren Problemzustandes." In BpB (Bundeszentrale für politische Bildung) (ed.) (2001).

Heinemann, Isaac (1931). "Antisemitismus." In Wilhelm Kroll (ed.) (1931). *Paulys Realencyclopädie der classischen Altertumswissenschaft*. Suppl. Vol. 5. Stuttgart: Druckenmüller.

Heinsohn, Gunnar (1988). *Was ist Antisemitismus? Der Ursprung des Monotheismus und Judenhass: Warum Antizionismus?* Frankfurt: Skarabäus bei Eichborn.

Heitmeyer, Wilhelm (ed.) (2002–2012). *Deutsche Zustände*. Ser. 1–10. Frankfurt: Suhrkamp.

Heitmeyer, Wilhelm (ed.) (2005a). *Deutsche Zustände*. Ser. 3. Frankfurt: Suhrkamp.

Heitmeyer, Wilhelm (2005b). "Gruppenbezogene Menschenfeindlichkeit: Die theoretische Konzeption und empirische Ergebnisse aus den Jahren 2002, 2003 und 2004." In Wilhelm Heitmeyer (ed.) (2005a).

Heitmeyer, Wilhelm (ed.) (2006). *Antisemitismus in Europa: Ergebnisse empirischer Studien*. Frankfurt: Suhrkamp.

Helas, Horst, Dagmar Rubisch, and Reiner Zilkenat (eds.) (2008). *Neues vom Antisemitismus: Zustände in Deutschland*. Berlin: Dietz.

Hentges, Gudrun (1999). *Schattenseiten der Aufklärung: Die Darstellung von Juden und 'Wilden' in philosophischen Schriften des 18. und 19. Jahrhunderts*. Schwalbach/Taunus: Wochenschau.

Herbert, Ulrich (ed.) (1998). *Nationalsozialistische Vernichtungspolitik, 1939–1945: Neue Forschungen und Kontroversen*. Frankfurt: Fischer.

Herbert-Quandt-Stiftung (ed.) (2007). *Zwischen Erosion und Erneuerung: Die gesellschaftliche Mitte in Deutschland—Ein Lagebericht*. Frankfurt: Societäts-Verlag.

Herbig, Albert F. (1992). *"Sie argumentieren doch scheinheilig!" Sprach-und sprechwissenschaftliche Aspekte einer Stilistik des Argumentierens*. Frankfurt: Lang.

Herr, Moshe David (1988). "The Sages' Reaction to Antisemitism in the Hellenistic-Roman World." In Shmuel Almog (ed.) (1988).

Herrmann, Steffen K., Sybille Krämer, and Hannes Kuch (eds.) (2007). "Verletzende Worte: Die Grammatik sprachlicher Missachtung." Bielefeld: Transcript.

Heyder, Aribert, Julia Iser, and Peter Schmidt (2005). "Israelkritik oder Antisemitismus? Meinungsbilder zwischen Öffentlichkeit, Medien und Tabus." In Wilhelm Heitmeyer (ed.) (2005a).

Hoffmann, Michael (1998). "Gestaltungsstrategien und strategisches Gestalten." In Michael Hoffmann (ed.) (1998). *Beiträge zur Persuasionsforschung*. Frankfurt: Lang.

Holz, Klaus (2001). *Nationaler Antisemitismus: Wissenssoziologie einer Weltanschauung*. Weilerswist: Hamburger Edition.

Holz, Klaus (2004). "Die antisemitische Konstruction des 'Dritten' und die nationale Ordnung der Welt." In Christina von Braun and Eva-Maria Ziege (eds.) (2004).

Holz, Klaus (2005). *Die Gegenwart des Antisemitismus: Islamistische, demokratische und antizionistische Judenfeindschaft*. Hamburg: Hamburger Edition.

Homann, Ursula (2002). "Goethe und das Judentum." *Goethe-Blätter* 1. Bonn: Bernstein. http://www.ursulahomann.de/goetheunddasjudentum/komplett.html. Accessed 2 September 2012.

Horkheimer, Max (1946/2002). "Der soziologische Hintergrund des psychoanalytischen Forschungsansatzes." In Ernst Simmel (1946/2002a).

Horkheimer, Max (1961/[5]1997). "Über die deutschen Juden." In Max Horkheimer. ([5]1997). *Zur Kritik der instrumentellen Vernunft*. Frankfurt: Fischer.

Hortzitz, Nicoline. (1988). *"Früh-Antisemitismus" in Deutschland (1789–1871–2): Strukturelle Untersuchungen zu Wortschatz, Text und Argumentation*. Tübingen: Niemeyer.

Hortzitz, Nicoline (1999). "Die Sprache der Judenfeindschaft." In Julius H. Schoeps and Joachim Schlör (eds.) (1999).

Hortzitz, Nicoline (2005). *Die Sprache der Judenfeindschaft in der frühen Neuzeit (1450–1700): Untersuchungen zu Wortschatz, Text und Argumentation*. Heidelberg: Winter.

Hove, Odd Sverre (2008). "The Cut-and-Omit TV News: Norway." In Manfred Gerstenfeld (ed.) (2008).

Hradil, Stefan and Holger Schmidt (2007). "Angst und Chancen: Zur Lage der gesellschaftlichen Mitte aus soziologischer Sicht." In Herbert-Quandt-Stiftung (ed.) (2007).

Hundsnurscher, Franz and Edda Weigand (eds.) (1986). *Dialogenanalyse: Referate der 1. Arbeitstagung Münster 1986*. Tübingen: Niemeyer.

Hutton, Christopher M. (1999). *Linguistics and the Third Reich: Mother-Tongue Fascism, Race and the Science of Language*. London: Routledge.

Jaecker, Tobias (2004). *Antisemitische Verschwörungstheorien nach dem 11. September: Neue Varianten eines alten Deutungsmusters*. Münster: Lit.

Jäger, Margret and Siegfried Jäger (eds.) (2002). *Medien im Krieg: Der Anteil der Printmedien an der Erzeugung von Ohnmachts- und Zerrissenheitsgefühlen*. Duisburg: DISS.

Jäger, Siegfried ([3]2001). *Kritische Diskursanalyse: Eine Einführung*. Duisburg: DISS.

Jäger, Siegfried and Margret Jäger (2003). *Medienbild Israel: Zwischen Solidarität und Antisemitismus*. Münster: Lit.

Jäger, Siegfried, Margret Jäger, Gabriele Cleve, Ina Ruth, Frank Wichert, Frank Jessen, Jan Zöller, and Alfred Schobert (2003). *Die Nahost-Berichterstattung zur Zweiten Intifada in den deutschen Printmedien unter besonderer Berücksichtigung des Israel-Bildes: Analyse diskursiver Ereignisse im Zeitraum von September 2002 bis August 2001*. Duisburg: DISS.

Jensen, Uffa and Daniel Morat (eds.) (2008). *Rationalisierungen des Gefühls: Zum Verhältnis von Wissenschaft und Emotionen, 1880–1930*. Paderborn: Fink.

Jucker, Andreas H. (1986). *Dialogstrategien in englischen Nachrichteninterviews*. In Franz Hundsnurscher and Edda Weigand (eds.) (1986).

Kahneman, Daniel (2011). *Thinking, Fast and Slow*. New York: Farrar, Straus and Giroux.

Kalb, Marvin and Carol Saivetz (2007). "The Israeli–Hezbollah War of 2006: The Media as a Weapon in Asymmetrical Conflict." *Harvard International Journal of Press and Politics* 3, 12.

Kämper, Heidrun (2005). *Der Schulddiskurs in der frühen Nachkriegszeit: Ein Beitrag zur Geschichte des sprachlichen Umbruchs nach 1945*. Berlin: de Gruyter.

Kämper, Heidrun (2007). *Opfer—Täter—Nichttäter: Ein Wörterbuch zum Schuldiskurs, 1945–1955*. Berlin: de Gruyter.

Katz, Jacob (1980). *From Prejudice to Destruction: Anti-Semitism, 1700–1933*. Cambridge, MA: Harvard University Press.

Katz, Jacob (1986). *The Darker Side of Genius: Richard Wagner's Anti-Semitism*. Hanover, NH: Brandeis University Press.

Katz, Jacob (1990). *Vom Vorurteil bis zur Vernichtung: Antisemitismus, 1700–1933*. Berlin: Union.

Kaufmann, Tobias and Manja Orlowski (eds.) (2002). *"Ich würde mich auch wehren . . ." Antisemitismus und Israel-Kritik: Bestandsaufnahme nach Möllemann*. Potsdam: Weber.

Kiener, Franz (1983). *Das Wort als Waffe: Zur Psychologie der verbalen Aggression*. Göttingen: Vandenhoeck & Ruprecht.

Kilian, Jörg (2005). "Assoziative Stereotype: Sprachtheoretische, sprachkritische und sprachdidaktische Anmerkungen zum lexikalisch verknüpften Mythos, Aberglauben, Vorurteil." In Dietrich Busse, Thomas Niehr, and Martin Wengeler (eds.) (2005). *Brisante Semantik: Neuere Konzepte und Forschungsergebnisse einer kulturwissenschaftlichen Linguistik*. Tübingen: Niemeyer.

Kinne, Michael and Johannes Schwitalla (1994). *Sprache im Nationalsozialismus*. Heidelberg: Groos.

Kirchhoff, Sabine, Sonja Kuhnt, Peter Lipp, and Siegfried Schlawin (^{3}2003). *Der Fragebogen: Datenbasis, Konstruktion und Auswertung.* Opladen: Leske & Budrich.

Klamper, Elisabeth (ed.) (1995). *Die Macht der Bilder: Antisemitische Vorurteile und Mythen.* Wien: Picus.

Klein, Josef (1994). "Medienneutrale und medienspezifische Verfahren der Absicherung von Bewertungen in Presse und Fernsehen: Typologie und semiotische Distribution." In Markku Moilanen and Lisa Tiittula (eds.) (1994). *Überredung in der Presse: Texte, Strategien, Analysen.* Berlin: de Gruyter.

Klemperer, Victor (1947/^{24}2010). *LTI: Notizbuch eines Philologen.* Stuttgart: Reclam.

Kloke, Martin W (^{2}1994). *Israel und die deutsche Linke: Zur Geschichte eines schwierigen Verhältnisses.* Frankfurt: Haag & Herchen.

Kloke, Martin W. (2005). *40 Jahre deutsch-israelische Beziehungen.* Bonn: BpB.

Kloke, Martin W. (2010). "Israelkritik und Antizionismus in der deutschen Linken: Ehrbarer Antisemitismus?" In Monika Schwarz-Friesel, Evyatar Friesel, and Jehuda Reinharz (eds.) (2010).

Klug, Brian (2004). "The Collective Jew." In Christina von Braun and Eva-Maria Ziege (eds.) (2004).

Königseder, Angelika (2011). "Boykott-Tag, 1. April 1933." In Wolfgang Benz (ed.) (2011). *Handbuch des Antisemitismus: Judenfeindschaft in Geschichte und Gegenwart.* Vol. 4: *Ereignisse, Dekrete, Kontroversen.* Berlin: de Gruyter.

Kopperschmidt, Josef (1989). *Methodik der Argumentationsanalyse.* Stuttgart: Fromman-Holzboog.

Krämer, Sybille and Elke Koch (eds.) (2010). *Gewalt in der Sprache: Rhetoriken verletzenden Sprechens.* Munich: Fink.

Kreis, Georg (2005). "Israelkritik und Antisemitismus: Versuch einer Reflexion jenseits von Religion und Nationalität." In Moshe Zuckermann (ed.) (2005).

Krieger, Karsten (2002). "Der Berliner Antisemitismusstreit, 1879–1881: Eine Debatte um die Zugehörigkeit der deutschen Juden zur deutschen Nation." In Wolfgang Benz and Angelika Königseder (eds.) (2002). *Judenfeindschaft als Paradigma: Studien zur Vorurteilsforschung.* Berlin: Metropol.

Kroucheva, Katerina (2009). "'. . . eine bestimmtere Erklärung mochten wir aus mehreren Gründen nicht verlangen': Kurze Einführung in die Theorie und Geschichte der Imagologie." In Hiltraud Casper-Hehne and Irmy Schweiger (eds.) (2009). *Kulturelle Vielfalt deutscher Literatur, Sprache und Medien: Sommerschule für Alumni aus Osteuropa und der Welt, 16–27. August 2009.* Göttingen: Universitätsverlag.

Küntzel, Matthias (2007). *Islamischer Antisemitismus und deutsche Politik: "Die Juden werden brennen, wir werden auf ihren Gräbern tanzen . . ."* Berlin: Lit.

Langenbucher, Wolfgang R. and Guni Yasin (2009). "Produziert die Logik des Journalismus Anti-Israelismus? Von den Schwierigkeiten, aus Israel zu berichten." In Christina Holtz-Bacha, Gunter Reus, and Lee B. Becker (eds.) (2009). *Wissenschaft mit Wirkung: Beiträge zur Journalismus- und Medienwirkungsforschung. Festschrift für Klaus Schönbach.* Wiesbaden: Verlag für Sozialwissenschaften.

Laqueur, Walter (2006). *Gesichter des Antisemitismus*. Berlin: Propyläen.

Leschnitzer, Adolf (1956). *The Magic Background of Modern Anti-Semitism*. New York: International Universities Press.

Levelt, Willem J. M. (1989). *Speaking: From Intention to Articulation*. Cambridge, MA: MIT Press.

Lichtenstein, Heiner (1999). "Vierundzwanzigstes Bild: Die 'Auschwitz-Lüge.'" In Julius H. Schoeps and Joachim Schlör (eds.) (1999).

Liedtke, Frank (ed.) (1995). *Implikaturen: Grammatische und pragmatische Analysen*. Tübingen: Niemeyer.

Lippmann, Walter (1922). *Public Opinion*. London: Allen & Unwin.

Löhner, Michael (1996). "Fallazien." In Gert Ueding (ed.) (1996). *Historisches Wörterbuch der Rhetorik*. Vol. 3. Tübingen: Niemeyer.

Longerich, Peter (1998). *Politik der Vernichtung: Eine Gesamtdarstellung der nationalsozialistischen Judenverfolgung*. Munich: Piper.

Low, Alfred D. (1979). *Jews in the Eyes of the Germans: From the Enlightenment to Imperial Germany*. Philadelphia: Institute for the Study of Human Issues.

Luhmann, Niklas (1996). *Die Realität der Massenmedien*. Wiesbaden: Westdeutscher Verlag.

Manstead, Anthony, S. R., Nico Frijda, and Agneta Fischer (eds.) (2004). *Feelings and Emotions: The Amsterdam Symposium*. Cambridge: Cambridge University Press.

Marcuse, Herbert (1984). *Schriften 8: Aufsätze und Vorlesungen, 1948–1969: Versuch über die Befreiung*. Frankfurt: Suhrkamp.

Marin, Bernd (1979–2000). *Antisemitismus ohne Antisemiten: Autoritäre Vorurteile und Feindbilder*. Frankfurt: Campus.

Markovits, Andrei S. (2004). *Amerika, dich hasst sich's besser: Antiamerikanismus und Antisemitismus in Europa*. Hamburg: Konkret Literatur.

Marrus, Michael R. (1986). "Is There a New Anti-Semitism?" In Michael Curtis (ed.) (1986). *Antisemitism in the Contemporary World*. Boulder, CO: Westview.

Marx, Konstanze and Monika Schwarz-Friesel (2013). *Sprache und Kommunikation im technischen Zeitalter: Wieviel Technik (v)erträgt unsere Gesellschaft?* Berlin: de Gruyter.

Mautner, Gerlinde (1998). "We are not like them and never have been: Zum persuasiven Potential der Wir-Gruppen-Konstruktion." In Michael Hoffmann and Christine Kessler (eds.) (1998). *Beiträge zur Persuasionsforschung: Unter besonderer Berücksichtigung textlinguistischer und stilistischer Aspekte*. Frankfurt: Lang.

Meibauer, Jörg ([2]2001). *Pragmatik: Eine Einführung*. Tübingen: Stauffenburg.

Meibauer, Jörg (2007). "Zitat und Lüge." In Elke Brendel, Jörg Meibauer, and Markus Steinbach (eds.) (2007). *Zitat und Bedeutung*. Hamburg: Buske.

Meibauer, Jörg (ed.) (2012). *Hassrede/Hate Speech: Interdisziplinäre Beiträge des gleichnamigen Workshops, Mainz 2009*. Giessen: Giessener Elektronische Bibliothek.

Mertens, Lothar (1995). "Antizionismus: Feindschaft gegen Israel als eine neue Form des Antisemitismus." In Wolfgang Benz (ed.) (1995). *Antisemitismus in Deutschland: Zur Aktualität eines Vorurteils*. Munich: DTV.

Meyer, Michael (1966). "Great Debate on Antisemitism: Jewish Reaction to New Hostility in Germany, 1879–1881." In *Leo Baeck Institute Yearbook*. No. 11.
Miller, George A. (1995). *Wörter: Streifzüge durch die Psycholinguistik*. Frankfurt: Zweitausendeins.
Milson, Menahem (2008). "Arab and Islamic Antisemitism." *Inquiry and Analysis* Ser. 442, May 27, 2008. http://www.memri.org. Accessed 2 September 2012.
Mitscherlich, Alexander and Margarete Mitscherlich (1967). *Die Unfähigkeit zu trauern: Grundlagen kollektiven Verhaltens*. Munich: Piper.
Müller, Hildegard (2006). "Deutschlands Verantwortung in Europa: Antisemitischem Denken, Reden und Handeln entegegenwirken!" In Klaus Faber, Julius H. Schoeps, and Sacha Stawski (eds.) (2006).
Nagel, Michael and Moshe Zimmermann (eds.) (2013). *Judenfeindschaft und Antisemitismus in der deutschen Presse über fünf Jahrhunderte: Erscheinungsformen, Rezeption, Debatte und Gegenwehr*. Bremen: Édition lumière.
Naumann, Michael (ed.) (2002). *"Es muss doch in diesem Lande wieder möglich sein . . .": Der neue Antisemitismus-Streit*. Munich: Ullstein.
Neugebauer, Wolfgang (2003). "Israelkritik als neuer Antisemitismus?" *Schalom: Zeitschrift der Österreichisch-Israelischen Gesellschaft* 3–4.
Niedermüller, Peter (1999). "Zweiundzwanzigstes Bild: 'Der Kommunist.'" In Julius H. Schoeps and Joachim Schlör (eds.) (1999).
Niklas, Hans and Änne Ostermann (1976). *Vorurteile und Feindbilder*. Munich: Urban and Schwarzenberg.
Nipperdey, Thomas and Reinhard Rürup (1994). "Antisemitismus." In Otto Brunner, Werner Conze, and Reinhart Koselleck (eds.). *Geschichtliche Grundbegriffe: Historisches Lexikon zu politisch-sozialen Sprache in Deutschland*. Vol. 1. Stuttgart: Klett-Cotta.
Nirenberg, David (2013). *Anti-Judaism: The Western Tradition*. New York: W. W. Norton.
Nolte, Paul and Dagmar Hilpert (2007). "Wandel und Selbstbehauptung: Die gesellschaftliche Mitte in historischer Perspektive." In Herbert-Quandt-Stiftung (ed.) (2007).
Nonn, Christoph (2008). *Antisemitismus*. Darmstadt: Wissenschaftliche Buchgesellschaft.
Ohde, Christina (1994). *Der Irre von Baghdad: Zur Konstruktion von Feindbildern in überregionalen deutschen Tageszeitungen während der Golfkrise 1990–91*. Frankfurt: Lang.
Operario, Don and Susan T. Fiske (2001). "Stereotypes: Content, Structures, Processes and Context." In Rupert Brown and Samuel Gaertner (eds.) (2001). *Blackwell Handbook of Social Psychology: Intergroup Processes*. Malden, MA: Blackwell.
Orland, Nachum (1999). "Dreiundzwanzigstes Bild: 'Der Israeli': Antizionismus und Antisemitismus." In Julius H. Schoeps and Joachim Schlör (eds.) (1999).
Ortak, Nuri (2004). *Persuasion: Zur textlinguistischen Beschreibung eines dialogischen Strategiemusters*. Tübingen: Niemeyer.

Ottmers, Clemens ([2]2007). *Rhetorik*, Stuttgart & Weimar: Metzler.

Pallade, Yves (2008a). "Antisemitismus in Deutschland: Politikwissenschaftliche Analysen." In Lars Rensmann and Julius H. Schoeps (eds.) (2008).

Pallade, Yves (2008b). "Aktueller Antisemitismus in der Bundesrepublik Deutschland." In Horst Helas, Dagmar Rubisch, and Reiner Zilkenat (eds.) (2008).

Parkes, James (1963). *Antisemitism*. London: Vallentine Mitchell.

Parkes, James (1981). *The Conflict of the Church and the Synagogue: A Study in the Origins of Antisemitism*. New York: Atheneum.

Paul, Hermann ([10]2002). *Deutsches Wörterbuch: Bedeutungsgeschichte und Aufbau unseres Wortschatzes*. Rev. Helmut Henne, Heidrun Kämper, and Georg Objartel. Tübingen: Niemeyer.

Paulsen, Wolfgang (1981). "Theodor Fontane: The Philosemitic Antisemite." In *Leo Baeck Institute Yearbook*. No. 26.

Pelinka, Anton, Karin Bischof, and Karin Stögner (eds.) (2009). *Handbook of Prejudice*. Amherst, NY: Cambria.

Pelinka, Anton and Ruth Wodak (eds.) (2002). *"Dreck am Stecken": Politik der Ausgrenzung*. Vienna: Czernin.

Perkuhn, Rainer and Cyril Belica. (2004). "Eine kurze Einführung in die Kookkurrenzanalyse und syntagmatische Muster." IDS Mannheim. http://www1.ids-mannheim.de/kl/misc/tutorial.html. Accessed 9 February 2016.

Pew Research Center (ed.) (2008). "Unfavorable Views of Jews and Muslims on the Increase in Europe." Washington, DC: Pew Research Center.

Pfahl-Traughber, Armin (2002). *Antisemitismus in der deutschen Geschichte*. Opladen: Leske and Budrich.

Pfahl-Traughber, Armin (2007a). "Antisemitische und nicht-antisemitische Israel-Kritik: Eine Auseinandersetzung mit den Kriterien zur Unterscheidung." *Aufklärung und Kritik* 1.

Pfahl-Traughber, Armin (2007b). "Ideologische Erscheinungsformen des Antisemitismus." *Aus Politik und Zeitgeschichte* 31.

Pohl, Rolf (2010). "Der antisemitische Wahn: Aktuelle Ansätze zur Psychoanalyse einer sozialen Pathologie." In Wolfram Stender, Guido Follert, and Mihri Özdogan (eds.) (2010). *Konstellationen des Antisemitismus: Antisemitismusforschung und sozialpädagogische Praxis*. Wiesbaden: Verlag für Sozialwissenschaften.

Poliakov, Léon (1983). *Geschichte des Antisemitismus*. Vol. 5: *Die Aufklärung und ihre judenfeindlichen Tendenzen*. Worms: Heintz.

Poliakov, Léon (1985). *The History of Anti-Semitism: The Littman Library of Jewish Civilisation*. London: Routledge.

Pollak, Alexander and Nina Eger (2002). "Antisemitismus mit Anspielungscharakter: *Über Analogien zwischen den Äusserungen Haiders gegenüber Muzicant* und NS-antisemitischer Argumentation." In Anton Pelinka and Ruth Wodak (eds.) (2002).

Pörksen, Bernhard ([2]2005). *Die Konstruktion von Feindbildern: Zum Sprachgebrauch in neonazistischen Medien*. Wiesbaden: Verlag für Sozialwissenschaften.

Porst, Rolf (2008). *Fragebogen: Ein Arbeitsbuch*. Wiesbaden: Verlag für Sozialwissenschaften.

Prager, Dennis and Joseph Telushkin (2003). *Why the Jews? The Reason for Antisemitism*. New York: Simon & Schuster.

Priester, Karin (2003). *Rassismus: Eine Sozialgeschichte*. Leipzig: Reclam.

Pulzer, Peter G. J. (1966). *Die Entstehung des politischen Antisemitismus in Deutschland und Österreich, 1867–1914*. Gütersloh: Mohn.

Pulzer, Peter G. J. (2003). "The New Antisemitism, or When Is a Taboo Not a Taboo?" In Paul Iganski and Barry Kosmin (eds.) (2003). *A New Antisemitism? Debating Judeophobia in 21st-Century Britain*. London: Profile Books.

Quadfasel, Lars (2005). "Für das Gute, gegen die Juden. Die Modernisierung des Antisemitismus." In *Initiative Antisemitismuskritik* (ed.) (2005). *Israel in deutschen Wohnzimmern: Realität und antisemitische Wahrnehmungsmuster des Nahostkonflikts: Dokumentation einer Veranstaltungsreihe in Hannover 2003*. Stuttgart: ibidem.

Quasthoff, Uta (1973). *Soziales Vorurteil und Kommunication—Eine sprachwissenschaftliche Analyse des Stereotyps: Ein interdisziplinärer Versuch im Bereich von Linguistik, Sozialwissenschaft und Psychologie*. Frankfurt: Anthenäum.

Quasthoff, Uta (1987). "Linguistic Prejudice/Stereotypes." In Ulrich Ammon, Norbert Dittmar, and Klaus Mattheier (eds.) (1987). *Sociolinguistics/Soziolinguistik: Ein internationales Handbuch zur Wissenschaft von Sprache und Gesellschaft*. Sub-vol. 1. Berlin: de Gruyter.

Raabe, Tobias and Andreas Beelmann (2011). "Development of Ethnic, Racial, and National Prejudice in Childhood and Adolescence: A Multinational Meta-Analysis of Age Differences." *Child Development* 6, 82.

Rabinovici, Doron (2006). "Altneuhass: Moderne Varianten des Antisemitismus." In Klaus Faber, Julius H. Schoeps, and Sacha Stawski (eds.) (2006).

Rabinovici, Doron, Ulrich Speck, and Natan Sznaider (eds.) (2004). *Neuer Antisemitismus? Eine globale Debatte*. Berlin: Suhrkamp.

Raphael, Freddy (1999). "Sechstes Bild: 'Der Wucherer.'" In Julius H. Schoeps and Joachim Schlör (eds.) (1999).

Rauscher, Hans (2004). *Israel, Europa und der neue Antisemitismus: Ein aktuelles Handbuch*. Vienna: Molden.

Reichel, John (in progress). "NS-Vergleiche in öffentlichen und halböffentlichen Diskursen." Dissertation. Berlin. Technische Universität.

Reinfrank, Timo (2008). "Globalisierter Antisemitismus im 21. Jahrhundert: Zur Arbeit gegen den aktuellen Antisemitismus in Deutschland." In Horst Helas, Dagmar Rubisch, and Reiner Zilkenat (eds.) (2008). Reinfrank, Timo and Tobias Ebbrecht (2004). "Antisemitismus im 21. Jahrhundert: Über die neuen (alten) Formen des deutschen Antisemitismus." In Zentrum demokratische Kultur (ed.) (2004). *Antisemitismus und Antiamerikanismus in Deutschland*. PDF Bulletin 5. Leipzig: Klett.

Reinharz, Jehuda (1975). *Fatherland or Promised Land? The Dilemma of the German Jew, 1893–1914*. Ann Arbor: University of Michigan Press.

Reinharz, Jehuda (ed.) (1987). *Living with Antisemitism: Modern Jewish Responses*. Hanover, NH: University Press of New England.

Reinharz, Jehuda (2010). "Aktuelle Judenfeindschaft: Ein Vergleich zwischen den USA und Deutschland." In Monika Schwarz-Friesel, Evyatar Friesel, and Jehuda Reinharz (eds.) (2010).

Reisigl, Martin and Ruth Wodak (2001). *Discourse and Discrimination: Rhetorics of Racism and Anti-Semitism*. London: Routledge.

Rensmann, Lars (2004). *Demokratie und Judenbild: Antisemitismus in der politischen Kultur der Bundesrepublik Deutschland*. Wiesbaden: Verlag für Sozialwissenschaften.

Rensmann, Lars (2006). "Der Nahost-Konflikt in der Perzeption des Rechts- und Linksextremismus." In Klaus Faber, Julius H. Schoeps, and Sasha Stawski (eds.) (2006).

Rensmann, Lars and Julius H. Schoeps (eds.) (2008). *Feindbild Judentum: Antisemitismus in Europa*. Berlin: Verlag für Berlin-Brandenburg.

Richter, Maria, Judith Eck, Thomas Straube, Wolfgang H. R. Miltner, and Thomas Weiss (2010). "Do Words Hurt? Brain Activation During Explicit and Implicit Processing of Pain-related Words." *Pain* 148.

Rokeah, David (1988). "The Church Fathers and the Jews in Writings Designed for Internal and External Use." In Shnuel Almog (ed.) (2006).

Römer, Ruth (1985). *Sprachwissenschaft und Rassenideologie in Deutschland*. Munich: Fink.

Sahm, Ulrich W. (2006). "Deutsche Medien und der Nahostkonflikt." In Klaus Faber, Julius H. Schoeps, and Sasha Stawski (eds.) (2006).

Salovey, Peter, Marja Kokkonen, Paulo N. Lopes, and John D. Mayer (2004). "Emotional Intelligence: What Do We Know?" In Manstead, Antony S. R., Nico Frijda, and Agneta Fischer (eds.) (2004).

Salzborn, Samuel (2005). "Katholischer Antisemitismus." *Blätter für deutsche und internationale Politik* 8.

Salzborn, Samuel (2008). "Uncovering Latent Anti-Semitism in Germany: Report on a Pilot Study." *Yalkut Moreshet* 5.

Salzborn, Samuel (2010a). "Halbierte Empathie: Antisemitische Schuldprojektion und die Angst vor der eigenen Vergangenheit." In Monika Schwarz-Friesel, Evyatar Friesel, and Jehuda Reinharz (eds.) (2010).

Salzborn, Samuel (2010b). *Antisemitismus als negative Leitidee der Moderne: Sozialwissenschaftliche Theorien im Vergleich*. Frankfurt: Campus.

Salzborn, Samuel and Sebastian Voigt (2011). "Antisemiten als Koalitionspartner? Die Linkspartei zwischen antizionistischem Antisemitismus und dem Streben nach Regierungsfähigkeit." *Zeitschrift für Politik* 3.

Sartre, Jean-Paul (1948). *Betrachtungen zur Judenfrage: Psychoanalyse des Antisemitismus*. Zurich: Europa.

Schapira, Esther and Georg M. Hafner (2006). "Entlastungsantisemitismus in Deutschland." In Klaus Faber, Julius H. Schoeps, and Sasha Stawski (eds.) (2006).

Schapira, Esther and Georg M. Hafner (2010). "Die Wahrheit unter Beschuss: Der

Nahostkonflikt und die Medien." In Monika Schwarz-Friesel, Evyatar Friesel, and Jehuda Reinharz (eds.) (2010).

Scheler, Max (1912/[4]1955). "Das Ressentiment im Aufbau der Moralen." In Max Scheler ([4]1955). *Vom Sturz der Werte: Abhandlungen und Aufsätze*. Berne: Francke.

Scherer, Carmen (2006). *Korpuslinguistik*. Heidelberg: Winter.

Scherer, Klaus (2004). "Feelings Integrate the Central Representation of Appraisal-Driven Response Organization in Emotion." In Anthony Manstead, S. R., Nico Frijda, and Agneta Fischer (eds.) (2004).

Scherr, Albert (2011). *Verbreitung von Stereotypen über Juden und antisemitischer Vorurteile in der evangelischen Kirche*. Expertise: Freiburg.

Scherr, Albert and Barbara Schäuble (2007). "'Ich habe nichts gegen Juden, aber . . .': Ausgangsbedingungen und Perspektiven gesellschaftspolitischer Bildungsarbeit gegen Antisemitismus. Berlin: Amadeu Antonio Stiftung." http://www.amadeu-antonio-stiftung.de/w/files/pdfs/ich_habe_nichts_2.pdf. Accessed 2 September 2012.

Scherr, Albert and Barbara Schäuble (2008). "'Wir' und 'die Juden': Gegenwärtiger Antisemitismus als Differenzkonstruktion." *Berliner Debatte Initial* 19.

Schmitz-Berning, Cornelia (1998). *Vokabular des Antisemitismus*. Berlin: de Gruyter.

Schoeps, Julius H. and Joachim Schlör (eds.) (1999). *Antisemitismus: Vorurteile und Mythen*. Munich: Piper.

Schwarz, Monika ([3]2008). *Einführung in die Kognitive Linguistik*. Tübingen: Francke.

Schwarz, Monika and Jeannette Chur ([5]2007). *Semantik: Ein Arbeitsbuch*. Tübingen: Narr.

Schwarz-Friesel, Monika (2007). *Sprache und Emotion*. Tübingen: Francke.

Schwarz-Friesel, Monika (2008). "Sprache, Kognition und Emotion: Neue Wege in der Kognitions-Wissenschaft." In Heidrun Kämper and Ludwig M. Eichinger (eds.) (2008). *Sprache—Kognition—Kultur*. Berlin: de Gruyter.

Schwarz-Friesel, Monika (2009a). "Worte wie Waffen: Wie Antisemitismus und Antiisraelismus über Begriffe und Vergleiche in der bürgerlichen Mitte salonfähig geworden sind." *Jüdische Allgemeine*, 26 February 2009.

Schwarz-Friesel, Monika (2009b). "Der Tatort Sprache in Deutschland: Antisemitismus im öffentlichen Kommunikationsraum." *Tribüne* 189, 48.

Schwarz-Friesel, Monika (2010a). "'Ich habe gar nichts gegen Juden!' Der 'legitime' Antisemitismus der Mitte." In Monika Schwarz-Friesel, Evyatar Friesel, and Jehuda Reinharz (eds.) (2010).

Schwarz-Friesel, Monika (2010b). "Tatort Sprache: Aktueller Antisemitismus in Deutschland als verbale Strategie." In Martin Neef and Christina Noak (eds.), *Sprachgeschichten: Eine Braunschweiger Vorlesung*. Bielefeld: Verlag für Regionalgeschichte.

Schwarz-Friesel, Monika (2011a). "Dem Grauen einen Namen geben? Zur Verbalisierung von Emotionen in der Holocaust-Literatur: Prolegomena zu einer Kognitiven Linguistik der Opfersprache." *Germanistische Studien. Jubiläumsausgabe 10: Sprachen und Emotionen*.

Schwarz-Friesel, Monika (2011b). "Das unbekannte Land Israel: Textlinguistische Analysen zur De-Realisierung." Unpublished manuscript.

Schwarz-Friesel, Monika (2012). "'Dies ist kein Hassbrief—sondern meine eigene Meinung über Euch!' Zur kognitiven und emotionalen Basis der aktuellen antisemitischen Hass-Rede." In Jörg Meibauer (ed.) (2012).

Schwarz-Friesel, Monika (2013a). "'Juden sind zum Töten da' (studivz.net, 2008): Hass via Internet: Zugänglichkeit und Verbreitung von Antisemitismen im World Wide Web." In Konstanze Marx and Monika Schwarz-Friesel (2013).

Schwarz-Friesel, Monika (2013b). "Explizite und implizite Formen des Verbal- Antisemitismus in aktuellen Texten der regionalen und Überregionalen Presse (2002–2010) und ihr Einfluss auf den alltäglichen Sprachgebrauch." In Michael Nagel and Moshe Zimmermann (eds.) (2013).

Schwarz-Friesel, Monika (2015). "Educated Anti-Semitism in the Middle of German Society: Empirical Findings." In H. Fireberg and O. Glockner (eds.) (2015). *Being in 21st- Century Germany.* Oldenburg: de Gruyter.

Schwarz-Friesel, Monika and Evyatar Friesel. (2012). "'Gestern die Juden, heute die Muslime . . .'? Von den Gefahren falscher Analogien." In Gideon Botsch, Olaf Glöckner, Christoph Kopke, and Michael Spieker (eds.) (2012). *Islamophobie und Antisemitismus: Ein umstrittener Vergleich.* Berlin: de Gruyter.

Schwarz-Friesel, Monika, Evyatar Friesel, and Jehuda Reinharz (eds.) (2010). *Aktueller Antisemitismus in Deutschland: Ein Phänomen der Mitte.* Berlin: de Gruyter.

Schwarz-Friesel, Monika, Konstanze Marx, and Sally Damisch (2012). "Persuasive Strategien der affektiven Verunsicherung im aktuellen Diskurs: Ironisieren, kritisieren und beleidigen in öffentlichen Streitgesprächen." In Inge Pohl and Horst Ehrhardt (eds.) (2012). *Sprache und Emotion in öffentlicher Kommunikation.* Frankfurt: Lang.

Schwitalla, Johannes ([3]2006). *Gesprochenes Deutsch: Eine Einführung.* Berlin: Schmidt.

Searle, John (1969). *Speech Acts: An Essay in the Philosophy of Language.* Cambridge: Cambridge University Press.

Shatzmiller, Joseph (1990). *Shylock Reconsidered: Jews, Moneylending, and Medieval Society.* Berkeley: University of California Press.

Simmel, Ernst (ed.) (1946/2002a). *Antisemitismus.* Frankfurt: Fischer.

Simmel, Ernst (1946/2002b). "Antisemitismus und Massen-Psychopathologie." In Ernst Simmel (ed.) (1946/2002a).

Simon, Marcel (1996). *Versus Israel: A Study of the Relations between Christians and Jews in the Roman Empire, AD 135–425.* Oxford: Littman.

Skirl, Helge and Monika Schwarz-Friesel (2007). *Metapher.* Heidelberg: Winter.

Smith, Eliot R. and Diane M. Mackie ([2]2000). *Social Psychology.* Philadelphia: Psychology Press.

Solomon, Robert C. ([3]2001). *Gefühle und der Sinn des Lebens.* Frankfurt: Zweitausendeins.

Soric, Aleksandar (2005). "'Bomben-Holocaust': Eine sprachkritische Analyse eines kontroversen Ausdrucks mit rechtsextremistischem Hintergrund." *Aptum: Zeitschrift für Sprachkritik und Sprachkultur* 2.

Sornig, Karl (1986). "Bemerkungen zu persuasiven Sprachstrategien." In Franz Hundsnurscher and Edda Weigand (eds.) (1986).

Stangor, Charles (ed.) (2000). *Stereotypes and Prejudice*. Hove: Psychology Press.

Stangor, Charles (2009). "The Study of Stereotyping, Prejudice, and Discrimination within Social Psychology: A Quick History of Theory and Research." In Todd D. Nelson (ed.) (2009). *Handbook of Prejudice, Stereotyping, and Discrimination*. New York: Psychology Press.

Staub, Ervin ([5]1995). *The Roots of Evil: The Origins of Genocide and Other Group Violence*. Cambridge: Cambridge University Press.

Stav, Arieh (1999). *Peace: The Arabian Caricature: A Study of Anti-Semitic Imagery*. New York: Gefen.

Stefanowitsch, Anatol and Stefan T. Gries (eds.) (2006). *Corpus-Based Approaches to Metaphor and Metonymy*. Berlin: de Gruyter.

Stephen Roth Institute (2010). *Antisemitism Worldwide, 2009: General Analysis*. Tel Aviv: Stephen Roth Institute for the Study of Contemporary Antisemitism and Racism.

Stern, Frank (1991a). *Im Anfang war Auschwitz: Antisemitismus und Philosemitismus im deutschen Nachkrieg*. Gerlingen: Bleicher.

Stern, Frank (1991b). "Philosemitismus statt Antisemitismus: Entstehung und Funktion einer neuen Ideologie in Westdeutschland." In Wolfgang Benz (ed.) (1991). *Zwischen Antisemitismus und Philosemitismus: Juden in der Bundesrepublik*. Berlin: Metropol.

Stern, Frank (1993). "Antisemitic and Philosemitic Discourse in Postwar Germany." *Folia Linguistica* 27, 3–4.

Stern, Frank (2002). "Dem Antijüdischen nach dem Munde geredet: Zur Entwicklung, Klassifizierung und Beurteilung antisemitischer und antijüdischer Äusserungen in der Bundesrepublik Deutschland." In Anton Pelinka and Ruth Wodak (eds.) (2002).

Taguieff, Pierre-André (2002). *La nouvelle judéophobie*. Paris: Mille et Une Nuits.

Teasdale, John D. (1999). "Multi-Level Theories of Cognition–Emotion Relations." In Tim Dalgleish and Michael J. Power (eds.) (1999). *Handbook of Cognition and Emotion*. Chichester: Wiley.

Toulmin, Stephen (1958). *The Uses of Argument*. Cambridge: Cambridge University Press.

Trachtenberg, Joshua (1943). *The Devil and the Jews: The Medieval Conception of the Jew and Its Relation to Modern Antisemitism*. New Haven, CT: Yale University Press.

United States Department of State (2008). *Contemporary Global Anti-Semitism: A Report Provided to the United States Congress*. http://www.state.gov/documents/organization/102301.pdf. Accessed 2 September 2012.

Van Dijk, Teun A. (1984). *Prejudice in Discourse: An Analysis of Ethnic Prejudice in Cognition and Conversation*. Amsterdam: Benjamins.

Van Dijk, Teun A. (2002). "Discourse and Racism." In David T. Goldberg and John Solomos (eds.). *A Companion to Racial and Ethnic Studies*. Oxford: Blackwell.

van Eemeren, Frans H. (2001). "Fallacies." In Thomas O. Sloane (ed.) (2001). *Encyclopedia of Rhetoric*. Oxford: Oxford University Press.

Volkov, Shulamit (1990). *Jüdisches Leben und Antisemitismus im 19. und 20. Jahrhundert: Zehn Essays*. Munich: Beck.

Volkov, Shulamit (2000). "Antisemitismus als kultureller Code." In Shulamit Volkov (ed.) (²2000). *Antisemitismus als kultureller Code: Zehn Essays*. Munich: Beck.

Volkov, Shulamit (2006). *Germans, Jews, and Antisemites: Trials in Emancipation*. Cambridge: Cambridge University Press.

von Braun, Christina (1999). "Viertes Bild: 'Blut und Blutschande.'" In Julius H. Schoeps and Joachim Schlör (eds.) (1999).

von Braun, Christina (2004). "Einführung." In Christina von Braun and Eva-Maria Ziege (eds.) (2004).

von Braun, Christina and Wolfgang Gerlach (eds.) (²2000). *Der ewige Judenhass: Christlicher Antijudaismus, Deutschnationale Judenfeindlichkeit, Rassistischer Antisemitismus*. Berlin: Philo.

von Braun, Christina and Eva-Maria Ziege (eds.) (2004). *Der "bewegliche" Vorurteil: Aspekte des internationalen Antisemitismus*. Würzburg: Königshausen and Neumann.

von Polenz, Peter (1999). *Deutsche Sprachgeschichte vom Spätmittelalter bis zur Gegenwart*. Vol. 3: *19. und 20. Jahrhundert*. Berlin: de Gruyter.

Wagner, Franc (2001). *Implizite sprachliche Diskriminierung als Sprechakt: Lexikalische Indikatoren implizierter Diskriminierung in Medientexten*. Tübingen: Narr.

Wahl, Klaus, Christiane Tramitz, and Jörg Blumtritt (2001). *Fremdenfeindlichkeit: Auf den Spuren extremer Emotionen*. Opladen: Leske & Budrich.

Weber, Matthias (2012). "Israel verliert bei den Deutschen an Ansehen." sterne.de, 23 May 2012. http://www.stern.de/politik/deutschland/stern-umfrage-israel-verliert-bei-den-deutschen-an-ansehen-1830648.html. Accessed 2 September 2012.

Weiner, Bernhard (1986). *An Attributional Theory of Motivation and Emotion*. New York: Springer.

Weinzierl, Erika (1995). "Stereotype christlicher Judenfeindschaft." In Elisabeth Klamper (ed.) (1995).

Weiss, Volker (2005). "'Volksklassenkampf': Die antizionistische Rezeption des Nahostkonflikts in der militanten Linken der BRD." In Moshe Zuckermann (ed.) (2005).

Welzer, Harald (2002). *Das kommunikative Gedächtnis: Eine Theorie der Erinnerung*. Munich: Beck.

Welzer, Harald (2005). *Täter: Wie aus ganz normalen Menschen Massenmörder werden*. Frankfurt: Fischer.

Wenzel, Angelika (1978). *Stereotype in gesprochener Sprache: Form, Vorkommen und Funktion in Dialogen*. Munich: Beck.

Wetzel, Juliane (2005). "Der schwierige Umgang mit einem Phänomen: Die EU und der Antisemitismus." In Moshe Zuckermann (ed.) (2005).

Wetzel, Juliane (2008). "Entwicklungen seit der Berliner Antisemitismus-Konferenz 2004." In Horst Helas Dagmar Rubisch, and Reiner Zilkenat (eds.) (2008).

Whine, Michael (2006). "Progress in the Struggle against Anti-Semitism in Europe: The Berlin Declaration and the European Union Monitoring Centre on Racism and Xenophobia's Working Definition of Anti-Semitism." *Post-Holocaust and Anti-Semitism* 41. http://jcpa.org/phas/phas-041-whine.htm. Accessed 2 September 2015.

Wistrich, Robert S. (ed.) (1991). *Antisemitism: The Longest Hatred*. New York: Pantheon.

Wistrich, Robert S. (ed.) (1999). *Demonizing the Other: Antisemitism, Racism and Xenophobia*. Amsterdam: Harwood Academic.

Wistrich, Robert S. (2003). "Confronting Antisemitism and Prejudice in the Media: New Strategies." Speech delivered at the International Conference on Antisemitism and Prejudice in the Contemporary Media. Hebrew University, Vidal Sassoon International Center for the Study of Antisemitism, Jerusalem. 18–12 February.

Wistrich, Robert S. (2005). *European Anti-Semitism Reinvents Itself*. New York: American Jewish Committee. http:www.ajc.org/atf/cf/%7B42D75369-D582-4380-8395-D25925B85EAF%7D/wistrich.pdf. Accessed 2 September 2012.

Wistrich, Robert S. (2007). "Antisemitism, the World's Obsession: An Interview with Robert Wistrich by Barry Rubin and Judith Roumani." *Covenant Global Jewish Magazine* 3, 1. http://covenant.idc.ac.il/en/vol1/issue3/Antisemitism-The-World-Obsession_print.html. Accessed 2 September 2012.

Wistrich, Robert S. (2010). *A Lethal Obsession: Anti-Semitism from Antiquity to the Global Jihad*. New York: Random House.

Wistrich, Robert S. (2011). *Muslimischer Antisemitismus: Eine aktuelle Gefahr*. Berlin: Edition Critic.

Wodak, Ruth (1990). "Opfer der Opfer? Der 'alltägliche Antisemitismus' in Österreich: Erste qualitative soziolinguistische Überlegungen." In Werner Bergmann and Rainer Erb (eds.) (1990). *Antisemitismus in der politischen Kultur nach 1945*. Opladen: Westdeutscher Verlag.

Wodak, Ruth (1997). "Aspects of Critical Discourse Analysis." *Zeitschrift für Angewandte Linguistik* 36.

Wodak, Ruth, Peter Nowak, Johann Pelinka, Helmut Gruber, Rudolf deCilla, and Richard Mitten (1990). *Wir sind alle unschuldige Täter: Diskurstheoretische Studien zum Nachkriegsantisemitismus*. Frankfurt: Suhrkamp.

Wolfradt, Uwe (2001). *Depersonalisation: Selbstentfremdung und Realitätsstörung*. Cologne: Kölner Studien-Verlag.

Wolgast, Eike (2001). *Die Wahrnehmung des Dritten Reiches in der unmittelbaren Nachkriegszeit (1945–46)*. Heidelberg: Winter.

Zick, Andreas (2010). "Aktueller Antisemitismus im Spiegel von Umfragen: Ein Phänomen der Mitte." In Monika Schwarz-Friesel, Evyatar Friesel, and Jehuda Reinharz (eds.) (2010).

Zick, Andreas and Beate Küpper (2006a). "Traditioneller und moderner Antisemitismus: Antisemitismus in modernem Gewand." http://www.bpb.de/politik/extremismus/antisemitismus/37967/traditioneller-und-moderner-antisemitismus. Accessed 2 September 2012.

Zick, Andreas and Beate Küpper (2006b). "Politische Mitte: Normal feindselig." In Wilhelm Heitmeyer (ed.) (2006). *Deutsche Zustände*. Ser. 4. Frankfurt: Suhrkamp.

Zimmer, Anja (2001). *Hate Speech im Völkerrecht: Rassendiskriminierende Äusserungen im Spannungsfeld zwischen Rassendiskriminierungsverbot und Meinungsfreiheit.* Frankfurt: Lang.

Zimmermann, Moshe (1986). *Wilhelm Marr: The Patriarch of Anti-Semitism.* New York: Oxford University Press.

Zimmermann, Moshe (2005). *Deutsch-jüdische Vergangenheit: Der Judenhass als Herausforderung.* Paderborn: Schöningh.

Zuckermann, Moshe (ed.) (2005). *Antisemitismus, Antizionismus, Israelkritik.* Göttingen: Wallstein.

INDEX

Note: Page numbers followed by n refer to notes, with note number. The letter *t* following a page number denotes a table; the letter *f* following a page number denotes a figure.

Library of Congress Cataloging-in-Publication Data

Names: Schwarz-Friesel, Monika, author. | Reinharz, Jehuda, author.
Title: Inside the antisemitic mind : the language of Jew-hatred in contemporary Germany / Monika Schwarz-Friesel and Jehuda Reinharz.
Other titles: Sprache der Judenfeindschaft im 21. Jahrhundert. English
Description: Waltham : Brandeis University Press, [2016] | Series: Tauber Institute series for the study of European Jewry | Includes bibliographical references and index.
Identifiers: LCCN 2016026225 (print) | LCCN 2016026739 (ebook) | ISBN 9781611689839 (cloth : alk. paper) | ISBN 9781611689846 (pbk. : alk. paper) | ISBN 9781611689853 (epub, mobi & pdf)
Subjects: LCSH: Antisemitism in language—Germany—History—21st century. | Stereotypes (Social psychology)—Germany—History—21st century. | Social perception—Germany—History—21st century. | Jews—Public opinion. | Public opinion—Germany | German language—Discourse analysis. | German language—Terms and phrases. | Germany—Ethnic relations.
Classification: LCC DS146.G4 S39513 2016 (print) | LCC DS146.G4 (ebook) | DDC 305.892/4043—dc23
LC record available at https://lccn.loc.gov/2016026225